WE SHALL BUILD ANEW

WE SHALL BUILD ANEW

STEPHEN S. WISE,

the JEWISH INSTITUTE *of* RELIGION,

and the

REINVENTION *of*

AMERICAN LIBERAL JUDAISM

===== SHIRLEY IDELSON =====

The University of Alabama Press
Tuscaloosa

The University of Alabama Press
Tuscaloosa, Alabama 35487-0380
uapress.ua.edu

Inquiries about reproducing material from this work should be
addressed to the University of Alabama Press.

Typeface: Adobe Jenson Pro

Cover image: Jewish Institute of Religion faculty and students, circa 1927; courtesy of
the Jacob Rader Marcus Center of the American Jewish Archives, Cincinnati, Ohio, at
americanjewisharchives.org
Cover design: Lori Lynch

Cataloging-in-Publication data is available from the Library of Congress.
ISBN: 978-0-8173-2131-4
E-ISBN: 978-0-8173-9410-3

To Alexis

Contents

Acknowledgments   ix

Introduction   1

PART I. CALL AND FIRST STEPS

1. Traditions of Dissent   9

2. There Is a Need and We Shall Meet It   28

3. A Seminary without Adjectives   44

4. The First Test   55

5. In Pursuit of European Scholars   69

PART II. THE MODEL BLOSSOMS

6. A New Yavneh   89

7. Rabbinical Training for Our Time   108

8. The First Cadre   130

PART III. METAMORPHOSIS

9. Early Transformation   153

10. Reform's Volte-Face   168

11. The Legacy Crystalizes   183

Conclusion   206

Notes   213

Bibliography   241

Index   253

Photographs follow page 144.

Acknowledgments

WHILE WORKING ON THIS BOOK, I HAVE LIVED IN OVERLAPPING WORLDS of *batei midrash*, houses of study, and I am indebted to the many teachers, including my students, from whom I have been privileged to learn.

At Hebrew Union College-Jewish Institute of Religion's New York School, the Reform seminary where I received my ordination and decades later served as dean, I was privileged to belong to a community devoted to scholarship, leadership, and the highest ideals of Judaism. There, my colleagues and students inspired me on a daily basis while also challenging and sharpening my thinking about the significance of JIR's history today. We were the direct descendants of Stephen S. Wise and the cadre he assembled at the institute, and while our predecessors surely could not anticipate how the school's ethos would change over time, its flourishing was thanks to the seeds they planted in the early 1920s.

My deep gratitude goes to David Ellenson, who was president of the college-institute when I began my research. Though this book ends prior to his presidency, I believe David embodied the best of the JIR vision while also making the crucial corrective of integrating a feminist outlook into his leadership. I was the beneficiary, enjoying the mentorship of this respected rabbi, scholar, and friend who recognized the importance of the JIR story and pushed me to complete the book.

The American Jewish Archives (AJA), which houses the Jewish Institute of Religion collection, is devoted to ensuring a strong future for American Jewish life by raising consciousness of its past. Gary P. Zola, executive director, could not have been more generous in sharing his wisdom, time, and boundless energy. Gary provided valuable insight and suggestions for the manuscript, as well as primary source material that clarified the record further. I also received ample assistance from the entire AJA team, including archivists Kevin Proffitt, Dana Herman, and Elisa Ho.

HUC-JIR's New York librarians were also extremely helpful. Yoram Bitton and Tina Weiss unearthed numerous JIR treasures, and Philip Miller recounted extensive memories of the faculty and students who worked and studied on West Sixty-Eighth Street before the school moved from its original quarters to Greenwich Village in 1979.

Historian Mark Raider has continually shared his deep knowledge of Stephen S. Wise and the American Zionist movement. He helped me create an analytical framework for some of the more difficult issues that arose in my research, and in the course of our many conversations, he became a cherished friend.

Others who shared their knowledge generously include scholar Jonathan Malino and Rabbis Paul Siegel and Isaiah Zeldin. Trudy Festinger, Stephen S. Wise's granddaughter, helped me understand the Wise family's approach to Judaism in the home. For contextual history of the Reform movement and women in the rabbinate, I relied on the important work of Michael A. Meyer, Pamela Nadell, and Lance Sussman, all valued colleagues.

I am also grateful to Jonathan D. Sarna, who has expressed his enthusiasm for this project since we first participated on a panel at HUC-JIR celebrating the institute's ninetieth anniversary in 2012. Later, he read my manuscript and contributed a wealth of valuable critique for which I am indebted. I am thankful, too, to have him as a trusted colleague at Brandeis University, where I also gratefully acknowledge my colleagues and students in the Hornstein Program and the Near Eastern and Judaic Studies department, as well as in the Graduate School of Arts and Sciences and the broader university community.

I was fortunate to study closely with Robert Seltzer, Gerald Markowitz, and Kathleen McCarthy in my doctoral program at the CUNY Graduate Center and Samuel Freedman at the Columbia University Graduate School of Journalism. Each of them influenced my thinking in important ways that are reflected in the writing of this book.

In the editing process, Elisheva Urbas and Debbie Sachs read every chapter and provided invaluable feedback. Elisheva also expanded my view of the JIR story's significance in contemporary American Jewish life, while Debbie shared a fascinating memoir from her grandfather, Sheldon Blank, longtime professor of Bible at HUC. They, together with my book-writing partner, Maynard Seider, provided thoughtful critique and a sense of companionship in an often isolating process.

At the University of Alabama Press, I am most appreciative of Daniel Waterman for his patience and attentiveness in shepherding the manuscript through the publication process, and Adam Mendelsohn and Mark Bauman for their assistance and confidence in the work.

Over the years spent writing this book, Kathryn Conroy, Sally Gottesman, Myriam Klotz, April Kuhr, Ruth Levine, Ellen Lippmann, Debbie Sachs, and Sheila Weinberg have been mainstays, giving me the strength and courage to speak, write, and act truthfully in the world.

I am also thankful for the love of my entire family. My parents, Martin and Paulette Idelson, were my first teachers and imbued in me a passion for learning.

Finally, I am most indebted to Alexis Kuhr, my partner, who generously critiqued many iterations of the manuscript and whose artist's eye enriched not only this project but all aspects of my life. *We Shall Build Anew* is lovingly dedicated to her.

WE SHALL BUILD ANEW

Introduction

IN THE FALL OF 1922, RABBI STEPHEN S. WISE AND THE FREE SYNAGOGUE opened the Jewish Institute of Religion (JIR), a nondenominational graduate-level rabbinical seminary in the heart of New York City. They had ambitious plans for the small school. American liberal Judaism had become stale and outdated, they believed, and was desperately in need of an overhaul. Confident that they offered a more modern, American, progressive, and even *Jewish* approach to Judaism, the founders sought to train a new generation of rabbis bent on spreading their vision and awakening American Jewish life.

Initially belittled and scorned by mainstream Jewish leaders, JIR ultimately played a central role in shaping American liberal Judaism into a dominant force in twentieth-century American religious life. Today, it is impossible to think of the liberal religious Jewish movements in the United States without their core commitments to *tikkun olam*, Zionism, and *klal yisrael*, yet a century ago these ideas, expressed in different terms but linked inextricably to Wise's rabbinate, made him and his congregation objects of contempt within the world they sought to change.[1]

Nonetheless, confident that demographic shifts underway in American Jewish life represented a powerful force for the change they sought, Wise and the Free Synagogue's lay leaders disregarded the opposition of current-day communal leaders and set their sights on a new breed of young American Jews who shared a very different sensibility and found Wise's message pertinent. In years past, Wise had little to offer the young men who wrote him, seeking a path to become rabbis in his mold, which blended the roles of pastor, preacher, and prophet. Now, JIR could provide that path. And by training not just a handful but a whole cadre of leaders, Wise and the founders hoped, the institute could galvanize a movement to promulgate the Free Synagogue's ideals in Jewish communities across America.

In building a seminary dedicated to altering the course of religious and communal life, the founders of JIR were at once rekindling the spark of radical Reform brought to the United States from Germany by a handful of nineteenth-century immigrant rabbis and joining a long-standing American tradition that traced back to the establishment of Harvard, the first training ground for ministers in the colonial period. Like Harvard, JIR was intended to be a center for higher learning in addition to clergy training. To this end, Wise, an early champion of freedom of the pulpit, similarly insisted on academic freedom at JIR, which went hand in hand with the school's nondenominationalism. He and the founders of JIR envisioned a school animated by faculty and students representing diverse interpretations of Judaism, including "orthodox, conservative, liberal, radical, Zionist and non-Zionist."[2]

From the outset, the institute faced the same struggles that confronted many earlier American seminaries: carving out a place within the denominational landscape, developing an effective model for the transmission of learning in accord with contemporary educational approaches, and procuring a reliable and adequate funding stream. Within the first few years of operation, certain ideas in each of these areas fell by the wayside, while others took root and began to flourish.

Soon JIR-trained rabbis, positioned in synagogues and educational institutions around the country, began to steer American Jewry toward the values for which the tiny seminary stood. In the decades to follow, American liberal Judaism would be transformed, as Wise's blend of American progressivism and Jewish nationalism became foundational. Indeed, just fifteen years after Wise declared from his pulpit at Carnegie Hall the need for a new generation of rabbis devoted to bringing about a "spiritual and moral reformation" in American Judaism, the Central Conference of American Rabbis (CCAR) officially adopted the liberal and Zionist outlook that reformation entailed, through passage of their "Guiding Principles of Reform Judaism."

Otherwise known as the Columbus Platform of 1937, and ratified by just one vote, this signaled the ideological about-face underway in the Reform rabbinate. While the institute itself was losing financial solvency by this time, from the standpoint of its long-term mission, no matter; soon all the non-Orthodox movements would follow the CCAR in embracing the key elements of Wise's ideology, and their seminaries would adopt JIR's most important innovations.

The institute's nondenominationalism took longer to gain traction, but by the early twenty-first century, as a growing number of American Jews viewed denominations with indifference, new rabbinical programs across the United States were embracing the pluralistic model first implemented at JIR in 1922. Several of these, including Boston's Hebrew College, soon posed formidable competition with their denominational counterparts for students as well as philanthropic dollars.

Today, American Judaism confronts challenges remarkably similar to those that emerged in the 1920s. In a world facing major political, environmental, and health crises, a young generation of American Jews is seeking new expressions of Judaism that reflect their values and concerns. As a result, American Jewish institutions are grappling with a surge in nondenominationalism, rapidly changing learning and prayer modalities, and challenges to prevailing funding models that rely principally on ultra-wealthy donors.

These were the very issues that led the founders of JIR to enter the fray of

American rabbinical training; they, too, wrestled with the tension between plu-ralism and denominationalism, the ongoing need for Jewish learning to evolve in form and content, and the difficulty of creating democratic Jewish life given the lopsided nature of Jewish philanthropy. The history of JIR offers a window into the origins of twentieth-century American liberal Judaism, including its trajectory of achievement over recent decades as well as its struggles today.

Yet, few know the story of the Jewish Institute of Religion. The institute's success introducing an outlook that would fundamentally alter American liberal Judaism became lost in the shadow of its demise as an independent institution. In 1950, JIR merged with Hebrew Union College (HUC), and by the time I arrived at HUC-JIR's New York campus as a rabbinical student in 1987, all but a few of the JIR-connected faculty were gone, and the institute was rarely mentioned. Like many of my classmates, I considered myself an "HUC student" and shared a common understanding of the school's history wherein Isaac Mayer Wise (no relation), the founder of HUC in 1875, figured prominently, while Stephen S. Wise, the founder of JIR, played just a bit role. In the marriage represented by the school's hyphenated name, to the few who bothered to notice, it was clear which legacy mattered.

Not until two decades later did I finally take note. By then, I was conducting historical research on how American religious groups have utilized seminaries to advance their religious ideal, while also serving as dean of HUC-JIR's New York campus. From that unique vantage point, eighty-five years after Stephen S. Wise and the Free Synagogue created the Jewish Institute of Religion, I decided to mine the school's neglected history, both as a lens for examining the power that past seminaries have held in shaping the religious landscape of the United States and to better understand the origin of issues facing the American Jewish community in our own day.

For the next few years, I lived a double life. By day, I did my work as dean in a seminary dedicated to strengthening the vitality of Judaism while also bringing Jewish wisdom to bear on the national and global events unfolding around us. By night, as a student of history, I read thousands of digitized archival materials con-cerning the challenges Wise and his colleagues confronted in 1922 as they dedi-cated themselves to the same purpose.

Strong parallels began to emerge, as I discovered how the central struggles facing contemporary American Jewish seminaries are rooted in events that took place a century ago. The founders of JIR, for example, before even opening the school, questioned the efficacy of denominationalism. In confronting the diffi-culty of imparting a vast body of knowledge across generational divides in literacy, culture, and technology, they introduced to rabbinical training the contemporary practices of secular graduate-level professional schools. And, faced with the diffi-culty of raising money for a school whose political orientation offended many of the Jewish community's wealthiest donors, they focused on drawing modest support from other sources rather than compromising their principles.

Each of the three sections in *We Must Build Anew*, arranged chronologically, investigates how JIR tackled these issues over time. Part 1, "Call and First Steps," places the impulse for opening JIR within the broader context of American and Jewish traditions of training clergy and then explores the founders' articulated need for a new seminary, as well as the fierce opposition they encountered.

From the outset, the practical challenges of running a Jewish seminary tested the institute's viability as a nondenominational institution. Even in the seminaries of war-torn Europe, where Wise traveled in order to hastily recruit an international faculty, JIR's nonalignment caused a fracas, and it remained a source of pride as well as difficulty throughout the life of the school. Part 2, "The Model Blossoms," examines how JIR's founding mission impacted faculty recruitment, led to bitter debates over the curriculum between scholars and rabbis with competing visions for the school, and created challenges in fundraising, where Wise could solicit individual donors from across the religious spectrum but failed to muster any institutional support beyond the Free Synagogue.

Despite these difficulties, the student body grew steadily, and the faculty, notwithstanding its high turnover, provided a new kind of rabbinical training that reflected the founding ideals of the institute. While several students left with their hopes of entering the rabbinate dashed, including highly accomplished women who were denied the right to ordination, JIR succeeded in launching a corps of rabbis and positioning them for maximal impact in the field.

Part 3, "Metamorphosis," explores the Jewish community's growing receptivity to these rabbis' leadership, particularly as the crises unfolding across the globe grew more urgent. While most of these clergy had been drawn to the institute in the 1920s out of a passion for social justice, Zionism, and Jewish peoplehood, none could have fully anticipated the heightened relevance of these commitments to American Jewry in the early 1930s. But now, this ideological approach shaped how the first generation of JIR rabbis, from pulpits across the country, led their congregations and communities in response not only to a devastating economic depression but also to the Nazis' rise to power in Germany, and European Jewry's pressing need for a haven in Palestine.

No rabbi fought harder on each of these fronts than Wise, who by 1936 was leading the American Jewish Congress, the World Jewish Congress, and the Zionist Organization of America. While his efforts and those of JIR alumni reflected precisely the mission of the institute, their manifestly outward focus took a toll on the school's already fragile infrastructure. Thus, part 3 also investigates the implications of subordinating the institute's longevity for the sake of more immediately achieving its broader goals.

As a feminist scholar and lesbian rabbi writing this book, I asked myself repeatedly why I find so compelling this story that revolves around a leading man—namely, Wise—and a school that for decades remained, with a few important exceptions, a male preserve. Not until 1972 did HUC-JIR finally ordain a woman as a rabbi, and it took another eighteen years for the school to officially end its discrimination against lesbian, gay, and bisexual admissions candidates. Other barriers were slow to be removed, as well; only in 2006 did the college-institute ordain its first transgender rabbi, and in 2009, its first African American rabbi.

While each change in admissions represented a first step toward equity and inclusion, upon entering the college-institute members of these previously excluded groups encountered not a path with guardrails intended to protect them as they pursued their professional aspirations but serious obstacles they had to navigate on a daily basis. In 2021, for example, a group of alumnae came forward with allegations that a recently deceased faculty member had sexually harassed his female students over a period of decades. In response, the school launched a broad independent investigation that revealed patterns of gender discrimination, sexual harassment, LGBTQ+ discrimination, bullying and disrespect, failure to provide accommodations, and racial discrimination at the college-institute spanning from the 1970s until the present.[3] *We Shall Build Anew* shows that the "old boys club mentality" mentioned repeatedly in the 2021 report as the backdrop for this pervasive misconduct dates back to JIR's founding in 1922, and gender discrimination as well as alleged sexual harassment has been part of the college-institute's history since long before the 1970s.

Still, while the struggle toward full equity and inclusion for all within Jewish life has a long way to go, the story of JIR reveals the central role seminaries can play in effecting deep change in the broader world—not only by opening the rabbinate to the full diversity of the Jewish people but also by challenging all forms of systemic oppression within Judaism and beyond. The various failures of past seminary leaders to do so have left Judaism diminished, and the all-male rabbinate is but one example; at the same time, forward-thinking clergy training has proven an effective path toward keeping Judaism dynamic and reflective of each new generation's highest ideals.

A century ago, the founders of JIR tested the idea that a single synagogue-sponsored seminary could alter the course of American Judaism. They rejected denominationalism, embraced contemporary innovations in Jewish learning, and challenged the outsize role of ultra-wealthy donors in Jewish life. Over the next three decades, under Wise's direction, the institute trained a cadre of rabbis characterized by Louis I. Newman, the first rabbi Wise ever ordained, as "prepared to go through fire" to espouse liberal causes at all costs, fight for the emancipation of the Jewish people from its oppressors, and achieve "the right to breathe freely in Zion."[4]

For historians and all who wrestle today with the legacy of twentieth-century liberal Judaism, the story of JIR reveals the roots of this ideological synthesis and how it entered the mainstream of twentieth-century liberal Judaism in defiance of institutional pressures within as well as beyond the Jewish community.

In the United States, where religious leadership has always mattered and seminaries have long been responsible for bringing about significant social change, creating a new kind of rabbi did, in fact, establish the path toward creating a new kind of American Judaism.

I

Call and First Steps

1

Traditions of Dissent

Since the earliest days of the colonial period in North America, enterprising clergy seeking to prepare disciples for leadership have created institutions of higher learning as a means of challenging, if not upending, the existing order.

The practice began, most famously, when the Puritan founders of the Massachusetts Bay Colony created Harvard College in 1636.[1] Based in the town of Cambridge, so-named to evoke a four-centuries-old English tradition of higher learning, the school itself reflected the very different values and new circumstances of religious dissenters planting roots in American soil. Harvard educated sons of the Puritan elite and succeeded in training three generations of Calvinist ministers before liberal, anti-Calvinists began to infiltrate the school's teaching staff and governing board in the 1690s. As Enlightenment thinking spread among Boston's Congregationalist ministers and on campus, the college began to veer away from the orthodoxy of its founders and toward a secular approach to learning.

Dissatisfied with Harvard's growing liberalism, a group of traditional Calvinists chartered their own collegiate school in 1701, which became Yale College in 1718. Meanwhile, Harvard continued down a steady path of liberalization and experienced a second split a century later when, following the appointment of a Unitarian to the prestigious Hollis Chair in Divinity in 1805, another group of dissatisfied Calvinists formed Andover Theological Seminary. Andover became the first graduate-level seminary in the country devoted exclusively to the training of clergy.

Until this time, the creation of colleges had proceeded gradually, with nine forming during the colonial period and another thirteen by 1800. All but one of these schools had a Protestant denominational affiliation and received colonial government support; none fell under church control; and, with the exception of Andover, none trained clergy exclusively.[2] Georgetown College was the exception, having been founded in 1789 as a Jesuit school dedicated to educating students of all religious backgrounds. Just one Catholic seminary existed in the country, St. Mary's Seminary of Baltimore, which four Sulpician priests opened in 1791 with an enrollment of five students.[3]

The scope of clergy training in the United States began to broaden rapidly around the turn of the century, as a revivalist movement swept across the nation,

inspiring large numbers of unchurched Americans to embrace new kinds of religious expression. Evangelical Christianity infused intense emotionality into
American Protestant life and encouraged followers to focus not only inward, on
their own individual grace, but outward, too. Protestant reformers intent upon
addressing the sins of the nation drew adherents into a "Benevolent Empire" of
organizations devoted to religious efforts such as Bible distribution, sabbath observance, temperance, missionary work, and more controversial causes such as abolition and women's suffrage. The religious fervor of the period fueled the growth
of existing denominations as well as the creation of new ones and greatly increased
the demand for clergy. As a result, the period 1820–1860 saw the emergence of
sixty-six new seminaries devoted primarily to producing Protestant ministers.[4]
Thanks to a rising number of Catholic immigrants, twenty-two diocesan seminaries were also in operation by 1843, though most proved to be short-lived due to a
shortage of both students and funding. Three Benedictine monasteries and four
provincial Catholic seminaries, based in the Northeast and Midwest, fared better.[5]

Religion, politics, and education converged at many of these seminaries, and
not always peacefully. At Lane Theological Seminary in Cincinnati, for example,
a bitter conflict broke out over abolition when, in 1835, the board of trustees attempted to quash the efforts of students and faculty advocating immediate emancipation and an end to slavery. The abolitionists broke away and then accepted an
invitation to join the new Oberlin Collegiate Institute, which they successfully
transformed into a powerful regional center for the antislavery movement.[6]

All of these religiously affiliated schools helped forge the values and political
trajectory of the nation. Religion, after all, offers cosmological notions about the
order of the universe and moral codes to guide human conduct within that order.
Rites and rituals performed in the confines of home or sanctuary reverberate in
the broader world. Personal religious transformation extends outward toward the
shaping of religious community and outward further as leaders steer a course for
their followers through the challenging issues of the day. Seminary founders have
played a role in charting the course of the country by bringing their faith to bear
not only on abolition but also on issues such as industrialization, wealth distribution, and war.

But conversely, American life has also played a role in charting the course of
seminaries. In response to the vicissitudes of politics and the economy, as well as
trends in culture, industry, higher education, and philanthropy, seminaries face
constant pressure to realign and change course. Harvard was just the first to acquiesce to the demands of a new generation by shedding the school's founding religious
values. Throughout American history, where religion and higher education have
intersected, new understandings have led to schism and change, and repeatedly,
dissenters have started new seminaries solely to promote their own approaches to
ministry and faith.

Later, when some of these faced decline—due to a precipitous drop in students, say, or the threat of financial insolvency—they either merged with a peer institution, radically altered their mission, or closed.[7]

The history of American Jewish seminaries did not begin until the mid-nineteenth century but followed a similar pattern. During the period from 1654, when twenty-three Jews arrived in New Amsterdam, to 1840, when the Jewish population in North America numbered roughly fifteen thousand, not rabbis but *hazanim* (cantors) and educated laity led worship, officiated at rituals, and arbitrated Jewish law for their local communities. Only after an influx of Jewish immigrants from Central Europe entered the United States in the decade following the revolutions of 1848, increasing the population of American Jewry by tenfold, did a handful of immigrant rabbis begin to reflect seriously on the need for an American Jewish seminary. "No Jewish community in history has ever thrived without a great academy, a *bet midrash gavohah*, at its center," writes historian David Ellenson, and now some of these rabbis sought to create one in America, too.[8] In imagining the contours of such an academy, they drew on the various European models they knew best, just as centuries earlier the Puritans had sought to import, with adaptations, the English model of higher learning familiar to them.

In the nineteenth century, with the development of Wissenschaft des Judentums, the scientific interpretation of Judaism, a new kind of European institution of Jewish learning emerged. These modern rabbinical seminaries, as distinct from traditional yeshivas, trained men for careers in scholarship as well as the rabbinate and required that their graduates earn a PhD from a secular university, as well. The first modern European Jewish seminary, the Istituto Convitto Rabbinico (later called the Collegio Rabbinico Italiano), emerged in Padua, Italy, in 1829.[9] Soon thereafter, one was attempted in Metz, France, but failed. In ensuing decades, several major institutions were established, including the Jewish Theological Seminary of Breslau, founded in 1854 by Zacharias Frankel to promote historical-positive Judaism; Jews' College, founded in London in 1855; the Israelitisch-Theologische Lehranstalt, founded in Vienna in 1862;[10] the Hochschule für die Wissenschaft des Judentums, founded in Berlin with a Reform orientation in 1872; the Rabbinical Seminary of Budapest, founded in 1877;[11] and the Neo-Orthodox Rabbiner-Seminar fuer das Orthodoxe Judentum, founded in Berlin in 1873.[12] Of these, the Jewish Theological Seminary of Breslau and Berlin's Hochschule had the strongest influence on the non-Orthodox rabbinate in the United States.

Most prominent among American-based rabbis seeking to draw upon this European model was Bohemian-born Isaac Mayer Wise (no relation to Stephen S. Wise), who came to the United States in 1846 and was quickly retained by Congregation Beth El in Albany, New York. There, he introduced a number of reforms and spoke his mind in ways that earned him loyalty from some but consternation from others, including a traditionalist faction. After a stormy four years, Beth El dismissed Mayer Wise, who together with his followers formed a new congregation, Anshe Emeth, which espoused Reform. In 1854, Mayer Wise moved to Cincinnati, home to a Jewish community of roughly three thousand (almost four times larger than Albany's), where he assumed the pulpit of Congregation Bene Yeshurun.[13] At this time, Cincinnati was the largest city in the West and one of the fastest-growing cities in the nation, and Mayer Wise had reason to believe it would become the urban center of the United States.

There, he began a decades-long effort to unite American Jewry. From the outset, however, in his efforts to shape an ideology as well as an institutional structure that could serve all of American Jewry, Mayer Wise, as a moderate Reformer, faced opposition from more radical Reformers, on one end of the religious spectrum, and traditionalists, on the other. Like their Protestant forebears in the United States, these immigrant rabbis, though few in number, lacked a shared approach to belief and practice. And during the latter half of the nineteenth century, they, too, split repeatedly and created increasingly traditionalist schools.

Had all gone according to Isaac Mayer Wise's original plan, Zion College would have been the nation's first Jewish institution of higher learning, preparing men for rabbinic ordination while also offering a range of secular subjects for students not intending to enter the rabbinate. A year after arriving in Cincinnati intent on founding the new school, Mayer Wise capably raised funds from local businessmen and organized associations in cities across the country to support the endeavor. However, after he proceeded to open Zion College without first consulting the membership of these associations, many withdrew their support and abandoned the project. Making matters worse, the Panic of 1857 hit shortly thereafter, and Mayer Wise lost the financial backing of his remaining Cincinnati base. Zion College soon closed its doors.[14]

A small group of German-born Reform rabbis in the Northeast made a separate attempt at establishing a rabbinical school in the United States during this period, but they, too, ran into difficulties. In 1859, Samuel Adler, who occupied the pulpit of New York City's Temple Emanu-El, began calling for a "scientific school" of Jewish theology to be based in New York, which would prepare rabbis in the scholarly *wissenschaftlich* approach of Germany's Reform rabbinate.[15] To hasten the process of providing American Jewry with new rabbis, he also began personally training at least one candidate, Chicago-based Bernard Felsenthal, on whom Adler conferred the title "*moreh harav*" (rabbi) in 1861.[16]

Felsenthal then joined Adler as well as David Einhorn, the prominent rabbi of Baltimore's Har Sinai Congregation, to develop plans for a school based at Emanu-El that would train rabbis. While the project was suspended during the Civil War, in April 1865, immediately upon hearing that General Robert E. Lee had surrendered at Appomattox, they resumed their efforts together with Emanu-El's lay leadership, and that June, Adler distributed flyers trying to enlist students for the school, to little avail.[17] Wondering if the school's identification with Temple Emanu-El was the problem—perhaps other congregations would never embrace a single synagogue's project—they temporarily tried changing its name to the American Hebrew College, to no avail.

Yet another effort to establish a seminary met with greater success, in the form of Maimonides College in Philadelphia, opened by the Board of Delegates of American Israelites in 1867. The board, founded in 1859 and made up of representatives from more than twenty congregations in the Northeast, selected *hazan* (cantor) Isaac Leeser, the foremost Orthodox leader in the United States, as provost. With a mission to serve Jews of all ideological perspectives, the school initially seemed positioned to prosper. Leeser, however, died unexpectedly after just four months in the position. Though he had retained some highly regarded faculty for the school during his brief tenure, the school subsequently struggled financially and could not retain students. After just six years, in 1873, Maimonides College closed its doors.[18]

That year the tide finally turned, when a significant step was taken toward fulfilling Isaac Mayer Wise's dream of establishing the first American Jewish seminary with staying power. After the Zion College debacle, he had strategically focused his sights on creating a rabbinical school (rather than a Jewish college with a broader mandate) and a union of congregations to sustain it. Now the president of his congregation, Moritz Loth, inspired by Mayer Wise but acting on his own initiative, galvanized thirty-four congregations from the South and the West to convene in Cincinnati for the purpose of forming the Union of American Hebrew Congregations (UAHC), which was established in July 1873. By 1875, it had grown to seventy-two congregations, and reflecting Wise's deep commitment to a true union of American Jewry, the UAHC included Reform as well as traditional congregations. Holdouts included congregations in the Northeast represented by the Board of Delegates of American Israelites, but in 1876 the UAHC and the board, representing different regions and serving different purposes, began exploring a merger.[19]

As Isaac Mayer Wise intended, the UAHC's primary focus was supporting a rabbinical seminary, and with the funding they provided, he succeeded in opening Hebrew Union College (HUC) in Cincinnati in 1875. With Wise at the helm, the college had a strong president, broad (if not deep) financial support, and a structure that gave a wide base of congregations some measure of control.[20]

The Jews of Cincinnati, numbering between eight and twelve thousand, infused these endeavors with their own unique spirit. For several decades until the end of the Civil War, Cincinnati had been home to the largest, wealthiest, and most influential Jewish community in the West, and as Jonathan D. Sarna has written, Cincinnati Jewry perceived themselves as "a Jewish version of the American dream, a 'sort of paradise,' not yet fully realized, but surely moving in the right direction." Indeed, Max Lilienthal, a rabbi and one of the architects of Reform Judaism who had followed Mayer Wise from New York to Cincinnati in the 1850s, declared of their chosen city, "here is our Zion and Jerusalem."[21] Having achieved economic success and substantial acceptance into the social and cultural fabric of the city, many felt duty-bound not only to work for local civic improvement but also to provide the American Jewish community with a new kind of Judaism free of traditional dictates and conducive to American life in the latter half of the nineteenth century.[22]

To be sure, by 1875, Eastern cities including New York, Philadelphia, and Boston were far outpacing Cincinnati in terms of growth, as was Chicago, which thanks to the routing of the railroads, was becoming a national hub for the grain market, meatpacking industry, and other manufacturing. San Francisco, meanwhile, was now home to the nation's second-largest Jewish community, numbering twenty thousand. Still, recognizing New York and San Francisco were worlds apart, Isaac Mayer Wise, as well as the officers and main financial supporters of the union and the college, still had reason to believe their own community of Cincinnati would continue to play a central role in national Jewish life.

Certainly, HUC in 1875 was well positioned to carry out its mandate to train the nation's rabbis. The school's base grew even stronger three years later when the board of delegates agreed to merge with the UAHC, making the union broader and more diverse.[23]

Mayer Wise initially intended Hebrew Union College to be a nonpartisan seminary that would train American rabbis to serve the entire American Jewish community, including all congregations regardless of where they fell along the ideological spectrum.[24] During its first year, the college retained one paid instructor to teach nine young students, most from poor families and reliant on the school for support. These students enrolled in an eight-year program that would include high school as well as college studies. The curriculum focused on classical Jewish texts, including the Bible, Talmud, Midrash, and Codes, and though based in some ways on the German seminary model, it included no biblical criticism or other contemporary scholarship that traditionalists would find offensive. "Doctrinal issues were purposely avoided," according to historian Michael A. Meyer, and "Wise did not want the College branded as Reform or radical in any respect."[25]

Meanwhile, in New York, Temple Emanu-El's efforts to build a rabbinical school had finally begun to gain traction in the early 1870s, thanks to increased financial support from lay leaders and the enthusiastic agreement of their rabbi, Gustav Gottheil, to serve as the school's superintendent. Gottheil, who was born in Prussian Poland and trained in Berlin, had been an assistant to the radical Reformer Samuel Holdheim and then worked in a congregation in Manchester, England, before moving to New York. Known for his liberal ideas and his outspoken opposition to slavery in England, Gottheil opened Emanu-El Theological Seminary with an enrollment of thirty students.

None too pleased with this competition in the Northeast, the Cincinnati-based leaders of the UAHC now pressured the congregation, which had only recently joined the union (together with the others represented by the board of delegates), to shut down their nascent seminary. At first, the congregation refused to comply, but eventually the two sides reached a compromise. The UAHC agreed to cover about half of the school's budget, as long as Emanu-El offered only a preparatory program for students who intended to complete their rabbinical studies at HUC.[26] With that arrangement, Isaac Mayer Wise neutralized the threat these radical Reformers had posed, and for a brief moment but one institution in the United States provided full rabbinical training: Hebrew Union College.

However, just as Harvard lost its monopoly when dissenters began creating schools of their own, so, too, did HUC. No sooner than the college's first ordination ceremony in 1883, where the reception featured a feast of unkosher seafood and meats mixed with dairy, did Mayer Wise's inclusive vision begin to collapse. The "trefa banquet," as the incident became known later, was attended by rabbis and other guests representing a broad religious spectrum including traditionalists. Serving that group such delicacies as littleneck clams, soft-shell crabs, shrimp salad, lobster bisque, and frogs legs triggered an ideological debate that would play out in Jewish newspapers across the country for the next two years. Though it appears Isaac Mayer Wise never intended for the dinner to provoke controversy, in the face of harsh criticism afterward, he took the offensive rather than apologizing for the menu, thereby fueling polarization. Ultimately, according to the historian Lance Sussman, the episode contributed to the long-term factionalization of American Jewish life.[27]

Indeed, a decisive break took place two years later, when radical and moderate Reform rabbis convened in Pittsburgh in response to a call from Kaufmann Kohler, a Bavarian-born immigrant rabbi in the radical Reform camp, who was David Einhorn's son-in-law as well as his successor at New York's Temple Beth El. When Kohler urged endorsement of a statement of principles far more radical than the moderate views of Isaac Mayer Wise, the assembled rabbis navigated the tension by electing Mayer Wise president but then unanimously passing an eight-paragraph platform for modern Judaism that reflected Kohler's outlook and by which no traditionalist Jew could abide. "We consider ourselves no longer a nation, but a religious community," read the platform, which not only rejected Jewish peoplehood but also adherence to laws related to diet, priestly purity, and dress.

In response, Conservative supporters of the UAHC and HUC, their religious outlook repudiated, now rejected both enterprises, even though neither organization ratified the document, and Mayer Wise himself expressed dissatisfaction with this "Declaration of Independence," as he called it. A group of Orthodox and

Conservative leaders from Philadelphia and New York, under the leadership of Sabato Morais and Henry Pereira Mendes, Sephardic rabbis formerly involved with Maimonides College, began planning a traditional seminary of their own, and in 1886 the Jewish Theological Seminary (JTS) opened in New York with Morais as president.[28]

JTS would promote modern scholarship in conjunction with traditional Jewish observance, and its founders hoped to make their institution inclusive of the broad spectrum of American Jewry who fell to the right of Reform. Thus, the faculty of JTS included Conservative as well as Orthodox Jews. But even this narrower model of inclusivity could not remain intact for long; just as the founders of JTS had challenged HUC from the right, so, too, would a contingent of Orthodox Jews from the growing immigrant community pose a similar challenge to JTS.

Hardly interested in modern scholarship, this group sought to import to America the traditional yeshiva model of learning they had experienced in Eastern Europe.[29] And so, the same year JTS was founded, Yeshiva Etz Chaim opened in the Mariampol Synagogue on the Lower East Side.[30] Whereas JTS would ordain college-educated, English-speaking rabbis who could promote Americanization while preserving Jewish tradition, the founders of Etz Chaim opposed modernization and instead sought to replicate the Lithuanian yeshiva system.[31] Here, students ranging in age from nine to fifteen years studied full-time, spending most of the day learning Talmud and Jewish law, and only in the late afternoon learning Hebrew and engaging in secular study mandated by New York State.[32]

Geographically, just as the founders of the UAHC and HUC had reason to view their location in Cincinnati as a strategic asset in the mid-1870s, the founders of JTS and Etz Chaim likely never doubted the importance of making New York their home in the mid-1880s. New York's Jewish population in 1880 was already the largest in the country by threefold when it numbered roughly sixty thousand, and by 1885 that figure had nearly doubled and was continuing to grow exponentially due to an influx of Eastern European immigrants. The city's overall population was now approaching 1.5 million.[33]

Despite the clear need for more Jewish educational opportunities in New York at this time, just before Etz Chaim got off the ground, further uptown, the Emanu-El school closed its doors. As a preparatory program for the college in Cincinnati, it had attracted neither many students nor donors, and tensions between the UAHC and the congregation had never dissipated. In 1885, when Emanu-El paid for two students to study at the Hochschule, the liberal Jewish seminary in Berlin, Isaac Mayer Wise complained that they should have been sent to HUC; in response, Gottheil claimed the students were too advanced for study at the college. That year, however, the congregation finally concluded that their endeavor was untenable and ended its support.

The founders of Etz Chaim encountered very different challenges during this period. While the yeshiva had little trouble attracting students throughout the 1890s, an increasing number of its graduates were turning to the more liberal JTS for rabbinical training. To provide an Orthodox alternative to JTS, in 1897 the Etz Chaim leadership created the Rabbi Isaac Elchanan Theological Seminary (RIETS), which attracted a steady stream of students. Etz Chaim and RIETS maintained a close relationship and eventually merged in 1915 under the new leadership of Bernard Revel, a thirty-year-old scholar trained in Lithuania and then at Dropsie College.[34]

By this point, amid a wave of immigration that ultimately brought nearly three million Eastern European Jews into the United States between 1880 and 1925, American Jewry's demand for rabbis had greatly increased. Three seminaries attempted to accommodate, serving three increasingly distinct streams of American Judaism: HUC (Reform) in Cincinnati, and JTS (Conservative) as well as RIETS (Orthodox) in New York.

For a young Stephen S. Wise seeking to become a rabbi in the early 1890s, none of these seminaries, nor the streams of Judaism they represented, held much appeal. At age twenty-two, he had in mind a different approach, which resembled that of his father, Aaron Wise, who descended from five generations of rabbis and had a rebellious spirit of his own.

The son of Joseph Hirsch Weisz, chief rabbi of Erlau and one of Hungarian Jewry's leading opponents of religious reform, Aaron, too, had initially followed in his father's footsteps. However, after studying for the rabbinate at the Orthodox seminary in Eisenstadt led by Esriel Hildesheimer, who later founded the Rabbiner-Seminar in Berlin, and then earning a doctorate at the University of Halle, he began moving in a liberal direction. In 1870, he married Sabine de Fischer Farkashazy and entered the family's porcelain business, his father-in-law's condition for approving the marriage. After organizing a workers' strike in protest of the factory's poor conditions, however, Aaron lost his welcome there and decided the time had come to move to the United States. Thus, in the spring of 1874, at age thirty and just a month after the birth of Stephen, his second child, he traveled in steerage to New York, where he started work as a bricklayer. Soon Congregation Beth Elohim in Brooklyn invited him to serve as their rabbi, and now back in the family business of choice, he brought over his wife and children.[35] Two years later, he accepted a position at Rodeph Sholom, a Conservative congregation in Manhattan, where he remained until his death.

Aaron Wise raised his family on East Fifth Street in Manhattan and socialized in many different milieus. While the family spoke German in the home and kept company with the uptown Jews of Rodeph Sholom, Aaron also cultivated in his children an affinity for the Eastern European immigrants living on the Lower East Side. From a young age, Stephen felt drawn toward these downtown Jews.

In 1886, Aaron Wise became involved with the founding of JTS, and he also belonged to a tiny circle of proto-Zionist rabbis that included Temple Emanu-El's Gustav Gottheil, in whose after-school religious classes he enrolled young Stephen. During this period, Aaron enlisted other friends to teach Stephen as well, including Henry Gersoni, who offered instruction in Hebrew, Max Margolis, and Alexander Kohut, who taught Talmud to Stephen, alongside Kohut's own son George, as well as another boy, Joseph Hertz. The three eventually took courses at JTS, together, too. Aaron Wise's ideological flexibility and ability to work with colleagues across a broad spectrum of belief, and his encouraging Stephen to take in all manner of viewpoints, strongly informed his son's commitments, particularly his prioritization of Jewish peoplehood over any particular theological perspective.

Stephen entered City College at the age of thirteen, where he concentrated in Greek and Latin, studied a great deal of English literature, and learned public speaking by participating in school debates. He also continued his Jewish studies, taking private Hebrew lessons with Arnold B. Erlich, a Hebrew linguist and Bible commentator, and later with Alexander Kohut. By the end of his junior year, he knew he wanted to enter the rabbinate, and he transferred to Columbia to study with Richard Gottheil, Gustav's son, who headed the Semitics Department.[36] Then, after earning his BA with honors in 1892, he spent a memorable summer in the Adirondacks at a summer school run by the philosopher Thomas Davidson. This experience contributed to his rabbinical training as well, for Davidson's focus on remedying the practical problems of modern society inspired Wise to translate these ideas into Jewish terms.[37]

Wise deepened this line of thinking while continuing his preparation for the rabbinate in Vienna, where he spent the next academic year studying privately with Adolf Jellinek, a prominent liberal rabbi who actively engaged in civic affairs. Wise had initially considered studying at HUC and managed to get Isaac Mayer Wise's reluctant agreement to his remaining in New York while preparing for the college's qualifying exams, so he could simultaneously pursue his doctoral studies at Columbia.[38] However, even with permission to prepare in absentia, rather than moving to Cincinnati to take the preparatory classes HUC generally required, Stephen abandoned the idea and chose to work with Jellinek. A powerful preacher who regularly drew large crowds to Vienna's Great Synagogue, Jellinek was also a scholar of Midrash and kabbalah. He took Wise under his wing and modeled a deep commitment to caring for the Jewish people everywhere. In the spring of 1893, Jellinek bestowed on his student private *semikhah* (ordination).[39]

The newly minted Rabbi Stephen S. Wise returned to New York that summer and, as planned, entered the doctoral program at Columbia. The following spring, he launched his career as assistant to Rabbi Henry Jacobs at Congregation B'nai Jeshurun, a conservative synagogue. There, he organized a religious school as well as the Sisterhood for Personal Service to aid needy immigrant families downtown.[40] Within a year, Jacobs became ill and died, and twenty-one-year-old Wise was elected to take his place.

During this period, Wise and his friend (and now academic advisor) Richard Gottheil began organizing a nascent Zionist movement in the United States. In the summer of 1897, they founded the Federation of American Zionists, and the following summer, Wise attended the Second World Zionist Congress in Basel as a reporter for the New York *Journal*. The gathering proved life-changing, with Wise particularly inspired by the movement's leader, Theodor Herzl. "At Basle [*sic*] I became a Jew in every sense of that term," he wrote. "Judaism ceased to be a type of religious worship. The Jewish people became my own." For the next two years, he spoke and wrote extensively trying to build support for Zionism in the United States. Still, despite his compelling oratory, the movement's focus on European antisemitism had little resonance with American Jews, and he attracted few followers.[41] Among those openly opposed was Isaac Mayer Wise, still head of HUC and the UAHC, as well as the Central Conference of American Rabbis, which had been founded in 1889 as an association for HUC graduates. After the first Zionist Congress met in 1897, Isaac Mayer Wise began denouncing the idea of a Jewish state and in 1899 called Herzl's idea "Ziomaniac."[42]

Stephen Wise's speaking did, however, open an important new opportunity for him in the summer of 1899, when a West Coast tour for the Zionist movement took him to Portland, Oregon. There, members of Congregation Beth Israel were so impressed with the charismatic 25-year-old, they invited him to become their rabbi.[43]

While the opportunity to leave New York for an adventure in this beautiful part of the country appealed to Wise, he could not make the decision alone. He had met Louise Waterman, an artistic and intellectual young woman who shared his rebellious spirit, love of reading, and passion for social justice. The couple shared an interest in the life of the spirit, though Louise, daughter of wealthy German Jewish parents who belonged nominally to New York's Temple Emanu-El, found inspiration not in Reform Judaism but the Ethical Culture movement. Founded two decades earlier by Felix Adler, son of Temple Emanu-El's Rabbi Samuel Adler, Ethical Culture dispensed with theology and instead prized universal fellowship, intellectual engagement, and social reform. The movement now had a strong presence in New York, and Louise participated actively, attending Adler's Sunday morning sermons regularly and teaching art in the city's settlement houses.[44]

To Stephen's good fortune, Louise, too, was eager for an adventure, and the couple agreed they would marry and then move to Oregon. Over the next year, Stephen completed his term at B'nai Jeshurun as well as his dissertation, a translation of an ethical treatise by Solomon ibn Gabirol, the eleventh-century Jewish philosopher and poet. Then, in the summer of 1900, he ventured back to Portland alone to get settled and begin his work at Beth Israel. In November, he returned to New York for the wedding, where Gustav Gottheil officiated together with

Kaufmann Kohler, a prominent Reform rabbi and friend of the Waterman family.[45] Finally, that winter, the couple headed west together, where they established their new home and prepared to build a family.

A Turning Point for American Jewish Seminaries

While 1900 was, personally, an eventful year for Stephen and Louise, a major development of a different kind made it pivotal in American Jewish life, as well. The death of Isaac Mayer Wise in March marked the end of an era, most especially for the Reform movement, whose three foundational institutions he had founded and led: the Union of American Hebrew Congregations, Hebrew Union College, and the Central Conference of American Rabbis. And although Stephen was balancing a full-time job and his dissertation defense at the time, he likely caught the debate regarding HUC and JTS that unfolded in multiple issues of New York's *American Hebrew* immediately following the traditional thirty-day mourning period for the great Reform leader.

Three years earlier, the seminary had lost its own president, Sabato Morais, and begun to languish. Now that *both* schools lacked permanent heads and struggled financially, the newspaper launched a symposium titled "One Institution for Rearing Rabbis? Shall Our Theological Colleges Unite—Is it Possible, Is It Desirable?" Jacob Schiff and Louis Marshall, two of the most powerful figures in the American Jewish community, led off the discussion with a proposal to merge the two struggling institutions into a single school based in New York and dedicated to serving all Jews across the country. Both prominent Reform Jews affiliated with New York's Temple Emanu-El—Schiff, a banker and philanthropist, and Marshall, a corporate lawyer—they were, in a sense, putting Isaac Mayer Wise's original inclusive vision, albeit an East Coast version, back on the table. Schiff wrote:

> The question much near to me is, how can Judaism be maintained as an active force in the daily life of our people, so that they may not become swamped by materialism and indifference, as is seriously threatened. In a serious effort for this maintenance of Judaism, the orthodox and reform Jews can, should and must join hands, and in no way can they better do this, than by the joining in the creation of a strong institution, from which sincere, earnest and capable men shall become graduated—true Jews, who shall be able to be teachers, leaders and missionaries among our people.

Marshall, then chairing a $500,000 endowment campaign for HUC, agreed:

> By consolidation, two financially feeble institutions can be developed into one strong body . . . united, much can be accomplished that cannot be done by a

house divided against itself. The best Jewish scholarship could then be enlisted toward the advancement of our cause. The interests of all classes of Jews
throughout the country would be concentrated. There would exist none of
the excuses for indifference which now obtain. There would not be that waste
of energy and of money which the continuance of the two schools, where one
would be ample to meet all requirements, would entail. There would be unity
in matters of essential importance, where now there is discord. Every dictate
of reason and of sentiment favors consolidation. Naught but unworthy personal prejudices can stand in its way.[46]

In the exchange of letters that followed, scholars, prominent rabbis, and lay
leaders from a range of religious perspectives argued vociferously. Those who opposed a merger included Reform as well as Orthodox Jews. Some believed mix-
ing "the oil of orthodoxy with the water of reform" was impossible, while others
feared the amalgamation would dilute sacred principles and lead to indifference.
The leadership of HUC and JTS also opposed the idea, unwilling to compromise
ideologically or to cede control of their respective institutions. Soon Schiff and
Marshall abandoned the merger idea for a bold plan of a different sort.

Working in secret, they invested their resources in taking over the seminary
and remaking it into a new institution. To hide the change from public view, they
reincorporated the school with just a slightly different name—the Jewish Theological Seminary *of America*—and installed a new board. The reorganization
shifted control to a wealthy group of Reform Jews, mainly from Emanu-El, who
placed the new seminary on solid financial footing by endowing it with half a million dollars.[47]

From the start, Marshall and his band of donors fully intended for the seminary to remain a Conservative institution promoting an Americanized form of
halakhic Judaism.[48] It would be more flexible than RIETS regarding traditional
Jewish practice but still far from Reform Judaism, which had little appeal among
Eastern European Jews. Viewing the seminary as a force for the preservation of
Judaism among the immigrant community, they enlisted the renowned British
scholar Solomon Schechter to serve as president. Under his leadership, the school
had little difficulty attracting students attempting to Americanize while leading
active Jewish lives, just as Marshall and Schiff had hoped.

A year after Schechter's appointment at JTS, Kaufmann Kohler was named
the new president of HUC and began charting a course for the college and Reform
Judaism that centered on ethical monotheism and preserved the movement's social
and cultural mores.

In the meanwhile, out in Oregon, Stephen Wise was introducing a new approach, unlike the Judaism taught at either the seminary *or* the college—and
his career was taking off. From the outset, he demonstrated the commitment to

civic engagement and Progressive activism that would characterize his rabbinate for the rest of his life. Regularly citing the Social Gospel teachings of Gladden, Rauschenbusch, and other liberal Protestant thinkers and utilizing the pulpit as his base, he attacked Oregon's gambling and liquor interests, supported women's suffrage and union rights, promoted interfaith dialogue, participated in the Oregon State Conference of Charities and Corrections, helped found the Peoples' Forum of Oregon, and served as a commissioner on the state's Board of Child Labor. The congregation largely supported Wise's independence, and over the six years he spent in Portland, he began to develop a national reputation.[49]

The story of his return to New York is well-known. In 1905, the board of trustees of Temple Emanu-El, in search of a new rabbi, invited Wise to interview and deliver a trial sermon. He had preached there once before, in 1900, but as recently as 1903 had turned down a similar invitation. He knew the congregation well, and as his biographer notes, by this point, "Temple Emanu-El stood for all he loathed in Reform Judaism, a rich complacency indifferent to the ills of the world, deaf to the ethical commands of the Hebrew prophets."[50] Nonetheless, this time Wise agreed and performed well enough for the board to ask him the terms under which he would accept an appointment. In response, Wise expressed just one stipulation, which he had told Beth Israel in Portland, as well: He could preach freely and express any view on any topic he deemed important, without submitting his sermons for board review.[51]

Unlike the Portland lay leaders, Louis Marshall, then secretary to the board, objected vociferously. "The pulpit should always be subject to and under the control of the Board of Trustees," Marshall wrote Wise, and should the rabbi and board ever differ irreconcilably, the rabbi shall either acquiesce, or exercise "the privilege of resigning."[52]

With battle lines drawn, Wise now withdrew his candidacy and returned to Portland but chose nonetheless to escalate the conflict by publishing a lengthy "Open Letter to the Members of Temple Emanu-El of New York," which the *New York Times* printed in full. Here Wise reported telling the board, "The chief office of the minister is not to represent the views of the congregation, but to proclaim the truth as he sees it . . . how can a man be vital and independent and helpful, if he be tethered and muzzled?" His lengthy letter to the synagogue membership also included the following: "A free pulpit, worthily filled, must command respect and influence; a pulpit that is not free, howsoever filled, is sure to be without potency and honor . . . even schisms at the worst are not so much to be feared as the attitude of the pulpit which never provokes dissent because it is cautious rather than courageous, peace loving rather than prophetic, time serving rather than right serving. The minister is not to be the spokesman of the congregation, not the message bearer of the congregation, but the bearer of a message to the congregation."[53]

The debate over ministerial independence had a long history in the United States, and notwithstanding Wise's argument, not all who opposed an entirely free pulpit were intent on quashing dissent. Rather, in the spirit of a long-standing American anticlerical tradition, some sought to challenge the hierarchy, privilege, and unchecked authority they believed clergy used all too often to empower and enrich themselves.[54]

Wise, however, by refusing to capitulate before the titans on the Emanu-El board, effectively depicted himself in the public eye as a David taking on Goliath, and the conflict helped him attract a popular following while further rankling his targets. The approach would soon become a staple for the thirty-two-year-old rabbi and positioned him perfectly for his next move: opening his *own* congregation in New York, a synagogue free in every respect and representing all that Emanu-El did not. He finished out his term at Beth El and then returned East with Louise and their family, which had now grown to include two children, James and Justine. And a year after the Emanu-El conflict hit the papers, on the last Sunday in January 1907, Wise garnered *New York Times* coverage once again when he led a crowded service at Times Square's Hudson Theatre and preached on the meaning of a "Free Synagogue."[55]

Dues, pews, and the pulpit would be free, Wise explained. Thus, rather than charging for membership, the congregation would rely solely on voluntary contributions. Rather than assigning specific pews to wealthy donors, as was customary in many congregations at the time, seating would be open.[56] And, of course, the preacher would be free to speak independently, along with the broad array of guests with whom Wise planned to share the pulpit. Office-holding would be free and open to women on the same terms as men, and to cultivate widespread appreciation for the Jewish heritage, courses in Hebrew, Bible, and medieval and modern Jewish studies would be offered free to the general public. Of equal importance, Wise made clear, the congregation would actively engage with the most challenging issues of the day, for "not charity but social service, building upon the rock of social justice, will be the watch word of the Free Synagogue."[57]

As he had in Portland, Wise continued translating into Jewish terms many of the democratic and egalitarian aims of the Social Gospel movement he admired. Indeed, in pursuit of those aims, the establishment of the Free Synagogue was just one step toward a broad transformation Wise had planned for all of American Judaism, he told his audience in the Hudson Theatre. Congregational life had come to a standstill, he believed, even in New York City, where the Jewish population had tripled over the previous twenty years. But just as bold reformers of the past had successfully renewed Judaism to meet the needs of their day, he signaled great change was again in the offing: "We . . . must recognize and proclaim that the Jewish reformation was not an isolated act or a series of acts, but is a continuing, never-ending process. Petrified reform may fittingly be placed by the side of

ossified orthodoxy in the museum of religious antiquities, but there is a Jewish reformation that is not dead, that has but begun to live."[58]

Over the next two months, Wise brought together a small group of influential men and women willing to lend their financial support to the endeavor. Henry
Morgenthau Sr. made a gift of $5,000 and agreed to become acting chairman
when the congregation formally organized in April, and even several members of
Emanu-El contributed gifts of $10,000 each, including Jacob Schiff.[59] Schiff sup-
ported a variety of endeavors that offered the immigrant community a middle path
between Orthodoxy and secularism, and the Free Synagogue fit that characterization well.

After unanimously selecting Wise to serve as their rabbi, the congregation set
out to find an uptown meeting place more suitable than the Hudson Theatre while
also opening a downtown branch at the Clinton Hall auditorium on the Lower
East Side. There, Wise regularly led Friday night services and a Sunday evening forum on social problems, and despite the vehement opposition of traditionalists, he
began drawing crowds that climbed from 250 to 500–600 during the downtown
branch's ten-year existence.[60]

The Free Synagogue, which affiliated with Reform Judaism despite Wise's
criticisms of the movement, focused on three areas of work: religious, educational,
and social service.[61] In October 1907, they opened a religious school, and with
membership growing rapidly, a few months later they moved Sunday morning services into the Universalist Church of Eternal Hope on West Eighty-First Street;
here, too, large crowds came to hear him preach.[62] To expose the congregation to
a broad range of viewpoints, Wise began sharing the pulpit with guest preachers,
a practice he would continue throughout his career.

By October 1910, the Free Synagogue's membership exceeded five hundred,
and that year they moved High Holy Day and Sunday morning services to Carnegie Hall, where weekly attendance ranged between sixteen hundred and two thousand people.[63] Finally, in 1911, the congregation purchased several brownstones
on West Sixty-Eighth Street, where they established their permanent home. Still,
to accommodate the crowd, Wise continued to hold High Holy Day and Sunday
morning services at Carnegie Hall.

Though Wise's charismatic preaching attracted many followers, his congregants' devotion to him also stemmed from the care and attentiveness he displayed
in shepherding them through the important milestones of their lives. They also
took pride in the Free Synagogue's distinguishing features, most especially the
Social Service Department, which stood out from its inception. Housed initially
at Bellevue Hospital before the move to Sixty-Eighth Street, and led by Rabbi
Sidney Goldstein, a graduate of HUC, the department engaged congregants
in a wide range of activities including the provision of medical social work at
Bellevue and Lebanon hospitals, making and donating clothes for the poor, and

running two summer camps for economically disadvantaged youth. In 1916, under the department's auspices, Louise Waterman Wise founded a child adoption agency, which in ensuing years removed thousands of Jewish orphans from state-assigned asylums where they languished and placed them in Jewish homes across the country.[64]

Wise's own influence began to extend far beyond the Free Synagogue, due to his activism in a variety of secular and Jewish causes during this period. After the Triangle Shirtwaist Factory fire, for example, he fought for greater factory safety standards and, together with Jane Addams, successfully urged President Taft to instate a Commission on Industrial Relations. He opposed child labor, defended union rights, actively worked for women's suffrage, worked on behalf of the American Civil Liberties Union, and pressed for racial equality, in part by helping to found the National Association for the Advancement of Colored People. He also challenged Tammany corruption and, to much criticism, endorsed reformist candidates in municipal as well as state and national elections. Like many Progressives, Wise left the Republican Party in 1921 and cast his support for presidential candidate Woodrow Wilson, with whom he had recently established a personal relationship that would grow stronger during Wilson's presidency.[65]

When war broke out in Europe in the summer of 1914, the American Jewish Committee galvanized aid for European Jewry while the Federation of American Zionists (FAZ), which Wise and Gottheil had started years earlier, attempted to address the needs of the Yishuv in Palestine.[66] At the time, however, the FAZ had little support and a membership of just fourteen thousand.[67] The jurist Louis D. Brandeis, recognizing the organization lacked the structure and resources it needed, agreed to take over. To serve alongside him, he enlisted Wise and Julian Mack, a judge on the US Court of Appeals in Chicago who had broken with his prominent Cincinnati family's anti-Zionism.[68] The men formed a close and active alliance and, drawing on the latest theories of cultural pluralism, attempted to convince American Jewry that loyalty to the United States and Zionism went hand in hand, for a strong Jewish community contributed to a strong America.

While lending aid to the Yishuv in wartime posed no dilemma for Wise, taking a stance on US involvement in the war was another matter. As an outspoken pacifist, he had long opposed militarism, and in the summer of 1914, together with John Haynes Holmes, Lillian Wald, Jane Addams, and others, he helped build a broad anti-war coalition. However, as the war escalated in Europe, Wise came to view American engagement as inevitable, and in April 1917, when President Wilson abandoned neutrality, Wise dismayed many of his friends in the peace movement by supporting the American war effort. Though the stance cost him his friendship with Addams, his allegiance to Wilson benefited the Zionist movement in a significant way later that year, when Wise and Brandeis successfully urged the president to approve a British statement supporting efforts to create a Jewish homeland in Palestine. Wise and Brandeis then helped draft the Balfour Declaration, which the British issued that November.[69]

Soon thereafter, Wise took the highly contentious step of establishing a democratically elected alternative to the non-Zionist American Jewish Committee. In December 1918, in anticipation of the Versailles Peace Conference scheduled to begin that January, he founded the American Jewish Congress (AJC) with the initial purpose of advocating, from within the American delegation, for Jewish minority rights in Eastern Europe as well as the right of Jews to a national home in Palestine. A month later, he and Louis Marshall, together with other delegates, accompanied President Wilson to Versailles and presented their case as a united Jewish front.

By 1920, with the delegation's work completed, Wise disbanded the congress, which had initially been set up on a temporary basis. However, he soon reestablished it as a permanent organization with a broader long-term mission: advancing Zionism and protecting Jewish rights in the United States and abroad.

Meanwhile, energized by the Free Synagogue's growth, Wise and the lay leadership were building a "Free Synagogue movement" by establishing satellite synagogues that followed the migratory pattern of upwardly mobile Jews in the New York area who were leaving the congestion of downtown for middle-class neighborhoods and cities uptown, in the outer boroughs, and beyond. After successfully opening congregations in the Bronx (1914), Washington Heights (1917), Flushing (1918), and Newark (1920), they set their sights nationally.[70] They had no intention of creating a new branch of Judaism, however; rather than opting out of Reform Judaism, they sought to spread the "Free Synagogue spirit" by working for change from within. All of the satellite congregations paid dues to the Reform movement, and for the most part, they retained graduates of HUC as their rabbis.[71]

Like many American religious leaders before him, Wise long harbored a dream of training a new generation of clergy in his own approach. "The practical experience, training and discipline they could get under me!" he wrote Louise in 1909. "I am just aflame with the idea and I will do it."[72] A year later, he broached the possibility with Richard Gottheil. "Could not some of us get together in New York, with a view of training men for the Jewish ministry? That is to say, men who have a college education, not unbred or underbred boys, but educated men? We must consider this carefully."

Assuming neither he nor Wise had the time required to establish a full-fledged rabbinical seminary, Gottheil made an alternate proposal. "Perhaps we might be able to do what my father did: direct the training of a few select men," he wrote.[73] As a beneficiary of Gustav Gottheil's customized training, as well as Adolf Jellinek's, Wise understood just what this would require, and without abandoning his original, more ambitious idea, he now kept an eye open for a suitable mentee.

By this point, having seized the opportunities America's uniquely open society presented, and utilizing his skills as a charismatic preacher and adept organizer, Wise had invented a new kind of rabbinate, well-suited to the conditions of the moment. Uninterested in overseeing the details of ritual practice or dispensing legal opinions based on traditional codes, he also chose not to dedicate himself to scholarship, though he recognized its importance and read voraciously on a wide variety of subjects. Rather, his rabbinate centered on his devotion to the Jewish people everywhere and to the prophetic tradition of social justice. At once a Jewish nationalist, a patriotic American, and a humanist, he considered these commitments fully congruent.

In his passion, Wise launched fiery criticism at those he believed impeded progress, particularly the rich and powerful, and in that milieu especially, he made a fair share of enemies. More frequently, however, with that same passion he expressed his affection for others and built friendships and alliances with an astoundingly diverse and influential array of scholars, Progressive reformers, labor leaders, politicians, and clergy. He also attracted many young people. Some, especially immigrant children attempting to integrate their Jewishness with their American identity in ways relevant to the issues of their day, found inspiration in Wise's synthesis and sought to emulate him.

Still, it was not until 1915 that Wise first implemented his plan to personally train candidates for the rabbinate. While visiting the Panama-Pacific Exposition in San Francisco that year, he met a fiery twenty-one-year-old Zionist leader named Louis I. Newman who wanted to become a rabbi. From Rhode Island and a graduate of Brown University, Newman was now earning a master's degree in Semitics at the University of California while also serving as national president of the intercollegiate Menorah Association and studying privately with Martin A. Meyer, rabbi of San Francisco's Temple Emanu-El.[74] With Meyer's consent, Wise invited Newman to move to New York City to join the staff of the Free Synagogue while continuing his studies with Richard Gottheil at Columbia. Newman agreed and, after completing his master's degree at Berkeley, returned East to begin assisting Wise while also working on his PhD. Just as Jellinek had trained Wise, Wise now trained his own young disciple.

For two years, Newman worked under Wise's direction supervising the Bronx Free Synagogue and directing the religious school program at several Free Synagogue branches while completing the course requirements for his doctorate.[75] And then, on July 19, 1918, Wise, together with Sidney Goldstein and Martin Meyer, led a special Service of Ordination for Newman at the Bronx Free Synagogue, where the new rabbi would now serve.

Looking back, Wise considered Newman the first "pre-graduate" of the Jewish Institute of Religion.

2

There Is a Need and We Shall Meet It

BY 1920, STEPHEN S. WISE'S FREE SYNAGOGUE HAD GROWN TO 1,100 members and opened four satellite congregations in the New York area, including three since 1917. While Wise's charismatic leadership, powerful oratory, and national reputation had no doubt fueled the Manhattan-based congregation's expansion, the proliferation of Free Synagogues led by far less prominent rabbis in the Bronx, Washington Heights, Flushing, and Newark indicated the stand-alone appeal of the "free pews, free dues, and free pulpit" model. Hoping to build on the momentum, Wise and his lay leadership now created a plan for national expansion: The time had come, they believed, to open their own seminary. By imbuing a whole cadre of rabbis with the "Free Synagogue spirit" and then propelling them into Jewish communities across the United States, they could win adherents in every pocket of the country and expand exponentially.

They knew that the opposition would be strong, and indeed, as word spread about the Free Synagogue's plan, leading Jewish newspapers across the country began editorializing. Given that the Reform movement's Hebrew Union College already prepared liberal rabbis, did the Jewish community need another rabbinical school? How radically different would the training be? Moreover, lest the whole endeavor stem from a desire to replicate the popular but at times incendiary Stephen S. Wise, did American Jewry *really* want more rabble-rousing rabbis like him stirring up trouble?

If the crowds who flocked to hear Wise preach at Carnegie Hall each Sunday morning provided any indication, then at least for a large number of Jews in New York City, the answer to that last question was a resounding yes. As Wise's booming voice filled the auditorium week after week, he resembled in many ways the Social Gospel ministers who had called for fundamental change in American Protestantism a generation earlier. Throughout his career working on behalf of Progressive causes, he had repeatedly accused the Reform movement of failing to live up to the values of social justice expressed in the Pittsburgh Platform and of bowing before the influence of wealth. As he continued to assert this message, his following only grew.

Now, from the dais, he launched a full-scale public critique. The Reform movement was in crisis, Wise warned, suffering from spiritual malaise, moral decline, and a lack of leadership.

WISE'S CRITIQUE OF REFORM JUDAISM

The spiritual problem related to aesthetics as much as faith; having begun in nineteenth-century Germany as an intellectual revolt bent on expunging the irrational beliefs that permeated Orthodox Judaism, the Reform movement in the United States had, in Wise's view, gone too far, by excising the poetry and supernal beauty at the very heart of the tradition. A rationalist and non-legalistic approach need not deaden the senses, he believed; a freethinker could be a mystic, and liberal Judaism ought to offer an inspiring and compelling vision of God.[1]

In the realm of ethics, Wise charged Reform Judaism with failing to apply the teachings of the Hebrew prophets to present-day life. In particular, he asserted, the movement disdained poor and working-class Jews and neglected their needs. "A religion cannot be limited to one social economic class without an entailment of grave moral and spiritual consequences," he warned. "And liberal Judaism almost exclusively became a religion of the rich and well-to-do." As a result, the movement had grown out of touch with the needs and concerns of the populace and functioned only at the periphery of Jewish life.[2]

Finally, Wise believed, Reform Judaism had a leadership problem. Whereas daring and militant pioneers—including rabbis like Samuel Holdheim and Abraham Geiger of Germany, and David Einhorn, Samuel Adler, and Isaac Mayer Wise who emigrated to the United States—nobly and passionately strove to realize the prophetic ideals of Israel, the current generation failed to carry the mantle. "Who can imagine these pseudo-Liberals of today waging a real battle for Liberalism," he lamented, "such as was waged by them whom they feign to follow?"[3]

To survive in the twentieth century, American liberal Judaism required revitalization and a dramatic reorientation. "Israel needs an awakening, Israel needs a renaissance, Israel needs a genuine spiritual and moral reformation," he declared. "Not that a handful of the elect in the Jewish cathedrals may be pleased, nor yet that the Jewish masses may be flattered, but in order that truth may be served."[4] The task, Wise believed, demanded a corps of rabbis who shared two fundamental commitments: applying the prophetic insistence on justice and righteousness to the social and economic problems of the day; and serving Jews of all beliefs and backgrounds in the name of building a united and robust Jewry. However, no such corps existed, and Wise claimed he knew why.

First, no American rabbinical school had any inclination to prepare this type of rabbi. The traditionalists at both the Jewish Theological Seminary (JTS) and the Rabbi Isaac Elchanan Theological Seminary (RIETS) focused primarily on rabbinics and training rabbis to be authorities in halakhic practice. And Hebrew Union College, though liberal on matters of Jewish law and ritual, did not provide an environment conducive to the Eastern European immigrants' left-leaning or Zionist viewpoints; their focus, rather, was on training students in Reform Jewish theology and religious practice, which spoke to few of the growing number of Eastern European Jews in the United States. The typical Reform temple, for example—formal in nature, with services conducted mainly in English and following strict rules of decorum—hardly appealed to Jews who looked to their synagogue (if they looked to one at all) as a place not only to pray but also to engage in service, study, and socializing.[5]

Second, HUC, the most liberal of the three seminaries, had failed to produce rabbis at a rate that correlated with the Jewish community's growth over the previous two decades. Whereas the number of congregations in the Reform movement more than doubled between 1901 and 1921, soaring from 91 to 237 (representing 36,110 members), the number of rabbis ordained at the college during that period never exceeded the 1901 figure of ten and during eight of those years was five or less.[6] As a result, scores of liberal synagogues were encountering a nationwide shortage of non-Orthodox rabbis and finding themselves unable to hire a rabbi at all. The issue was hardly a lack of candidates for the rabbinate, Wise believed; indeed, for years he had been receiving letters from young men seeking to follow in his path and lamented how little he could offer them.

That would be a problem no longer, Wise determined; he and his followers at the Free Synagogue would create a seminary of their own. They envisioned the school as a national center for the Free Synagogue movement, generating rabbinical leadership not only for their growing number of satellite congregations but also for Jewish communities of all kinds across the country. Their training would draw broadly from the practices of European and American Jewish seminaries as well as university-based American divinity schools, but the approach would also differ in significant ways.

In the tradition of many past seminaries, in Europe as well as the United States, Jewish as well as Christian, this new seminary, too, would have as its mission the catalyzing of, in Wise's words, an awakening, a renaissance, a moral and spiritual reformation.

With Antecedents in Mind

The historical record, however, did not bode well for the endeavor. The demise of the Emanu-El Theological Seminary decades earlier in New York City, for example, represented a cautionary tale. Though established by one of the most prominent Reform synagogues in America during the immediate aftermath of the Civil War, the school never managed to gain stable footing either in terms of funding or en-rollment, even under the capable leadership of Gustav Gottheil, the congregation's rabbi. A generation later, Wise and his friend Richard Gottheil both attributed the Emanu-El Seminary's failure to measures taken by Isaac Mayer Wise and other Reform leaders in the 1870s who were anxious to eliminate a competing school in New York just as they were founding Hebrew Union College in Cincinnati. In-deed, when Wise enlisted Richard to help him found his new seminary, the two men determined not to let the same forces thwart their success this time around.

But they also knew that in 1900 HUC had successfully opposed a second at-tempt to establish a liberal seminary in New York, this time the proposed HUC-JTS merger that Jacob Schiff and Louis Marshall had advanced. That idea failed, too, after the Cincinnati-based Reform leadership vociferously objected, leading the two philanthropists to revitalize JTS, instead.[7] While Schiff subsequently contributed to several of Stephen S. Wise's endeavors, including the Free Syna-gogue, he had died in 1920, and now neither Marshall nor any other major Re-form Jewish philanthropists were likely to lend their support. Wise, after all, had spent the last decade challenging their control over Jewish communal life, and few, even those who did appreciate the merits of establishing a liberal seminary in New York, had Schiff's patience for his antagonism. Although the 1900 idea of consol-idating HUC and JTS at least made financial sense (why maintain two schools if one sufficed?), the creation of an entirely new seminary in the 1920s offered no fiscal advantage whatsoever.

Wise understood that just as Gustav Gottheil had met resistance in 1877, as had Schiff and Marshall in 1900, establishing JIR would trigger yet another battle with the Reform movement's Cincinnati-based leadership. By this time, however, the balance of power had shifted dramatically, and the Cincinnati Jewish commu-nity could no longer claim the central role in American Jewish life it had once held. Chicago had eclipsed Cincinnati in becoming the dominant city of the Midwest, while New York, with a Jewish population of 1.6 million, was now the center of Jewish life in the United States. Cincinnati's Jewish community, by contrast, num-bered twenty-five thousand.[8]

Despite these changes, Cincinnati remained a special place in the minds of many American Jews, who continued to regard the city as the true seat, even the Jerusalem, of Reform Judaism. That said, Eastern reformers like Stephen S. Wise had devel-oped a substantial following, too—if not the elite members of Temple Emanu-El, then a growing number of second-generation immigrants coming of age in the sec-ond decade of the twentieth century.

Since the British had issued the Balfour Declaration in 1917, these Jews in-creasingly supported Zionism, and despite the country's overall shift to the right, many were also working alongside other New Yorkers to turn the City into a bastion of liberalism with pockets of radicalism. Recent progressive losses were many: the Republicans' gaining control of the House and Senate in 1918, Warren Harding's lead in the 1920 presidential race, increasing repression of political dissent, a lag in union organizing, and a resurgence in nationalist, racist, and anti-immigrant sentiment. Yet the nation's new conservatism only deepened the sense of urgency progressive Jews brought to their agenda. And while few of these Jews thought in terms of applying the principles of "prophetic Judaism" to democratic institutions and the industrial economy, they embraced leaders who did. Within this new generation of American Jewry, tens of thousands looked to Wise as their most prominent spokesman.

In rendering Wise's ideals into a blueprint for the school and its daily operations, Wise and the founders decided to proceed gradually, taking advantage of all the resources they could muster, beginning with the city where they lived. New York, a refuge for immigrants from around the world and a liberal haven in an increasingly conservative nation, was becoming a global center for Jewish intellectual and religious life. Meanwhile, Wise's network of contacts was extending nationally and internationally, thanks to his leadership over the previous two decades in Jewish as well as Progressive causes. Surely, no one was better positioned to establish a center for liberal rabbinical training in Gotham.

SUMMER SCHOOL 1920

In their first concrete step toward establishing a full-fledged rabbinical seminary, Wise and the lay leadership decided to test their idea by offering a summer school. As a young man in the 1890s attempting to formulate his own religious and political credo, Wise had relished the mentorship he received attending Thomas Davidson's summer school in the Adirondacks. Now he could provide students with a similar kind of mentorship while also experimenting with an urban educational framework and assessing its appeal.

The eight rabbinical students and fourteen ordained rabbis who participated in the 1920 "Summer School for Rabbis and Rabbinical Students" experienced, from the start, an immersion in the values of the Free Synagogue movement. The well-known Jewish publisher Charles Bloch, chair of the Council of Free Synagogues, welcomed the students at the opening of the program, and over the next month the congregation's trustees feted students regularly at luncheons where they discussed issues in contemporary Jewish life. Lay leaders from the New York–area satellite congregations also met with the students, teaching them about the Free Synagogue model and urging them to incorporate it into their own communities, which extended as far as Iowa and Texas. Several prominent congregational rabbis also gave visiting talks at the school.

The coursework that summer covered a mix of scholarly topics and professional development. Wise taught Practical Problems of Jewish Ministry, addressing the significant challenges facing contemporary rabbis, the opportunities and duties of the pulpit, the power of the sermon, and congregational relationships. F. J. Foakes-Jackson, a liberal church historian who held the Briggs Professorship at Union Theological Seminary, taught Early Christianity and Judaism. Sidney Goldstein's course, Synagogue and Social Service, focused on different aspects of organizational and synagogue leadership. To provide firsthand exposure to the problems plaguing New York's Jewish immigrant community, including the tenements and sweatshops on the Lower East Side, Goldstein augmented his lectures with site visits to social service agencies and organizations throughout the city.

In addition, Max Margolis of Dropsie College, a staunch Zionist, taught Making of the Hebrew Scriptures. As Wise knew well, Margolis had experience training rabbinical students, having taught for several years earlier in his career at Hebrew Union College. That episode, however, had not ended well, for in the spring of 1907, Kaufmann Kohler had forced Margolis along with two other Zionist faculty members to resign from the college for dissenting from Reform ideology as articulated in the Pittsburgh Platform.[9]

The controversy showed how Kohler had completely broken with Isaac Mayer Wise's much more ecumenical approach to running the college, insisting instead that a seminary had to reflect and enforce the dogma of its denomination. Some leading American rabbis at the time disputed this notion of what the college should be, Stephen S. Wise among them.

Indeed, a number of years later, Wise got involved when another dispute broke out at the college over similar issues. This one involved student James Heller and his classmates on the board of the Literary Society, who had invited Horace Kallen to speak on campus but then rescinded the invitation under pressure from HUC authorities who objected to Kallen's Zionism. The students apparently wrote Kallen saying the decision to cancel had been made "over our heads," and they feared "appearing disloyal" to the college, which further incited Kohler to take disciplinary action against the students for insubordination. Kallen, who believed proper rabbinical training required academic freedom, reached out to Wise, who joined forces with Rabbi Max Heller, James Heller's father, in lodging a grievance before HUC's board of governors. They contended that the college's censorship reflected poorly on Isaac Mayer Wise's "broad toleration," apparently to some effect, for the governors resolved that political Zionism could henceforth be discussed by faculty as well as students as long as they were "sincerely religious."[10]

Still, neither the governors nor Kohler believed that a seminary should foster full academic freedom when its mission was, after all, to promote a particular religious outlook. Wise and Heller, by contrast, had no interest in promoting ideological uniformity among faculty and students; rather, they believed religious training should prepare students to think independently in an environment welcoming of diverse viewpoints. This was yet another area where the approach of the Free Syn-agogue's summer school in 1920 differed from HUC's.

That fall, the congregation's lay leadership deemed the experiment a success. Students had the opportunity to study "the Principles and Methods and Ideals of the Free Synagogue and to become infected with the spirit of our Organization," wrote Israel Thurman, a progressive attorney and longtime member of the congregation, and they gained new practical skills as well as a deeper understanding of the changing role of the rabbi and synagogue in contemporary American society. A Free Synagogue brochure boasted, "Immediate and direct contact with the Jewish population of the Metropolis . . . proved a revelation to many students and served to open their minds to the various ways in which Jewish life expresses itself." A rabbi must understand all of this, the brochure explained, in order to become an intelligent and serviceable leader.[11]

Convinced that no other seminary was similarly focused on equipping rab-binical students with the skills and outlook they were now providing, the Free Synagogue leaders decided to build on the foundation they had just created by repeating the summer school in 1921, once again gearing it toward two different constituencies: rabbinical students seeking educational opportunities not available in their own seminaries; and practicing rabbis who sought the tools they needed to better serve their communities in small towns and cities with little access to train-ing of any kind. The curriculum, again, would focus only minimally on the study of classical Jewish texts and more on the latest thinking and practices in progres-sive religious circles.

In addition, they began to flesh out their plans for the seminary they would call the Jewish Institute of Religion. Recognizing that the Free Synagogue, as a member congregation of the Reform movement, would have to articulate how and why their new school would differ from Hebrew Union College, Wise, Gold-stein and the board began drafting an internal document that explained, in broad strokes, their critique of HUC and their plan for moving forward: The college no longer attracted top candidates, and it failed to equip its graduates with the skills they deemed necessary to fill the pulpits of forward-looking, progressive Ameri-can congregations. If the Free Synagogue ideal of "a vital Jewish Faith in America" was to be realized, the time had come to equip a new group of men with profes-sional training for the rabbinate on a par with that of other professions such as medicine or law. Toward this end, unlike HUC (or any American Jewish semi-nary, for that matter), JIR would admit only college graduates or the equivalent, a practice increasingly being adopted by university-affiliated Protestant divinity schools. Moreover, whereas HUC underwrote most students' tuition, room, and board, thereby attracting young students who had few other options, the Jewish Institute of Religion would end what they called the practice of "granting subsi-dies as a bait to prospective Rabbis"; rather, JIR would charge tuition while also procuring employment for all students and providing scholarship assistance only to those most in need.[12]

Next, they assembled a rudimentary budget. Assuming the institute would pay rent to the Free Synagogue for the use of its space on Sixty-Eighth Street, and the two organizations would share administrative and secretarial costs, the group anticipated annual expenditures totaling roughly $40,000–$50,000.

Professors (4–5):	$20,000–25,000
Visiting teachers (2–3):	$5,000–6,000
Library:	$5,000
Free Synagogue House rent and maintenance:	$5,000–10,000
Administration (secretary, printing, sundries):	$5,000

They did not identify a source for these funds.[13]

Taking the Case to the Reform Movement

A few months later, in the spring of 1921, the Free Synagogue lay leaders formally apprised the Reform movement of their intention to establish the Jewish Institute of Religion. They knew they were entering sensitive political terrain, for they were about to openly challenge the denomination to which they belonged. Keenly aware that the UAHC leadership in Cincinnati would perceive their plan to open a new school as an act of provocation in the context of hostilities that went back over half a century, they attempted to explain the considerations that now led them to offer their own training for men entering the liberal Jewish ministry. However, in contrast to the arguments they had shared internally, which maligned the college to no small degree, they presented to the union a letter outlining a more complex and diplomatic rationale. And then Wise took a step that might temper the anticipated opposition—he invited one of the most influential Reform rabbis in the Midwest, Emil G. Hirsch of Chicago Sinai Congregation, to serve as JIR's honorary president.

Hirsch and Wise, despite their twenty-three-year age difference, had much in common, most notably their longtime involvement with Progressive causes, their rousing preaching, and their ability to galvanize their congregations in social activism. Hirsch, in fact, had a direct connection to three radical Reform rabbis, for he was the son of Samuel Hirsch and was married to the daughter of David Einhorn, which also made him a brother-in-law of Kaufmann Kohler. Born in Luxembourg in 1852, Hirsch moved to the United States at age fourteen when his father accepted the pulpit at Keneseth Israel, a Reform congregation in Philadelphia. After graduating from the University of Pennsylvania in 1872, he pursued his rabbinical training at the Universities of Berlin and Leipzig, as well as at the newly established

Hochschule, where he studied under Abraham Geiger and developed a friendship with classmate Felix Adler.[14] Both young men would soon come under the sway of the Social Gospel movement, though Hirsch applied this progressive approach with Judaism rather than following Adler into Ethical Culture.

After returning to the United States, Hirsch served in several different Reform congregations before assuming the pulpit of Chicago Sinai in 1880, where he became one of the nation's most prominent Reform rabbis. A powerful advocate for social justice and eloquent preacher on prophetic Judaism, Hirsch also edited the *Reform Advocate*, wrote prolifically, participated widely in Jewish affairs, and served as a professor of rabbinical literature and philosophy at the University of Chicago. When the Great War broke out and he put his support behind Germany, however, many of his congregants turned on him, and by May 1921, he was past the height of his influence and in a weakened position.

Wise, one of Hirsch's few remaining friends, was aware of this and also knew that Hirsch harbored resentment for not having been selected to head HUC, where he had been a long-standing member of the college's board of governors. And so, both Wise and Hirsch saw great symbolism in Hirsch's assuming the honorary presidency of JIR.[15]

At the outset, the Free Synagogue made it clear to the UAHC that they regarded JIR not as a local endeavor but as a national one and that changes in American Jewish demography since the establishment of HUC in 1875 figured prominently in their thinking. The Jewish population of the United States had increased tenfold in the nearly fifty years since HUC's founding, and the number of adherents to liberal Judaism had grown accordingly. Anticipating the Reform movement's claim that one liberal seminary—Hebrew Union College—sufficed, they pointed to the nationwide shortage that had left a considerable number of small- and medium-sized congregations unable to hire a rabbi.

In light of this recent population growth, they argued, no single institution could adequately train all the rabbis required to serve the nation's increasing number of Jews "of the liberal mood or persuasion." American Jewry needed a second liberal school, this one based in the New York metropolitan area, now home to the largest Jewish community in world history. The city and its environs contained fully one-tenth of the world's Jews—at 1.5 million, nearly five times the number in Warsaw, the city that now held the second-largest Jewish population in the world. The local universities and libraries now housed a wealth of scholarly resources, and a rich array of Jewish cultural activities and communal organizations were thriving from Brooklyn to the Bronx. To achieve a high level of scholarship while also developing an understanding and love for Jewish life in all its diversity, the JIR founders claimed, young men training to become rabbis and effective leaders for twentieth-century American Jewry required access to all of this.[16]

Moreover, in their broader effort to professionalize the rabbinate, the Free

Synagogue also announced two new approaches JIR would take to the training
of rabbis. First, JIR would train college graduates exclusively. Ideally, with a secular undergraduate education in hand, students entering JIR would already have
the skills necessary to pursue serious study and could devote themselves solely to
their rabbinical coursework. In addition, the institute would emphasize training
in the areas of religious pedagogy and social service. These, they asserted, required
expertise and occupied a more significant part of the modern rabbi's job description than pulpit responsibilities. HUC and JTS, too, offered practical training but
only to a limited degree, whereas JIR would make the practical component central
in the curriculum. Through contact with the city's schools of social work, and by
supplementing coursework with opportunities for "laboratory practice" in Jewish
New York, JIR would prepare students to play "a directive and even inspiring part
in the social ministry of our age."[17]

This approach harkened back to Wise's view that American liberal Judaism
mandated engagement with, rather than aloofness from, the most challenging social and economic issues of the day. Wise believed this attention to current conditions would distinguish JIR from the institutions of Reform, which had become
disengaged and reticent to get involved with issues plaguing the industrial economy, such as factory conditions, child labor, and tenement housing.[18] In contrast,
the JIR model would link religious leadership directly with activism, drawing on
the Protestant tradition of Oberlin College, the University of Chicago Divinity
School, Union Theological Seminary, and the handful of other urban university-
affiliated divinity schools where Social Gospel theologians maintained a strong
presence.

Reflecting another of Wise's priorities, the Free Synagogue letter also stated,
"it is hardly necessary to add that we shall be governed by the principle of academic
freedom."[19] The Free Synagogue lay leaders knew that for Wise, few principles
mattered more than freedom of expression. This commitment dated back at least
to 1899, when Wise demanded a free pulpit in his negotiations with Congregation Beth Israel in Portland, and the issue became central again in 1906, when he
turned down the pulpit at New York's Temple Emanu-El, claiming the board refused to grant him the autonomy to preach as he saw fit. In the same spirit, Wise
had founded the American Jewish Congress in 1918, in part to give voice to disen-
franchised constituencies he believed the American Jewish Committee refused to
recognize. And most recently, in response to the Palmer Raids of 1919 and 1920,
in which the nation's attorney general, Mitchell Palmer, began arresting thousands
of so-called radicals amid a spreading fear of Communism, Wise joined the effort
to create the American Civil Liberties Union.

The Free Synagogue's embrace of academic freedom, like its calls for a liberal
seminary in New York, represented a particular challenge to HUC. Wise and other
critics believed that Kaufmann Kohler, having purged those he deemed heretics in

the past, continued stifling the expression of viewpoints he opposed, particularly student and faculty support for socialism and Zionism. Just days before the Free Synagogue sent off their letter to the UAHC, Wise made clear to Richard Gottheil his view that little had changed at the college. "Kohler seems kindly and benevolent because of the length and whiteness of his beard, but in many ways he is malevolent and vindictive and almost inquisitorial in his intolerance of Zionism," he wrote. "It is his attitude toward Zionism and Zionists that has empoisoned the atmosphere of the HUC and made it the thing that it is become."[20]

This, of course, went unstated in the Free Synagogue letter, but the message was clear. In prioritizing the social ministry and academic freedom, the authors sent an unmistakable signal that the seminary soon to be led by Stephen S. Wise would be more than open to political radicalism as well as Zionism. Anyone who knew Wise, Goldstein, and the progressive Free Synagogue laity could be sure that at JIR the faculty could hold a variety of beliefs, a broad range of ideas would be freely discussed, and students would be encouraged to reach their own conclusions.

Tackling the issue of admissions, the Free Synagogue assured the UAHC that they did not seek to compete; they failed to share, however, that university graduates were already seeking admission in anticipation of the institute's opening in the fall of 1922. "We look forward to your approval of our plans and most earnestly invite your co-operation in their working out," they concluded.[21]

One day after the Free Synagogue sent off their missive to the UAHC, Wise preached at Chicago Sinai, where the congregation was honoring Hirsch, their rabbi, on the occasion of his seventieth birthday. There, Wise announced from the pulpit,

> I offer Dr. Hirsch a birthday gift in the name of the Free Synagogue. We are about to establish in New York a Jewish Institute of Religion for the training of men for the Liberal Jewish Ministry, young Jewish graduates of American colleges and universities. As the founder, I offer Dr. Hirsch the Honorary Presidency and a visiting Professorship of Jewish Theology in this Institute. Long before this, with his profound and versatile scholarship and his power of inspiration over youth, Dr. Hirsch should have been called to the leadership of an institution to train young men for the Liberal Rabbinate. This opportunity we bring him, assuming that Sinai will have the wisdom and generosity in the larger cause to let Dr. Hirsch come to us and teach for at least one month every year, that our youth, fitting themselves for his calling, may sit at his feet.[22]

Hirsch immediately accepted the offer and appealed to the congregation for donations to JIR. Two members quickly pledged one thousand dollars each, and discussion ensued about the possibility of raising a much larger sum to establish an Emil G. Hirsch Professorship at the institute.

Meanwhile, in Cincinnati, the UAHC executive board appointed a select committee to confer and craft a response to the Free Synagogue.

SUMMER SCHOOL 1921

In the interim, Goldstein and Thurman were busy lining up faculty for the second summer school. The preponderance of left-leaning scholars and experts they invited likely attracted some prospective students while deterring others, but overall matriculation in the summer program of 1921 increased by seven from the previous year to twenty-nine. Of these, twenty-two students enrolled full-time, including seven from the junior and senior classes of HUC and four practicing rabbis. The synagogue provided fewer one-hundred-dollar scholarships than it had in 1920, and as a result, the program ran at a lower cost despite the higher enrollment.

In its second iteration, the curriculum placed an even greater emphasis on linking religious teachings with political theory and engagement. By bringing in Social Gospel thinkers from leading Protestant seminaries and nondenominational university-affiliated divinity schools, as well as rabbis and Jewish communal leaders from Wise's circle, the Free Synagogue developed a pioneering approach they called Jewish social ministry.

Charles Foster Kent, professor of biblical literature at Yale and author of several books on early Jewish history, explored the biblical roots of social justice in his course, The Social Principles of the Prophets and Jesus, based on his recent book of the same title. Presenting the Hebrew prophets and Jesus as teachers and reformers addressing the political and social conditions of their time, Kent elucidated biblical principles that pertained, in his view, to such contemporary topics as the rise of democracy, the philosophy of wealth, and the making of a common citizenry. He charged his students with continuing to reinterpret and apply biblical principles in the shaping of modern-day society—a vital task of clergy, he argued, as purveyors of religious tradition.

While Kent provided a scholarly perspective connecting the Bible with contemporary social reform, Goldstein brought in some of the most active and progressive Protestant clergy in New York to share their experiences. The summer school featured lectures by five Christian ministers, among them Wise's good friend Rev. Dr. John Haynes Holmes of the Community Church (formerly the Messiah Church), well-known for his socialist and pacifist views; Percy Grant, minister of the Episcopalian Church of the Ascension, also known for his socialism and labor activism; and John Lovejoy Elliott of the Society for Ethical Culture, a leader in the settlement house movement and cofounder of the National Association for the Advancement of Colored People.

Goldstein himself offered a Jewish counterpoint in his course, The Synagogue and Industrial Programs, in which he challenged his students to consider the question, "What form of industrial organization promotes and realizes the Jewish ideal of social justice?" Focusing on the role of rabbis and synagogues in addressing the problems of labor and capitalism, Goldstein geared the course toward helping students question industrialism with knowledge and authority. In his view, rabbis had a responsibility to move their congregations, including employers as well as workers, toward "the correction and reorganization of industrial life."[23]

Goldstein focused more specifically on teaching students how to incorporate social service into their synagogues, working with children as well as adults. He also lectured on religion and psychotherapy and invited local rabbis to address such practical topics as religious school curriculum, theories of religious education, and mental hygiene among Jews. In addition, Goldstein convened a roundtable of experts on synagogue life and subjects, including immigration, the Jewish "delinquent," care for the Jewish sick, religious education, and mental health in the Jewish community. A member of the Free Synagogue board, Frederick Guggenheimer, discussed synagogue organization and administration, including the generation of income and budget making.

Once again, students attended classes in the morning and participated in afternoon site visits to Jewish institutions and agencies where they had the opportunity to meet with executive officers. And again, the teaching of classical texts from a Wissenschaft perspective made up just a small component of the curriculum, including only Bible Backgrounds: Bible Lands and Bible Peoples taught through the lens of anthropology and geography by William Worrell, a professor at Hartford Theological Seminary and former director of the American School of Archaeology in Palestine. No courses focused exclusively on Jewish texts other than the Bible, reflecting the summer school's aim of exposing students to experiences they lacked at their own seminaries, most notably an activist approach to the rabbinate.

The great disappointment of 1921 was Wise's inability to teach, due to illness. He had been scheduled to offer Practical Problems of the Ministry but managed to attend only the first luncheon, where he addressed the students, and to send a message to be read at the summer session's closing meeting. Adding to the toll of physical illness, he had suffered a great disappointment at the Zionist Organization of America's convention in Cleveland that June when the movement split over the establishment of the Keren Hayesod (the fundraising effort now also known as the United Israel Appeal); following a vote of no confidence, he and the entire Brandeis contingent resigned en masse. The defeat disappointed Wise, though while he remained active in the movement, it also relieved him of a major responsibility and enabled him to devote more time to opening his seminary.

At the conclusion of the summer of 1921, Wise and the Free Synagogue assessed the experimental model they had created. On the one hand, both summer sessions had provided participants with an approach to rabbinical training different from any that had come before, for virtually every aspect of the curricula signaled a departure, including the heavy emphasis on social service, interfaith study, and practical rabbinics. Though the Social Gospel thinkers and reformers had a strong foothold in the more liberal Protestant seminaries at the time, nothing comparable existed in any rabbinical school. Indeed, no comparable approach existed in the rabbinate, where few spoke out as publicly as Wise did on divisive political issues. Wise and the Free Synagogue hoped their new school would counteract this reticence and that the summer courses, guest lectures, and field trips linking religious teaching with political activism represented a step in that direction. All of these could be integrated into a full-time rabbinical course of study.

However, as Wise and the founders now prepared to open a major American seminary, the summer school model, groundbreaking as it was, would not suffice. In one critical regard, JIR needed to resemble the other Jewish seminaries rather than stand apart—first and foremost, a rabbinical school required Jewish scholars. While the assembly of leading Protestant thinkers and Jewish practitioners might help JIR gain recognition as a progressive force in American Jewish life, on the most practical level the institute needed to provide instruction in subjects including Mishnah and Talmud, Jewish codes and commentaries, as well as history, philosophy, and liturgy. As Wise well knew, the *academic* stature of the institute would determine the school's standing in the Jewish community. Here, Wise could not compete with Kaufmann Kohler, the president of HUC, or with Cyrus Adler, the president of JTS (and certainly not with Adler's predecessor, Solomon Schechter), all highly accomplished scholars. This shortcoming only heightened the importance of hiring a distinguished faculty for JIR.

At this point, a two-pronged approach was requisite. The Free Synagogue would offer a third iteration of the summer school, once again focused on practical training, this time polling rabbis in small communities across the country to provide the most relevant program possible. At the same time, Wise would begin the process of recruiting Jewish scholars for JIR's inaugural, full-time faculty.

Beginning the Search for Faculty

Knowing better than to take on this crucial task alone, Wise enlisted his longtime allies Julian Mack, a member of the Harvard College Board of Overseers, and Richard Gottheil, still on the faculty at Columbia, to help conduct a global search. Both men brought extensive contacts in the Jewish world, as well as valuable experience in academe, and together they surveyed major institutions that retained faculty conducting Wissenschaft des Judentums. In Europe, these included the rabbinical schools Wise referred to as "the five seminaries in German-speaking lands" (two in Berlin, and one each in Breslau, Budapest, and Vienna), Jews' College in London, and a few universities in England, Germany, and Austria. The United States offered fewer academic homes for these scholars, for no American college or university currently housed a professorship in any Jewish field outside of Semitics; that left HUC, JTS, Dropsie College, and a handful of Hebrew teachers' institutes.

The initial group of scholars who made it onto the JIR wish list in 1921 included an impressive mix of Europeans and Americans: Harry Austryn Wolfson, a young philosophy professor at Harvard; Max Margolis, who taught biblical philology at Dropsie; Raphael Mahler, a historian teaching in Jewish secondary schools in Poland; Israel Efros, a philosopher and Hebrew poet who had just two years earlier founded the Baltimore Hebrew College and Teachers Training Institute, which he now directed; Jacob Mann, a historian recently moved from England and now teaching at the school in Baltimore; Ismar Elbogen, a professor of history and liturgy at the Hochschule in Berlin, which he also unofficially directed; Felix Perles, a rabbi and biblical scholar in Koenigsberg; Israel Abrahams, a teacher of Talmudic and rabbinic literature at Cambridge University; and just one New Yorker, Mordecai Kaplan, who taught Midrash and philosophy at JTS, where he also led the Teachers Institute.

The list grew as Wise and the others cast the net wide, recognizing that not all scholars would necessarily be a good fit for JIR and that some of the best might have little interest in abandoning their current positions to join the nascent seminary. Over the ensuing months, an increasing number of Europeans, especially, came under consideration. This reflected the market, for just as Europe housed the majority of institutions supporting Jewish scholarship, European scholars engaged in this work far outnumbered their counterparts in the United States or elsewhere. True, in addition to JIR, other new centers of Jewish learning were also in the works, with Bernard Revel in the process of creating Yeshiva College in New York, and Judah Magnes and Chaim Weizmann working to open Hebrew University in Jerusalem. Nevertheless, while these initiatives signaled a shift, neither had yet come to fruition. For now, JIR's recruitment efforts seemed promising in part because Jewish scholars had such limited opportunities.

By the fall of 1921, Wise and the Free Synagogue had successfully created a prototype for rabbinical training that aligned with their ideals and introduced some of the key innovations they hoped would distinguish JIR. They were now ready to convert the summer school into a full-scale seminary. By grounding students in the Free Synagogue approach and then sending them out as rabbis to serve in communities across the United States, they hoped to bring their ideals to the rest of the country.

Having informed the Reform leadership of their plans, they would soon learn whether or not the UAHC was interested in cooperation. Despite the Free

Synagogue's assurance that they would not compete with the college, Wise had no reason to expect a favorable response. Neither the radical Reformers of the nineteenth century nor even Jacob Schiff and Louis Marshall had succeeded in challenging HUC's hegemony, and though conditions had changed dramatically in recent decades, the Reform leadership's hostility toward Wise and what he represented had not. Long considered among the most influential arbiters of American liberal Judaism, they were unlikely to welcome Wise's effort to reorient the endeavor in a whole new direction.

In light of JIR's ideological deviation from the Reform movement and the anticipated opposition, Wise would have to think carefully about how to position the new school within the broader landscape of American Judaism. His commitments to a free pulpit, the democratization of Jewish communal life, and universal social and economic justice failed to map neatly onto the denominational axis. Moreover, while prioritizing "the oneness of Israel" over ideological distinctions might prove attractive to the European faculty he hoped to recruit, among American Jews, it challenged the very basis on which the contours of religious life were increasingly being drawn.

3

A Seminary without Adjectives

W ISE STOOD WITH FEET PLANTED IN TWO VERY DIFFERENT WORLDS IN 1921: the Reform movement where, though he had a significant number of allies, he found himself in constant tension with the dominant ethos; and the milieu of Eastern European Jewish immigrants and their children, where a growing base eagerly embraced his priorities and leadership. The Free Synagogue mirrored Wise's approach, affiliating with Reform while building branches and satellite congregations in places like the Lower East Side, the Bronx, and Newark. In these Eastern European enclaves, many Jews lacked a strong allegiance to any particular denomination and found far more compelling Wise's focus on social justice, Zionism, and the democratizing work of the American Jewish Congress.

Now, by inviting the UAHC to cooperate with them in opening JIR, Wise and the Free Synagogue were testing the limits of the Reform movement's tolerance for their approach. It was one thing, after all, for an individual Reform rabbi or dues-paying congregation to espouse contrary views. But a seminary? Could a religious movement endorse the training of clergy by a group antagonistic to its creed? True, the Free Synagogue committee had argued cogently that a much-needed new school in New York City would augment rather than compete with HUC, and perhaps some of Wise's influential allies might convince the movement to acquiesce. Reform leaders who knew Wise, however—and just about all of them did—could not be blamed for suspecting that JIR's real mission was to prepare a new generation of rabbis to upend the very approach they and their predecessors had worked tirelessly over decades to establish.

If cooperation proved impossible, the Free Synagogue would need a backup plan. Most obviously, following the example set by the founders of JTS and RIETS, they could abandon the Reform movement entirely and stake out a new position on the ideological spectrum, albeit to the left rather than the right of HUC. The possibility raised a new set of questions, derisively articulated by an opinion writer for the *Jewish Times* of Baltimore:

> Do our eyes deceive us or have we read correctly the announcement that the Free Synagogue of New York will, at an early date, establish a seminary for the training of *Liberal* rabbis? This is, indeed, an astonishing bit of information,

viewed in relation to the Hebrew Union College. Will the new seminary graduate only those who guarantee that they will not be subservient to a Board
of Trustees and that they will not permit their lectures and sermons to be
censored? Is this a new movement in American Jewry . . . ? Does it mean that
radicalism will be rampant? . . . We were always under the impression that the
liberalism of the Hebrew Union College made the sky the limit. But, perhaps
there is a special brand of liberalism that has not been covered by the HUC,
which omission will be supplied by the Free Synagogue Seminary.[1]

Though the *Jewish Times* called this piece "Slightly Facetious," for Wise these
questions were dead serious. And whereas a year earlier he would have answered
most of them in the affirmative—JIR *would* focus on training liberal rabbis, with
the aim of spreading the burgeoning and in some respects radical Free Synagogue
movement—he now discerned a new path and began to pivot.

If the Reform movement refused to cooperate, he realized, he did not necessarily have to locate JIR to the left or right of anyone. Why should the institute
occupy just one spot on the denominational axis, when neither his followers nor
his ideological commitments really fit there? Why not, instead, create a school that
embodied his belief in "the oneness of Israel"? In conceiving of this broad approach,
Wise identified the "omission" in American Jewish life that JIR could fill.

Doing so, however, would mark a departure from his modus operandi—he
preferred working with one foot in the Reform camp, the other in the broader Jewish world. Therefore, holding out hope that JIR, like the Free Synagogue, could
have a formal relationship with the Reform movement, he refrained from articu-
lating his new idea publicly, lest doing so derail efforts at cooperation. An amicable
arrangement, if unlikely, was still the best path forward.

But now, if none emerged, Wise had his Plan B.

ENGAGING REFORM

Wise's anxiety about reaching an agreement increased that fall, thanks to another
tactical decision he made: refraining from fundraising for JIR until an agreement
with the UAHC could be reached. Since May, talks had been repeatedly postponed,
and the delay now threatened his ability to raise much money for the institute before
opening day. His sense of urgency grew in November when Hebrew Union College appointed Julian Morgenstern as acting president, in preparation for Kaufmann
Kohler's retirement at the end of the academic year. Morgenstern, a protégé of Kohler,
would continue business as usual, Wise believed, making further delay impossible.

"Had Cincinnati chosen a great person as leader, I might have put everything
aside and waited a few years," Wise told his friend Louis Grossmann, a faculty member at HUC. "But the new regime makes it the more compelling that we inaugurate

this work and appeal to a new group of men in America to come into the ministry and help to give them their start in the call that is yours and mine."[2]

Finally, in late December, Daniel Hays, chair of the UAHC, and several other UAHC board members met with a contingent of the Free Synagogue's lay leadership, including Lee K. Frankel, president of the congregation. A nationally recognized leader in Jewish social work, Frankel had gained prominence early in his career at the United Hebrew Charities of New York City, where as an academically trained full-time agency head, he pioneered the professionalization of the field. Now a vice president at Metropolitan Life, he remained an influential force who lent his expertise generously to such organizations as the National Jewish Conference of Charities and the New York School of Social Work, as well as to the growing number of Jewish federations being formed in metropolitan areas across the country.[3]

The negotiations did not go well, however. The UAHC not only refused to entertain any agreement for cooperation, but also objected to a new seminary operating *beyond* their auspices. The Reform movement's leadership had a single purpose: to dissuade the Free Synagogue from opening the institute at all.

After restating the arguments for opening JIR, the Free Synagogue delegation implored the UAHC to take a cue from Europe. Over the last century, they contended, at least four different rabbinical institutions had been founded in Germany and Austro-Hungary, yet never had one sought to avert the rise of another. When Hays, not surprisingly, remained unmoved and refused to back down, Frankel made it clear that JIR would open in October regardless, with Stephen S. Wise as president and Emil G. Hirsch as honorary president. They had more than a dozen applicants for admission and anticipated more.

By the end of the meeting, neither side ruled out some form of cooperation, and they agreed to convene again.

"The understanding was definitely and amicably reached that our institute is to be and to go on," Wise subsequently told Hirsch, "and that the thing to consider is not to avert its rise but how to bring about relations of cordiality and comradeship between the two organizations." Wise still hoped that the UAHC leadership, in a conciliatory spirit, would bring JIR under its wing. As long as he and Hirsch were free to shape the new school as they desired, he would raise money for HUC as well as JIR.

Some sort of merger may even be attempted, Wise added, or an arrangement whereby the union supported JIR to a degree. "But that support must not be conditioned by our submerging within the Union, or our dependence upon the College and the Union," he cautioned.[4]

That winter, a heated debate unfolded in the Jewish press over the plan to open a new seminary. Opponents' chief concern was that JIR threatened to draw donors away from HUC, which trained rabbis well and in sufficient numbers.[5]

But Wise had a very different view of fundraising, which he shared in a lengthy missive to Leo Franklin, a congregational rabbi in Detroit and a former president of the CCAR, who publicly opposed the Free Synagogue's undertaking. Many mistakenly believed that American Jews designated a fixed sum of money for educational, social, and philanthropic purposes so that every expenditure left less overall, Wise wrote. Instead, "needs create sources, and I often find that giving to one institution leads to generosity to parallel institutions."[6]

As to the current market for rabbis, far more pulpits existed than rabbis to fill them, and the shortage had driven up rabbinic salaries. As a result, scores of congregations could not afford the considerable sum needed to hire "even the youngest and most immature men" just graduating from HUC. At the same time, these new rabbis could reject half a dozen pulpits before selecting one deemed best adapted to their gifts, abilities, and tastes. Wise would not be satisfied, he wrote, "until I help to make it possible for every congregation in America to secure a Jewish teacher and preacher for itself."[7]

And once again, Wise disingenuously insisted that the impetus to create a new school did not stem from a critique of the college. "Our founding of the JIR . . . is no more in disparagement of the HUC or an attempt to compete with it than the founding of new colleges and universities in different sections of the country constitutes competition with the older colleges and universities," he wrote. Instead, simply, the time had come to establish a liberal seminary in the demographic and cultural center of American Jewish life, where students could receive professional training for the contemporary rabbinate. HUC's work was honorable and necessary, and the Free Synagogue entered the field aiming only to be friendly and helpful.[8]

In February, the Free Synagogue razed six dwellings on Sixty-Eighth Street just west of Central Park and began construction of a five-story structure that would temporarily house the institute along with the congregation's religious school, child adoption bureau, and other activities. Wise hoped to build a much larger "great synagogue" within five years, at which time the institute could occupy the entire Sixty-Eighth Street premises; until then, the school would operate in the upper stories.[9] Construction of the synagogue house cost $250,000, of which $170,000 had already been raised.[10]

In early March, negotiations with the UAHC continued, this time with the participation of Julian Morgenstern, HUC's acting president. When Frankel asked if the UAHC was now genuinely amenable to cooperation, Morgenstern answered affirmatively, though he also said any recommendation made by their committee would have to be approved by the UAHC board's executive committee.

On this basis, the Free Synagogue group considered cooperation a real possibility, though internally, they lacked consensus about how best to move forward. While Frankel and most of the others supported some kind of agreement, Israel Thurman, a progressive leader active not only in the Free Synagogue but also in the UAHC, argued that JIR should remain under the sole aegis of the Free Syn-agogue, autonomous of any other organization.[11] Perhaps he had a sense of what was to come.

Despite Thurman's objections, two weeks later, the Free Synagogue proposed a "Basis for Discussion" to the UAHC's New York delegation: JIR would become an activity of the UAHC and would coordinate with Hebrew Union College but at the same time remain independent and entirely autonomous. The JIR Board, created by the Free Synagogue, would remain a self-perpetuating body, with no more than 20 percent of its number appointed or elected by the UAHC. JIR and HUC could, pending mutual agreement, exchange professors, students, and course credits. In the area of fundraising, the UAHC would provide JIR a minimum of $45,000 per year for three years, after which the institute's budgetary needs would be reevaluated; in return, Wise and JIR's officers would place themselves at the dis-posal of the UAHC to raise funds for HUC as well as JIR, crediting all funds they secured to a joint College and Institute Fund.[12]

The Free Synagogue men left the meeting under the impression that their proposal had been received positively and that the UAHC group planned to pres-ent it to their executive committee for approval by April 15, just a few weeks away. Wise was still holding off on fundraising, pending the outcome of these negotia-tions, and he had plans to travel to Europe in early June to secure faculty for the institute. Whether he would be fundraising for JIR as well as HUC per the pro-posal, or JIR alone should the union reject it, time was running out; he needed to get on with raising the money.[13] But given the positive news, he was willing to wait a little longer.

Charles Shohl, president of the UAHC, however, reported no such amicable discussion. In his view, the Free Synagogue had issued an ultimatum, threatening that if the UAHC did not agree to their "Basis for Discussion" proposal quickly, Wise would immediately set out for the West and deliberately target HUC's sup-porters in order to raise money for the Jewish Institute of Religion.[14] The Free Synagogue group denied issuing any such ultimatum and offered to send repre-sentatives to meet directly with the UAHC executive committee, but the UAHC declined; the union's president and vice president would take up the matter alone.

While waiting for the UAHC to render its decision, Wise and the Free Syna-gogue refrained from fundraising but continued apace with other steps, including the critical one of creating a board. To the temporarily dubbed Committee on the Jewish Institute of Religion, which primarily included members of the Free Syn-agogue's lay leadership, Wise now added a few strategically selected allies from other circles.[15]

Richard Gottheil, in whom Wise had long ago confided his dream of creating a rabbinical school, brought a unique perspective due to his father's failed battle to keep the Emanu-El Theological Seminary alive in the face of Reform opposition.

The younger Gottheil and Wise both saw JIR as a means to redress this past wrong, and Wise knew there were ways Gottheil could help from his position at Columbia.

Julian Mack, the federal judge in Chicago who had spent years working alongside Wise and Louis Brandeis leading the Zionist Organization of America (ZOA), brought his own academic ties as a member of the Harvard College Board of Overseers.[16] Mack, interestingly, grew up in Cincinnati where his family was prominent in Jewish affairs, and his brother Ralph was a member of HUC's board of governors. Julian, now a member of Hirsch's Chicago Sinai, had broken from his family over Zionism and expressed enthusiasm upon receiving the invitation from Wise. "Reform or radical Judaism as represented by Sinai and the Free Synagogue has always seemed to me to need just such an institute of religion as you propose establishing," he wrote, and then revealed his top priority for JIR. "What we want in the rabbinate, in addition to the broad and liberal point of view, is the soundest scholarship—a scholarship that fits the student for active service as well as for the scholarly life."[17] For Mack, a curriculum like the summer schools', which focused primarily on social service and interfaith study, would not suffice, and Gottheil surely agreed. Wise, too, recognized the need to assemble a faculty who could teach traditional subjects like Bible, rabbinic literature, history, and philosophy, and he enlisted Mack and Gottheil in part for their academic connections and ability to help recruit scholars.

JIR board member Charles Bloch also came from a prominent Cincinnati family closely aligned with the college. Indeed, Charles's aunt, Theresa Bloch, was Isaac Mayer Wise's wife until her death in 1874 (the couple had ten children together), and Edward Bloch, Charles's father and Theresa's brother, had founded Bloch Publishing together with Wise in 1854. The company published Wise's newspapers, the *Israelite* and the German-language *Die Deborah*, as well as his liturgies and hymnals, before expanding into a broader array of Jewish literature. Charles entered the business in 1878 and took over its Chicago operations in 1885, founding the *Reform Advocate* in 1891 with Emil G. Hirsch as editor. After receiving overall control of the company from his father, Charles moved it to New York in 1901, where he built it into the largest Jewish publisher in the English-speaking world. He became highly involved in New York's Jewish affairs, including at the Free Synagogue and, now, JIR.

The librarian and scholar George A. Kohut, another member of the JIR board, also brought an understanding of Jewish publishing, though his focus was more on the global trade in Jewish books and manuscripts, many of which were moving from ravaged Jewish communities in Eastern Europe into the United States. The son of Alexander Kohut, a Talmudist who had helped found JTS, Kohut could surely help JIR establish its own library while also advising on faculty recruitment.

Emil G. Hirsch's presence on the board brought academic standing, thanks to his appointment at the University of Chicago,[18] and signaled that a prominent figure in the Reform rabbinate (if controversial, as well) shared the ethos of the Free Synagogue. Hirsch had recently fallen gravely ill, but Wise hoped that when he recovered, in addition to serving as honorary president, he would also teach theology as a visiting professor. "It will be great for you to have disciples in teaching of a really liberal Judaism," Wise wrote.[19]

Several female philanthropists distinguished JIR's board from the all-male leadership of the other Jewish seminaries at the time. Bertha Guggenheimer, a friend of Wise's from Lynchburg, Virginia, was a generous donor to Zionist causes and an activist in Hadassah. Mary Fels, a talented writer and editor based in New York City, was also an avid and philanthropic Zionist. The widow of a wealthy soap manufacturer, she shared her late husband Joseph's critique of capitalism, and long after his death in 1914, she continued to promote Progressive causes, including labor reform, civil rights, and women's suffrage.[20] And Louise Waterman Wise was a Zionist leader as well as a pioneer in the fields of health and child welfare and led some of the Free Synagogue's major social service efforts, most notably the child adoption agency.

The demand for a new kind of seminary was urgent and insistent, the board asserted at their first meeting in late March, and given the Free Synagogue's achievements and ideals, no one was more qualified to establish it. Moving forward immediately was imperative.

As to brass tacks, Wise would temporarily direct the school, and to enlist students, he would tour American universities with the aim of inspiring young men who might otherwise never consider the rabbinate. They approved an annual budget of $30,000, based on the Free Synagogue contributing $10,000 and the balance raised from friends of the Free Synagogue movement throughout the country. Notably, they omitted the UAHC from potential funding sources; clearly, the new board held out little hope for a cooperative arrangement. Over the next few months, they would begin procuring pledges, publicly aiming to raise a total of $50,000 per year; providing they could secure at least $30,000 for each of the next three to five years, they would open the school in September.[21]

Meanwhile, Daniel Hays traveled to Cincinnati and, with no official UAHC meetings scheduled, informally convened as many members of the executive board and HUC's board of governors as possible. Speaking before the fifteen men who assembled, Hays explained that his committee had unsuccessfully tried to dissuade the Free Synagogue from establishing the Jewish Institute of Religion.

This group, too, opposed the opening of JIR. The best interest of American Judaism would be served not by founding a new institution in New York, they agreed, but by uniting all efforts and strengthening support for the historical institution in Cincinnati. Hebrew Union College provided adequate training, a distinguished faculty, and an ideal location. Given years of financial investment in college buildings, including a library and a new dormitory, the college had an "inalienable claim" on the allegiance of every alumnus, every Reform congregation, and every man in the liberal Jewish ministry.[22]

And so, the group of fifteen unanimously rejected the Free Synagogue proposal in its entirety. In doing so, they objected particularly strongly to one element: the JIR group's insistence on remaining independent. Should a second institution for the training of rabbis ever come under the auspices of the Union of American Hebrew Congregations, Hays told Frankel soon after the meeting, the union would require total control. Under no circumstances would this body of more than two hundred congregations ever hand over authority, in perpetuity no less, to a single synagogue.[23]

Could the Free Synagogue have expected any other response? They had asked the Reform movement to endorse and fund the creation of a competing seminary while ceding its control to one of the college's most vocal antagonists. Reform leaders who worried that JIR's success would come at a steep price for HUC would find little assurance in Wise's offer to raise money for both schools. In proposing such untenable terms, the Free Synagogue revealed its ambivalence about placing JIR under the auspices of the Reform movement.

For Wise, this ambivalence went back to his youth, when he had attempted to work out an arrangement with Isaac Mayer Wise that presaged the current situation. In the 1890s, of course, Wise had had no intention of starting a school; he simply wanted to conduct his *own* preparatory studies in New York under the auspices of HUC. But even after Isaac Mayer Wise acceded to his request, at least by letting him prepare independently for the college's qualifying exams rather than attending classes in Cincinnati, the young Wise had abandoned the idea in favor of studying with Jellinek in Vienna.

Now he seemed to be involving the Free Synagogue and Union in a similar gambit, and one unlikely to yield genuine cooperation. This time, even some of Wise's friends found the tactic unreasonable. Rabbi Max Heller of New Orleans, who often supported Wise, made clear his objections. "Frankly," he wrote, "I was surprised at you and your friends placing before the Union a plan which called for so large an appropriation and promised to return so small a measure of control."

Still, Heller did not agree with the UAHC's claim that one seminary sufficed for Reform Judaism. Over the next two decades, he predicted, so many children of the Orthodox would become Reform that an additional seminary would urgently be needed. For this reason he encouraged the two sides to continue negotiating with the aim of reaching a harmonious agreement.[24]

Neither continued negotiations nor harmonious relations, however, lay ahead. Though the UAHC's rejection of the Free Synagogue proposal still had to be approved by its executive board at their June meeting, both sides considered the decision final. The Union had opposed the Free Synagogue's opening of a new school from the start, and now that the congregation intended to proceed nonetheless, the union refused to associate with the school in any way: no affiliation, no board representation, no joint fundraising, no cooperation.

Wise and the Free Synagogue were now on their own. The deadlock with Reform left them having to raise significant funds but also free to pursue a new path. Wise had never been comfortable with the denominational order, and it was now time for Plan B, which promised only to incite the Reform leadership further.

"Training Men for the Ministry without Using Adjectives"

Until now, Wise and his associates had focused on creating a distinctly liberal and Zionist rabbinical program, with the summer schools a first step in this direction. But the idea of welcoming students and faculty of *all* viewpoints more closely aligned with Wise's commitment to free speech and Jewish unity, as well as his desire to challenge the denominational model.

Doing so would buck a historical trend, for ever since Isaac Mayer Wise's inclusive plan for Hebrew Union College collapsed when traditionalists walked out of the notorious "*trefa* banquet" in 1883, the idea of a rabbinical school open to a broad range of religious perspectives had gone by the wayside. Instead, the Reform, Conservative, and Orthodox movements were turning their seminaries into brain trusts tasked with staking out distinct ideological positions. Kaufmann Kohler, for example, devoted his presidency at HUC to ensuring that the college promulgate the principles and teachings unique to Reform Judaism and pressured faculty and students to assert prevailing Reform dogma. That said, seminary leaders could not always maintain the degree of allegiance they sought to enforce. Students at RIETS, the Orthodox rabbinical school, for example, went on strike in 1908 demanding that secular subjects be added to the curriculum.

Just as Stephen S. Wise had repudiated denominational inculcation by choosing as a young man to study privately with Jellinek for the rabbinate, his new plan would offer the next generation of rabbis an opportunity to do the same but within a seminary setting. Undaunted by Isaac Mayer Wise's nineteenth-century failure to unite the Orthodox and Reform behind one school, he knew the crux of his idea, as well as the historical context, were now very different.

To begin with, unlike Isaac Mayer Wise, Stephen S. Wise harbored no illusion that JIR would become the sole source of rabbis for all of American Jewry; he intended for the institute to augment the existing seminaries, not to supplant them. Understanding that diehard Reform, Conservative, and Orthodox Jews would continue to gravitate to their own schools, Wise set his sights on those Jews who were not motivated primarily by denominational loyalty.

In addition, whereas Isaac Mayer Wise attempted to build a broad alliance at the college by positioning himself as a moderate and excluding the radical Reformers, Stephen S. Wise took a very different tack. Amid a national Red Scare in which left-leaning faculty were being forced to resign from colleges and universities across the country and while American Jewish seminary heads were trying to curtail Zionist activism in their ranks, Wise envisioned the Jewish institute of Religion welcoming pacifists, Zionists, and independent thinkers of all viewpoints to the faculty as well as the student body. In 1920s America, encouraging the free expression of diverse viewpoints within a Jewish seminary represented neither a moderate stance nor an effort to build a broad alliance, but rather a challenge to institutional and communal leaders constrained by the prevailing fear of radicalism. Indeed, following a long-standing American seminary tradition, Wise would utilize the school to cultivate dissent.

More specifically, by taking this path, Wise would signal that at JIR, unlike any other American rabbinical school, the bond of Jewish peoplehood would outweigh ideology. In this sense, his nonsectarian plan was anything but neutral. An unaffiliated, pluralist, free-speech-promoting rabbinical school—the antithesis of even the liberal HUC—would surely vex every Jewish denominational leader in the country. Whereas for Stephen S. Wise, the idea made all the sense in the world.

It made sense to several of his confidants, too. Wise had been quietly sharing his nondenominational vision with them that winter, after the stalled December round of negotiations.

"I am not sure that we shall limit the work and make it an institute for the training of men for the Liberal Jewish ministry," he told Louis Grossmann. "I wonder ... if it would not be a finer thing to let young men come to us whether Zionist, or anti-Zionist, whether Liberal, conservative or orthodox, and help them to prepare for the ministry, and then when they have had their training let them choose the way they shall go. I somehow feel that this plan will appeal to you, for as we grow older we see how fatuous and impermanent are the labels we have magnified in the past."[25]

He presented the idea slightly differently to Mack, explaining that JIR *would* be liberal, not by representing a single perspective but "liberal enough to welcome and respect men whether reform or orthodox, Zionist or anti-Zionist."[26] Wise appreciated the liberal spirit of some of his colleagues who, like his own father, maintained more traditional practices. Mack loved the idea, seeing this nonaligned approach as wholly in sync with the "radical Judaism" he associated with Chicago Sinai and the Free Synagogue. In addition, having rejected the anti-Zionism of his own family, Mack believed deeply that ideological differences did not preclude Jewish unity.

Wise also consulted Hirsch. "Would you approve of the plan of training men for the ministry without using adjectives, whether liberal or orthodox or conservative?" he asked. "It would in a sense work itself out, for I suppose orthodox men would not come to us, but would it not be better for men to come and make their choice after they have been with us and have come to understand. It would seem to me we could do a much more catholic and in some senses Jewish work if we were to follow this procedure. We would not of course conform to the things that the conservative or orthodox might expect of us, but excepting for that would it not be a fine and big thing to make it possible for conservative men to come and to be taught?"[27]

Hirsch, still unwell, responded with enthusiasm. On the occasion of the Free Synagogue's fifteenth anniversary, he wrote a note in shaky script to the congregation, rejoicing in their achievements and conveying his high hope for the Jewish institute of Religion. The Free Synagogue had brought his own Chicago Sinai out of loneliness and solitude, he wrote; the two congregations were sisters, with shared high aims and convictions—and those convictions, including freedom of thought and expression, would lie at the heart of JIR. He spelled out his conception for the institute, based on his own experience attending the Hochschule during its own founding years in the 1870s:

> I have in mind a school which will encourage independence of thought in its student. We shall subscribe to no doctrine unless approved by our own searching, probing into the original Jewish sources. We want our men to have a deeper understanding of the social outlook. That after all is Judaism's message and Religion's function. Humanize! I remember the Hochschule in Berlin. Geiger on the faculty with Cassel, Lewi, Steinthal, a representation of every opinion only bound together by the love and passion for truth. We students were not asked to accept but we were helped to think and to search independently. . . . Freedom of thought on theology is the birthright of the Jew . . . but freedom as Sinai and you understand is also freedom to discuss the distracting problems of our social conditions. Our Prophets certainly have pointed the way. It is this freedom which is denied by many to the pulpit. We claim it as our obligation would we be worthy of the successorship to Isaiah and Amos. Your progress, a tribute to the rare abilities and ardor of your leader, but also is a ringing response which the old Jewish cry for justice found in your hearts.
>
> It is because we and you have this freedom of Judaism at heart that we are vitally interested in creating the Institute of Religion.[28]

For Wise, the path was now clear. This twentieth-century American version of the Hochschule, as Hirsch envisioned the school, would embody "the oneness of Israel" and promote free inquiry. Broad inclusiveness, rather than affiliation with any single religious movement, would go hand in hand with academic freedom.

With this approach now central to the institute's mission, Wise had just a few months to enlist his boots on the ground—the scholars and teachers necessary to make this vision real.

4

The First Test

Wise sought faculty who could position JIR as a global center for Jewish scholarship on par with the best in the world and, at the same time, train forward-looking rabbis capable of leading American Jewry through the challenges that lay ahead. JIR's teachers would instill students with Jewish learnedness, professional skills, religious depth, and more. "Israel needs an awakening," Wise had preached at Carnegie Hall, where his Sunday morning services were now drawing crowds upward of 1,600 people on a weekly basis, and he wanted mentors who could inspire their students to assume the mantle of rejuvenating American Jewish life.

To hire this inaugural faculty, he would have to encroach upon the handful of educational institutions where they currently worked—and not just sell them on the idea in principle but convince them to join him.

In the recruitment effort ahead, JIR's nondenominational approach offered a strategic advantage. Rather than ruling anyone out due to creed or mode of Jewish practice, he could hire a diverse faculty and thereby expose students to a wide range of competing ideas. Moreover, since no other American rabbinical school promised full academic freedom, JIR might appeal to those who held controversial views regarding, say, Zionism or socialism.

But the approach also came with a significant vulnerability. The movement-affiliated seminaries offered collegiality and influence through their network of like-minded scholars and rabbis, and even though they struggled financially, they also provided a modicum of job security thanks to their broad bases of support. Wise could promise none of this. Assuming no breakthrough in negotiations with the UAHC, the institute would remain utterly dependent on a single synagogue as its lifeline. And with the Reform movement now galvanizing opposition to the institute across the country, how would JIR faculty be received in the broader community of Jewish scholars? Would the luminaries Wise sought risk joining this precarious venture?

With insufficient funds to pay the faculty, no one yet hired, and a heated battle playing out in the national Jewish press, Wise might reasonably have delayed opening JIR for another year in order to secure the institute's finances, methodically appoint faculty, and let tensions with the Reform movement cool down. Instead, he moved ahead, exuding confidence that belied the actual state of affairs.

"We must have three or four outstanding men in heads of departments, giving much of their time and strength to research," Wise wrote Harry Lewis, a British rabbi who had moved to New York years earlier whom he hoped to hire. "And then we need a staff of men to do the day-by-day teaching, men who will, as it were, fit the young men so that they shall be ready for the great masters who are to be at the head."[1] In addition, he would also enlist visiting lecturers to address such topics as comparative religion, recent developments in Jewish scholarship, and current events.

Recruiting These "Outstanding Men"

Enlisting professional scholars posed the greatest challenge—one Wise had been able to defer while setting up the summer schools, which had been designed solely to *augment* the rabbinical training students received elsewhere. They made no claim to offer more than a few courses in traditional Jewish studies, emphasizing instead social service and comparative religion, the areas in which the other institutions were weak or offered no courses at all. With the institute now responsible for providing *all* aspects of rabbinical training, courses like Bible, rabbinic literature, and Jewish thought—virtually none of which had been offered in the summer programs—would form the bulk of the curriculum. Of equal significance to Wise, the institute's academic reputation would rise or fall based on the scholars he enlisted to teach in these fields.

It was a complicated endeavor. Given the paucity of academic positions for Jewish Wissenschaft scholars worldwide, few were likely to risk leaving a secure post to join the new institute. On the other hand, for those scholars lacking such a post, or in difficult circumstances, JIR represented a rare opportunity.

This was particularly true for those in Central and Eastern Europe, where important institutions of higher Jewish learning were suffering amid postwar social and economic unrest. For Jewish scholars caught in the maelstrom, the idea of joining Wise's institute in New York might appeal, offering at minimum a temporary respite and exposure to New York's thriving Jewish life—if not a full-out exit strategy.

While Jewish scholars in the United States did not confront such dire circumstances, they faced scant employment prospects. University chairs were limited to Semitics, and though institutions like HUC, JTS, and Dropsie College did hire faculty in a breadth of fields, rarely were more than a few positions open at any one time. Additionally, none of these Jewish institutions offered the full academic freedom that Wise promised, which, combined with the opportunity to work alongside him in shaping American Jewish life, Zionist and left-leaning scholars would have found particularly compelling.

Now that Wise was ready to begin reaching out, he introduced criteria that would help narrow down the extensive wish list compiled earlier by Mack and Gottheil.[2] The list identified European and American Jewish scholars making significant advancements in their field, a sine qua non for JIR's permanent faculty. That said, Wise's primary aim was to build not a research center but a seminary. And just as his own mentors—men like Adolf Jellinek and Thomas Davidson— had inspired him, he wanted faculty who could instill in a new generation of rabbis not only the book knowledge they would need to serve effectively but also the love of Judaism they would need to awaken that same passion in others. He harbored no illusion that more than a few of the young, first- or second-generation immigrants attending JIR were destined to become professional scholars; his mission was to give them the tools to invigorate American Jewish life as *rabbis*.

As a result, Wise wanted a chance to assess candidates in person. This was particularly true of the Europeans, for he was wary of re-creating what he perceived to be the dominating and overly stiff German presence at HUC and JTS. "I don't want German scholars but Jewish teachers," he told Louis Grossmann.[3] He would delay reaching out to them until June, when he could take a steamship to Europe and spend the summer continuing the search.

For now, he focused on recruiting several leading figures closer to home. Two were Wissenschaft scholars: Harry Austryn Wolfson, a historian of philosophy who held a recently created position at Harvard, and Max Margolis, the Bible professor at Dropsie College who had taught in the Free Synagogue's 1920 summer school. Wise also targeted Mordecai Kaplan, a radical rabbi and intellectual making waves in New York as founder of the Society for the Advancement of Judaism and head of the Teachers Institute at JTS, and Nissan Touroff, cofounder and dean of the new Hebrew Teachers College (HTC) of Boston, which had just opened six months earlier. While a diverse group by way of professional expertise and personal religious orientation, all four were prominent figures in their fields, and all four were Zionists.

Wise was particularly interested in securing an arrangement with Harry Wolfson, who, at age thirty-four, was the youngest of the four men. Born in Russia, he had received rigorous religious training as a youth studying at the renowned Lithuanian yeshiva in Slobodka before his family immigrated to New York in 1903. There, he continued his studies at the Rabbi Isaac Elchanan Theological Seminary, but after the director discouraged him from becoming a rabbi because of his poor social skills, he moved to Scranton, Pennsylvania, and taught Hebrew while attending high school.[4] He subsequently earned his bachelor's degree as well as his doctorate at Harvard, developing an expertise in medieval Jewish philosophy.

In 1915, Harvard hired Wolfson as an instructor in Jewish literature and philosophy. While the appointment was trailblazing, it came with an exceptional provision: The university would not pay his salary. Julian Mack, on Harvard's board of overseers at the time, together with Judge Irving Lehman of the New York State Court of Appeals stepped in to raise funds for his wages, and on this basis, Harvard repeatedly renewed Wolfson's one-year position.[5]

In 1921, the university promoted Wolfson to assistant professor and granted him a multi-year contract under the same funding terms. Nonetheless, he and his allies well understood the tenuousness of his appointment. Mack, through his position on the board, was particularly aware of how prevalent antisemitism was at Harvard, where President Abbott Lowell's desire to limit Jewish student enrollment found strong support among alumni. Lowell's refusal to pay Wolfson's salary stemmed from a similar desire to exclude Jews from the faculty.

That fall, Horace Kallen, the Harvard-trained philosopher who had recently helped found the New School for Social Research, urged Wise to pursue Wolfson for JIR. Not only did he bring prodigious learning in all fields Jewish, from Talmudic texts to contemporary social problems, but at Harvard Wolfson had also proven himself to be a support for the Jewish students, who gravitated toward him in times of crisis, whether academic or personal. "I do not know of a young man of so solid attainment and rich promise, both as scholar and teacher," Kallen told Wise. Like the RIETS director in an earlier period, Kallen also saw in Wolfson a social awkwardness—"a fear of women, an immense shyness, and a gaucherie in adaptation and utterance"—but "these things could be immensely improved by judicious training," he added, and they did not seem to matter in his contact with the young men who were his students.[6]

Wise reached out, and Wolfson responded with qualified interest. Although he had no desire to leave Harvard, he was willing to serve JIR as a visiting professor on a reduced schedule commuting from Boston. The specifics of the arrangement remained to be worked out, but Wise had finally secured a scholar who fit his ideal: brilliant and devoted to his students.

Margolis, the second of the American Wissenschaft scholars pursued by Wise that spring, was open to hearing an offer. An accomplished biblical philologist, Margolis was best known for having overseen the Jewish Publication Society's new translation of the Bible into English, completed in 1917. He had been in his position at Dropsie College since 1909, and as the JIR negotiations began, he made it clear he intended to take every measure to avoid conflict with Cyrus Adler, who ran Dropsie as well as JTS. Insisting on the utmost confidentiality, he directed that all JIR correspondence be sent not to his office at work but to his home address in Germantown.[7] Margolis knew how dangerous rankling a seminary head could be, as an earlier such conflict had uprooted his life.

As a young scholar, trained first in Europe and later at Columbia, he had landed his first academic position at Hebrew Union College, where he taught Hebrew and Semitic languages for five years and enjoyed a collegial relationship with the

president, Isaac Mayer Wise. Enticed to take a position in Semitics at the University
of California at Berkeley in 1899, he returned to HUC in 1905 when the college's
new president, Kaufmann Kohler, offered him a professorship in Hebrew exegesis.
This time, however, Margolis's stay in Cincinnati proved disastrous. In the intervening years, he had been swayed by Ahad Ha'am's writings to become a Zionist. Accustomed to the free atmosphere at Berkeley, upon his return to HUC, Margolis chafed
under Kohler's strict control of the faculty, and the two men repeatedly clashed over
compensation, the content of the curriculum, and other matters. Margolis did not
overtly teach Zionism in his courses, but when Kohler discovered that he was inter-
preting prophetic literature—the urtexts of Reform's universalism—through a Jewish nationalist lens, he became enraged. Kohler had already removed the instruction
of Modern Hebrew from the curriculum, and he saw Margolis's ostensible subter-
fuge as "poison instilled in sugar-coated pills." Insisting that academic freedom had
its limits in a seminary, he reassigned the courses to another faculty member, and in
response, Margolis resigned.[8]

After spending a year working for the Zionist movement in Europe and conducting research, he returned to the United States and began working on the JPS
Bible translation. A year later, he accepted the appointment at Dropsie, where he
remained.[9] Now, at the age of fifty-five, he had no interest in further conflict. Wise
acceded to his requests for secrecy and awaited his response.[10]

Convincing Wolfson and Margolis to leave their posts would likely be an uphill
battle, because JIR could hardly compete with either Harvard or Dropsie when it
came to academic resources. Wise had much more to offer, however, when it came
to rabbis and Jewish educators—namely, an opportunity to join forces with the
most prominent and powerful rabbi in the nation. His record of leadership in the
American Jewish Congress, the Zionist movement (albeit recently deposed), and
virtually every major Progressive cause positioned him well to recruit like-minded
colleagues. Moreover, on the Eastern seaboard, he did not need to look far for outstanding candidates.

Of all the Americans under consideration, Wise set his highest hopes on Mordecai Kaplan, a leading intellectual and controversial rabbi in the New York Jewish
community. Kaplan had studied in his youth at the Orthodox Etz Chaim yeshiva
but then earned his BA at City College, and his ordination at JTS in 1902. Well-
versed in traditional Jewish literature and Wissenschaft scholarship, he also had
broad knowledge of contemporary philosophy and sociology. And though Kaplan
followed Orthodox law in his personal religious practice and Wise did not, the
two men, both sons of rabbis, had much in common. They each prioritized Jewish
unity above sectarian divides and promoted their own religious and cultural program for the revitalization—or, in Kaplan's terminology, the reconstruction—of
Judaism. Both had embraced cultural Zionism when few rabbis did; each spoke

out on controversial political issues such as women's suffrage and the rights of labor, even when doing so alienated Jewish communal leaders and philanthropists;
and, in imagining a new, more vital form of American Judaism, each had created a
unique kind of synagogue center to advance their ideas—the Free Synagogue, in
Wise's case, and in Kaplan's, actually, two: first, the Jewish Center, an Orthodox
congregation he opened in 1918 but where his increasingly liberal views proved
untenable, prompting his resignation in 1921; and the recently established Society for the Advancement of Judaism (SAJ).

In addition, just as Wise hoped to build a cadre of rabbis to advance his vision
for American Judaism, Kaplan was doing similar work at JTS, where in 1909 Solomon Schechter had appointed him principal of the new Teachers Institute and, a
year later, professor of homiletics in the Rabbinical School, as well. By 1922, Kaplan had steered the Teachers Institute, located downtown, on a course very different from that of the Rabbinical School uptown. While both were vibrant centers
for higher Jewish learning, the Teachers Institute reflected the influence of Ahad
Ha'am's cultural Zionism in conjunction with John Dewey's philosophy of expe-
riential education; all courses in the formal program were conducted *ivrit b'ivrit*
(solely in Hebrew), for example, and extension courses in English were offered to
the broader community.[11] Here, some of the most influential teachers on Kaplan's
staff advanced a secular approach he did not share. At the Rabbinical School, by
contrast, traditional scholarship held pride of place, particularly in the area of Talmud, and the entire faculty other than Kaplan were Orthodox.

Many of these faculty had long and vociferously objected to Kaplan's radical-
izing influence at JTS, and in the spring of 1922, provoked by an article he had
recently published in the *Menorah Journal*, they were up in arms. In his "Program
for the Reconstruction of Judaism," Kaplan had urged the revitalization of Jewish
life through new modes of practice and the creation of a Jewish cultural center in
the Land of Israel.[12] His unique blend of religious liberalism and Zionism, which
entailed the rejection of Orthodox as well as Reform Judaism, enraged not only
his faculty colleagues but also JTS donors and alumni. A formidable group exerted
intense pressure on Cyrus Adler to fire Kaplan over his heterodox views.[13]

Amid the conflict, Wise reached out and tried to recruit Kaplan for JIR. This
was, in fact, his second attempt; in 1920, recalling that Kaplan had once considered
joining the Free Synagogue movement, Wise had invited him to help organize the
institute, possibly even run it, but Kaplan had declined.[14] Now Wise pitched the
idea of teaching just a single course. Kaplan expressed interest, but after conferring
with Adler, he once again said he had to decline. Wise then upped the ante, offering full-time work and promising Kaplan everything he lacked at JTS—the joy
of teaching in freedom, the appreciation and cooperation of his students and colleagues, and a voice in determining the direction of the school.[15]

While Wise and his trustees awaited a response, Richard Gottheil, who had met with Kaplan, believed the maverick rabbi might accept—if only he could stop worrying about losing the support of his allies who had "gone through the fire" with him and might perceive this as too radical a move.[16]

Wise also reached out that spring to Nissan Touroff. Having previously spent over a decade in Palestine running a teachers' seminary and then establishing and directing the Hebrew educational system, the Russian-born educator had perfect credentials to lead the new school.[17] Like Kaplan's Teachers Institute, the Hebrew Teachers College where Touroff was now dean had also stemmed from a cultural Zionist milieu and attracted a cohort dedicated to bringing about a rejuvenation of Jewish life in Palestine and the diaspora.

Touroff believed JIR could play a revolutionary role in Jewish life on a grander scale, and when Wise invited him to join, he responded enthusiastically. Not wanting to leave HTC in the lurch, he and Wise agreed that until a new dean could be found to replace him, he would serve part-time at JIR, teaching his courses *ivrit b'ivrit* and simultaneously heading the Department of Modern Hebrew Literature and Language and the Department of Religious Education.

Of course, it would have been preferable to have Touroff start full-time, given his experience establishing new schools, and the same was true of Wolfson. Still, the presence of these two leading figures on the inaugural JIR roster marked a significant achievement.

Now, if only Wise could prevail upon Margolis or especially Kaplan to join JIR, the newly formed institute could boast a faculty rivaling that of every one of its peer seminaries. In addition to hiring these major figures, lining up "day-by-day" teachers was critical, too, not so much for the cachet they might bring JIR but because, beyond Wise, these were the men who would actually teach the students how to be *rabbis*.

Here, Wise needed instructors for the introductory-level courses in traditional Jewish fields of study, as well as practitioners who could break new ground in additional areas he deemed essential: social service especially, but also chaplaincy, homiletics, and interfaith dialogue. In response to broad societal shifts underway within and outside the American Jewish community, these fields had changed dramatically since the turn of the century, and in order for JIR-trained rabbis to serve effectively as modern rabbis, they required up-to-date training.

Seeking a chaplain who could oversee religious services at the institute while doing double duty as an instructor in Jewish literature, Wise reached out to Harry Lewis. A gentle and kind man with a passion for social justice, Lewis, at the time, worked in the municipal prison system as a New York City chaplain. Born in Manchester, England, of Sephardic background, he had trained to become a rabbi at Montefiore College, a small seminary in the seaside town of Ramsgate. He and Wise shared a relationship that went back over a decade when Lewis took a temporary leave from his pulpit at the Manchester Congregation of British Jews for a stint guest-preaching at the Free Synagogue. Later, frustrated at his inability to implement reform at his synagogue, he resigned, and in 1913, immigrated to the United States.[18]

Lewis possessed a breadth of Jewish knowledge and published articles in Hebrew as well as English on diverse topics, including the Book of Isaiah, the Jews of London, and "Liberal Judaism and Social Service."[19] Wise invited him to teach Midrash and biblical exegesis while also serving as chaplain, and Lewis accepted immediately.[20]

When it came to social service, no one had more synagogue-based experience than Sidney Goldstein, and Wise now designated him head of the institute's Social Service Department. The department would hold a prominent place at JIR, allowing Goldstein to offer courses on a wide array of topics, including Jewish social welfare policy, marriage and sexuality, psychology and mental illness, alcohol abuse, and more.

Finding an appropriate instructor of homiletics proved a more difficult challenge. Who would have the hubris to teach preaching under the watchful eye of Stephen S. Wise, whose oratory regularly filled Carnegie Hall? At Kohut's suggestion, Wise invited Joel Blau, an HUC graduate and rabbi of Temple Peni-El, a Conservative congregation in Washington Heights, who could teach Midrash, as well. Blau, however, failed to reply.[21]

Meanwhile, several of Wise's Protestant colleagues who had taught in the summer schools signed on without hesitation. Wise wanted these visiting lecturers to have a visible presence at the school, teaching at least one course each year on some aspect of Christianity. Doing so mirrored the Hochschule's practice of inviting non-Jewish speakers weekly.[22] Long dedicated to interfaith alliance, here Wise had two goals: honoring Christian scholars who put their reputation at risk by rejecting antisemitic interpretations of the Bible; and exposing JIR students to diverse religious perspectives. "I want the men who are to become the students at the Institute to get the non-Jewish viewpoint of teachers and scholars like yourself who have messages of inspiration to bring," Wise wrote to Charles Foster Kent, the Yale biblical scholar who had taught in the summer school of 1921, "who have messages and inspiration to bring."[23] Moreover, visiting lecturers from leading university-affiliated divinity schools brought the identical modern approach to theological education that Wise wanted to introduce into Jewish seminary life, and those who taught from a Social Gospel perspective could also help cultivate a similar mindset in JIR-trained rabbis.

Kent agreed to return, as did George Foot Moore, a Presbyterian minister and historian of religion at the Harvard Divinity School. An expert in Ancient Near Eastern studies who earlier in his career had chaired Hebrew at Andover, Moore was an advocate for modernizing theological education through the inclusion of sociology, social psychology, and social ethics—a strategy closely aligned with

Sidney Goldstein's plan for JIR's Social Service Department.[24] Wise garnered commitments for the 1923–1924 academic year, too, from F. J. Foakes-Jackson, the Church historian at Union Theological Seminary, and Kirsopp Lake, a New Testament scholar at Harvard Divinity School.

By June, JIR had a pool of Protestant scholars on board to lecture and engage students in interfaith dialogue. Together with the Social Service Department and a school chaplain, these were a first in American rabbinical training.

OPPOSITION MOBILIZES

Meanwhile, the Reform movement leadership, having failed to dissuade Wise and the Free Synagogue from moving forward, took the battle public. In a letter alerting Reform congregations across the country to the Free Synagogue's plan, the president of the UAHC, Charles Shohl, made an explicit bid to choke JIR of the critical assets the school needed to open by urging all member congregations to withhold support:

> We are content to have Dr. Wise set out immediately for all the money he can get. We realize that the field is limited and that Dr. Wise's success may mean diminished revenue for the Hebrew Union College but we refuse to be thrown into a panic. We have resources which cannot be minimized or overlooked. We have two hundred graduates who will not suffer the institution founded by Dr. Isaac M. Wise of sainted memory to fail. We have the support of every man in the Liberal Jewish ministry. We have 241 congregations belonging to the Union who will not lend themselves to our undoing. We face the issue with equanimity, awaiting the judgment of our rabbis and congregations.

Shohl also disclosed elements of the Free Synagogue's proposed "Basis for Discussion" and his charge that they had issued an ultimatum, namely, that if the UAHC did not render a decision within fifteen days, Wise would immediately tour the West to raise money for his "proposed college in New York."[25]

This charge infuriated Wise. The Free Synagogue had not demanded but simply *requested* an early answer, he told Hirsch, and the UAHC committee had amicably agreed to render a decision by April 15. He would demand that Shohl repudiate his "false and foul statement."[26] The Free Synagogue then further escalated the battle by distributing a pamphlet of their own, *Open Letter to the President of the Union of American Hebrew Congregations from Committee of Free Synagogue on the Jewish Institute of Religion*, which divulged correspondence documenting the negotiations and offered a counterclaim in response to Shohl's attack. "There was not the slightest intimation in the course of our last conference that the plan in its entirety or in any of its details was unfriendly or antagonistic either to the Hebrew

Union College or to the Union of American Hebrew Congregations. Throughout the conferences, Dr. Wise and others of us gave personal expression to our deep and unfeigned interest in the union to which the Free Synagogue belongs, and in the college, the chief institution under its care, three of whose graduates are Dr. Wise's associates in the ministry of the Free Synagogue." They called on the UAHC executive board to address Shohl's statement and give them a hearing before rendering a decision.[27]

The open letter achieved little. Hirsch praised its content but despaired that it had come too late. "I doubt whether it will move the Cincinnati folks to repentance," he wrote Wise. "They have done the mischief . . . judging my own Congregation which, like all others, was flooded by these Cincinnati communications, they have succeeded in prejudicing the minds of even my closest friends against our proposed institute. From all sides I hear the question 'Why must we have two schools; isn't one enough?'"[28]

Wise's longtime ally John Haynes Holmes commiserated, having recently come under attack for publishing a critique of the Unitarian church structure. "It is getting awful slams from the denominational papers . . . positively vicious," he wrote, which he was inclined to take as "proof positive that my case against the whole sectarian system and all its works is sound." He framed the fervency of Reform's opposition as a measure of Wise's effectiveness. "They know you are doing what they should and would have done if they had the courage and vision," Holmes told Wise.[29]

The next attack came not from the Reform lay leadership but from Kaufmann Kohler, who, stepping down after two decades as president of HUC, used his farewell sermon to address the situation. Kohler understood that the appeal of JIR, as well as its threat, was the compelling nature of Wise himself and the vision he offered American Jewry. To the faculty, students, alumni, and supporters who filled the sanctuary in Cincinnati on that May day, he praised the college for uniting and centralizing the forces of progressive Jewry. He then took aim at JIR:

> All the more deplorable is the attempt in certain quarters to split the power, the unity and the authority of the Hebrew Union College as the center of American Reform Judaism by the proposed creation of Jewish Institute of Religion which could be just colorless and non-descript enough to suit certain classes of men in a Free Synagogue, or of a Hochschule of the University type which would be so broad and all-inclusive in its character as to give equal place to all religious systems and shades of thought, and whose professors should represent all possible stand-points, however diametrically opposed to each other. And out of such an Institute Rabbis, preachers and teachers are to emanate who are to mould character and inspire reverence for God and things godly!

"The Hebrew Union College need not fear competition," he proclaimed. With half-a-century's tradition, congregational support, a full faculty, and dormitories to be erected, "it will under God's Providence remain what it was hitherto under Isaac M. Wise's Presidency and mine—the center and watch-tower of American Reform Judaism, safe and secure for all time."[30]

Notwithstanding Shohl's so-called equanimity, Wise's feigned interest in Hebrew Union College, and Kohler's confident forecast, blood was boiling on all sides. Still, the UAHC agreed to allow representatives of the Free Synagogue to address the board at their upcoming June meeting.

≈

While Kohler inveighed from Cincinnati, his counterpart at JTS and Dropsie, Cyrus Adler, was impeding JIR's faculty recruitment efforts closer to home. Adler's powerful hold, Wise was discovering, extended to some of the leading figures Wise coveted for his new enterprise.

The heavier blow came from Kaplan. While the experience of being wooed by Wise and Gottheil stood in marked contrast to the hostility Kaplan was encountering at JTS, after serious consideration, he declined, fearing that were he to abandon the Teachers Institute now, it would go to pieces. When Wise revised the offer once again, proposing that Kaplan continue directing the Teachers Institute *and* join JIR, Kaplan said he had raised the possibility, but Adler would not permit it.[31]

Wise expressed regret and told Kaplan he was making the wrong decision. "I am not thinking of your gain in a low sense, but I am thinking of the opportunity I would have coveted bringing to you," Wise wrote, "namely, teaching under the most favoring auspices . . . in the spirit of freedom of cooperation and of eager appreciation. The Institute would have welcomed your service."[32] For his part, Kaplan rued the decision in his personal diary, blaming his weak will, fear, and indecision for not doing what he ought "to be of greatest service to the Jewish cause."

"Will I have the courage to cross the Rubicon of my career?" Kaplan asked himself.[33]

Both men, Wise *and* Kaplan, were distraught, recognizing the tremendous potential that would have come from their shaping the institute together. The men held one another in high regard and recognized shared goals as well as their different strengths. Wise excelled at social activism and organizing institutions, whereas Kaplan was making his mark as a theologian, philosopher, and teacher. As Kaplan's biographer has argued, "the combination of Kaplan the thinker and Wise the activist would have been formidable."[34]

Margolis, by contrast, set his terms much too high. In response to his demands for a $10,000 salary (double what Wise planned to pay), the title dean of the faculty, a lifetime appointment, and a pension of $5,000 for his wife should she survive him, the JIR men refused even to offer a counterproposal.[35] Instead, Wise offered him a position on the board, assuring him a unanimous election.[36]

This, however, brought out Margolis's fear of Adler. Hurt at not receiving a counteroffer and frightened about the consequences of having engaged in the discussion at all, he met with Mack in June to address his concern. "The specific thing he wanted to talk over with me was the danger of even hinting to Adler his becoming Trustee or lecturer," Mack told Wise. "I told him that I would have a talk with Adler without mentioning him, bringing up only the Kaplan matter, and in that way sound Adler out. I appreciated fully the possibility that his own position would be endangered if Adler felt that he was even considering any connection with us."[37]

≈

Decisively, negotiations between the Free Synagogue and the Reform movement came to a formal conclusion at the UAHC board meeting in June. After all the vituperation of the year gone by, the willingness of both sides to meet showed that neither was interested in severing the relationship altogether. Still, it was a foregone conclusion that the Reform movement would not take on JIR as a "coordinate activity" as the Free Synagogue had initially proposed and that any sort of meaningful cooperation was off the table.

Julian Mack and Lee K. Frankel agreed to represent the institute at the HUC board meeting, on one condition. They told Wise he must raise $45,000 for JIR immediately, in hand or pledged over the next three years. Among the few who knew JIR's real financial state of affairs, they would only go to Cincinnati if they could announce to the Reform leadership that all funds necessary for the institute to open were in place. Wise understood and agreed.

"I must work like a Trojan in the next ten days in order to raise that amount," he told Hirsch.[38] Hirsch worried, too. "Everywhere the Cincinnatians are at work belittling you and the Institute," he replied. "They argue and not without effect that the institute never will become real."[39]

Nonetheless, an appeal that Mack, Frankel, and Wise issued together, according to a report Wise sent Hirsch soon after, raised all the money JIR needed and more. This was thanks principally to the Free Synagogue's appropriation, which included $30,000 annually over the school's first three years, plus an additional $47,000 during this period guaranteed, should Wise not secure this amount through his own fundraising across the country ("I know I will," he told Hirsch).[40]

In the end, Mack alone made the Free Synagogue presentation, addressing the UAHC and HUC Boards at 2:00 P.M. on June 11, 1922.[41] Speaking dispassionately, he explained that the Free Synagogue had been motivated to negotiate with the UAHC not out of fiscal concern but hoping that joint fundraising would increase funding from untapped sources to their mutual benefit. The past month alone had demonstrated that such sources existed, he claimed, citing the large amount recently raised (it is not clear if he identified the single source of most of these funds). In any case, he also announced that twenty to twenty-five prospective students now wanted to enroll.[42]

Mack then addressed Shohl's charge and insisted that had the UAHC committee expressed their displeasure with the JIR proposal for cooperation from the outset, the Free Synagogue would have withdrawn it at once and asked the UAHC representatives for alternative suggestions. The UAHC committee should not have conveyed satisfaction with the proposal if, in fact, they were not satisfied.

Shohl responded apologetically, according to Mack. Regarding the UAHC president's letter to congregations across the country, board members seemed split. Mack had the impression that while some of the Cincinnati men would have been willing to launch an offensive even stronger than Shohl's, others, including the major philanthropist Julius Rosenwald, disapproved of the president's letter. Perhaps to avoid further division, the board chose neither to approve nor to condemn the letter, and members of the New York–based UAHC committee stated clearly that the Free Synagogue had acted with integrity and should in no way be subject to censure. In the same spirit, Mack urged continued discussions and expressed hope for a large measure of cooperation not only between JIR and HUC but also with JTS.[43]

That the UAHC Board did not endorse Shohl's letter represented a small victory, but more importantly, Wise and the Free Synagogue had reached a significant turning point. JIR's position as the sole independent and nondenominational seminary within the landscape of American Jewish life was now public and official.

Paradoxically, while JIR's nondenominationalism reflected Wise's belief in the unity of the Jewish people, the school would have to compete in a world of coalescing denominations. And while the Wissenschaft seminaries in Germany had *not* sought to avert one another's rise, when the JIR founders turned from rhetoric and experimentation to constructing buildings and hiring faculty, HUC and JTS responded fearsomely. Notwithstanding Wise's stated aim "only to be friendly and helpful," they knew a threat when they saw one: Not only did Wise bring a sizable following among the Eastern European Jews, who demographically represented the future of American Jewish life, but he also brought a formidable record of institution-building. Now, they believed, Wise aimed to wrest control of rabbinical training in order to bring about a radical vision for Jewish renewal.

Kohler and Adler fervently believed *their* seminaries were the standard-bearers in creating authentic Jewish life and ensuring Jewish survival in America, and Wise and the Free Synagogue were hostile intruders bent on upending all that they and their predecessors had built over decades. Moreover, if the JIR group succeeded in diverting precious resources like funders or faculty away from either the college or the seminary, they could do great harm. The leaders of both denominational seminaries quickly took defensive postures, to real effect. In the search for faculty, for example, while Wise reached out to individuals and not institutions, matters of institutional loyalty and infighting factored significantly, if not determinatively, in the results. Adler's refusal to sanction any cooperation between the seminary and the new institute rendered irrelevant any interest Mordecai Kaplan may have had in a joint faculty position or Max Margolis in joining JIR's board.

Unwelcome in the landscape of American Jewish seminaries, Wise and the Free Synagogue nonetheless made significant strides that spring in establishing their new model. Wise's success hiring teachers representing some of the most progressive strains in American Jewish and religious pedagogy laid to rest criticism that his nondenominational seminary would be "colorless and non-descript." With Nissan Touroff teaching his courses *ivrit b'ivrit* and functioning essentially as a one-man Hebrew teachers' institute, JIR would bring the pragmatic Hebraist model for the first time to the training of rabbis. Sidney Goldstein would provide in-depth exposure to the Free Synagogue's unique approach to congregation-based social service. Harry Lewis would bring his experience as a Liberal congregational rabbi in England to teaching the critical skills of liturgical leadership. And Wise's Protestant colleagues from Harvard, Yale, and Union Theological Seminary would provide ample opportunity for interfaith dialogue involving scholars rooted in the Social Gospel tradition.

Thanks to the Free Synagogue, these men could all be paid. Moreover, given the number of applications coming in, it was clear they would have plenty of students, too.

With the institute scheduled to open in four months, Wise had yet to hear from Blau about homiletics, and he still lacked a librarian, but these arrangements could be delegated to Goldstein and others. He needed to turn his full attention to enlisting professional Jewish scholars—the "great masters" he hoped would put JIR on the map as a global center of higher Jewish learning.

It was time to get himself to Europe.

5

In Pursuit of European Scholars

Bᵧ the early 1920s, a transatlantic migration of Jewish Wissen-schaft scholarship from Europe to the United States had been underway for decades, accelerated by the recruitment efforts of various seminary heads. Solomon Schechter, for example, one year after leaving his position at Cambridge University to become president of JTS in 1902, had returned to Europe together with Talmud professor Louis Ginzberg in order to recruit faculty for the seminary. In Germany that summer of 1903, Schechter hired a young Alexander Marx, who had just defended his doctoral thesis, as professor of Jewish history and librarian at JTS and the University of Strasbourg's Israel Friedlaender to teach biblical literature and exegesis.[1] Similarly, Kaufmann Kohler, upon assuming the presidency of HUC in 1903, set out to increase the number of German-trained faculty put in place at the college by Isaac Mayer Wise, though Kohler did so by drawing on his network of contacts rather than by making the trip. Schechter and Kohler, themselves renowned scholars trained in the German university system (and in top yeshivas before that), were paradigmatic of the colleagues they sought, and as a result largely of their efforts, HUC and JTS by 1922 had become centers for Wissenschaft in their own right.[2] Stephen Wise, however, did not take an entirely favorable view of the achievement, contending that the German approach to teaching at these American seminaries took all the life out of learning. "How can I take a man from Germany now?" he wrote Gottheil. "Have not Cincinnati and the Seminary here been ruined by the Teutonically-minded leaders, Schechter, Wise, Kohler and all the rest?"[3]

Indeed, one of Wise's closest advisors opposed his making the trip, arguing that faculty fresh off the boat from Europe could hardly prepare JIR students to meet the needs of contemporary American Jewry. "You ought to recruit your entire force in America," wrote George A. Kohut, who had himself trained at the Hochschule and the University of Berlin.[4] A scholar and educator devoted to preserving Jewish books and manuscripts from around the world, and also to publishing new work, Kohut knew well the community of Jewish scholars in the United States. There was no shortage of viable candidates, he assured Wise, "they only have to be sought."

Wise, however, for all his complaints about "Teutonically-minded leaders," fully intended for scholars from Berlin and Breslau, as well as London, Vienna, and Budapest, to play a prominent role at the institute, for ideological as well as practical reasons.

Ideologically, Wise was claiming for the Jewish Institute of Religion the birthright that all modern Jewish seminaries shared: the tradition of Wissenschaft des Judentums, which he considered revolutionary at heart and still relevant. He venerated the movement's founder Leopold Zunz (1794–1886), who had pioneered the effort in Germany in the 1820s to integrate the scientific study of Judaism into secular culture. The scholarly investigation of Jewish classical texts in relation to the historical contexts that formed them, Zunz believed, would vanquish age-old antisemitic misconceptions by revealing an intellectual tradition on par in scope and depth with all the world's great cultures. Fighting for the establishment of Jewish studies within German universities, he argued, went hand in hand with the battle for full equality. Wise shared this view and bemoaned the fact that a full century later, Zunz's dream remained unfulfilled not only in Germany but in the United States, as well.

Wise also admired Zacharias Frankel (1801–1875) and Abraham Geiger (1810–1874), who had extended Zunz's project to the founding of seminaries. Unlike Zunz, Frankel and Geiger viewed the critical approach to Jewish texts as a *religious* endeavor, aimed not at secularizing Jewish learning but at laying the groundwork for a non-Orthodox religious awakening.[5] Moreover, they believed that rabbis like themselves, as purveyors of Jewish knowledge, had a crucial role to play in this effort. Their seminaries, the Juedisch-Theologisches Seminar of Breslau (founded in 1854) and the Hochschule (founded in 1872), together with the Orthodox Rabbiner-Seminar established by Esriel Hildesheimer in Berlin in 1873, succeeded in sparking a rejuvenation of Jewish intellectual life.

In the decades since their founding, alumni of these seminaries formed a transnational network of scholars who spread the Wissenschaft seminary model beyond Germany, not only to institutions in the United States but also to the Jews' College in London (founded 1855); the Israelitisch-Theologische Lehranstalt in Vienna (founded 1893); the Rabbinical Seminary of Budapest (founded 1877); and the Collegio Rabbinico Italiano in Florence (founded in Padua in 1829, reopened in Florence in 1899). By 1922, every one of these schools had flourished under the direction of Breslau graduates, and Wise planned to visit each of them after his stops in Germany, with the exception of the seminary in Florence, where the director, Samuel Hirsch Margulies, had died just a few months earlier. In addition to recruiting faculty, Wise would also have an opportunity to view firsthand the conditions of the Jewish communities in each of these cities.

JEWISH EUROPE IN TRANSITION

Wise had last traveled to Europe in January 1919 as a delegate to the Versailles Peace Conference, where he had advocated for Armenian independence, safeguarding Jewish rights throughout Europe, and securing a Jewish homeland in Palestine. Since that time, he had led the American Jewish Congress's efforts to provide humanitarian relief to Jews suffering in the aftermath of the war. And while the vast majority of that aid went to Eastern Europe, where Jews continued to endure pogroms and mass displacement, Jewish communities in Germany, Austria, and Hungary were also in turmoil. No longer the citizens of a vast empire, these Jews now belonged to nations constrained within treaty-imposed borders and buckling under sanctions that included exorbitant reparations and demilitarization.

The Jews of Germany and Austria had to navigate countervailing currents. On the one hand, thanks to progressive reforms put in place under the Weimar Republic in Germany and the Social Democrat–led government in Austria, they had gained rights and protections that made possible unprecedented economic, social, and political advancement. At the same time, however, the prevailing strife was proving fertile soil for reactionary forces. Though Jews had served loyally in the armies of the Central Powers, right-wing nationalist groups were now blaming them for the loss of the war and the ensuing economic misery. Germany and Austria alike experienced a dramatic spike in antisemitism, visible not only in an increase in physical attacks on Jews by extremist groups but also in growing efforts within mainstream society to curtail Jewish participation in universities and public life. By 1922, it was clear in both countries that the postwar liberal reforms Jews had hoped might finally enable full integration into society were not going to put an end to entrenched antisemitic discrimination any time soon.

As German Jews' hope for acceptance dimmed, many began to look inward, exploring aspects of the Judaism their parents and grandparents had left behind in pursuit of assimilation. As a result, a growing number of projects promoting Jewish culture and Zionism emerged, including Martin Buber's journal *Der Jude* and Hayyim Nahman Bialik's publishing house Dvir. A stream of leading Jewish writers and poets who, like Bialik, had arrived from Russia were turning Berlin into a center for Hebrew literature. Liberal, Orthodox, and Zionist organizations and youth movements were flourishing, and in 1922 several new schools had recently emerged, including Eugen Täubler's Akademie für die Wissenschaft des Judentums and Franz Rosenzweig's Lehrhaus. With the popularization of Wissenschaft des Judentums, Germany's three seminaries were growing during this period, as well.[6]

In Vienna, too, Jewish culture was flourishing. A center of Zionist activity since Theodor Herzl established the movement there in the 1890s, the city now became a hub for European Jewish youth en route to Palestine. Yiddish publishing was thriving, Yiddish theater was experiencing a revival, and here, too, new Jewish educational institutions had recently opened, including the Realgymnasium (a Zionist-leaning school for children) and a Hebrew teachers' academy.[7] Unfortunately, since the war's end, the city's seminary, the Israelitisch-Theologische

Lehranstalt, had been struggling with a financial crisis and now relied on American Jewish relief aid in order to stay afloat.

In Hungary, by contrast, Jews were faring far worse, with no such renaissance in Jewish culture. There, following the collapse of a brief Communist-led government in 1919, the national army—composed of right-wing counterrevolutionaries led by Admiral Miklós Horthy—carried out the notorious "White Terror," targeting Jews as well as labor and political activists and killing more than three thousand, including between one thousand and thirteen hundred Jews. Tens of thousands of Jews were deported, and many others, including Jewish scholars and intellectuals, fled the country.[8] And, in 1920, the National Assembly passed numerus clausus, the first "Jewish Law" in post–World War I Europe, which capped the number of Jewish students allowed in institutions of higher education at 6 percent. This corresponded to the percentage of Jews in the general population but was far lower than current representation in some of Budapest's major universities, where Jews made up roughly a quarter of the students. When Prime Minister István Bethlen formed a coalition government in 1921, state-sponsored violence subsided, but attacks on synagogues and Jewish groups continued and Zionist activities were banned.[9]

England was another story altogether. Here, where fifty thousand Jews had served in the armed forces during the war, the British empire's victory and expansion afterward held special significance for the Jewish community. Now, not only were they enjoying upward mobility and greater social integration within England, but thanks to passage of the Balfour Declaration and the new British Mandate for Palestine, they could also claim an ascendant position among world Jewry. The declaration, an official statement issued by the British government in 1917 supporting the establishment of a national Jewish home in Palestine, signaled to the world that the aims of the Zionist movement were now achievable. And notably, three leaders from the American wing of that movement had helped draft the text—Wise, together with Louis Brandeis and Felix Frankfurter.

Indeed, as an actor on the international stage, Wise had demonstrated repeatedly that his commitment to the "oneness of Israel" extended globally. His love for the Jewish people continually motivated him to respond to the crises in Eastern and Central Europe with urgency and to advance the Zionist cause in every practical way. Similarly, his commitment to Judaism's prophetic call led him to fight for non-Jewish victims of oppression in the United States as well as abroad. Now, as he anticipated visiting England, Germany, Austria, and Hungary in search of scholars, he brought more than just a deep appreciation for the Wissenschaft tradition; he understood that at stake were matters of life and death. To fight the battles of the moment and those that surely lay ahead, he needed teachers who shared and could instill in a new generation the same passion he felt for the Jewish people and Jewish values.

To be sure, amid the cataclysmic change brought by a war that had shattered four empires, Wise believed the nineteenth-century goals of the Wissenschaft movement—achieving full emancipation for the Jews and stimulating a religious awakening—had lost none of their urgency. Moreover, he intended for the institute's scholarly arm to be strong; just as no rabbi could claim legitimacy without learnedness, so, too, no Jewish seminary could claim legitimacy without distinguished faculty. Nonetheless, in the path he was forging, Wissenschaft scholarship would hold an equal, rather than paramount, place alongside other, more worldly but desperately important priorities. In light of the international struggles of the Jewish people, he believed, rabbis needed to be equipped with far more than academic knowledge to lead the way. Scholarship, after all, could not alleviate suffering. Scholarship could not provide refuge. Scholarship could not create a just world.

For Wise, there was nothing incongruous about this model; it mirrored his own rabbinate, writ large. Unlike Kohler and Schechter, he had never attended a German seminary, and while he had earned a doctorate and he valued Jewish learning, his achievements were elsewhere, in his singular mix of Jewish religious and political leadership.

WISE PURSUES EUROPE'S SCHOLARS

When Wise set sail for England on June 13, 1922, just two days after Mack's meeting with the UAHC and HUC boards in Cincinnati, he had reason to be hopeful; truthfully, things had mostly gone his way thus far, though not without difficulty—and *not* in the realm of recruiting Jewish scholars. Nevertheless, while ambitious to secure a full faculty for JIR in just over two months, he continued to harbor concerns regarding the German approach. Thus, he set out with a plan to minimize risk to the institute. He would visit the European centers of Jewish learning and meet their faculty and then invite a select few to teach on a visiting basis for just a semester or two. This would provide ample opportunity for classroom observation, without jeopardizing anyone's position elsewhere. Over time, he would offer permanent positions to those who established a genuine rapport with students while the others returned as planned to their posts in Europe.[10] "I know it savors of the trial method," Wise told Hirsch, "but it's a serious matter to ask men to come from another country unless one is quite sure one can offer him a life place."[11]

LONDON

Immediately upon arriving in London on June 20, Wise learned the storm over JIR had reached Europe and threatened to jeopardize his recruitment efforts. Indeed, his very first meeting, a luncheon with Israel Abrahams, the liberal Jewish theologian who had succeeded Schechter as Reader in Rabbinic Literature at

Cambridge, began badly. In response to Wise's invitation to teach, Abrahams re-
acted adversely, explaining that he had good friends involved with HUC and did
not want to take sides.[12] Wise explained how negotiations with the UAHC had
unfolded, expressed hope that the two schools would soon share friendly relations, and then, arguing that teaching at JIR did not indicate bias, worked hard
to persuade Abrahams to come to the institute for a semester. By the end of the
meeting, Abrahams seemed less worried. He agreed to teach on a visiting basis if
he could gain the approval of Claude Montefiore, the head of England's Liberal
Jewish movement, and he coached Wise on the merits of various scholars, particularly those based in Germany (at present he felt there were none in England "big
enough" to join JIR as a full-time professor).[13]

The following Saturday, Wise preached at the liberal Jewish Religious Union
and then met with Abrahams, Montefiore, and Israel Mattuck. A Harvard-
educated graduate of HUC (class of 1910), Mattuck had left the United States to
become senior minister at London's newly established Liberal Synagogue in 1912,
when he was just under thirty years old. Over the ensuing decade, the synagogue
had flourished along with Liberal Judaism in England, thanks to the efforts of the
"Three M's"—Montefiore, Mattuck, and Lily Montagu, a religious organizer and
driving force behind the movement.[14] Wise, however, found Montefiore and Mattuck, too, unsympathetic to JIR. Both men opposed Zionism even after passage of
the Balfour Declaration, as did Abrahams, but this seems not to have been their
primary concern. Montefiore, rather, had read negative editorial statements in the
Israelite, the Cincinnati-based Jewish weekly, and Wise felt that Mattuck objected
out of loyalty to his alma mater.[15] Wise, however, once again explained the impetus
behind the creation of JIR, reviewed the negotiations, and then suggested to Abrahams that he come to the United States and lecture not only at the institute but at
the college, as well. The suggestion seemed to put Abrahams at ease, and Wise felt
the men were, by the end of the meeting, "quite won over." None seemed to hold a
deep grudge; Mattuck invited Wise to preach at his synagogue, Montefiore helped
him hone his faculty recruitment strategy, and Abrahams agreed not only to teach
that fall but also to sell his library to the institute.[16]

While in London, Wise corresponded with Ismar Elbogen, head of the Hochschule, and with Hirsch Perez Chajes, the chief rabbi of Vienna, seeking guidance
for his upcoming European tour. Elbogen responded generously, offering to introduce Wise to the scholars of Berlin and providing a list of those Wise should meet in
other cities. Notwithstanding his stated concerns that those in Breslau and Vienna
might be too Orthodox to have any interest in JIR and that Budapest's seminary
was currently suffering a shortage of teachers, Elbogen was overall encouraging and
assured Wise he would find the selection of scholars in Europe "all too abundant."[17]

Meanwhile, Montefiore urged Wise to pursue Elbogen himself, for he was the
foremost Jewish historian in Germany, now unofficially directing the Hochschule

while also helping to lead the Liberal Jewish movement in Germany. A graduate of the Breslau seminary, Elbogen had taught at the Collegio Rabbinico Italiano in Florence for three years, before joining the faculty at the Hochschule in 1903. There he taught hundreds of students preparing to serve as rabbis, scholars, or educators and became one of the preeminent intellectual leaders of Reform Judaism in Germany. His major scholarly work at this point was a comprehensive study of synagogue liturgy, and he was now editing several different projects, including a history of the Jews of Germany.[18]

Montefiore also recommended Chaim Tchernowitz, an important Hebraist as well as one of few Talmud scholars from Russia who embraced the Wissenschaft approach. Tchernowitz, who went by the pen name "Rav Tzair," had a unique background. Born in 1871 in the Russian town of Sebezh, he had studied in Kovno, where he received rabbinical ordination from Yitzhak Elhanan Spektor in 1886. He then founded a progressive yeshiva in Odessa, which combined traditional study with Wissenschaft research and offered tracks for teacher training as well as Jewish and general studies. A friend and disciple of Ahad Ha'am, Tchernowitz attracted young intellectual Zionists to the yeshiva, including Hayyim Nahman Bialik and Yehezkel Kaufmann.[19] After converting the school into a rabbinical seminary in 1907, he stepped down in 1911 to visit Palestine and then pursue a doctorate at the University of Würzburg, where he wrote his dissertation on the Shulhan 'Arukh.[20] Elbogen mentioned Tchernowitz, as well, but knew he was planning to settle soon in Palestine and assumed that would rule him out.

As to other suitable faculty in England, just as Elbogen had warned about the orthodoxy of the scholars of Breslau and Vienna, Montefiore saw no possibility beyond Abrahams for the same reason.

Before leaving London, however, Wise did secure another nonresident faculty member: Protestant scholar and Unitarian minister Robert Travers Herford, who specialized in rabbinical literature and directed the Dr. Williams's Library and Trust, a small theological library in London. Like Charles Foster Kent and George Foot Moore, Herford challenged the antisemitic bias that had become dominant in Christian scholarship, particularly in his treatment of the rabbinic period.[21] When Herford initially declined Wise's invitation, Wise tried to persuade him, citing the debt Jewish students and thinkers owed him for his courage in "redeeming the name of the Pharisees from agelong unjust obloquy." Herford seemed moved, according to Wise, and agreed to offer two courses during JIR's 1923 summer school, one on the Pharisees and a second on Pirkei Avot.[22] "I have long wanted to be the medium of presenting you to Jewish and Christian scholars and they to you," Wise told Herford.[23]

With the Hochschule his next major destination, Wise stopped en route in Paris. "Am on the trail of Dubnow, said to have been expelled from Kovno," he wrote Sidney Goldstein, referring to the Jewish historian Simon Dubnow from

Belorussia.[24] Dubnow had recently left his teaching post at the government-supported "Jewish People's University" in Petrograd and then come under consideration for a professorship in Jewish history at the University of Kovno in Lithuania, but that fell through due to faculty opposition. Goldstein urged Wise to pursue Dubnow, believing he might be convinced to come to JIR for a semester or two,[25] and Wise seized upon the idea. "It would be a tremendous thing to bring him to America even if we could not keep him," Wise told Hirsch.[26] Wise did not find Dubnow in Paris, however, and after guest preaching at the city's synagogue, he continued on to Berlin.[27] While later that year, Dubnow moved to Berlin, it appears that he and Wise never met.

BERLIN AND BRESLAU

When Wise crossed the border from France into Germany, he entered a nation in financial and political chaos. Just two weeks earlier, a right-wing nationalist group had assassinated the Weimar government's Jewish minister of foreign affairs, Walther Rathenau, setting off widespread panic and a flight of capital that spurred rapid depreciation of the mark and hyperinflation.[28] Nonetheless, the two institutions he planned to visit, the Hochschule and the Juedisch-Theologisches Seminar of Breslau, remained in operation.

Wise held the Hochschule in particularly high esteem, due perhaps to the liberal seminary's strong influence on close colleagues like Hirsch and Kohut, as well as Richard Gottheil, Felix Adler, and many others. For fifty years, Americans seeking to become Jewish scholars had been crossing the Atlantic to study at the Hochschule, and they continued to do so in the aftermath of the war, for the United States still had no equivalent institution of higher Jewish learning. "As late as 1922 a young instructor at the Hebrew Union College desiring to do graduate work had no choice but to study in Germany," the American Jewish historian Jacob Rader Marcus would write later about beginning his own studies that year at the Hochschule and the University of Berlin.[29] But like the seminary in Vienna, the Hochschule, too, was now experiencing financial difficulties and becoming increasingly dependent on aid from the American Jewish community.[30]

Finances aside, however, the school was now enjoying a period of growth, thanks to the resurgence of interest in Wissenschaft des Judentums.[31] Embracing the trend, the Hochschule under Elbogen's unofficial direction expanded its role beyond the training of rabbis and scholars to include, as well, men and women exploring Judaism out of their own search for meaning. The biblical scholar Nehama Leibowitz, who studied as an undergraduate at the Hochschule during this period (and at the University of Berlin, as well), recalled being exposed to critical scholarship in an open, liberal atmosphere. There, she felt at home studying alongside rabbis and intellectuals, including her *hevruta* (study) partner, fellow student Leo Strauss. He helped her with Greek philosophy, and she helped him with Hebrew.[32]

On July 4, the morning after Wise's arrival in Berlin, he headed to the Hochschule, where he attended classes and met with two members of the faculty, Julius Guttmann and Harry Torczyner. Both men impressed him. Guttmann, a philosopher of religion and historian of Jewish philosophy, had joined the Hochschule in 1919 when he was called to succeed Hermann Cohen, who had died the previous year.[33] Torczyner, a Hebrew philologist and Bible scholar, had also joined in 1919, after leaving his previous post at the University of Vienna.[34]

Wise found Guttmann's teaching especially informative and clear. "He held his students and was most stimulating," he noted, adding, "he is quiet, thoughtful, the typical German scholar, rather cloistered and not quite forceful but a nice wholesome personality, and, I should say, a gentleman." While Guttmann seemed keen to come to the United States, Wise declined to invite him; his field would parallel Wolfson's, and for the moment, the institute could not afford the luxury of having two men in the Philosophy Department. Guttmann, like Montefiore and Elbogen, also recommended Chaim Tchernowitz, despite the Talmudist's intention to move soon to Palestine. America might tempt Tchernowitz for a year or two, Gutmann told Wise, as long as the call to JIR ultimately furthered his plan.[35]

In contrast to Guttmann, Torczyner struck Wise as having a tempestuous nature but brilliant nonetheless. And Torczyner, too, was interested in coming to the institute, offering to teach Bible while also heading the "Neo-Hebraic Department." "I am told he speaks it well and writes it perfectly," Wise noted. Bringing Torczyner for the fall posed yet another challenge, though; he currently held the rotating position of rector at the Hochschule and could not easily leave on short notice.

That evening, Wise stopped by Elbogen's house, where he found a note from the historian indicating that he would be back in two days. The message went on to urge Wise in the meantime to cable Felix Perles, a rabbi and biblical philologist based in Koenigsberg, who would be visiting Berlin later in the week. Wise had previously heard about Perles from Abrahams, who called him "the greatest scholar of his generation." From a prominent German Jewish family—his Breslautrained father had been the rabbi of Munich, and his mother was a well-known writer—Perles had a wide range of scholarly interests including Biblical criticism, medieval Hebrew poetry, liturgy, and more, and he had also been active in the Zionist movement for more than two decades.[36] Wise cabled him, then prepared to head for Breslau the next day in order to meet the Talmudist Michael Guttmann. He, too, had a strong record, as a graduate of the Budapest seminary who had lectured on Jewish law at the Budapest seminary for fifteen years prior to joining the Juedisch-Theologisches Seminar faculty in 1921. At this point, however, Wise decided all would depend on the outcome of negotiations with Perles and Elbogen, whom he viewed as the top two Jewish scholars in Europe.

In Berlin that July Fourth evening, Wise reflected on the impact of his trip thus far. "Of one thing I am persuaded, though I have made no definite commitments . . .

namely, that my coming to Europe ought to be richly productive and of good to the JIR for years to come. I am enabled to make my program clear, Lehrfreiheit, as the atmosphere of Jewish study and Jewish loyalty. I have the feeling that before another week I shall have most of the great scholars of the four seminaries enrolled as members of the visiting staff and perhaps some of the best of them as our permanent teachers; they seem to like the plan of trial visits."[37]

In Breslau, the Juedisch-Theologisches Seminar impressed Wise, as well. This seminary, like the Hochschule, had expanded its program and now trained not only rabbis and scholars but also teachers and youth leaders. And here, too, the faculty included a Zionist presence, reflected in the fact that the seminary was now offering instruction in Modern Hebrew. Nonetheless, Wise chose not to extend an invitation to Guttmann or anyone else there; instead, he still focused on the Hochschule faculty, while in Breslau he wrote up an ambitious proposal and sent it off to Elbogen.[38]

"As you know," he explained, "I am engaged in seeking teachers throughout Europe. But in addition to our Regular and permanent teachers, we are desirous of conferring upon our students the benefit of contact with and inspiration from the foremost Jewish scholars of European lands."[39] To that end, Wise proposed an arrangement whereby the Hochschule would provide JIR with a visiting professor on an annual basis. JIR, in exchange, would not only cover travel expenses and an honorarium for each scholar but also provide an additional thousand dollars in general support for the Hochschule, reflecting his belief that seminaries on both sides of the Atlantic bore responsibility for one another. He invited Elbogen to inaugurate the rotation by teaching at JIR in the upcoming fall semester.[40]

When the two men finally met later that week, Elbogen seemed favorably disposed toward the overall arrangement. Although hesitant due both to his responsibilities running the Hochschule and to his wife's reluctance to see him leave Germany for such a long period, he agreed to request approval from his board. Wise would have to wait. In the meantime, his meeting with Perles went well, and Wise invited him, too, for the fall semester.

While in Germany, Wise was acutely aware of rising antisemitism, as well as the flourishing cultural activity of a Jewish community turned inward. "Certainly in communities such as Berlin, one feels the pulse of Jewish life," he wrote, singling out the stimulating effect of the poet Bialik. "But the most healthy token of Jewish life in the German-speaking lands," he added, "is to be found in the spirit and influence of the schools of Jewish Wissenschaft."[41]

A STAY IN VIENNA INTERRUPTED

Wise's next stop was Vienna, where he visited the Israelitisch-Theologische Lehranstalt. Modeled on the Juedisch-Theologisches Seminar in Breslau and directed for decades by Adolf Schwarz, a Breslau-trained Talmudist known to be Frankel's favorite student, the Lehranstalt attracted excellent faculty and a capable but small student body drawn largely from Galicia and other parts of the Austro-Hungarian Empire. Amid the school's current financial difficulties, Chajes, who was widely regarded as the spiritual leader of Austrian Jewry and devoted considerable effort to sustaining all of the community's struggling educational institutions, helped keep the Lehranstalt afloat through successful appeals to American Jewish philanthropists.[42] In fact, in response to a recent request from Chajes geared specifically toward assisting the school's student body, Wise, in his letter from London, had offered to help.

Recognizing Chajes was not in a position to leave Vienna for a visiting lectureship at the institute, Wise extended an open invitation to teach sometime in the future. In the meanwhile, he requested recommendations of younger scholars who would make strong candidates for JIR's faculty now.[43] Chajes offered several names, and Wise planned to meet them—but recent international news prompted him to delay. In less than two weeks, the Council of the League of Nations would vote to entrust Britain with the mandate to administer Palestine.[44]

The League's resolution, citing the Balfour Declaration, charged Britain with establishing the conditions necessary to secure for the Jews a national home in Palestine.[45] The vote marked a significant step on the path toward Jewish statehood. For Wise, who had devoted himself to the cause ever since attending the Second World Zionist Congress in 1898, it represented a personal victory, as well. Putting his meetings with Chajes's colleagues on hold, he resolved to head to Jerusalem in order to join the festivities now being planned.

On the way to Trieste, where he would board a steamer for Alexandria, he stopped in Venice but regretted not having time to visit Florence in order to meet the Italian historian and biblical scholar Umberto Cassuto, the new director of the rabbinical seminary there. Cassuto, too, was on Wise's list of candidates for a visiting lectureship.

While in Trieste, Wise received good news: The Hochschule's board had consented in principle to the annual faculty exchange, and Perles had accepted the invitation to teach in the fall.[46] Wise immediately let Goldstein know and permitted him to publicize the entire list of faculty engaged thus far, plus the additional Hochschule faculty he hoped would join the exchange over the next few years: Julius Guttmann and Harry Torczyner, as well as Leo Baeck, lecturer in Midrash and homiletics, and rabbi of the liberal Fasanenstrasse Synagogue.

In addition to these faculty developments, Wise had much else on his mind when he wrote Goldstein. "Has the building actually begun?" he asked. "I have begged [Joseph] Levine to work promptly re 46 West 68. We must have a house of the JIR at once—offices for faculty, ourselves, students and library . . . and what of applications from students? Are there no more? We must have classes Preparatory. Berlin and Breslau both have them." Noting he still had work to do in Vienna,

Budapest, and Berlin, Wise allowed his excitement to outshine his anxieties. "I never was more keen to begin work than today in relation to JIR," he wrote. "We can make it, *b'h*, a truly serviceable work in and for Israel."[47]

PALESTINE

Wise enjoyed a heady two-week stay in Palestine.[48] He met with leaders of the Zionist movement and with British officials in Jerusalem, and after all fifty-one member countries in the League of Nations endorsed the resolution, he joined the celebrations surrounding the official beginning of the British Mandate. Afterward, he reflected in his diary:

> And as I review the lands I visited and the peoples again seen, it comes to me with the force of an unshakeable conviction that in more ways than one may Zionism prove to be the saving strength of the people of Israel. There was brought low great numbers of Jews everywhere on the Continent of Europe. Insecurity and proscription are become their portion even in newly established countries.
>
> One thing lends security and dignity to their status, namely the Balfour Declaration and its reaffirmation by the League of Nations. If there had been no Zionism before, it would have become necessary to invent it. For there is persecution from without and defection for one reason or another from within. Against these there stands as a veritable bulwark the purpose of the Jewish people ratified in England's will and supported by the League of Nations' word. Resting in the ancient faith, the Jewish people is resolved to rebuild with unflagging hope and unimpairable will the land, which is Eternal in its challenge, summoning inspiration to the Jew.[49]

With the institute opening in just two months, Wise headed back to Vienna via Trieste, where he found a letter waiting from Elbogen, who had decided he *would* come to New York to teach in the fall semester. Elated, Wise now expressed a larger vision he had been harboring regarding the role the Hochschule director could play. "I warn you now that we shall do everything in our power to keep you in America," Wise wrote back, "for you are the one man to be the head of the Jewish Institute of Religion, and the leadership and presidency will be yours if by any means you can be persuaded to accept the post."[50]

Wise could not contain his excitement. Elbogen and Perles, he believed, were the two outstanding Jewish scholars of the Continent, having a place in Bible and history comparable to that of the seminary's Louis Ginzberg in Talmud. He was overjoyed to have enlisted the former. "Perles is a tremendous scholar but I have lost my heart for Elbogen. If I were thirty years younger, I would say that I was daft about him. He is one of the dearest, finest men I have ever met," Wise wrote

Charles Bloch, now a member of the JIR board. "If he were willing to stay with us, he would be the president of the JIR. You will all feel about him just as I do. He has such beauty of character and I know what he has done in Berlin."[51]

At this point, every European scholar Wise had invited to teach thus far had accepted: Elbogen from Berlin, Perles from Koenigsberg, and Abrahams and Herford of London.[52] Goldstein, who was regularly sending Wise updates on developments in New York, was also pleased, for the European faculty would bring prestige and power to the institute, positioning JIR to reawaken an interest in Jewish learning in America and to act as an agent more broadly in stimulating Jewish thought, life, and culture.[53]

Cognizant of the deteriorating conditions in Europe, Goldstein had a more ambitious vision for the institute as a whole; nonetheless, he clearly had concerns about the demands being placed on Wise and their toll on his well-being. "As I said to you some time ago, the Institute will have a large part in shaping the new stage of Judaism that must emerge out of the present moral and spiritual collapse and chaos," he wrote Wise. "If you will only guard your health and conserve your strength the Institute will mean the resurrection of the spiritual life of Israel in America."[54]

WORD FROM NEW YORK: JOSHUA BLOCH AND NISSAN TOUROFF

Goldstein, likewise, had good news to report. While Wise was enlisting the Europeans, he had been busy recruiting instructors who could teach the institute's introductory courses.[55] To that end, he had successfully secured a librarian who could also teach Bible. Joshua Bloch, born in Lithuania in 1890, had immigrated to New York City at a young age and attended several different schools before earning his PhD at New York University in 1918.[56] Thanks to his developing expertise in Semitic languages and literature, in addition to the invitation from JIR, he also received an offer for a professorship at the University of Texas in Austin.

Knowing that Wise wanted a serious scholar to oversee library acquisitions and recognizing the unlikelihood of finding another candidate qualified to serve as both librarian and instructor in Bible, Goldstein worked hard with members of the board to create a package Joshua Bloch would accept.[57] Unable to match Texas's salary offer of $5,500–6,000, they instead offered $2,500 for part-time work as librarian and instructor, supplemented by $1,500 for additional part-time work at the publishing house of board member Charles Bloch (no apparent relation). Wanting to remain in New York, Joshua Bloch agreed.

Wise was pleased and eager to put the new librarian to work. The nucleus of JIR's collection had already been established through the purchase of the library of Marcus Brann, former chair of history and librarian at the Breslau seminary, in combination with Wise's extensive private collection, which he donated to the institute. Wise directed Bloch to get the Brann library onto the shelves and usable as quickly as possible.[58]

Meanwhile, in negotiations with Touroff, the institute had once again run into difficulties matching another institution's competing salary. Whereas JIR planned to offer senior faculty $5,000, Goldstein reported that the Hebrew Teachers College was paying Touroff $6,000, which Wise considered "rather stiff." For the time being, at least, they could put off reaching a decision; Touroff, who was also starting on a part-time basis, had agreed to $2,000 for the year plus travel expenses. "One thing I would urge upon you, unless it be too late," Wise wrote board member Charles Bloch, who was assisting Goldstein. "Don't make any arrangement with T. for more than the first year. Let us move slowly in the matter of permanent commitments."[59] The instruction cohered with Wise's general approach to bringing faculty but now reflected a new concern in light of his hiring successes: how JIR would cover its steadily mounting costs.

VIENNA AND BUDAPEST

Before heading back to New York, Wise had several more scholars to meet in Vienna and Budapest, but he now hesitated to issue any further invitations. In part, he wanted to wait until Elbogen could survey the situation, hoping to benefit from his experience and judgment. More importantly, however, he began to worry about accumulating expenses. He had already spent a good deal on furniture and books for the new school, and now he needed two thousand dollars to cover steamer tickets for Elbogen and Perles, as well as their additional living expenses.[60]

"I am just a little disturbed about the budget," Wise told Charles Bloch. "Not really disturbed, that is hardly the word, but a little 'nervus.'" Having already committed about $35,000—the total allocation for the year ahead—he knew he should not let that figure rise above $40,000.[61] He kept this in mind when meeting Samuel Krauss, the Vienna Lehranstalt's scholar of rabbinics and archeology.[62] Krauss's credentials were impeccable, his work prodigious, and he was interested in joining JIR.[63]

While still torn over Krauss, Wise began considering yet another professor, University of Hamburg's Julian Obermann, an expert in Semitic languages and literature. However, his concern about finances continued to gnaw. "I am still in a quandary about Obermann," he wrote Goldstein. "Everyone praises him. His work on Ghazali is a really big and important thing, and still I hesitate, wondering whether we are not going to be top-heavy in the matter of teachers, and also whether we are not over committing ourselves in the way of expenditures."[64] Wise, in due course, decided to let the matter rest; he had what he needed to open the institute with fanfare in the fall, and now knew he would have little trouble recruiting more for the 1923–1924 year.[65]

Finally, Wise headed to Hungary, his native land and home to the last of the seminaries on his itinerary. In Budapest, he met with the rector of the Rabbinical Seminary, Ludwig Blau. A rabbi, Talmud scholar, and historian, Blau too was eager to serve as a visiting professor at JIR and offered to teach Talmud, Greek papyri from a Jewish standpoint, and more general courses on Jews and world culture. Wise, however, would not commit.

Before leaving the country, Wise came face to face with the devastating reversals confronting the Jews of Hungary. First, he ventured into the past, making a pilgrimage to the birthplaces of his parents: Erlau, where his father had descended from five generations of rabbis, and Herend, where his mother had grown up in a wealthy family, enjoying the success of her father's porcelain factory. And then Wise confronted the present, in an extraordinary meeting he arranged with Miklós Horthy himself, the leader of the national army that had terrorized the Jewish community who was now head of state. In "two hours of frankest talk," Wise encountered the Hungarian leader's "undisguised and unashamed medievalism" and his resolve to ruthlessly crush everything that might endanger "the integrity of the Hungarian State."

He left the country in despair. "Up to 1918, on a par with England and Italy in its attitude toward its Jewish citizenship," he wrote in his diary, "Hungary under the Black regime has descended to a depth the occupancy of which places it on a par with Poland and Roumania at their worst."[66]

Banquo's Ghost: An Attempt to Torpedo the Hochschule Agreement

Back in Vienna, Wise received an alarming letter. "Banquo's ghost appeared here in the shape of Dr. Schulman," Elbogen wrote, referring to Samuel Schulman, the rabbi of New York City's Temple Beth El and a graduate of the Hochschule. "All of a sudden, he felt his debt of gratitude towards his Alma mater, and held it his duty to inform the board of trustees about the evil the Hochschule was going to do to American Jewry as a whole and to Reform Judaism especially" by cooperating with JIR.[67]

Apparently, Schulman, after visiting the Hochschule and discovering the arrangement, had warned them that Felix Warburg and Cyrus Adler, who controlled the Joint Distribution Committee (JDC), were entirely opposed to JIR and to Stephen S. Wise. Whether or not he made a direct threat, Schulman, who had been urging Adler to raise the JDC's appropriation to the Hochschule, had frightened the board with the idea that any sort of cooperation with JIR would cost them their JDC relief aid.[68] Schulman also seems to have suggested that Wise, having supported America's entry into the war, did not have Germany's best interests at heart.

Schulman made a strong impression on the Hochschule governors, Elbogen told Wise, particularly the chairman, Albert Mosse. "Poor old Mosse says that he can't agree to the contract unless he has seen you and received further information from you personally," Elbogen wrote, and urged Wise to return to Berlin immediately. If he delayed, the board would not approve the arrangement.[69]

Wise immediately demanded a suspension of the Hochschule agreement until the charges were disproved, and cabled the JIR contingent in New York to inform them of the situation.[70] A meeting with Elbogen and the Hochschule board
had become necessary, the message read, due to "Schulman's slanderous destruc-
tive intrigues." From New York, JIR trustees Mack and Frankel cabled a statement
for Elbogen to share with the board. Expressing pleasure that Elbogen and Perles
would be teaching at JIR in the fall, the cable read:

> Dr. Stephen Wise president is endorsed and supported by large group in
> American Israel including Oscar Strauss, Abram Elkus, Emil Hirsch, Justice
> Brandeis, Adolph Lewisohn, Nathan Straus, Mrs. Joseph Fels, Prof. Gott-
> heil. Fifty thousand dollars per year guaranteed for first three years, and fu-
> ture positively assured. One quarter million dollars building being erected.
> Over twenty-five students already registered. Institute will greatly strengthen
> liberal Judaism. Does not aim to rival but to cooperate in every way possible
> with Cincinnati and other seminaries. Dr. Wise a commanding influence in
> American Israel and leader in every liberal movement in American life, hav-
> ing confidence of Jews and non-Jews. We rejoice over and heartily welcome
> cooperation with Hochschule.[71]

Louis Brandeis sent a similar cable assuring the Hochschule that Wise had shown
devotion and leadership in every Jewish and liberal cause and had earned his complete confidence.[72]

Wise returned to Berlin and met with Elbogen and Mosse to address Schulman's threat. First, he asked whether Schulman had been authorized by the JDC
to assess the merits and needs of the Hochschule and to discuss the proposed arrangement. Wise questioned Schulman's claim to represent Warburg and Adler,
in part because he knew that Adler had arranged for Judah Magnes to investigate
conditions at all three German seminaries that summer, in order to help him determine how much relief aid to allocate to each institution. Even if Schulman did
have Adler's authorization, was he empowered to threaten the Hochschule with
punitive measures on behalf of the JDC? Such a threat, if authorized, would profoundly dishonor those in whose name Schulman purported to speak, Wise said.

As to the charge regarding Wise's attitude toward Germany, Wise assured
Mosse he had an interest in the well-being of the German people, which would
remain intact regardless of the outcome of the Hochschule negotiations. At the
same time, he objected to the insinuation, "even as I have no doubt, you would
resent a corresponding inquiry on my part touching your attitude towards your
country in relation to its foreign policies."[73]

Wise learned that Schulman might have also suggested that in the postwar
political environment, the Hochschule's entering into a cooperative agreement

with an American institution would expose Jews in Germany to danger. Cognizant of the postwar climate in the United States, Wise responded: Would not he be hurt by bringing two German scholars to JIR in its first year?[74]

Elbogen, in favor of cooperation with JIR, attempted to allay Mosse's concerns. However, at this point, Wise refused to proceed with the agreement to pay the Hochschule for regular visiting faculty until he knew whether Warburg and Adler had authorized the threat. Still, he insisted that Elbogen be granted a leave of absence from October through January, for his teaching at JIR had already been set and publicly announced.[75]

Following the meeting, Elbogen confirmed his plan to teach at JIR that fall, but as a "private person" rather than as a representative of the Hochschule.[76] Schulman's threat had taken a toll, but it had not derailed Wise's plan; the institutional partnership between JIR and the Hochschule would proceed, informally rather than officially.

As Wise sailed back to the United States, word about his successful trip began to spread. "Rabbi Stephen Wise is almost due from Europe," a columnist wrote in the *Detroit Jewish Chronicle*, "with several trunks full of professors for his proposed Jewish institute."[77] Notwithstanding the overstatement, Wise could now return to New York confident that the faculty he had enlisted—if only for a short time—promised to inaugurate the institute as a center for Jewish scholarship in the same league as HUC and New York's JTS. Typical of Wise, the process had been anything but gradual or quiet; he had announced his plans to enlist the "great masters" of Europe and then, in a matter of just eight weeks, visited five major institutions in four different countries, securing three men for the fall, one for the following summer, and a growing waiting list of others eager to join as soon as he could bring them.

That significant gaps remained on the faculty seems not to have troubled Wise, despite his stated goal for the institute to represent a wide diversity of perspectives. Just as Montefiore and Elbogen had predicted, he had enlisted no Orthodox faculty; indeed, in Berlin he declined to visit the Hildesheimer seminary, where his father had once studied, and over the entire summer in Europe, it appears he never reached out to a single Orthodox scholar.

Furthermore, the faculty lacked women, an absence on which Wise did not comment in his notes. At this time, the field of Wissenschaft Jewish scholarship was almost entirely closed to women, due to barriers at secular universities as well as the Jewish seminaries. Outside the field of Semitics, the universities, where women were making inroads in other fields, provided no opportunity for advanced Jewish scholarship. The rabbinical seminaries, the only places where advanced Jewish scholarship *was* offered, barred entry to women. As a result, not only did the rabbinate remain an all-male preserve, but Wissenschaft des Judentums did, as well. It is true that the Hochschule had now created a slight opening, by admitting women as candidates for teacher certification in Judaica and allowing them to study alongside rabbinical students. However, even if these women pushed the bounds by seeking entry into either the rabbinate or the world of Jewish scholarship—and some eventually did—none had yet achieved that in 1922, when Wise was hiring.

That said, in his initial foray into faculty hiring, he had succeeded to a large degree not only in enlisting able scholars but also men representing a range of interpretations and approaches, just as he had hoped. The new faculty would include Europeans and Americans, Jews and Protestants, scholars and practitioners, as well as Zionists and non-Zionists.

Whether or not the European scholars could bring about Wise's vision for JIR remained to be seen. More than the Atlantic Ocean separated them from the Americans; Abrahams, Elbogen, and Perles would bring to the institute very different experiences of Jewish higher learning as well as Jewish religious and communal life. Nevertheless, Wise had also discovered commonalities. The Hochschule provided a genuine openness to diverse perspectives, just as Hirsch had experienced fifty years earlier; the Breslau seminary had taken to offering Modern Hebrew; and, together with the Lehrenstalt in Vienna, they seemed to have a strong cohort of Zionist students and faculty. These advances reflected not only the growing influence of Eastern European Jews in each of these cities but also, as Wise noted in his diary, the fact that more Jews than ever before were resolving that had Zionism not yet existed, it would have to be invented now.

Undeniably, the conditions Wise witnessed that summer on a continent still reeling from war served to bolster his determination to make JIR a force not only for the advancement of Jewish learning but also for Jewish political, cultural, and social change. Goldstein had stated the aim well: Out of the present moral and spiritual collapse and chaos, JIR would hasten a new stage for Judaism, nothing short of the resurrection of the spiritual life of Israel in America.

II

THE MODEL BLOSSOMS

6

A New Yavneh

SOON AFTER WISE DISEMBARKED IN NEW YORK FROM THE RMS *Aqui-tania* in early September 1922, word of his success in Europe began fueling bold aspirations for the Jewish Institute of Religion within Jewish and scholarly circles in the United States. In the wake of the cataclysmic war, many recognized that European Jewish learning needed to be salvaged from utter collapse—not as some relic of the past but to provide the foundation for a flourishing Jewish life elsewhere, in more favorable conditions. By bringing scholars out of the wreckage to teach a new generation in the United States, JIR could make a singular contribution toward nothing less than a renaissance of the Jewish spirit in America.

Indeed, for Jewish leaders like Nissan Touroff and Mordecai Kaplan, the unique approach to scholarship and rabbinical training planned for JIR evoked the rabbinical academies that had ushered in a new epoch in Jewish life two millennia earlier. Following the destruction of the Second Temple in 70 CE, as the center of Jewish religious and cultural life lay in ruins, these academies served as a base from which the rabbis of Palestine created a radically new approach to religious life, meaningful to Jews in their profoundly changed conditions. Cognizant of the precarious conditions facing present-day Eastern and Central European Jewry, Touroff told Wise privately he would call JIR "Yavneh," after the ancient academy most recognized for providing a path of Jewish survival in the face of exile.[1]

While Wise made no such historical claim, his own aspirations for the institute were broadening, as well. Deeply moved by the burdens weighing on the Jewish communities and communal leaders he had just visited in Germany, Austria, and Hungary, he believed more than ever that American Jewry now bore the chief responsibility not only for revitalizing twentieth century Judaism in the United States but also for securing the well-being of Jews around the globe. Toward these ends, he began developing concrete ways that JIR could spread its influence among Jews in the United States while simultaneously leading the American *wissenschaftlich* Jewish seminaries in a unified effort to aid their peer institutions in Central Europe.

But lofty goals would mean little unless the Jewish Institute of Religion could withstand its practical challenges, and in September 1922 the school still lacked permanent faculty, reliable funding, a physical home, and a president-designate who could take over for Wise. Even more critically, with opening day scheduled immediately after the High Holy Days on October 9, the institute needed students, a curriculum, and fieldwork assignments posthaste.

As Rosh Hashanah approached, Wise knew his vision for JIR as a catalyst for change would be tested in the year ahead. Creating a renaissance in American Jewish life would surely take years; preventing the collapse of the European Jewish centers of learning currently in crisis required acting immediately. Both would entail navigating an array of forces far beyond any single individual's control.

STUDENTS

I shall always look forward with great interest to future news concerning the Jewish Institute of Religion, because I believe it will fill a crying need in American Israel. If you keep your standard high and select men for ordination who not only have brilliant minds and know how to preach but also, more especially, have their whole souls attuned to the spirit of God, you will render an invaluable service to American Israel.
—Letter to Wise from congregational rabbi in the Middle West
Cited in *Free Synagogue Bulletin*, November 27, 1921[2]

With the requirement that students earn their BA *prior* to enrolling, Wise hoped the institute would attract students prepared to begin advanced study upon entry and capable of attaining the requisite learning and skills through a highly focused three-year graduate program. Whereas neither HUC nor JTS could have imposed this admissions requirement at the time of their founding without severely limiting their pool of applicants, JIR ran no such risk. Young Jews were pouring into urban colleges and universities at such high rates that alarmists spoke of an "invasion."[3] In 1918, for example, Columbia University experienced a 40 percent rise in Jewish students, and NYU a 42 percent rise. By 1920, Hunter College had 80–90 percent Jewish students, as did the City College of New York (CCNY), which some derogatorily referred to as "the College of the Circumcised Citizens of New York."[4]

This influx generated a backlash, particularly at elite schools where many Jewish students outshone their classmates in intellectual pursuits while demonstrating little interest in the social mores of monied collegiate culture. Columbia, for example, lowered its Jewish population in 1922 to 22 percent by instituting a quiet quota system (Jews still made up nearly half the students elected to Phi Beta Kappa that year), and quotas were also enacted at Syracuse, Princeton, Rutgers, and other eastern universities.[5]

The issue became headline news when a controversy erupted over admissions at Harvard, where the Jewish student population had risen from 10 percent in

1920 to 15 percent in 1921, and then to 20 percent in 1922. At the end of May that year, President A. Lawrence Lowell proposed a 15 percent numerus clausus on Jewish student admissions, and unlike his peers, he defended the approach publicly. The cap would reduce antisemitic prejudice, he argued in the *New York Times*, for when the number of Jews was small, "the race antagonism was small also."[6] That he was also a staunch advocate for immigration restrictions undercut what little credence he might have otherwise had in the Jewish community, and his plan provoked outrage.[7]

Two JIR men played a central role in galvanizing opposition to the policy—Julian Mack, the sole Jew on Harvard's board of overseers, and Harry Wolfson, whom, at Mack's behest, Lowell appointed to a faculty committee tasked with investigating the issue.[8] Though Lowell claimed to have temporarily lifted the quota pending that committee's report, in September the issue became national news once again when Harvard released a new application that, for the first time, questioned applicants about their race. "Jews See Race Ban in Harvard Queries," the *New York Times* reported, and though the university insisted this data would not factor into admissions, some Jews began urging a boycott of Harvard, which one Jew, according to the *Times*, supposedly dubbed an "intellectual Ku Klux Klan."[9]

Not surprisingly, higher Jewish learning did not flourish in this climate. Only a handful of university Semitics programs offered Jewish studies to begin with, and prior to the quota debates these tiny graduate programs were already contracting as Jewish donors steered their philanthropy to more pressing causes.[10] And though the Wissenschaft movement by this time had produced an impressive number of Jewish historians and philologists, in 1921 no European or American colleges or universities had yet appointed any full-time faculty in Jewish scholarly fields outside of Semitics, such as history or philosophy. Now, with prominent universities trying to curb Jewish enrollment rather than catering to this growing constituency, there was little reason to hope that the dream of Leopold Zunz, who sought a home for Wissenschaft des Judentums in secular academe, would ever come to fruition in the United States.

Beyond the world of higher education, by contrast, young men and women with an interest in Jewish intellectual, cultural, religious, and political life had access to an unprecedented and exciting world of opportunity. In New York, especially, wide varieties of religious life, Zionism, Hebrew renewal, Jewish leftism, and Yiddish art, music, and theater were all flourishing, with young Jewish thinkers expressing their views on much of this in the *Menorah Journal* and other literary organs.[11]

HUC and JTS, though navigating financial challenges of their own, were also growing stronger. The College had recently hired five new faculty members, ordained its largest class ever in 1921, and was now benefiting from the National Federation of Temple Sisterhoods' $250,000 campaign for a new dormitory on campus. The seminary, which had graduated more than 140 rabbis by this time and housed the thriving Teachers Institute, was fundraising as well, with a $100,000 campaign underway. Both schools could boast major libraries and eminent scholars, and a national shortage of rabbis virtually guaranteed jobs for all of their young graduates entering the profession.

In September 1922, women seeking to become rabbis had reason to hope they could share in that opportunity, as well. Until now, though nineteen American Protestant denominations ordained women, not a single Jewish seminary in Europe or the United States had followed suit. But in light of recent developments at HUC and in the CCAR, it appeared that might soon change. For the preceding two years, faculty at the college had been debating the issue, raised initially by Martha Neumark, a student at the college who, with the strong backing of her father, David Neumark, professor of philosophy, was pressing for women's ordination. Others within the Reform movement, too, were pressing for women's entry into the "Jewish ministry," including Carrie Simon, founding president of the National Federation of Temple Sisterhoods, who voiced her support in an article in the *Union Bulletin*, "What Can the Women Do for Judaism?" in October 1921.[12] In March 1922, the HUC faculty had voted in favor, and momentum for the idea grew in July when the CCAR, at their Cape May meeting, voted 56–11 for a resolution that read "women cannot justly be denied the privilege of ordination." By August, with the CCAR's endorsement of women's ordination, Martha Neumark had every reason to believe that, upon completion of her studies at the college, she would be ordained as the first female rabbi. The only step that remained was for the board of governors to accept the CCAR's recommendation.[13]

A few years earlier, when the matter was still hypothetical, Wise appeared to support rabbinical ordination for women, encouraging a fifteen-year-old girl who advanced the idea in the Free Synagogue's newspaper in 1919 "to go on and prepare yourself."[14] During the same period, he fought hard for passage of the Nineteenth Amendment granting suffrage to women, a milestone that inspired others to battle for women's rabbinical ordination. Now, as JIR's admissions requirements were being finalized, he could at last open the door to the rabbinate that had been closed to women for two thousand years—and Harry Lewis urged him to take the lead. "I am glad to see that this is coming to the front," he had written Wise shortly before the CCAR vote and just before Wise left for Europe. "It would be a fine thing if you could get some women students at the Institute from the very first."[15]

A month later, from Vienna, Wise told Charles Bloch that as soon as he returned from Europe, they needed to consider the matter carefully. "I think we shall have to content ourselves for a time with a pronouncement to the effect that women will be admitted in a year or two, just as soon as satisfactory arrangements can be made in respect to housing, etc.," he wrote.[16] Despite the debate underway at HUC and within the CCAR, in forming the first class of students at JIR, Wise chose not to open a path for female rabbis.

With more than a million and a half Jews living in New York City, Wise never doubted the institute's ability to attract students, and as it turned out, enrolling the first entering class required little effort. Young men had long wanted to train with him, and many were now expressing interest in attending JIR.

Long before any formal recruitment efforts began, Wise functioned as a one-man publicity department, trumpeting the institute during his many speaking engagements across the country. As early as 1920, Goldstein reported that twelve men definitely planned to apply, should the summer school expand into a full-fledged program—and sure enough, by January 1922, about a dozen applications had been received. "That number seems excellent, viewing the fact that I have made no attempt to secure them," Wise told Hirsch.[17] For the time being, applicants interviewed with members of the board who functioned as a preliminary admissions committee until the new faculty could take over.[18] By June, the number had reached twenty, and in early August three more applied.[19]

Despite the steady stream of applicants, Wise and the board did not leave recruitment entirely to chance. While HUC and JTS, serving different religious constituencies, did not pose a substantial threat to one another, JIR—aiming to attract students from a wide range of Jewish perspectives—would have to compete directly with both seminaries. And though as a nondenominational school, JIR had the advantage of drawing from a broader pool, HUC and JTS each offered a venerable history, more resources of every kind, and far greater stability. Most important, their eminent faculty—including Talmud scholars Louis Ginzberg at the seminary, for example, and Jacob Lauterbach at the college —were permanent, unlike the rotation of Europeans Wise had lined up for JIR.

Competing for students was hardly new in Jewish education; yeshivas and Jewish seminaries had often jockeyed for enrollment, and in the market economy of 1920s America, such competition fit well within the broader culture. To attract applicants, HUC and JTS regularly published ads in the Jewish press. HUC touted its history as the oldest rabbinical school in the United States, along with its beautiful and spacious grounds facing the University of Cincinnati, and a library housing more than forty thousand volumes of Hebraica and Judaica; similarly, JTS promoted its "commodious building," a library holding 57,077 books and 1,828 manuscripts, a synagogue where students delivered sermons, and the Teachers Institute. Over the summer, JIR pursued this path as well, using a publicity strategy outlined by board member and publisher Charles Bloch.

Not everyone in the JIR camp supported the consumerist approach, however; when Wise sought approval from Hirsch over the summer for a similar advertisement in the *Menorah Journal*, the older rabbi expressed his distaste. "It is '*Marktschreirich* [sic]," he wrote, and "smacks too much of 'Department Store.'"[20]

Wise nonetheless went ahead with the ad but kept it fairly modest, including only a list of faculty and departments of study, along with a drawing of the Sixty-Eighth Street building under construction.

As the advertising generated additional inquiries, Wise, Goldstein, three board members, and a faculty representative took over admissions interviews, and the incoming class grew to twenty-five, including a few "conditional" students. In addition, several women were accepted as "special students," eligible to enroll in courses for credit but not for acceptance into the rabbinical program. Hebrew Union College and the Hochshule took this approach, as well; indeed, it was just this exclusion that Martha Neumark and fifty-six members of the CCAR were now challenging in the battle for women's ordination.

Enrolling in JIR's first class entailed a certain degree of risk. The institute was affiliated with just a single synagogue, scorned by denominational leaders, and still under construction, with faculty and much else in flux. For many, the opportunity to train for the rabbinate under the direction of Stephen S. Wise overrode these uncertainties; regardless of what shape the institute would eventually take, with Wise at its center, they wanted to join.

Philip Bernstein, a member of the first class, recalled how Wise's engaging personality drew him to the institute. Bernstein, having just finished college at Syracuse University, returned home to Rochester, New York, in order to help his ill father with the family business. That year, after deciding to enter the rabbinate, he met with a representative from either HUC or JTS (he declined to say which) who seemed to suggest, in Bernstein's words, that the rabbinate required "saintliness, piety, goodness, sweetness and light." The more the man spoke, the less Bernstein could imagine himself attending this school. Later that spring, he met Wise in Syracuse. "The first thing he did was to reproach me for not accepting the cigar offered by the president of the local temple," Bernstein recalled. "This was the beginning of a long and uplifting process of instruction." Playfulness runs through other student accounts, as well; Wise had an easy way with young people, and Bernstein was not the only one who, upon meeting him for the first time, became a disciple.

The seismic forces rupturing Jewish life across the globe that led many of the faculty to Sixty-Eighth Street impacted JIR's earliest students, as well—and some, particularly those from Europe, had encountered the most devastating of these forces directly. At the same time, in many ways, the student body reflected the diversity of American Jewry at the start of the 1920s.

About half of the institute's first class were born abroad, in places including Poland, Russia, and Austria. One, Zwi Anderman, received his rabbinical and doctoral training at the Israelitisch-Theologische Lehranstalt in Vienna and taught at the gymnasium level in the embattled city of Lemberg prior to immigrating to the

United States. Another, Lutsk-born Benjamin Hoffseyer, had studied at a Hebrew college in Jaffa and the University of London before coming to JIR.[21]

Many of the American-born students came from New York, but others hailed from cities and towns around the country including Baltimore, Rochester, Kansas City, Pittsburgh, and even Guthrie, Oklahoma. While a preponderance of students earned their BA at City College, the entering class also included graduates from the Cooper Institute of Technology, Harvard University, the New School for Social Research, New York University, Syracuse University, the University of California, and Yale University. Two, Max Meyer and Morris Rose, also studied at the NYU Law School, though it does not appear that either earned degrees in the profession.[22]

Some students, European- as well as American-born, brought a left-leaning political orientation; Bernstein, for example, entered the institute as a devout pacifist, and others arrived having already worked in the field of social service. And, not surprisingly, quite a few were Zionists, including Anderman, who had been involved in the movement dating back to his youth in the Ukraine.[23]

Many were religiously in flux and on a trajectory toward greater liberalism. Those raised in Orthodox households who were leaving halakhic practice behind included Abraham Dubin and Morris Rose, who had each attended the Jacob Joseph School before earning their undergraduate degrees at City College. Dubin then enrolled at the Rabbi Isaac Elchanan Theological Seminary but after a short time moved to Kaplan's Teachers Institute at JTS before applying to JIR.[24] He was "going through spiritual development from orthodoxy to conservatism and from conservatism to liberalism," Sidney Goldstein later observed.[25] Morton Berman, a Phi Beta Kappa graduate of Yale, came to JIR after spending a year in the rabbinical program at JTS. "He finds the religious life in this institution too narrow, and the social programme altogether too restricted," Wise told Mack.[26]

Unlike Dubin and Berman, Meyer hadn't attended rabbinical school previously, but he did come from a family that included five generations of rabbis.[27] Wise hoped Meyer would not be the only student representing a long rabbinical lineage; he was holding a place at the institute for his own son James, who was currently a senior at Columbia. James Waterman Wise, like his father, held left-wing political views as well as a passionate commitment to Zionism.

The few women who enrolled as "special students" also brought impressive credentials. Dora Askowith, for example, entered with an academic record that only Anderman could match. Born in 1884 in the Lithuanian city of Kovno, Askowith immigrated to Boston as a child, attended Barnard College from which she graduated with honors, and then earned her MA and PhD in history at Columbia. She now taught history in New York public high schools and lectured in Jewish fields at Hunter College, where she founded Hunter's Menorah Society and advocated for Jewish students. A Zionist active in Jewish communal affairs, she had served on Hadassah's early Central Committee, was active in the American Jewish

Congress, and had a record fighting for women's rights. At JIR, she planned to pursue an academic career, not the rabbinate.[28]

By contrast, Irma Lindheim, who also enrolled at this time, *did* want to become a rabbi. Born into an assimilated German Jewish family in New York and the niece of JIR board member Bertha Guggenheimer, Lindheim had the experience and wherewithal to challenge barriers that stood in her way. In 1917, at age thirty-one, this heiress and mother of four enlisted for active service in the Motor Corps of America and rose to the rank of first lieutenant. Soon thereafter, she discovered Zionism and dedicated her life to the cause. As chair of the Seventh Zionist District, she worked with Henrietta Szold, Julian Mack, and others, and drawing upon her father's inheritance, she bought a New York brownstone and converted it into an educational and cultural center for Hadassah, where she worked with Mordecai Kaplan on programming.

After the war, however, Lindheim experienced several setbacks. First, her husband, Norvin Lindheim, who had been barred from armed service because his firm did business with German companies, was wrongfully convicted in 1920 of conspiring to defraud the United States and sentenced to prison (in 1928, the conviction was overturned). A year later, the Brandeis faction of the American Zionist movement with which she had aligned herself lost political control, resulting in the closure of the Hadassah center.[29] At that point, Lindheim stepped away from Zionist work in order to study Judaism, and when she asked Wise if she could enroll at JIR, he responded enthusiastically. Lindheim rented a studio apartment a block from the institute and prepared to focus on her studies, which would include coursework in child development with John Dewey at Columbia's Teachers College, as well.[30]

In all, fifteen rabbinical students as well as ten "conditional" and "special students" were willing to cast their lot with the fledgling institute that October. They were older on average than students at other seminaries and untroubled by the fact that JIR had little infrastructure in place and no track record. Fundamentally, they were drawn to study with Wise, who modeled the possibility that progressivism, Jewish nationalism, and religious life could coexist and promised that, together, they could lead a renewal in American Jewish life.

Before the start of classes, while waiting for their course schedules, the rabbinical students learned where they would be working. A sizable fieldwork program had developed over the summer, thanks largely to Charles Bloch, who, by late August, had lined up weekly, weekend, and High Holy Day pulpits in New York City and the surrounding area extending into Long Island, upstate New York, and Pennsylvania. In addition to providing educational value and income for the students, the fieldwork program brought congregations into JIR's orbit of influence. And thanks in part to the shortage of rabbis, Bloch was able to find an assignment for every rabbinical student in time for Rosh Hashanah, which fell in late September. "Don't forget about my big son," Wise wrote to Bloch from Vienna, "who I think is quite ready to step in and take some place for the Holy Days."[31]

As in any fieldwork program, students learned on the job—at least, that was the aim. But leading High Holy Day services must have been particularly daunting for JIR's entering class, for none had yet received even a single day of instruction at their new school, which was yet to open. Philip Bernstein reflected on his first fieldwork experience in a baccalaureate sermon he preached at the institute two decades later. "I presume that our class experienced more and learned less than any in the history of the Institute," he said. "Without being able even to read the Torah I was sent for the Holidays in the fall of 1922 to New Castle, Pennsylvania, where I was soon preaching on this subject, 'Jews of Newcastle, Wake Up.'"

"It was fortunate for me," he added, "that they did not."[32]

While the twenty-one-year-old Bernstein, of strong spirit but lacking the basic knowledge required to competently fulfill his responsibilities, was traveling nearly four hundred miles by train to his student pulpit on the Ohio-Pennsylvania border, his teachers at JIR were beginning to hash out a plan for how he and his classmates would acquire the learning they so desperately needed. Wise chose to stay out of the curriculum process for the most part, intentionally leaving this to the faculty—which was well and good in theory, but in practice, until shortly before opening day, the faculty never met.[33]

Now, with Elbogen and Perles en route via steamer, the initial work fell to Kohut, Lewis, Touroff, Bloch, Newman, and a few other New York rabbis who would be teaching that fall. Two meetings were scheduled to get the work done, but over twelve days in late September and early October, during which a majority of the men were also leading Shabbat Shuvah, Yom Kippur, and Sukkot services for their congregations, the group met five times trying to devise a plan.[34] They mapped out a rudimentary curriculum that included traditional seminary topics as well as subject matter that would set JIR apart, namely, Modern Hebrew language and literature and social service.[35]

That American colleges and universities offered little to no Jewish studies rendered incoming students' undergraduate transcripts virtually useless when it came to distinguishing between those who would require introductory coursework versus those prepared for higher level study. Only on the Friday before the start of classes did the faculty get a sense of the challenges ahead, when they met individually with students at the Free Synagogue to evaluate reading and comprehension of biblical as well as Modern Hebrew, familiarity with Mishnah, and knowledge of Jewish history. They also observed whose spoken English required improvement.[36]

The interviews revealed wide-ranging knowledge and skills within the entering class. Morris Rose, for example, who had spent several years as principal of New York's Hebrew Orphan Asylum School and taught at a Talmud Torah before entering the institute, had a strong background in biblical Hebrew and classical texts. Leo Reichel spoke fluent Hebrew, but his English was deficient; perhaps concerned that this might jeopardize his standing, Reichel brought letters of support from his rabbis. Morton Berman, who had a year of study at JTS under his belt, could read and translate Hebrew and had studied Tractate Berakhot of the Talmud. While Philip Bernstein could read Hebrew fairly well, he could translate little, and his grammar needed help; as a result, the committee recommended that he enter as a "special student" rather than a regular student. Benjamin Goldstein, by contrast, had taken three years of Hebrew at the University of California and knew Mishnah Yoma as well as some history. Bernard Turner, a teacher at the orphan asylum, had a strong knowledge of biblical Hebrew and history but only fair skills in grammar and Mishnah; the committee decided to place him in the first year with the option of trying a second-year placement. Henry Schorr, who taught Talmud in a Talmud Torah, entered at an advanced level, whereas Benjamin Parker, who knew little Hebrew, began his studies on a conditional basis.

To accommodate the students' various academic levels, the faculty divided them into three groups. Several, designated "conditional" (including Philip Bernstein), required preparatory coursework in Bible, grammar, and prayerbook. These students could take courses for credit during the fall, but like their female classmates, they could not enroll in the rabbinical program, with a critical difference: If they passed their fall semester classes, they would become "regular students" in the spring. The remaining students were classified as either "Beginner" or "Advanced."[37]

The night before opening day, the faculty met at Wise's home and completed the first-year curriculum. All rabbinical students would take the same distribution of courses (a few of which would be offered with separate sections for the two different levels of proficiency): history, Bible, Jewish religion, Talmud, Midrash and homiletics, liturgy, social service, principles and methods of education (in Hebrew), and Modern Hebrew literature and composition, which Touroff would teach in Hebrew alone.[38] The faculty adopted the modern Sephardic pronunciation of Hebrew and hoped the students could also take an hour of Aramaic with Gottheil each week.[39] Attendance at daily chapel services would be required for all, and the institute would also hold a service for the public each Sabbath afternoon, beginning on Shabbat Bereshit a few weeks hence.[40]

It seems the faculty may have been experiencing second thoughts about some of the students' suitability for the rabbinate. At the end of their meeting, they stipulated that a letter be sent to all students. "Make clear: admission to JIR does not involve graduation."[41]

Beit Hamidrash Lechochmat Yisrael

Monday morning at nine o'clock on October 9, 1922, the third day of the Festival of Sukkot, JIR's first academic year commenced. With construction still underway on the Free Synagogue House being built on West Sixty-Eighth Street, students and faculty made their way to temporary quarters at Temple Israel on West 91st Street.[42]

Temple Israel had not been Wise's first choice—initially he approached Congregation B'nai Jeshurun, where he had launched his rabbinical career in 1893 and served until departing for Portland in 1900. To his chagrin, however, B'nai Jeshurun's Rabbi Israel Goldstein did not accede to Wise's request for temporary housing; rather, Goldstein insisted on asking the board "whether it would be proper for a Conservative Congregation, which pledges its unqualified loyalty and support to the Jewish Theological Seminary and to the United Synagogue of America, to house the Jewish Institute of Religion."[43] Wise, taking offense and preferring not to risk further rejection, rescinded his request and instead turned to Rabbi Maurice Harris at Temple Israel.[44] Harris, who had studied at the Emanu-El Theological Seminary before it closed in the 1880s and whose involvement with the institute dated back to the earliest organizational meetings in 1921, proved willing to risk opprobrium by his own Reform movement and agreed to lend the school space until construction was complete.[45] Louis I. Newman, his assistant rabbi and Wise's protégé, likely supported the decision.

That Temple Israel's provisional classrooms reflected Sukkot's emphasis on the temporary nature of all dwellings was apt, for almost everything about the institute seemed temporary, including the entire faculty with their visiting status and short-term contracts and the bare bones curriculum. Insisting that even his own position was temporary, Wise took the title acting president with the hope that a permanent appointment could be made soon. And though he envisioned Hirsch serving as honorary president for many years to come, this, too, was now up in the air, for the Chicago rabbi remained critically ill and lacked the strength to come to New York. Hoping his seventy-one-year-old friend would soon recover, Wise delayed opening ceremonies so that Hirsch could participate at a later date.

Two days into the semester, the fashionable steamer *Olympic* docked in New York Harbor, and the Hochschule's Ismar Elbogen disembarked together with Felix Perles. In anticipation, Wise planned to meet them personally at quarantine and arranged for Pier tickets for the faculty and board members so they could greet the men, too, as they stepped ashore.[46] A few hours later, the whole group convened at Wise's home for the first full faculty meeting, missing only Touroff.[47]

There, with high aspirations of their own, the faculty designated a Hebrew name for the institute: Beit Hamidrash Lechochmat Yisrael. The name aptly juxtaposed a traditional framework of Jewish learning with a modern one: The *beit midrash* idea, referring to the age-old "house of study" in synagogues and yeshivas, captured a vision of JIR as a force for the preservation of Judaism's ancient laws and teachings; *chokhmat yisrael*, by contrast, literally "the wisdom of Israel," referred to modern scholarship of the kind produced through Wissenschaft des

Judentums and appealed to those who hoped to create at JIR a center for scholarship resembling either the German or American university model. Still others
prioritized the school's mission to modernize the rabbinate by preparing students
to lead a renaissance for American Jewry, including a renewal of Modern Hebrew.
JIR, the new name declared implicitly, would encapsulate all of this, honoring the
old *and* the new.

Very quickly, however, the challenge of translating this ambitious idea into
practice became evident, as the faculty realized that almost all the students needed
introductory coursework in just about every subject area. Those not raised with
some traditional, yeshiva-style Jewish learning knew little Hebrew, with the exception of Hoffseyer, who had lived in Palestine. And despite the fact that all had
earned bachelor's degrees, only the handful who had completed coursework in Europe or at JTS had any experience with the *academic* study of Judaism, which
American undergraduate programs did not offer.

How could the faculty design a graduate-level program for a student body
with no scholarly training in the traditional fields of Jewish learning and vastly
divergent levels of Hebrew? Clearly in the first year, the faculty would have to do
spade work, Wise told Gottheil, "making the men grind pretty hard at more or
less elementary things until they are thoroughly prepared to do advanced work."[48]

Yet in the faculty's effort to provide a strong foundation, they discovered that
by requiring so many hours in the classroom, they had left students with little time
to complete their assignments. Goldstein, Elbogen, and Blau reluctantly agreed to
pare down their course offerings by an hour each week, pending a larger discussion about the curriculum as a whole. Opening up space in the overcrowded class
schedule, though necessary, did not address the students' need for *more* instruction, not less.[49]

Complicating matters further, faculty members brought their personal biases
to student assessment, in some cases perpetuating attitudes Wise was endeavoring
to change. Some complained about students' heavy Yiddish accents, poor English
grammar, and loud voices and wanted students to abandon inflections that marked
them as members of the working-class immigrant community from which they
came. While Wise had founded the institute, in part, to move American liberal
Judaism *away* from this sort of cultural and class bias, which he saw as endemic in
the Reform movement, not all JIR faculty appreciated hearing the Eastern European Jewish patois in their classrooms.

Neither did they appreciate a disciplinary problem that was quickly developing: perpetual lateness to class, if not absence altogether. With hopes dashed that
graduate students would require little supervision, by early November faculty re-
sorted to keeping a daily record of attendance, allowing a maximum of three unex-
cused absences.[50] When this failed to alleviate the problem, they began taking roll
before the daily morning chapel service and instituted a system of bells to mark the

start and dismissal of classes.[51] Wise and Goldstein threatened repeat offenders with suspension and reminded students that admission to JIR did not guarantee graduation. They had to meet *all* requirements, not only the "technical" ones.[52]

The faculty, meanwhile, were finding it increasingly difficult to agree on what, exactly, those requirements should be. One question led to another. Given the students' meager background in Jewish studies, how could the curriculum provide adequate breadth *and* depth of knowledge? Related, how much time would a proper JIR education require? All agreed on a minimum residency requirement of two years for advanced students, but some sought to increase that to three years or more. Wise dismissed out of hand a proposal to require summers, for most students required that time to earn much-needed income.

Extended discussions of a thesis requirement exposed the tension between scholarly and professional training that lay at the heart of the curricular debates. Historically, in a bow to the German seminaries' requirement that all rabbinical candidates also complete a university doctoral program, HUC and JTS both required the writing of a thesis. However, while this may have provided the appearance of mastery, their curricula rarely provided doctoral-level proficiency in any particular field, despite the large number of superb Wissenschaft scholars both seminaries retained. American rabbinical students seeking doctoral-level Jewish study tended to augment their studies at HUC or JTS by attending a European university. Now, however, deteriorating conditions on the Continent increased the need for advanced Jewish studies in the United States.

Toward that end, Blau proposed that all senior theses directly relate to some aspect of Jüdische Wissenschaft.[53] Goldstein disagreed, arguing that the primary aim of the institute was to train men for "service in American Israel" rather than the pursuit of pure scholarship. After all, wasn't the whole idea for JIR to take a radically different, more modern and American approach? Following extensive discussion, the faculty sided with Goldstein and in December declared that all theses must address "a phase of Jewish life and learning," subject to their approval.[54]

Wise, in response to the directive, asked the faculty whether the curriculum should also provide for students interested in Jüdische Wissenschaft alone, and not the active ministry. Yes, the faculty agreed, the institute should take on this role, as well.[55] Optimistically, they believed JIR could do it all, training rabbis as well as scholars, in the tradition of the Jewish academies of Europe but with a modern American sensibility.

Jewish newspapers reporting on Elbogen's and Perles's teaching at JIR that fall hailed the German Jewish scholars for taking just this approach. "Old world but by no means old school" and "modern thinkers in every sense of the word," the *American Hebrew* declared. The two men, in various interviews with the press, emphasized two distinct points: the importance of rebuilding Jewish life in Europe, where, despite the Great War's bloodshed and continuing persecution, large numbers of Jewish youth were still drawn to study Torah; and, at the same time, their view that Jewish culture must henceforth emanate from the United States.

They welcomed Wise's effort to bring European professors to America, they told the *American Hebrew* in October, for rather than jeopardizing their home institutions, the initiative promised to infuse a fresh American perspective into organizations otherwise "practically doomed to stagnation."[56] But they also emphasized the importance of strengthening higher Jewish learning in the United States. Willingly or not, Perles said, America is to be the child that shall lead and inspire whatever may be salvaged from the wreckage of the European debacle. Sharing this view, the *Detroit Jewish Chronicle* anticipated that other scholars would follow Elbogen and Perles in coming to the United States to spur research on the part of native-born Americans and that "within another few years the center of Jewish scholarship will be shifted from the Old World to this."[57]

The prediction matched Wise's aspiration for JIR perfectly—the young and tenuous seminary would extricate Europe's top scholars out of the turmoil and draft them into the work of reshaping American liberal Judaism.

To that end, Wise did everything possible to maximize the impact of Elbogen's and Perles's visit by engaging the two scholars with the broader American Jewish community in ways that spread their learning while also heightening the institute's profile. He opened their afternoon courses to rabbis, seminarians, students at teachers' institutes, religious school instructors, and others.[58] He had Elbogen deliver a series of evening lectures on Jewish history and advertised them in venues as disparate as the Yiddish press and university Semitics departments. And he sponsored speaking tours for both men, Perles in Baltimore and Elbogen in the Midwest. Elbogen covered a particularly wide range of topics, addressing the Chicago Rabbinical Association on "Current Spiritual Movements in German Jewry," for example, and speaking to the Anti-Defamation League on antisemitism. He lectured at HUC on early Christian attitudes toward Judaism, and he spoke to a Menorah Club, too, on "The Place of Zunz in Jewish History and Literature."

FETING JEWISH SCHOLARS AND SCHOLARSHIP

As long as Emil G. Hirsch remained critically ill, Wise delayed any sort of opening ceremony for JIR, but when the fall semester drew to a close, he held a reception in honor of Elbogen and Perles that served a similar purpose. Hosted by mining magnate and Reform Jewish philanthropist Adolph Lewisohn in his newly renovated mansion on Fifth Avenue, over one hundred of New York's most influential religious, educational, and social leaders and their spouses gathered on December 6, 1922, to fete the two German scholars.[59] Lewisohn, who supported a wide variety of Jewish and social causes and held permanent membership on the JTS board, was also known for throwing boisterous parties in his mirror-lined, ivory-and-gold ballroom—indeed, just a few weeks later, he would host more than two hundred guests for a "burlesque" auction of caricatures of paintings in his famous modern art collection, for sale in Russian rubles.[60]

The JIR reception was a far more sober affair, where speakers of national renown spoke of the crises brewing in Europe as well as the United States, emphasized the importance of bringing more German scholars like Elbogen and Perles to teach American Jewry, and underscored the critical role they expected JIR to play in reshaping American Judaism. For Wise and the institute's faculty and board, many of whom had spent the fall focused on details related to students, curriculum, and finances, the evening offered an opportunity to focus on the significance of their work on the world stage. Cumulatively, the ambitions expressed that evening represented a complex mandate for the tiny school, replete with challenge.

Wise stage-managed the event from the start, honing the guest list to reflect the various arenas where he hoped JIR would wield influence and selecting speakers who could galvanize support for his broad vision. In addition to the faculty and lay leadership of JIR and the Free Synagogue in attendance, prominent figures included philanthropists Louis Marshall, Adolph S. Ochs, and Nathan Strauss Jr.; the rabbis of Manhattan's largest synagogues; Rebekah Kohut, the social welfare leader, and progressive reformer Lillian Wald; as well as a good number of judges and newspaper publishers. Representatives from the broader world of higher education included the chancellor of New York University, Elmer E. Brown; the educator John Dewey; and the scholar F. J. Foakes-Jackson, of Union Theological Seminary.[61]

Not everyone accepted Wise's invitation, however. Notably, while JTS professors Mordecai Kaplan, Israel Davidson, and Alexander Marx were present, along with several from Dropsie College, neither Cyrus Adler nor a majority of the JTS faculty attended, though all were invited.[62]

The evening began with a call for religious unity, offered by the opening speaker, Arthur C. McGiffert, president of Union Theological Seminary (UTS). Citing a dangerous self-interest now prevalent in American society, McGiffert emphasized the importance of training a new generation of religious leaders imbued with deep knowledge of their heritage as well as the skills necessary for modern-day ministry, and he welcomed the institute as a partner of UTS in this complicated work.[63]

The focus then turned to contemporary Jewish scholarship, as Mordecai Kaplan laid out a historically grounded vision utterly in sync with Wise's activist approach to the rabbinate.[64] The Jewish scholarly tradition originated as a form of resistance to persecution and a means of survival, he said, citing rabbis like Akiba and his disciples who two millennia earlier had resisted the Roman campaign of destruction by creating academies of their own, along with the Sanhedrin. Likewise, he urged, contemporary scholars must dedicate their teaching to saving the soul of the Jewish people. "Nothing so hurts the cause of Jewish scholarship," he said, "as when it becomes a means of escape from the problems of Jewish life." At the same time, he said, Jewish scholars must also devote themselves to reviving the universal human heart by eliminating bigotry, dogmatism, and intolerance from all spiritual pursuits.[65] Elbogen and Perles exemplified this model, he concluded, not only in their efforts to rebuild European Jewish life currently in ruins but by giving the struggling cause of Judaism in the United States a new lease on life. Kaplan credited Wise for bringing them to New York and contributing signally to a Jewish spiritual renaissance in America.[66]

Harvard Divinity School's George Foot Moore spoke next, extending a "hand of fellowship" from the oldest theological faculty in America to the youngest and spelling out what he saw as the institute's mission: "It should be more than a place where the tradition of learning is carried on and knowledge extended by research, fundamental as that is; more, again, than a training school for the practical work of the minister of religion in our time, necessary as that is. Its specific task, as I apprehend it, is to produce leaders in thought and action."[67]

The sole speaker to make no mention of the Jewish Institute of Religion was Daniel Hays, the UAHC board member who had played a central role in the previous year's failed negotiations. Still, acknowledging progressive Judaism's need for serious Jewish learning, he thanked Wise for bringing Elbogen and Perles to the United States and urged him to bring them again for a permanent stay.

The two honorees turned the evening's focus to Wissenschaft des Judentums, the scholarly movement to which they had devoted their lives. Wissenschaft offered the key to Jewish self-understanding, according to Perles, a goal long impeded by Jewish internal divisiveness but at last attainable through JIR's unique approach. "Our faculty has members of different habits of life and thought, and relies upon the power of science to provide the pupils with the necessary knowledge," he said. "Science is the only bridge which can bring together the different groups existing in our midst and tie the bonds of connection with the non-Jewish world." Perles pointed to the Lewisohn reception itself as an embodiment of his larger hope for the institute, with leaders of different religious groups as well as the academic community meeting together in harmony.[68]

Elbogen echoed Kaplan's framing of Jewish learning as a means of resistance, but with a very particular end goal. "For a century, ever since Leopold Zunz inspired and initiated a scientific investigation of Judaism, Jewish scholars have been taught to break down the spiritual ghetto, to make our distinctly Jewish studies a part of general culture. This has been the real aim of Jewish scholarship during the last hundred years," he said, "and it ought still to be our aim for the future—the embodiment of our studies in the Universitas Literarum."[69]

Given the precariousness of Jewish life in Germany, however, Elbogen predicted that the flourishing of Jewish studies in the twentieth century would take place not in his home country, where the movement began, but in the United States. Reflecting on the construction of JIR's new home on Sixty-Eighth Street, which he had observed over the course of the fall semester, he said, "I wish that we, too, could work as do these masons," laying the foundation for a new center of Jewish scholarship in America.[70] But with his own institution, the Hochschule, imperiled by economic and political crises worsening by the day, he had recently turned down Wise's invitation to join JIR permanently in order to resume his responsibilities in Berlin; though hopeless about the future of Jewish learning there, he would nonetheless return home. Perles, too, had chosen to go back to Koenigsberg.

Anticipating their departure later that winter, Wise remained hopeful that both men would teach again at JIR in the future. Bringing the evening's celebration to a close, he saluted his German colleagues who had crossed the Atlantic to help launch the institute. Refusing to say goodbye, he instead insisted they would meet again: "*Meine Herren, auf wiedesehen!*"[71]

EUROPEANS AND THE FIVE SEMINARY FUND

The perilous state of the Hochschule and its peer institutions weighed heavily on Wise, who believed the American Jewish seminaries had a responsibility to raise financial support for their struggling European counterparts. Still troubled by the threat Schulman had made to withdraw the Joint Distribution Committee's funding from the Hochschule in retribution for the German seminary's cooperation with the institute, Wise hoped to unite HUC, JTS, and JIR in collectively sending $2,000 annually to each of the five Wissenschaft seminaries of "German-speaking lands," including those he had visited in Berlin, Breslau, Vienna, and Budapest, plus the Orthodox Rabbiner-Seminar in Berlin. He also hoped the American seminaries would jointly sponsor a tour of the United States by representatives from these seminaries, with the aim of stabilizing them financially. This seemed "a more fitting and dignified way to secure funds than to let the JDC continue its help," he told Chajes, head of the Vienna seminary.[72]

However, lacking a modus vivendi with either Adler at JTS or Morgenstern at HUC, Wise soon dropped both ideas and instead committed to sending $1,000 per year to each of the five seminaries on behalf of JIR alone. "It is very difficult to get our friends of the Seminary and of Cincinnati to move," he told Chajes, "and so I thought that the lesser gift immediately would be better than a possible larger gift in the remote future."

While relations with HUC and JTS remained hostile (notwithstanding the harmony Perles had lauded at the Lewisohn gathering), Wise pursued further cooperation with the European seminaries and continued reaching out to scholars across the Continent whom he had not yet met. Leo Baeck, on behalf of the

Hochschule, assured Wise that despite the difficulties of the previous summer, the faculty rejoiced over JIR's opening and fully intended to continue sending a rotation of visiting professors.[73] And Julian Obermann, a Semitics professor at the University of Hamburg whom Gottheil had recommended, accepted Wise's invitation to teach at the institute in the upcoming spring semester.[74]

With Elbogen's decision to return to Berlin, Wise also had to resume his search for a president and quickly pinned his hopes on another European—Israel Abrahams, the leader of Liberal Judaism in England, who was also due in New York shortly to teach for the spring semester. The selection would have attested to the institute's commitment to freedom of thought, for Abrahams, widely considered a Jew without label thanks to his broad-minded approach to religious life, shared neither Wise's left-leaning politics nor his Zionism.[75] That his predecessor, Solomon Schechter, had left Cambridge in 1902 to assume the presidency of JTS provided a historical resonance Wise also no doubt appreciated. The JIR board, however, rejected Wise's proposal to invite Abrahams to serve as JIR's acting president, for sentiment was building in favor of selecting an American—even Elbogen, after considering the position, had determined this would be best.[76] Wise agreed to continue as acting president until a replacement could be found.[77]

That winter, the American Jewish community mourned the passing of one of its leading rabbis, Emil Gustave Hirsch, who died of pneumonia at age seventy-one on January 7, 1923.[78] With Hirsch's death, Wise lost a powerful confidant, ally, friend, and partner in building the institute. Fifty years earlier, Hirsch, as a young graduate of the University of Pennsylvania, had utilized financial support from Temple Emanu-El to follow in the footsteps of his father, Samuel Hirsch, the pioneering radical Reform rabbi from Germany, by traveling to Berlin to enroll in the rabbinical program at the Hochschule during its own inaugural year.[79] In the decades since, he had built a powerful urban rabbinate at Chicago Sinai and become one of Reform Judaism's foremost leaders in the United States. With his passing, no one again would advocate for JIR as a new Hochschule in America nor hold the position of honorary president.

CONCLUSION

Construction of JIR's new home, at the cost of roughly half a million dollars, came to completion just in time for the spring semester. The stately four-story Collegiate Gothic structure, clad in large, rectangular-cut pale Manhattan Schist stone with limestone-trimmed windows and doors, housed the institute's classrooms and offices, a one-hundred-seat chapel, and the newly named Hirsch Library, which had eight thousand volumes already and was growing rapidly under Joshua Bloch's direction.[80] Indeed, the collection now included the Brann collection and Wise's substantial personal library, which he donated, as well as books and manuscripts

from the collections of Richard Gottheil, Emil G. Hirsch, and Alexander Kohut—with more acquisitions arriving monthly, largely from the private collections
of American rabbis.[81]

Thanks primarily to Wise's publicity efforts that fall, enthusiasm for JIR was
spreading far beyond the rarified milieu of leaders and scholars like those who
attended the Lewisohn dinner, into the broader non-Orthodox Jewish world, including a growing number of congregations across the region seeking to hire JIR
students. And no wonder, given all that was being promised. JIR would soon produce rabbis both Jewishly learned and possessing a broad social outlook grounded
in the strivings of contemporary American Jewry, an editorial in the *Reform Advocate* told readers. The institute would also be a graduate school for those seeking to
specialize in some branch of Hebraic learning. Soon, the *Advocate* predicted, the
institute would rank with the famous rabbinical academies in Breslau, Budapest,
and Berlin while at the same time possessing "the essential flavor and content of an
American school of learning."[82] It was a lot to deliver.

7

Rabbinical Training for Our Time

JIR's formidable new home belied the tenuousness of the nascent school. To deliver the world-class training Wise promised, this so-called new Yavneh required a stabilized faculty and an agreed-upon curriculum, along with a viable plan for funding the large set of costs not covered by the Free Synagogue's annual contribution.

The situation would be challenging enough were the school operating in a vacuum with no competitors and unlimited resources. But in 1923, others, too, also saw higher education as a meaningful path toward Jewish renewal, and several groups were creating new initiatives of their own, in Jewish as well as secular contexts. JIR, while still building its fragile infrastructure, would have to contend with all of these, particularly in the pursuit of scholars and donors.

A few of these endeavors were underway in New York. That year, Bernard Revel, who now ran RIETS, announced his intention to establish Yeshiva College, where he planned to bring Jewish and secular studies together within an Orthodox institution.[1] At the other end of the religious spectrum, HUC opened its own School for Teachers, located at Temple Emanu-El and directed by a recent CCNY graduate, Abraham Franzblau. In addition, the National Conference of Jewish Charities was planning a Graduate School for Jewish Social Work, to train professionals for the rapidly expanding federation and community center movements.[2]

Others pinned their dreams for Jewish renewal on secular American colleges and universities, which they hoped might finally offer higher Jewish learning. At Harvard, for example, while the current battle focused on ending the admissions quota, men like Mack and Judge Irving Lehman, the early funders of Wolfson's position, had their sights on the larger goal of establishing a home for Jewish studies within the university. In addition, Louis I. Newman, the young rabbi Wise had privately ordained and who was now assistant rabbi at New York's Temple Israel and had agreed to teach at JIR, was drawing significant attention with his proposal for the establishment of a "Menorah University." Open to Jewish as well as non-Jewish students and faculty, the school Newman envisioned would offer secular as well as Jewish studies in a non-Orthodox environment. "The curriculum of the Jewish University would be 'universal,' liberal and free," Newman wrote, but the idea had yet to take any concrete form.[3]

In Jerusalem, Judah Magnes was leading an even more ambitious project—the establishment of Hebrew University, devoted to sustaining Jewish cultural identity across the world. This national institution, as Magnes envisioned it, would not only offer a wide array of Jewish studies but would also advance the application of humanistic Jewish values to matters of universal concern.[4] Albert Einstein delivered the university's inaugural lecture in February 1923, the same month JIR moved into its new building.[5]

Each of these efforts, if successful, would eventually supply the Jewish world with plenty of Jewish scholars and teachers. In the short term, however, in building their own faculty, they all had to draw from the same small pool of scholars spread across Europe, North America, and Palestine. And while the shifting center of Jewish learning, from Europe to the United States and Palestine, was already discernible in 1923, scholars were still moving in all directions. Germany, for example, continued to exert a pull, and not only for those who had built their lives and careers there, like Elbogen and Perles; in June of that year, for example, three young HUC graduates (Sheldon Blank, Nelson Glueck, and Walter Rothman) sailed on the steamer *Manchuria* to Hamburg, where Jacob ("Jake") Rader Marcus '20 met them at the port. After Jake introduced the newcomers to German beer at a sidewalk cafe, the group spread out to different locations to learn German and then reconvened that fall at the University of Berlin, where Marcus was studying under Elbogen. Blank, Glueck, and Rothman transferred to the University of Jena in the spring, and all four remained in Germany for several years to earn their doctorates.[6]

Initially, by virtue of Wise's trial system, visiting faculty came to the institute for brief periods of time by design. Their short-term contracts provided the institute as well as each professor an opportunity to evaluate the fit after spending a semester or year together. Clearly, Wise had little trouble attracting scholars, notwithstanding the few, including Kaplan, who had rejected his advances; now, among those currently teaching, he needed to identify his top candidates and entice them to stay while continually finding replacements for those he did not select. Ultimately, he aimed for a core faculty to coalesce over time.

In the earliest years, the constant coming and going of faculty posed a particular challenge given the institute's need to develop an effective curriculum. Rather than dictating what should be taught, Wise and the board set few parameters and mainly emphasized the importance of exposing students to a wide range of viewpoints. "Academic freedom is the bedrock of Judaism," Mack had declared at the inauguration of the new building. "This means a freedom of teaching for the faculty, of learning for the students."[7] In a similar vein, Wise insisted that students experience the full curriculum before affiliating with any particular stream of Judaism. "As far as it is at all necessary for a man to utter the shibboleth of reform, or orthodoxy, or conservatism, this should so be done—if at all—after a man has gone to the sources of Jewish life and history—not before."[8]

But what should be taught, and how? And what about the women in the student body? These questions threw the faculty into a bitter debate that would last several years, in no small part because the cast of characters kept changing.

Wise stayed out of that debate for the most part. As long as he brought capable faculty to the institute, they could work out the curriculum, whereas the task of fundraising rested on his shoulders alone. Here, too, he would have to compete with rival institutions targeting the same handful of major American Jewish donors. In the quest for dollars, as well, JIR's uniqueness as a nondenominational seminary would be tested. On the one hand, Wise could solicit donors across the spectrum of Jewish religious belief and practice. At the same time, the institute's nondenominationalism was hardly pareve (neutral); rather, the inclusion of a broad range of Jewish perspectives stemmed directly from Wise's commitment to Zionism and liberalism. With anti-Zionist and conservative funders unlikely to join the endeavor, Wise had to come up with ways to generate revenue that would prove viable over the long term.

In the spring of 1923, with the institute newly ensconced in a beautiful building, a critical two-year period began, in which the focus turned to establishing the academic and financial infrastructure necessary for JIR to endure over time and make a lasting impact on American Judaism.

Aspirations Collide

Everyone in the institute's orbit, it seemed, wanted a say, and discussions over faculty hiring, women's status in the rabbinical program, the content of the curriculum, and funding models revealed a wide range of aspirations for JIR. The fluid situation created, on the one hand, a great sense of possibility; at the same time, those seeking to shape the school's direction often brought a healthy dose of self-interest. As a result, debates often turned contentious.

Stabilizing the institute required, more than anything else, a core group of full-time permanent faculty who could develop the curriculum, establish agreed-upon standards for teaching and research, and mentor the students as they prepared for the rabbinate. Thus far, only Wise and Goldstein had a long-term commitment to teach at JIR, thanks to the Free Synagogue's willingness to share their time with the institute. The congregation also agreed to share their new music director, Abraham W. Binder, an Orthodox young Zionist composer and choral director recently graduated from Columbia and the New York College of Music. Wise appointed Binder head of the institute's Department of Jewish Music.[9]

Elbogen and Perles, though, were soon heading back to Germany, and Abrahams would leave for England at the end of the semester. Wolfson and Touroff held full-time positions elsewhere and traveled to New York as little as possible—in fact, to Wise's regret, by mid-spring Touroff realized he could not sustain the commute from Boston; he would teach Jewish Education and Hebrew in the 1923 summer school but not join the permanent faculty for two more years.[10] Most others, mainly local rabbis, were teaching at JIR part-time.[11]

The burden for recruiting more faculty fell largely on Wise, who had a knack for identifying promising candidates and the ability to astutely navigate institutional politics.

HARRY AUSTRYN WOLFSON AND THE HARVARD DEAL

In the spring of 1923, Wise focused on finalizing the hire of thirty-five-year-old Harry Wolfson, assistant professor of Jewish literature and philosophy at Harvard. For the past year, Wolfson had agreed to do little more at JIR than attend an occasional faculty meeting and consult on the curriculum, but now, with his Harvard contract set to end at the conclusion of the 1923–1924 academic year, he was ready to work out an arrangement, as long it entailed continued teaching at Harvard.[12] Mack agreed to help broker a deal, utilizing his role as a board member at JIR as well as the university.

Meanwhile, in April, the battle over Harvard's quota system took a major turn. On the basis of a recommendation from the committee on which Wolfson served, the board voted unanimously to maintain its "traditional policy of freedom from racial or religious discrimination" in admissions.[13] Yet, while the official numerus clausus quota appeared to be ending, the committee's recommendation of a new "highest seventh" plan complicated matters.[14] Ostensibly aimed at garnering more students from prep schools west of the Mississippi in the name of broader regional representation, the plan effectively replaced the quota with a new tool Lowell could use to limit Jewish admissions.[15] The development added to Wolfson's anxiety that Lowell might refuse to renew his contract.[16]

Mack, however, succeeded in brokering a joint appointment that worked well for Wolfson and benefited Harvard, at the expense of JIR. Wise would appoint Wolfson as full professor beginning in the fall of 1923, with the understanding that he would teach one semester at each institution on an annual basis.[17] For the one year remaining in Wolfson's contract at Harvard, the university would cover $3,500 of Wolfson's compensation out of the funds Mack and Lehman had raised, and JIR would cover $1,500. However, beginning in the 1924–1925 academic year, JIR would cover Wolfson's annual salary of $5,000 in full, though he would continue to teach at Harvard for half the year. "Professor Wolfson is to be Professor of Jewish Philosophy and History," JIR's executive committee agreed at their May 1923 meeting, "and his services are to be given by the Institute for one term in each year to Harvard University, for which services, after 1924 *Harvard is not to pay* [emphasis added]."[18]

Wise must have repressed his revulsion when he told Lowell that JIR was pleased to foot the bill: "The Jewish Institute of Religion believes that through this division of his labors the field of usefulness for Professor Wolfson will be greatly widened, and it is happy to tender his services to Harvard in recognition of the interest of Harvard in the Hebrew language and in Semitics from its very earliest day."[19]

Harvard would pay nothing to retain this top scholar on its faculty; rather, JIR, with no means yet to cover its own bills, would subsidize the oldest, richest university in the country.

HENRY SLONIMSKY

While the Wolfson negotiations were underway, Wise got wind that a Jewish philosopher at Hebrew Union College, Henry Slonimsky, was also interested in joining JIR. Slonimsky's nomadic life, and his political and artistic engagement, differed dramatically from Wolfson's cloistered existence. Born in Minsk but raised in Philadelphia, he attended Haverford and the University of Pennsylvania and then enrolled at the University of Marburg, where he studied with Hermann Cohen, founder of the Neo-Kantian school. After earning his doctorate in 1912, he moved to Paris, where he joined Ezra Pound's literary circle, and then went on to London, where he developed a lifelong friendship with the poets Richard Aldington and Hilda "H.D." Doolittle.[20] With the outbreak of war, he returned to the United States and taught at Columbia for a year before joining the faculty at Johns Hopkins.[21] After six years there, he resigned in 1921 and moved to Cincinnati, where he spent a short time doing settlement work before HUC appointed him full professor in Jewish education and ethics.[22]

But now at odds with Kaufmann Kohler, Slonimsky wanted to join JIR, and he had a wealthy high school classmate from Philadelphia, Albert M. Greenfield, willing to underwrite his salary if Wise hired him.[23] Wise learned this from Jacob Billikopf, head of Philadelphia's Federation of Jewish Charities, who wanted to help broker an arrangement. Though interested, Wise refused to negotiate unless Slonimsky provided a written statement saying he wanted to leave HUC.[24] "Even though universities have the habit of calling men from one Faculty to another, we naturally are chary of doing anything that may seem to be unfraternal in relation to Cincinnati," he told Billikopf.[25]

JULIAN OBERMANN

If Slonimsky was quietly looking for a path *to* JIR, Obermann was already looking for a way out. Hoping Yale might be interested in an arrangement similar to Wolfson's, he garnered support from George A. Kohut, who had donated his father's library to the university 1915 and remained a significant donor.[26] Kohut arranged a trip to New Haven and introduced Obermann to university officials, who offered to take on Obermann as a research associate if JIR covered his salary and expenses, estimated at $1,000.[27]

The proposal triggered a debate within the JIR board over the merits of faculty taking university teaching posts while employed by the institute. Mack, pointing out that the Yale proposal basically matched the Harvard arrangement, believed JIR would benefit from these university connections. But Wise opposed the idea, seeing no parallel between Obermann, an unknown figure in the United States, and Wolfson, a prominent scholar already based at Harvard. Gottheil suggested that if they simply gave Obermann more time for research, he would have none left to devote to Yale or anywhere else.[28]

Ultimately, Wise held sway, though Obermann benefited, as well. The board promoted him from associate to full professor but stipulated that he serve JIR *exclusively*.[29] Obermann agreed, and at the conclusion of the academic year, Wise's "trial method" yielded JIR's first truly full-time appointment.

WOMEN

One of the first questions the faculty addressed in the winter of 1923 pertained to the admission of women into the rabbinical program. While Wise and the faculty took pains to create a path into the rabbinate for "the boys," they gave little thought to the matter until Irma Lindheim used her considerable influence to press for women's access.

In doing so, Lindheim must have understood that the future of women in the rabbinate now rested entirely on JIR. For despite the fact that both the HUC faculty and the CCAR had recently voted in favor of the ordination of women, that winter, just as JIR's second semester began, HUC's board of governors decided *against* ordaining women.[30] The battle Martha Neumark had been fighting was lost.

Lindheim now petitioned JIR for admission as a "regular student" in the rabbinical program, and the faculty considered her request at their February meeting. While they had no serious objections to admitting female students in principle, the minutes indicate, several expressed concern about how this might be implemented. Goldstein, generally one of the most liberal members of the faculty, opposed admitting women entirely—not even as "special students." The male students already demonstrated a lack of seriousness, he felt, and he wanted to cultivate a more severe atmosphere at the school, which could more easily be done without women around. According to Abrahams, admitting women would add to the burden of establishing JIR, and apparently all agreed that the school lacked proper facilities for women, such as dormitories. The matter would be postponed for about two years, they decided; in the meantime, while the three women already attending classes would be permitted to remain, henceforth the institute would admit no more.[31]

Lindheim pushed back, and after revisiting the matter over the course of the spring, the faculty reversed their earlier vote and in May unanimously recommended that "women be admitted to the institute upon the same basis as men, and that the conditions of admission, residence and graduation be applicable to women in the same way in which they are applied to the men." Reflecting this decision, the institute's 1923 charter included in its mission the training of "men and women for the Jewish ministry."

Still, the faculty urged "extreme caution" in the selection of students, and Wise never announced this momentous decision to the Jewish press.[32]

CURRICULUM BATTLE

The admission of women was hardly the only issue argued that spring; the faculty also spent untold hours in theoretical discussions regarding the mission of the school, and as they attempted to embody their divergent aspirations in a functional curriculum, they plunged into rancorous debate.

Perhaps the conflict was inevitable, given the diversity of scholars and rabbis attracted to JIR, the pressures of the "trial" method, and their lack of clarity regarding the school's overall mission. The group, collectively, had experienced virtually every form of Jewish schooling available in Europe, the United States, and Palestine in the early twentieth century, including apprenticeship with a rabbi, traditional yeshiva learning, liberal as well as Orthodox seminary training, and doctoral research in the German, British, and American university systems. None were assured long-term employment. And their task was complicated by the expectation that they train not only rabbis but also scholars, and maybe even social workers—for in the spring of 1923, Wise expressed openness to a proposal that JIR take this on, as well.

Fraught as the undertaking may have been, with the student body in place and growing, they had a job to do: create and implement a cogent curriculum that expressed JIR's core values and effectively trained leaders capable of transforming American Judaism.

Because JIR students generally had little background in Jewish studies, the accomplished scholars on the faculty faced the confounding task of having to teach graduate students the most rudimentary skills. The European faculty, accustomed to conducting high-level seminars, were particularly distraught, and those advocating a model wherein students conducted much of their research independently fought sharply with those who preferred an American approach characterized by significant classroom teaching and close student supervision. Increased classroom responsibilities threatened the faculty's ability to advance their own research, which was critical in order for the institute to become a true center of scholarship; the students, however, expected American-style classroom teaching and required introductory courses in every subject, including Hebrew.

Obermann took a strong stand in favor of instituting a seminar system, which would help the students learn to work independently and enable the faculty to bring "young men with profound ignorance to a real and sound knowledge."[33] Wise, however, strongly preferred an American progressive approach to education and made his views clear.[34] When Obermann did not relent, his proposal triggered a full-scale debate in April and May 1923 about how best to train twentieth-century American rabbis. "I remember it as if it were yesterday," wrote Irma Lindheim. "I used to hear all sides. It was in the development of the curriculum that the fundamental differences between the way the Institute had been planned on paper and the way it later developed, first appeared."[35]

Some critiqued the German approach as overly scientific, intellectual, and technical. If they taught students in this way, asked Rabbi Maurice Harris, how could the faculty ever touch upon the question of *faith?*

Others believed rabbinical students needed to master Hebrew and interpretive text skills before they could ever learn anything of Jewish significance. Given their rudimentary knowledge in both areas, Israel Abrahams proposed a two-tiered approach whereby the institute would retain instructors to help students acquire a grounding in elementary Hebrew and other subjects in their first two years, and then, in their final two years, they could work at a more advanced level in a seminar system under the guidance of the faculty.

Wolfson agreed about the need for elementary work, which he broadened to include survey courses in areas like Jewish literature and history, for students, he believed, required a breadth of knowledge prior to specializing in a particular field. But rather than outsourcing these introductory courses, they should be taught by the top faculty members from each department to ensure adequate training through weekly reading assignments, regular exams, and meetings with the instructor. He proposed Harvard's approach, whereby students spent approximately twelve hours in class each week, combined with a minimum of twenty-four additional hours in preparation each week. In light of this time commitment, Harvard students were prohibited from taking on any work beyond their actual studies, and Wolfson advised that JIR enforce a similar policy, pointing out that in American universities, graduate students with outside jobs were required to extend the amount of time they took to earn their degrees.[36]

Wise objected to the last stipulation, as JIR students were almost entirely self-supporting; otherwise, he favored Wolfson's approach. He urged the faculty to focus on creating a basic curriculum for now, and later they could work out a plan for those seeking to specialize in Jewish scholarship, religious education, or social service.[37]

While Wise intended for JIR to prepare students eventually for a variety of career paths, as reflected in the institute's letterhead ("A School of Training for the Ministry, Education, Research and Community Service"), the students, it turned out, were almost exclusively interested in becoming rabbis, and as the institute's second year began, this impacted the curriculum more than any philosophical discussion about what JIR should become. Now there was no question that meeting the educational needs of the rabbinical students was by far most pressing.[38]

Given the students' minimal background in Jewish studies, this meant focusing on elementary coursework. As Wise explained to Reuben Levy, recently arrived from Oxford, despite his expertise in Persian literature and Semitic languages, he needed to teach two sections of introductory Hebrew Bible, including one for students with minimal Hebrew reading skills. "While those men who are going in for [Jüdische] Wissenschaft will want Persian and Arabic," Wise wrote, "every man at the Institute, whatever calling he fit himself for, must have a knowledge of the Hebrew Bible."[39] Similarly, Joshua Bloch wanted to teach Greek but had to teach Bible, and Obermann had to offer Hebrew, though to the dismay of other faculty as well as the students, he took a classic philological approach rather than teaching ivrit b'ivrit.[40]

On top of all the elementary courses, the faculty still had to make room for advanced work. As the three-year curriculum grew overcrowded with courses, they considered requiring three six-week summer sessions and adding a preparatory year. Wise, however, rejected both ideas; the students needed to earn income over the summer, and JIR would remain exclusively a graduate school, without offering any precursory training. The faculty then unanimously recommended extending the program to four years, and the board approved.[41]

An Amalgamated Synagogue

The costs of the Wolfson and Obermann appointments, plus travel and honoraria expenses associated with the visiting European faculty, grew the budget beyond Wise's initial estimates. The institute needed a large infusion of cash, and when Central Synagogue's rabbi, Nathan Krass, announced he would be leaving for the pulpit fifteen blocks away at Temple Emanu-El, Wise seized on an idea. If the Free Synagogue and Central Synagogue merged into an "amalgamated synagogue," he could serve as rabbi for a so-called Central Free Synagogue, which, with the combined resources of both congregations, could easily commit to a contribution of $25,000 to JIR annually, at least for three to five years. He staked the plan on raising $2.5 million to build a sanctuary capable of seating three-to-four thousand congregants.

While Wise had long criticized "cathedral" Judaism, he harbored little doubt that this grand synagogue would be a step forward for American Jewry. And if his funding plan materialized, JIR would receive an infusion of at least an extra $30,000 over the next three years.[42] In truth, neither congregation fully supported the idea, but Central Synagogue held off on hiring a new rabbi, and merger negotiations began.[43]

Wise, however, was exhausted, and at the end of JIR's first academic year, his friend Martin Meyer publicly urged him to hire someone else to lead the institute. "Dr. Wise is too busy with his multifarious interests to give this the attention it demands," Meyer wrote in Emanuel, his synagogue publication.[44]

Wise agreed, but he had yet to find an ideal candidate prepared to take over the presidency, and with so much still in flux, this was hardly the time to step down. For now, he retreated to Camp Willamette, the family home in the Adirondacks, while Goldstein oversaw the 1923 summer school. Mack, too, agreed to pitch in that summer, by interviewing a new set of faculty candidates during a trip to Europe and Palestine for meetings with the Zionist movement.

1923–1924 FACULTY AND FINANCES: A POROUS STRUCTURE

Mack planned to meet with scholars in London and Berlin, where the Hochschule had finally agreed to send a regular rotation of faculty to JIR.[45] While this was good news, the recent curricular debate had made clear the inappropriateness of the German model, for which Obermann continued to advocate. And really, despite the value of Wise's trial method, the institute desperately needed to attract and retain more permanent faculty. This would be a lot easier, of course, if the institute could offer job security, but that was not yet the case. Thus, Mack could have only moderate expectations that his trip would yield just the kind of faculty member JIR needed.

MORDECAI KAPLAN AND CHAIM TCHERNOWITZ

To his surprise, however, soon after boarding the SS *George Washington* bound for Bremen, Mack found himself in discussion with the one man he and Wise sought for JIR above all others: Mordecai Kaplan who, like Mack, was en route to the Thirteenth World Zionist Congress in Carlsbad and had booked a berth on the same ship.

Kaplan had maintained collegial relations with Wise since turning down the JIR invitation a year earlier, not only speaking at the Lewisohn reception but later advising Wise on faculty salaries by sharing sensitive information from JTS.[46] Still, when Wise had invited Kaplan to teach a course in the summer school, Kaplan had regretfully declined.[47] "As matters stand at present," he wrote, "both the authorities of the Seminary and my colleagues on the faculty would interpret my participation in the work of the JIR as an act of disloyalty to the Seminary."[48]

Nonetheless, aboard the steamer that June, Mack asked Kaplan again if he would reconsider joining the institute, and Kaplan said he would. Mack cabled Wise, and Wise cabled back: "If Kaplan ready we are." The men agreed to work out the details in late August when all would be back in New York.

Mack's good fortune continued when he reached Europe. Though Elbogen remained reluctant to leave Germany, two other Hochschule faculty, Julius Guttmann and Harry Torczyner, were interested, and Guttmann agreed to teach in the spring of 1924. In London, Reuben Levy of Oxford wanted a stint at the institute, as well, and signed on for the fall of 1923. Arthur Marmorstein of Jews' College, however, declined; the prolific Rabbinics scholar feared that if he taught at JIR even for a semester, his Orthodox colleagues would dismiss him.[49] Hirsch Perez

Chajes, by contrast, chief rabbi of Vienna, considered becoming the institute's first Orthodox faculty member and agreed to at least make a visit in the upcoming year.

Back in New York, however, the Orthodox Talmudist Chaim Tchernowitz preempted Chajes by signing on to teach. He had arrived in New York from Berlin on his way to Jerusalem, where he planned to head the Department of Talmud at Magnes's new university. Among the first scholars to apply *wissenschaftlich* methodology to halakhic literature,[50] Tchernowitz came with high reviews from Elbogen, Montefiore, and others. Elbogen, in fact, had urged Wise to defray his travel costs by hiring him to teach a short course of lectures. The JIR faculty, however, thought otherwise—two Talmudists were already under consideration, Solomon Zeitlin and Henry Malter, both of Dropsie College. Why should the institute subsidize Tchernowitz's travel when he would be in town for so little time?[51]

Now it appeared Tchernowitz *would* have an extended stay, as the opening of Hebrew University had been pushed from 1924 to a later date. Wise appointed Tchernowitz for the year, hoping he would stay longer.[52]

The negotiation with Kaplan did not go as smoothly, and not for lack of trying on Wise's part. When the two men met in August, Wise quickly agreed to Kaplan's request to teach the psychology of religion and the interpretation of Bible and Midrash, and Kaplan expressed his gratitude.[53] "It is just such whole-souled friendship that I have missed, and that I have been longing for in all the years of my work at the Seminary."[54]

Wise, too, was thrilled. Kaplan would provide just the spiritual orientation to Jewish texts the students sought, and Wise envisioned the two men visiting universities across the country together, inspiring young men to join the rabbinate in ways the European scholars simply could not. For while they brought international stature to the institute and introduced students to Wissenschaft des Judentums, most of them had little understanding of American Judaism.

Goldstein had observed this, as well; after a year working alongside his colleagues from across the Atlantic, he had begun to wonder how they could possibly help students meet the unique demands placed on American rabbis. He also found them difficult, especially Obermann. "Is there not some way in which we can avail ourselves of German scholarship without the German scholars?" he asked Wise in frustration.[55] Mordecai Kaplan would bring just the fresh, contemporary approach the institute needed.

But Kaplan, too, proved a source of frustration. Not long after he showed Wise the letter of resignation he planned to submit to Adler, he reversed course entirely—leaving Wise bereft, once again.[56]

Joshua Bloch and the New York Public Library

More loss came that fall, but this time, it was Wise's doing. He enjoyed helping other institutions procure scholars, even, at times, from JIR's own faculty, and his support for Joshua Bloch and the New York Public Library in the fall and winter of 1923 was a case in point.

On the morning of October 2, 1923, the New York Public Library suffered a major loss when Abraham Solomon Freidus, chief of the Jewish Division, died of a heart attack at the foot of the library stairs on his way in to work. A well-known figure in New York's cultural world, many of the city's Jewish scholars and writers eulogized him at his funeral the next day.[57]

In response to the NYPL's immediate need for a replacement, Wise offered to lend out Joshua Bloch until a successor to Freidus could be appointed. Bloch and the library's director, Edwin Anderson, were both amenable, and Anderson promised not to impose on the institute's generosity. Anxious to hire a scholar who could build on Freidus's success turning the Jewish Division into a major collection, Anderson turned to Wise and Gottheil, among others, for guidance.[58] Wise recommended HUC's Adolph Oko, who had built a great library at the college, and he also spoke highly of young Bloch, though no one knew if he was up to the task.[59] Anderson took Oko and Bloch both under consideration.

Kohut agreed to run the JIR library in Bloch's absence. Books were flowing in, including several cases from the late Emil G. Hirsch's library, sent by his son-in-law Gerson Levi, and about one hundred and fifty volumes Richard Gottheil was donating from his own late father's library. These gifts were invaluable, for the institute had little money to build its collection; when the seminary in Vienna offered to sell its duplicates to JIR that fall, for example, the board could not justify the expenditure.[60]

Over the next few months, Bloch apparently proved himself, for in February Anderson decided to appoint him chief of the Jewish Division, unless Wise objected. "I should feel very much chagrined if we appeared to be annexing a loan without your full consent," Anderson wrote. Wise hoped Bloch could retain both posts, but when Anderson asked that Bloch quickly be freed of all his JIR responsibilities, Wise complied.[61]

In need of a replacement, JIR now turned to Oko, inviting him to serve as librarian while also lecturing during his first year, to test his teaching ability.[62] Oko, however, demanded a salary of $9,000, almost double what most JIR faculty were making, and when he refused to back down, the negotiations ended. For the time being, Kohut continued overseeing the library, hiring as his assistant twenty-three-year-old Ralph Marcus, a recent college graduate now pursuing a doctorate at Columbia under Gottheil, who had grown up in the Free Synagogue.[63]

Travails and a Hopeful Turn

That winter, tensions mounted with Wolfson, who failed to arrive to teach his classes, complained about his teaching schedule, and continuously postponed his start date.[64] A week prior to a JIR dinner in honor of Wolfson and Guttmann,

Wolfson cabled to say he could not attend. "I cannot do things in a hurry with all my desire to attend the dinner it will be impossible for me to make it," the cable read. "I hope it will come off successfully without my presence."[65] He eventually began teaching, but Wise's initial enthusiasm for the Harvard man, who was known to suffer from agoraphobia and hated to travel, was wearing thin.

Guttmann, too, disappointed. Though Wise had explicitly instructed the Berlin scholar to work on his English, "which, alas, constitutes almost the only medium between a teacher and the students of the Institute," Guttmann insisted on delivering his lectures on sociology and the history of religion in German.[66]

And then there was Obermann, still looking for an appointment elsewhere. Having failed to work out an arrangement with Yale, Obermann now proposed that JIR send his salary to Columbia so he could have an appointment there. Columbia could then pay him out of the JIR funding, he suggested, while he continued to teach at JIR for nothing. "He wants at all hazards to push himself into the faculty of Columbia University," Gottheil wrote Wise, though he knew the trustees at Columbia would never agree and was dumbfounded by the "devious" suggestion.[67] "I am troubled to think that you have to deal with a man who so entirely misunderstands our American methods," Gottheil added.[68] Obermann then offered another idea. Why not lighten his teaching load at JIR, increase his salary, and have him lecture at Harvard each spring in Wolfson's absence? Mack rejected the Harvard idea as infeasible, and the board rejected the rest.[69]

Developments on the faculty front finally took a turn for the better over the winter when Tchernowitz, adapting well, decided to extend his stay.[70] Then, in late February, Henry Slonimsky submitted his resignation to HUC's board of governors, and though students petitioned him to reconsider, in March he accepted an appointment at JIR as professor of ethics and the philosophy of religion.

Of course, every new hire put further strain on the budget, including Slonimsky's. While the Greenfield gift covered his salary for one year, JIR would thereafter have to bear the cost. Wise again asked for Greenfield's help, this time in convening a Philadelphia group who might be willing to cover Slonimsky's salary in perpetuity, but Greenfield demurred.[71] This was not Wise's first attempt to cover faculty costs in this way; a year earlier, when he attended the memorial service for Hirsch, he broached the possibility that friends of the renowned rabbi in Chicago might establish an Emil G. Hirsch Chair in Comparative Religion, but that, too, never materialized.

Two developments signaled that the financial situation might improve, at least in the short term. First, the synagogue merger seemed more and more likely, and with it, the increased contribution to JIR. In addition, the institute received a bequest of $163,000 from the estate of Hannah Heyman, a woman who had lived on modest means until her brother Jacob Semel, a hosiery dealer, left her nearly a million dollars. After Wise officiated at Semel's funeral, just six months before her own death, Heyman bequeathed the gift to JIR in her will and designated Wise as one of the executors.

The Heyman bequest enabled JIR to pay off the nearly $100,000 it owed the Free Synagogue on the construction of its new home, with plenty left over.[72] To celebrate, the Free Synagogue leadership considered creating a chair in honor of Wise, but he had another idea.[73] The synagogue owned three adjacent buildings on West Sixty-Eighth Street, and their maintenance costs had become burdensome.[74] Wise proposed that the institute purchase them[75] for conversion into a dormitory.[76] In May, JIR acquired the buildings at the cost of $110,000, paying $50,000 in cash and taking a $60,000 mortgage from the synagogue. Jubilant, Wise anticipated the "great and glorious day" when the Hannah Heyman Hall would be built.[77]

JIR's treasurer, Edmund Kaufmann, however, saw no point in erecting a dormitory—indeed, he had little enthusiasm for purchasing the buildings at all. "Would not it be well to consider seriously a sinking fund which could be used to carry the institute through some lean year?" he asked Wise.[78]

"You are quite right," Wise told Kaufmann. "At present we have nothing, no such income fund at all, and if the lean years should come, we would be very hard hit. How happy I would be if something could be done, towards that end!"[79]

And yet, Wise also went ahead and purchased a fourth building on the street for JIR, paying $17,000 out of personal funds he received as executor to the Heyman estate and taking on a $20,000 mortgage for the institute.

Scaffolding in Place

For the 1924–1925 academic year, Wise focused on bolstering the institute's instruction in Jewish education, homiletics, and Midrash. He appointed Isaac Kandel, a Romanian-born educator at Columbia's Teachers College, to begin teaching in the fall, and he invited David Yellin, a Palestinian Jewish educator, to offer courses in education as well as Hebrew literature and Bible in the spring.[80] A native of Jerusalem and a leading figure in the movement to revive the Hebrew language, Yellin had helped create the Jewish National Library, compiled a Hebrew dictionary, and published several textbooks on Hebrew instruction while also running a Hebrew teachers' college and participating in the political leadership of the Yishuv.[81] While at JIR, Yellin would also lecture at Columbia on Hebrew and Arabic literature.

Homiletics and Midrash proved a particular challenge. Who would teach preaching under Wise's watchful eye? Initially, he engaged Joel Blau, rabbi of New York's Temple Peni-El, but soon Blau was complaining about his compensation and status, and Wise had misgivings about his pedagogy.[82] Virtually all of his students, Wise observed, were imitating their homiletics instructor's mannerisms. "I am not trying to mould the Institute in my own image, and I do not propose to permit the students to be moulded after the image of one member of the Faculty," Wise recalled telling Blau.[83] After the situation came to a head in September, Wise took over the teaching of homiletics together with Nathan Krass, rabbi at Temple Emanu-El, and Blau promptly quit.[84]

"I promise you we shall not try to duplicate our inimitable selves," Wise told his friend Louis Grossmann, mindful of his earlier criticism of Blau, "for God knows one Krass is enough and one Stephen Wise is more than enough."[85]

In desperate need of a Midrash instructor, Wise yet again reached out to Mordecai Kaplan—and finally got a yes.[86] Having nearly resigned from the seminary a year earlier, perhaps Kaplan felt emboldened, and apparently Cyrus Adler now gave him a bit more latitude. Regardless, in the fall of 1924, JIR students could boast studying homiletics with Stephen S. Wise and Midrash with Mordecai Kaplan.

But with Kaplan a temporary appointment, like Kandel and Yellin, Wise had to continue scouring the shifting landscape of Jewish scholarship for faculty. From his efforts thus far, he knew that the benefits of working at JIR did not always outweigh the pull of other institutions, be they in Europe, the United States, or even Palestine. Two of the Europeans Wise had interviewed the previous summer—Samuel Krauss of Vienna and Ludwig Blau of Budapest—now planned to join Hebrew University,[87] Wolfson and Obermann seemed reluctant at best to teach at JIR, and some of the men Wise had wanted most—Kaplan and Elbogen—refused to leave their home institutions, despite difficult circumstances in each case.

Still, for the overall endeavor of American Jewish scholarship, Wise's hiring was starting to have significant consequences. The institute was effectively attracting capable faculty from other Jewish institutions of higher learning, as evidenced by the hiring of Bloch, Tchernowitz, and Slonimsky. To have continued impact at JIR and in the broader field, Wise had no choice but to make peace with the ongoing rotation of faculty at West Sixty-Eighth Street, which reflected the broader transformation underway in Jewish higher education as scholars across the globe felt pushed and pulled in various directions. More faculty would leave the institute, but plenty of others would seek to teach there.

Meanwhile, Jewish studies was finally beginning to inch its way into American secular higher education. For this advance, JIR was about to pay a significant price.

HARRY WOLFSON AND THE LITTAUER CHAIR

Wolfson was the next to go. First, in January, he received an invitation from Hebrew Union College to occupy the chair in Jewish philosophy recently left vacant with the death of David Neumark. Wolfson weighed the pros and cons: While JIR offered the intellectual and cultural life of New York City, the ability to remain at Harvard, and greater freedom, HUC promised a higher salary, more funds for research, and greater long-term stability. "The Institute, like my former instructor-ship, but on a larger scale, is being fed from hand to mouth by generous friends," he told Mack. "What would happen if the attention of the generous friends should someday be diverted elsewhere? How would the faculty be taken care of?"[88]

Wise and the board chose not to issue a counteroffer. For a second year, Wolfson had failed to show up to teach at the beginning of the spring semester, this time claiming he needed more time to complete his fall grading.[89] "If he have only blue, green or purple books to correct," Wise told Mack, Wolfson's chief sup-porter, "that might be done in New York."[90] Finally, after agonizing over the HUC decision, Wolfson declined the offer and resumed teaching at JIR. His arrange-ment with the institute, however, was tenuous.

In the late spring of 1925, Lucius Littauer, a Harvard alumnus and member of New York's Temple Emanu-El, established at Harvard the first chair in Jewish studies in the United States. Littauer, formerly a Republican politician who made his fortune in his father's glovemaking business, designated Wolfson as the recipi-ent, and Harvard complied without conducting a search. As holder of the Nathan Littauer Chair in Jewish Literature and Philosophy, Wolfson had the job security he sought, and he promptly resigned from JIR.[91]

For the Jewish scholarly world, the appointment represented "the embodiment of our studies in the Universities Literarum" for which Elbogen had yearned. But for JIR, despite the difficulties the Wolfson presented—his reluctance to teach, and the subsidy the institute had promised Harvard—his departure marked a sig-nificant loss. The philosopher's keen intellect and prominence had immeasurably advanced the institute's effort to become the great scholarly center envisioned by the institute's founders. Given the degree to which Wolfson's students at Harvard appreciated his teaching and guidance, ostensibly, if he had ever settled in at JIR, the students there would have benefited from his presence similarly.

But this was not to be, thanks to yet another Reform philanthropist from Temple Emanu-El, who made a landmark contribution elsewhere.

FUNDRAISING CHALLENGES
In one regard, the loss of Wolfson proved beneficial for JIR: No longer would the institute have to pay Harvard in order to retain him half-time on Sixty-Eighth Street. This came as particularly welcome relief, because just as Harvard was cel-ebrating the establishment of the Littauer Chair, negotiations for the synagogue merger, aimed in part at placing the institute on stronger financial footing, col-lapsed. Wise had failed to garner sufficient support for building a new sanctuary and then refused a compromise arrangement that would have entailed his perma-nently conducting services in two different sites.[92]

In truth, despite his initial enthusiasm, after two years of trying to work out an agreement, he was relieved the Free Synagogue could "cut loose" from Central.[93]

Unfortunately for JIR, however, any hope for increased contributions from an "amalgamated synagogue" evaporated.

The institute now held at least $80,000 in mortgage debt, and the school's 1922 budget of $35,000 had tripled to approximately $100,000 for 1925.[94] This included the support JIR continued to send the five seminaries in Europe, which Mack now urged Wise to endow with somewhere between $50,000 and $100,000.[95] Wise, however, could hardly create an endowment for the European institutions when he had none in place for JIR.

Recognizing faculty chairs as the single best way to ensure financial stability, not just for Harvard but for the institute, too, in the spring of 1925 Wise made several more attempts to establish these, soliciting members of Pittsburgh's Rodef Shalom Congregation for a chair in memory of their deceased rabbi, J. Leonard Levy, and appealing to Boston philanthropists for a chair in memory of Charles William Eliot, the Harvard president who had opposed a Jewish quota system, quite unlike his successor. Both efforts garnered modest gifts, but neither yielded a fully funded chair.

Wise tried another approach—creating a circle of about fifty to one hundred donors amenable to giving between one and five thousand dollars annually; here, too, he achieved only limited success.[96]

Ambitious fundraising underway by JIR's closest competitors at this time could not have helped matters. HUC was in the midst of $5 million endowment campaign chaired by Adolph Ochs, publisher of the *New York Times* and Isaac Mayer Wise's son-in-law, and JTS was pursuing a $1 million goal, similarly relying on wealthy Reform supporters, including Louis Marshall, Mortimer Schiff, and Felix Warburg, who in 1924 gave $215,000 to purchase adjoining properties on West 123rd Street to build a new home for the seminary's library.[97] JIR still lacked the support of these elite donors, and given the failed synagogue merger and the lackluster results of Wise's efforts to endow faculty chairs, the institute desperately needed a new funding structure.

Promising New Faculty

Yet, with or without an infusion of cash, continued implementation of the curriculum required replacing not only Wolfson but also Kaplan, Kandel, and Yellin. Here, at last, JIR's ability to retain leading scholars and practitioners from the United States as well as Europe mitigated the recent losses.

Locally, two protégés of Samson Benderly, the Zionist educator, joined the faculty: Shalom Maximon, a noted Hebraist and teacher, signed on to teach Midrash, and Isaac Berkson, a Columbia-trained psychologist known for his "Theories of Americanization," took the post in education.[98]

In the area of history, Wise decided to take a chance on two youthful scholars: twenty-four-year-old Cecil Roth of Oxford and thirty-year-old Salo Baron of the Hebrew Paedagogium in Vienna. Baron, the more accomplished, held doctorates in philosophy, political science, and law from the University of Vienna, as well as rabbinic ordination from Vienna's Israelitisch-Theologische Lehranstalt, and had already published two books challenging Heinrich Graetz's approach to Jewish history. Both men practiced a new methodology that would come to be called social history.

Finally, the JIR board decided to invite Israel Abrahams back for a semester. The school would benefit from the elder statesman's intellect and stature in the Liberal Jewish movement in England while his non-Zionism demonstrated JIR's continued openness to a range of viewpoints.

CURRICULAR INNOVATION

After four years of constant faculty turnover, in which JIR wrestled with the same forces in the broader world of Jewish scholarship that were pushing and pulling many individuals and institutions in multiple directions, a core group finally coalesced. And despite the tremendous flux, as well as the internal battles over the curriculum and its methodology, this group succeeded in creating an innovative course of study that effectively embodied the institute's mission. The unique academic infrastructure they built enabled faculty to teach out of their own traditions and areas of expertise while also providing students with ample opportunity to explore contemporary issues in Jewish life and the rabbinate. Because the vast majority of students sought to become rabbis, and not professional scholars or social workers, some faculty desiderata had to be let go. At the same time, in several important areas, the faculty broke new ground.

Faculty members like Obermann and Levy, who had hoped to mentor future scholars, realized the futility of any such expectation. Similarly, in 1925, when a Training School for Jewish Social Work opened in New York City (with the Free Synagogue's Lee K. Frankel as board vice president), JIR lost all impetus to provide this kind of training on-site. Instead, Goldstein, Slonimsky, and Baron would occasionally teach at the Training School of their own volition.[99]

While research and social work were dropped as distinct programs, both areas retained a strong presence in the rabbinical curriculum. In addition, now that a critical mass of core faculty shared a commitment to progressivism and Zionism, these, too, came to have a strong presence in the curriculum. Indeed, while a majority of courses covered traditional rabbinical seminary subjects, in other areas, JIR developed a unique approach to rabbinical training.

The traditional areas included Bible, Mishnah and Talmud, Midrash, and ethics. Substantial study was also required in theology and philosophy, with slightly less in history and liturgy. The students could also take a variety of electives, such as Arabic with Obermann, Medieval Hebrew poetry and biblical commentaries with Yellin, and cantillation with Binder. In addition, all seniors were required to complete a research thesis. This part of the curriculum resembled HUC's, but differed from that of JTS, which put far greater emphasis on Talmud and halakhah.

While delivering these traditional offerings, the curriculum also took an innovative approach aimed at creating a new kind of American rabbi. For the students, the opportunity to learn with Wise each week, both in and out of the classroom, was most influential. The institute's unique prioritization of social service, Hebrew, religious education, and comparative religion also helped shape the cadre of which Wise had long dreamed.

When not out of town, Wise was often the first to arrive at early morning chapel services, where he would hail the barely awake students with a cheery "good morning" as they arrived and join heartily in singing the prayers led by Harry Lewis. On Fridays, services began at a later hour and featured Abraham W. Binder at the organ and a student sermon of 15–20 minutes. The entire student body attended, and in Wise's preaching practicum, which immediately followed, they were asked to evaluate and criticize the sermon. A twenty-minute discussion ensued, in which Wise invited disagreement and urged the students to speak freely and independently.[100]

Finally, Wise would launch a critique of his own. Form and content both came in for a drubbing, recalled J. X. Cohen '29, citing the example of Henry Schorr '26, who delivered a sermon criticizing a point made by Horace Kallen in a recent talk on campus. After students had a chance to opine in the discussion that followed, Wise spoke. "When he had completed his dissection of the sermon and his cutting comments on the preacher, the poor sermonizer was ready for a stretcher. Dr. Wise literally lashed poor Schorr to pieces. He said his answer was no answer at all. Had Kallen heard it, Kallen would have rightly exclaimed 'behold, my judgments are vindicated.'"[101]

Jacob Rudin '28 remembered a similar experience after delivering his first trial sermon in the JIR chapel. "I had conceded to myself that others had preached better sermons. But I wasn't modest enough. Dr. Wise confided to me, in the presence of the assembled student body, that I had set new standards of ineffectiveness. Indeed, through all the intervening years, I have derived a perverse satisfaction from the belief that my record still stands unchallenged, nay, unapproachable. So we deviously give to failure a lustre that success itself might envy."[102]

Thursday afternoons, Wise and students in the upper classes sat around a circular table to discuss contemporary Jewish problems.[103] Here, imbuing them with his own approach to the rabbinate, he would begin by describing a pressing issue in Jewish life with which he was involved and then elicit the students' reactions.[104] In the discussion that followed, he listened carefully and often took detailed notes, for he considered the group, in many ways representative of a new generation of American Jews of Eastern European descent, a valuable sounding board.[105] The weekly meeting had a profound impact on students and represented, for many, the highlight of their contact with Wise.[106] Often, he shared a box of cigars provided by a congregant; though his doctor forbade him to smoke, he obviously enjoyed the male bonding.[107] The students learned the tools of a publicly engaged rabbinate and derived a model of Jewish leadership that fused the pursuit of social justice with Zionism.[108]

These were bolstered by other innovations in the curriculum. The emphasis on teaching Modern Hebrew *ivrit b'ivrit* and the Zionist approach to religious education reflected a prioritization of peoplehood over religious creed.[109] Goldstein's courses in social service ensured that students gained exposure to various strategies that rabbis and other communal leaders were using to address social and economic problems in the Jewish community. Comparative religion broadened the students' perspectives and fostered the intellectual openness and free exchange of ideas so central to JIR's ethos.

Students were also permitted to earn credit at neighboring academic institutions. Like Irma Lindheim, Philip Bernstein studied with John Dewey at Columbia Teachers College, and several students took courses at the New School for Social Research.[110] In this way, JIR benefited from the New York area's Jewish and scholarly resources, as the founders had hoped. And in due course, as JIR began to consolidate, those institutions began to benefit, as well, including not only the congregations that served as student pulpits but also the general public who attended the institute's extension courses and public lectures. By bringing serious scholars to Sixty-Eighth Street, JIR itself was becoming a highly regarded scholarly resource.

On top of the heavy course load, the students were also required to learn the practical skills of the rabbinate through fieldwork assignments in congregations across the metropolitan area and beyond.[111] These included mostly Reform congregations located in New York, Connecticut, New Jersey, and Pennsylvania, which students visited each Friday through Sunday.[112] A few students who held "all week" pulpits in the outer boroughs or nearby cities like Newark lived near their jobs and commuted into Manhattan to attend classes.[113]

The Reform movement's leadership could hardly have been pleased to see so many positions available for JIR students. If these worked out well, congregations might become favorably disposed toward supporting the institute, and in just a few years, they might hire JIR alumni to be their rabbis. In light of this unwelcome competition, the union and the college remained firm in their opposition to any form of cooperation with JIR. When, for example, the JIR board reached out to HUC to explore mutual recognition of course credits and an occasional exchange of faculty, Morgenstern declared these out of the question.[114] A better spirit might prevail in the future, he suggested, and perhaps the two schools would one day operate under the aegis of the UAHC; for the time being, however, no agreement could be reached.[115]

By the spring of 1925, JIR's initial growing pains were past. Wise had built a strong faculty, despite the endless rotation. Slonimsky was "making himself loved," Wise reported to Louis Grossmann, and quickly taking on extra responsibilities like serving as faculty representative to the board and co-teaching a course with Wise at Columbia during Richard Gottheil's sabbatical.[116] Tchernowitz, despite the imminent opening of Hebrew University, had decided to remain at the institute. Harry Lewis, the school's chaplain, was an unusually effective teacher, and Goldstein was pioneering the social service curriculum. In Bible, while Obermann continued to rile, students enjoyed studying with Reuben Levy. At least one prominent Christian scholar taught each semester, as well.

Retaining the faculty, rather than attracting them to the institute in the first place, had proven the greater challenge, as repeatedly, the institute lost gifted faculty to secular institutions of higher learning. But Wise had facilitated the Joshua Bloch arrangement with the New York Public Library, and he never had a chance at keeping Harry Wolfson once Harvard, his alma mater and home institution, made their offer. Wise also understood that these appointments, while dealing a blow to the institute, broke important new ground in the overarching field of Jewish higher learning.

In addition, for all the faculty turnover and turmoil over the curriculum, students were now receiving a solid grounding in Jewish texts, history, thought, and practice while also gaining exposure to contemporary best practices in social service and Jewish education, the major challenges facing global Jewry, and of course, Wise's approach to creating a publicly engaged rabbinate.

The Institute had truly become a nondenominational seminary, with all the challenges and strengths that model brought to bear. Securing a reliable stream of funding posed the greatest difficulty for the moment, but Wise, who always managed to scrape together what he needed, remained optimistic. Meanwhile, everyone at JIR could take immense pride in the school's independent *Scope and Purpose*, which began to appear in the institute's prospectus in 1925:

> The Jewish Institute of Religion, liberal in spirit, does not commit its teachers to any special interpretation of Judaism. All Jews possess in common the same literature, the same history, the same varied religious experiences, and these are studied scientifically in the classroom. The different interpretations of the literature, history and religion, the different constructions of Judaism and of Jewish life, orthodox, conservative, liberal, radical, Zionist and non-Zionist, are expounded to the students in courses given by men representing different points of view. Every member of the teaching staff is free to see and to state the truth as he sees it, and in the same way every student is free.[117]

Everything now in place at the institute—the faculty, curriculum and field-work program, as well as the board, the buildings, and the school's mission itself—represented an enormous investment dedicated to the training of a new kind of rabbi. Whether the outlay of time, money, and effort would pay off now depended on the biggest variable of all: the students themselves, and their capacity and willingness to take up the gauntlet.[118]

8

The First Cadre

ROM THE START, ENROLLING AT JIR ENTAILED RISK. THE VAST MAJORITY of students intended to become rabbis, yet they had chosen a seminary lacking any track record and maligned by Jewish leaders from every stream of American Judaism.

Still, they had reason for optimism. Thanks to the nation's economic boom as well as the Jewish community's population growth following decades of mass immigration, synagogue life was expanding. In the Reform movement alone, the number of congregations shot up from 209 in 1922 to 273 in 1925, creating an unprecedented demand for American rabbis. In 1924, while more than one hundred pulpits needed to be filled, only about twenty rabbis were ordained by HUC and JTS combined. "Slow as is the process of sending out Rabbis, and great as is the demand for them," the American Hebrew reported, "it is nevertheless the part of wisdom to fill the need only with high-minded, scholarly men who will be certain to stimulate the communities to which they are called toward a finer conception of Judaism and a more intensive living of its practical idealism."[1] The newspaper assured readers that more rabbis were in the pipeline, with 107 students currently enrolled at HUC, 75 at JTS, and 49 at JIR.

These men required training that addressed the new challenges facing American rabbis in the 1920s. In addition to meeting the usual demands—scholarship, liturgical leadership, life cycle observance, pastoral care, and religious education— they would have to navigate the changing demographics of their synagogues while also advocating for American Jewry's needs in society at large. The new expectations of rabbis included representing one's local Jewish community in interfaith settings and the public arena and addressing the widespread antisemitism being stoked by Henry Ford and others at this time, which had serious reverberations. Discriminatory policies in housing, employment, and education were becoming more prevalent, and in 1924 Congress enacted the Johnson-Reed Act, which effectively closed the nation's doors to more than ten million Eastern European Jews in need of refuge and relief.

JIR students received an in-depth tutorial on Wise's methods for melding pulpit responsibilities with public engagement around virtually every pressing issue of the day. At the Free Synagogue, he pastored to his congregants and oversaw a staff and volunteer team that ran the religious school, Social Service Department, and extension sites around the city. Every Sunday morning, he preached to a large crowd at Carnegie Hall, where the congregation continued to hold services. Through his sermons, which often garnered Monday headlines in the *New York Times* and other papers, Wise addressed Zionism, antisemitism, and immigration and much more. He criticized the growing wealth gap and advocated for the rights of labor; he discussed social concerns related to marriage, the family, and a perceived youth rebellion; and, with an eye always to the global situation, he warned about Mussolini's rise to power and urged greater US aid for European governments to maintain geopolitical stability and prevent another world war. Meanwhile, beyond the pulpit, as president of the American Jewish Congress, he lobbied the federal government to ease immigration restrictions and enact legislation that would protect Jews and other minority groups from discrimination. On the Zionist front, he rejoined the ZOA's leadership and agreed to chair the United Palestine Appeal's $15 million campaign.

Just as Adolf Jellinek had taken Wise under his wing, Wise regularly brought JIR students into his confidence, sharing the ways he worked at every level of Jewish life. And through weekly meetings, monthly dinners, and individual conferences with Wise, these students took in his perspective on a range of issues as well as his strategies for leadership and change.

At the same time, Wise insisted that the students form their own opinions rather than parroting him or anyone else. An independent and outspoken rabbinate, Wise hoped, would be one of JIR's significant contributions to American Judaism. "From the moment we entered the Institute he insisted upon absolute freedom for teacher and student alike," Philip Bernstein said, "and although undoubtedly hoping that most of the graduates would share his views, said and meant that he would be happy if the men would not agree with him."[2]

Throughout the 1920s, JIR students had ample opportunity to debate their views with classmates while also trying out their new skills in fieldwork placements around the metropolitan area. And after the institute's first class of rabbis graduated in 1926, they began bringing their approach into the congregations they served.

Their entry into the rabbinate immediately proved disruptive for the Reform movement, which encompassed many of the congregations they served. Until now, HUC had held a monopoly on rabbinical placement in UAHC congregations, and the CCAR functioned essentially as an alumni organization for the college. As JIR rabbis entered both spheres, advancing an outlook shared by a large swath of American Jewry, it was inevitable that the institutions of Reform Judaism would change—the only questions were when and how.

STUDENTS

The students came from diverse backgrounds and debated plenty. In the institute's earliest years, nearly half were born outside the United States, with less than a quarter from New York City. More than a few young men, upon hearing Wise speak for the first time, decided on the spot to change their career plans to follow him into the rabbinate. Robert P. Jacobs, for example, who graduated JIR in 1933, recalled his father taking him to the one-thousand-seat Loew's State Theater in downtown Syracuse in the fall of 1928 to hear Wise. "That one speech changed my life," he later recalled. "I would become a rabbi and go to his school for my studies."[3] Each year, admissions grew increasingly competitive as graduates of Harvard, Yale, Columbia, the University of Chicago, Cornell, City College of New York, and other schools sought to enroll.

JIR's nondenominationalism attracted students with varying approaches to traditional observance. "Religious practices take in the whole gamut of Jewish attitudes," observed a reporter who spent time at the school in the winter of 1924. "There are those whose daily use of 'Tefillin' begets the warm respect of the ultra-reform who wants all prayers in English and wants prayers cut down to the very minute. The 'Shomer Shabbos' who wears his hat regularly chums with the graduate of Western Reform Temple where hats are never seen."[4]

"The students disagree on everything but two," the reporter wrote. "On these two points, they are unanimous. Every student at the school is a thoroughgoing, intensively ardent Zionist. One wonders how it is that non-Zionists have not come to the school, but would they not soon be converted if they came? The students think in terms of Zionism, and their objections to reform Judaism (as generally presented) always include this matter of Zionism."[5]

"The second matter that wins the unanimous and hearty approval of the boys," the reporter noted, "is the love of the school. Only a fool would attempt to say which love were greater, for both are so blended together and harmonize. It is a school of Zionism; it is the Zionist strain that helps make the school strong and distinctive."[6]

Many brought experience in Young Judaea or the intercollegiate Menorah Association, groups that Wise frequently addressed during the many visits he made to college campuses each year on the lookout for JIR prospects.[7] Jacob Rudin '28 first met Wise as a junior at Harvard in 1923 when he attended a Menorah meeting on campus, where the rabbi "unsettled and disturbed him."[8]

"I heard a man speak as I had never heard a man speak before," Rudin recalled. "He dominated the room and all who were in it. His voice shook us as a wind shakes the reeds. He talked of a homeland for the Jews. He talked about justice in an unjust world. And he talked about a school he had just founded in New York, a school for the training of rabbis, where no special sectarian allegiance would be asked, where there would be room for all who came to study in truth, where the dream of a people would be articulated and finalized. I knew then and there that I would go to the JIR if Dr. Wise would have me."[9]

Another feature stood out to the reporter when he visited campus: "The strong personal admiration that the boys hold for the school's founder and acting president," which appeared as "little short of the best hero-worship." The students shared affection with one another, too, he added. They "good naturedly kid one another, and for those who live in the dormitory adjoining the school, spend a great deal of time together in work as well as play."[10]

Of course, Irma Lindheim and Dora Askowith, the two women enrolled as regular students, neither lived in the dorm nor shared in the camaraderie enjoyed by the male students. Bringing very different life experiences, and pathbreakers in their own unique ways, they likely had little interest in doing so. Lindheim, an heiress, stayed at an apartment near the institute all week, making weekend visits to her husband and five children on Long Island. She had a deep desire for Jewish learning and still sought ordination. Askowith, who had begun classes at JIR to deepen her knowledge while pursuing her academic career at Hunter College, lived on her own. Both women devoted themselves intensely to their studies and joined their classmates in expressing their views in the classroom as well as the chapel. Askowith, for example, preached on women in the rabbinate, arguing that nothing in Judaism justified their exclusion.

The student body also produced a journal where they debated a broad range of issues. In the May 1925 issue of the *Jewish Institute Quarterly*, editor John Tepfer '27 declared:

> We are not bound by any rigid expression of Judaism, its theory or practice. Just as little are we Reformed as Orthodox. We do not have to use up our energies supporting ancient and perhaps crumbling walls. We do not have to spend ourselves holding the door against hostile and unholy forces—science or nationalism—trying to break into our sanctum. No! we throw the doors wide open and invite all to come in . . .
>
> There is no use our saying we are but students and do not know enough. It is now we have to make our discoveries, formulate our experiences, analyze our concepts. Thus only can we become sure of the interpretation we are tomorrow going to give the world from platform and pulpit. We who have to convince others that Judaism, as we see it, is the highest expression of our entire modern life and thought, must first with the facilities offered by the Institute, find this expression for ourselves . . .[11]

In the pages of the *Quarterly*, students critiqued the various streams of Judaism, proposed new approaches to liturgy, and discussed matters of God and spirit.

Some wrote about their experience in the Great War, while others advocated pacifism or criticized American materialism. They explored the prophetic tradition's bearing on matters of social and economic justice and debated Jewish particularism versus universalism. Seeking to "revivify" or "reconstruct" liberal Judaism, various students embraced Hebrew renewal, Jewish scholarship, Yiddish culture, and Jewish arts and literature. Frequently, they discussed Zionism and the power of Jewish peoplehood to unite Jews across the religious spectrum.

The Field Activities program provided a laboratory in the Jewish community where students could test their ideas and hone their skills while also earning much-needed income. Amid the national shortage of rabbis, neither JIR's lack of affiliation with a particular stream of Judaism nor the students' Zionism impeded the institute from securing sufficient synagogue placements for the growing student body. Important for the institute as a whole, this indicated the degree to which congregational leaders regarded the new seminary as a legitimate training ground.

To build the program, Sidney Goldstein traveled across the region urging synagogue leaders to hire JIR students, and by 1925, a wide array of congregations were doing so.[12] Geographically, they reflected the migration of the Jewish community from the most densely populated neighborhoods of the city to the outer boroughs and eventually into suburban communities in upstate New York, Long Island, Connecticut, and New Jersey, with a few as far as Pennsylvania and Massachusetts.[13] Many congregations entered the system as High Holy Day positions and then grew into regular weekend pulpits; in addition, a small number of "all week" pulpits were located within or near the City, in places like Yorkville, Borough Park, Flushing, Staten Island, and Newark.[14] New students without year-long pulpits conducted High Holy Day services at venues ranging from the Eastview Penitentiary, which held overflow services, to the elite Harmonie Club on the Upper East Side.[15]

The Free Synagogue and its satellite congregations, still intent on preparing rabbis to lead the national movement they envisioned, also hired students. The Flushing Free Synagogue hired Max Meyer '26 as acting rabbi in 1923,[16] and in 1925, Jacob X. Cohen '29 became assistant director of the Free Synagogue's Social Service Department.[17] The Social Service Department also provided fellowships for two students each year to work at sites including Bellevue and Lebanon Hospitals,[18] Stuyvesant House (a settlement on the Lower East Side), the Bernard Cantor Memorial School at Clinton Hall, the Bronx School at the London Casino,[19] and the Stony Wold Sanitorium.[20] And every Shabbat afternoon during the academic year, students offered congregants a service in the chapel on West Sixty-Eighth Street, with upper-level students and faculty sharing preaching responsibilities and Abraham W. Binder directing a student choir.

In their senior year, students maintained a rigorous schedule taking courses and commuting to their pulpits, while also completing a thesis. At this point, a few left the program, but most eagerly anticipated receiving Wise's blessing and entering the rabbinate.

Lindheim and Askowith each chose to leave the institute for different reasons. Lindheim and her husband had been fighting his 1920 conviction for years, but in March 1924, Norvin finally served his jail sentence. The one-month experience proved grueling for both of them, and Irma's health took a turn for the worse. A year later, on doctor's orders to rest, she traveled to Palestine, where she decided to devote herself fully to Zionism. She withdrew from JIR and after returning to New York succeeded the legendary Henrietta Szold as national president of Hadassah. Askowith, by contrast, took a leave of absence from the institute after receiving a Barnard alumnae fellowship to conduct research in 1924–1925 at the American School of Oriental Research in Jerusalem and the American Academy in Rome. Upon return, she put off resuming her coursework to continue her research, writing, and teaching at Hunter. She also taught a Sunday afternoon extension course on comparative religion at JIR.[21]

Far more disappointing for Wise was his son James's decision to leave the institute shortly before graduating. As a student, he had published a short book, *Liberalizing Liberal Judaism*, which was roundly criticized in the *Jewish Institute Quarterly* by fellow student Philip Bernstein, who felt James's universalism went too far. The younger Wise did hold left-wing politics, but he was also as ardent a Zionist as his father. James told the *New York Times* that he left JIR because he lacked any sort of religious conviction, and while serving at his student pulpit in White Plains his unsuitability for the rabbinate had become clear. After withdrawing from the institute in the spring of 1926, James began editing *Opinion*, a journal published by the American Jewish Congress.[22]

ORDINATION

Undeterred by these departures, on May 26, 1926, six years after making public his vision for the school in a sermon at Carnegie Hall, Wise conferred on JIR's first ten graduates the Master of Hebrew Literature degree and the title rabbi.[23] The ceremony marked a milestone for everyone at the institute. As the graduates received Wise's blessing before the ark in the same chapel where they had attended so many morning services and delivered their trial sermons, they assumed not only the responsibility and privilege that came with the title rabbi but also the expectation that they would ably carry forth the mission of the institute. For, while entering the rabbinate would test them as individuals, the quality of their leadership would also reveal the efficacy of JIR and the return on years of investment by its acting president, faculty, and donors.

The ceremony garnered substantial coverage in the Jewish as well as the secular press. Honorary degrees were conferred upon Hayyim Nahman Bialik, whom

Tchernowitz hailed as "the national poet of the Jewish Renaissance," and Claude G. Montefiore, scholar and founder of liberal Judaism in England.[24] Wise selected a Zionist and a non-Zionist intentionally to celebrate the school's pluralism. While Montefiore could not attend the ceremony due to illness, Bialik addressed the gathering in Hebrew.

The faculty awarded prizes to students who had excelled in their disciplines. For outstanding academic performance, Morton Berman became the first recipient of the Guggenheimer Fellowship for a year of study in Palestine, which Irma Lindheim's aunt, Bertha Guggenheimer, had endowed through a gift of $25,000.[25]

In his own remarks, Wise called for greater exchange between Jewish and Christian seminaries. Proud that JIR had brought six Christian scholars to lecture in the four years since its founding, he deemed such interchange "absolutely essential for modern religious toleration."[26]

Then, lamenting the dearth of men preparing for the rabbinate, Wise addressed the power of the preacher in American life. "It is sometimes held that the day of the minister has passed, that the spoken pulpit word has no place in the life of the modern world," he said. "The truth is that men are just as ready today as ever to listen to the man who is an humble and unafraid truthseeker." He called upon the ten new rabbis to summon American Jews back to the high places of spiritual life and to an understanding of the genius of Jewish history.[27]

THE FIRST JIR RABBIS

For JIR's competitors, the visibility and symbolic value of the institute's first graduation likely garnered less concern than its success placing newly minted rabbis in full-time pulpits. HUC and JTS alumni now had to compete with graduates of Wise's "Zionist school," whose training set them apart, as did the expectations Wise had of them. He advocated strenuously, if behind the scenes, to secure placements for all graduating seniors, most of whom landed positions in Reform or Conservative congregations in the New York area. Of the first graduating class, Philip Bernstein went farthest afield, joining Temple B'rith Kodesh of Rochester, New York, one of the larger and older Reform congregations in the United States, as assistant rabbi.

Over the next few years, admissions proceeded apace, and the institute continued to attract students from across the country, including a good number from elite universities like Harvard and Columbia, as well as CCNY and other public schools.[28] And each May, a new crop of JIR graduates entered the rabbinate, with a Guggenheimer Fellow headed to Palestine for a year of study and Wise helping secure placements for all the others.

At times, graduates seeking pulpits ran into challenges. Within Reform congregations, especially, candidates with a Yiddish accent encountered pervasive discrimination, and lay leaders sometimes expressed reluctance to hire a JIR rabbi out of either anti-Zionism or loyalty to HUC. In frustration, Louis I. Newman, back in California, where he had assumed the pulpit of Congregation Emanu-El after the death of their rabbi and his former mentor, Martin Meyer, complained that just as Jews had to meet a higher bar than non-Jews to get jobs in the secular world, "so an Institute man must be much better than an HUC man."[29] Nevertheless, most alumni secured placements despite these obstacles, and by the fall of 1929, twenty-six held pulpits.

As the Free Synagogue founders of JIR had hoped, several graduates joined their growing movement. Wise hired Jacob Rudin '28 to serve as assistant rabbi at the Free Synagogue as well as JIR's director of field activities, and Jacob X. Cohen '29 became the congregation's associate rabbi. Cohen, who entered rabbinical school after a career in engineering, had already participated in the establishment of the Free Synagogue's Bronx branch and assisted in planning the new building on Sixty-Eighth Street. The Free Synagogue of Flushing hired Max Meyer as their permanent rabbi, Abram Goodman '28 helped found the Free Synagogue of Westchester, and Isadore Breslau '28 led the Washington Heights Free Synagogue for a short time before moving to Temple Israel in Waterbury, Connecticut.

While most alumni took positions in Reform congregations on the East Coast, some went to the South or the West. Morton Berman '26, after returning from his Guggenheimer Fellowship in Palestine and Europe, accepted a job in Davenport, Iowa, on Wise's advice that he experience American Jewish life outside New York, as Wise had as a young rabbi in Oregon. Benjamin Goldstein '26 went to Montgomery, Alabama, and Victor Eppstein to Havana, Cuba. Abraham Dubin and Joshua Goldberg took positions at Conservative congregations in Cedarhurst, Long Island, and the Astoria Center of Israel, respectively, and Zwi Anderman, Ephraim Fischoff, and Morris Rose went to more traditional congregations, as well.

Freshly ensconced in their communities, many of these new rabbis discovered that their views, once considered marginal, particularly in Reform congregations, were increasingly welcome among a new generation of American Jews. They brought their perspectives to bear at the grassroots, through their teaching, preaching, and pastoral presence. Gradually, they began implementing institutional change, too. For those in congregations founded by German Reform Jews, this often entailed integrating the new concerns of a growing Eastern European membership. In Rochester, for example, Philip Bernstein, who took over as senior rabbi after his predecessor died unexpectedly in 1927, introduced a "liberalism steeped in Jewish tradition." Under his leadership, the congregation instituted bar mitzvah ceremonies and Hebrew instruction and replaced Protestant music with Jewish repertoire.[30] Typical of his classmates, Bernstein also participated in local communal affairs, serving on the Rochester Housing Commission to work for fair housing, arbitrating labor disputes, and regularly speaking out on matters of economic and social justice at the City Club and elsewhere.

Many alumni also continued their work in the Zionist movement, fundraising for the United Palestine Appeal, or providing leadership for their local or regional district. Not all of Wise's former students shared his political views, however. By the late 1920s, as the situation in Palestine grew increasingly violent, a small but growing cohort, including Louis I. Newman and Morris Rose '26, were gravitating toward Vladimir Jabotinsky's more militant Revisionist camp.[31]

An Emerging Presence Within the Institutions of Reform

Whereas Wise knew that most JIR alumni shared his fundamental commitments, differing on matters of strategy rather than end goals, the leaders of Reform Judaism could not claim the same ideological support among the Reform rabbinate. As each year a growing number of JIR graduates garnered UAHC pulpits and joined the CCAR, forcing Reform leaders to fend off an incursion, the relative strengths of the two sides became apparent. In outlook, the JIR contingent more closely aligned with that large swath of American Jewry who had no compunction in hiring JIR rabbis. However, in resources and infrastructure, the institutions of Reform had far more strength. They needed each other, and though neither side extended an olive branch during this period, they each took steps that suggested a mutual recognition of Reform Judaism's changing ethos.

Much to the consternation of HUC's leadership, alongside the growing number of JIR men with UAHC pulpits and membership in the CCAR, rabbis and rabbinical students from the college were also increasingly adopting the priorities that Wise, and not the Reform leadership, had long been preaching. A handful of Zionist HUC alumni had worked alongside Wise in the past, including Max Heller '84, Abba Hillel Silver '15, James Heller '16, and Edward Israel '19. Now, younger HUC rabbis were also caught up in the Zionist fervor spreading through the American Jewish community, where membership in the Zionist Organization of America grew from just over twenty-four thousand in 1921 to sixty-five thousand in 1929. In espousing their views, students at the college during Morgenstern's presidency, unlike Kohler's, had complete freedom of expression.[32] Still, when it came to promoting Zionism, whereas JIR men had the institutional imprimatur of their seminary, HUC students and alumni placed themselves in opposition to their school's leadership, most of whom (excluding the educator Emanuel Gamoran) remained staunchly opposed.

HUC students also found compelling the prophetic mandate to battle for social and economic justice. Just as Philip Bernstein and many of his JIR classmates made this central to their rabbinates, so, too, did HUC graduates like Ferdinand Isserman '22, Maurice Eisendrath '26, and Joshua Loth Liebman '30. On these issues, they found much stronger support at the college, particularly from the more activist faculty members. Prominent among these was Abraham Cronbach, professor of social studies and an ardent pacifist. Ordained at HUC in 1906,

Cronbach had served with Wise as assistant rabbi of the Free Synagogue from 1915 to 1917, and while he never embraced Zionism, Cronbach was deeply committed to social justice and the pursuit of peace.[33]

Conceivably, JIR and HUC alumni of similar outlook could unite behind a shared agenda within the CCAR, but they faced challenges. Not all JIR rabbis joined the conference, though most with Reform pulpits did. Only a minority of this group, however, attended the national convention each year where critical debates, committee meetings, and votes were held. Finally, tensions between HUC and JIR alumni over competition for pulpits and committee assignments impaired their ability to strategize together. Still, the growing JIR presence within the conference empowered like-minded colleagues from HUC, and together they represented a potential bloc on key issues.

Recognizing an opportunity, Wise urged JIR graduates to participate in the CCAR and began holding a dinner for all alumni at each annual convention, where they could strategize together. By 1929, twenty of thirty-three graduates belonged (including Louis I. Newman, whom Wise considered an honorary alumnus), as did Goldstein, Slonimsky, and Lewis from the faculty, and Wise himself. They were starting to have a more significant presence on committees and in the organization as a whole.

That year, Wise received word that the UAHC, at its convention in San Francisco, had passed a resolution urging cooperation between HUC and JIR. The telegram came from Walter Hilborn, a board member of JIR as well as the Free Synagogue, who had long favored some sort of merger. While Hilborn assumed "the Institute will be rejoiced to consider every possibility of cooperation,"[34] Wise, blindsided, reached out to Newman in California, whose congregation had helped host the convention. "Was this extorted from the Union, was it done in a nice way, do they really want cooperation, or is it merely a sop?"[35] Wise asked.

Without answering his question directly, Newman made clear his suspicions regarding the union's motives. HUC had vested interests in Cincinnati, he told Wise, whereas the need for a liberal school in New York represented JIR's raison d'être. Should the Reform movement perceive JIR as weak and needing money, or Wise as raiding their "pork barrel," Newman warned, "they will press you at every point, and destroy the Institute, just for the sake of raising the 'prestige' of HUC." But, "if the Institute can go its own sweet way in the next few years, graduating capable men, placing them in good positions in the field, the difficulties will appreciably diminish." For now, Newman favored an open exchange of professors and students between the two seminaries, and he believed that eventually, with the passing of the old guard, opposition among Reform leaders, at least in New York, would disappear.[36]

While Wise neither initiated the 1929 move toward cooperation nor intended to propose any sort of shared funding arrangement, the relative financial strength of the two seminaries was undoubtedly in the backdrop, for JIR *did* need money. Over the preceding years, the budget had steadily increased, as Wise invested in faculty, books for the library, the *Jewish Institute Press* and, most extravagantly, real estate. By 1929, the institute had purchased four houses to the east of the JIR building at 40 West Sixty-Eighth Street and three more to the west.[37] Reflecting all of these expenditures and more anticipated, JIR's budget rose from $35,000 in 1922–1923 to a projected $145,000 for 1929–1930.[38]

The institute's primary funding base remained the Free Synagogue, which had ambitious fundraising goals of its own, including the purchase of a site on West 64th Street by Central Park where Wise once again hoped to build an edifice that seated twenty-five hundred. This time the projected cost was $1.5 million, and Wise wanted it done in time for the congregation's twenty-fifth anniversary in 1932.[39] While the Free Synagogue now contributed $25,000 annually to JIR (in addition to space, lay leadership, and the time and energy of their rabbis), with this new project on the docket, the congregation would never have the capacity to serve as the school's sole funder. Not even the UAHC, the representative body of *all* Reform congregations in the country, could maintain Hebrew Union College without the additional support of major individual donors.

Thus, Wise devoted much of his time to raising money for the institute. He solicited individuals, congregations served by JIR men, and community welfare funds in New York and throughout the country, hoping to endow a new library and student hall, as well as professorships, research fellowships, scholarships, summer sessions, and publications. At one point, Wise proposed enlisting one hundred donors to give $1,000 annually for five years, which, combined with the Free Synagogue's annual gift, would have covered most of the budget; like many other ideas, however, this fell by the wayside.[40] He did achieve moderate success, through gifts like that of Temple Beth El of Glens Falls, New York, which committed $1,000 annually for five years, and Bertha Guggenheimer, who died in 1927 and left $25,000 for the institute.[41]

Nevertheless, abundant obstacles stood in the way. For one, Wise continued to have little support within the wealthy German Jewish philanthropic circle whose power and authority he had challenged throughout his career. The institute also had to vie against an array of Jewish causes in need of funds, including relief for European Jewry, the Zionist movement, and the many Jewish organizations and institutions trying to establish themselves in the United States. Also, congregations sending dues to the UAHC had little inclination to pay more for a second school, even when they were benefiting directly from JIR students and rabbis. As a result, Wise was unable to build a substantial synagogue network for JIR and failed to secure the level of support the UAHC provided the college.

A new competitor for Jewish philanthropic dollars was also emerging, mostly undetected but already having a detrimental impact on JIR. Just as moguls like

Rockefeller and Carnegie gave large sums of money to secular institutions of higher learning as a path to respectability, some Jewish donors in the mid-1920s began doing the same. In 1923, a handful of Jews donated over $1.2 million to Harvard University,[42] and the following spring, Samuel Zemurray, a Jewish businessman in New Orleans, rejected appeals from Wise as well as Chaim Weizmann in favor of Tulane University, where he became a preeminent benefactor. Less than a year later, Lucius Littauer endowed the chair at Harvard, making it possible for Wolfson to leave JIR to pursue his research in a secular university.[43] Linda Rosenberg Miller, a widow and Temple Emanu-El member, followed suit, donating $250,000 to Columbia University to establish the Nathan J. Miller Chair in Jewish History, Literature and Institutions, in memory of her husband. In fact, in the midst of a global search to fill the world's first university chair in Jewish history during the summer of 1929, Columbia officials were negotiating with Elbogen, who had remained at the Hochschule since his visiting stint at JIR in 1922.[44]

Wise could take small comfort in the fact that HUC, even with the union's support, was also struggling financially. The college's expansion in the 1920s under Morgenstern had nearly tripled the budget, and with little to draw upon beyond sisterhood scholarships and an endowment of about $500,000, HUC needed a better funding model, as did the UAHC, which could cover neither HUC's costs nor its own.[45] To this end, beginning in 1924, the Reform leadership had taken several steps: First, to secure a regular stream of income for the union as well as the college, the union began assessing congregations a percentage of their annual expenditures rather than relying on membership-based dues and funds raised through annual drives.[46] Next, the college launched the campaign chaired by Ochs to raise its endowment to five million dollars.[47] Finally, at the insistence of Ochs, who chaired HUC's board of governors, as well, the college incorporated as a separate entity from the UAHC in 1926.[48] The Union, no longer responsible for covering the college's expenses in full, would continue to fund a portion of the operating budget while retaining ownership of the school's land and buildings and maintaining control over two-thirds of the board of governors.[49] But now the college could augment the Reform movement's support by raising funds independently, as a distinct legal entity operating under its own charter rather than as a subsidiary of the UAHC.[50]

These changes served the college well, and by the summer of 1929, the campaign had raised $3,600,000. Julius Rosenwald, head of Sears, Roebuck and Company, could take considerable credit for the success, having responded to Ochs's solicitation with a gift of $500,000 (he had given the same amount to Harvard in 1923, and in 1929 he also gave that amount to JTS),[51] conditional on the college raising the endowment to $4 million by July 1, 1929. In response to Ochs's challenge, the Guggenheim and Schiff families each matched Rosenwald's

gift, bringing the endowment to $4,350,000. As the historian of Reform Juda-
ism, Michael Meyer, has noted, 61 percent of this revenue came from just sixteen
people.[52]

A few HUC donors contributed to JIR, as well, including Rosenwald, who
had been one of the principal donors to a fund of $50,000 raised for the institute
in honor of Wise's fiftieth birthday back in 1924.[53] Though opposed to Zionism,
the Chicago-based philanthropist may have had a soft spot for the JIR due to the
long and close relationship he shared with his rabbi, Emil G. Hirsch, the institute's
honorary president until his untimely death. In fact, Rosenwald was among those
who hoped that HUC and JIR, together with JTS, might stop duplicating efforts
and eventually merge. "Our aim should be to bring about a consolidation of the
three main 'rabbi factories' of this country," Rosenwald told Ochs, and rather than
having any one school prevail over the others, "the trite saying, 'United we stand' ...
might be applicable."[54]

Rosenwald was not the only philanthropist urging a seminary merger during
this period. Louis Marshall, chairman of the board of JTS and a significant donor
to Yeshiva College, which opened in 1928, proposed the consolidation of *those* two
schools, as in his view they served, in effect, the same mission. Bernard Revel, head
of Yeshiva College, opposed the idea, however, and managed to fend it off. Primarily concerned that he would hold a diminished role alongside Cyrus Adler, Revel
was bolstered in his stance by the fact that Yeshiva College's faculty would never
agree to work alongside JTS's Mordecai Kaplan, whose radicalism they found as
abhorrent as Wise found it attractive.

The UAHC's interest in cooperating with JIR also failed to gain traction,
though discussions lacked the venom of 1922 and did not concern funding but
student admissions. The college was ordaining its largest class in history in 1929
and having difficulty securing pulpits for all sixteen of its graduates. Recognizing
that a growing number of Reform congregations were now hiring JIR-trained rabbis, the union sought an agreement whereby the two seminaries would limit admissions at a ratio of two to one, HUC to JIR. In return, HUC would allowing its
students to take courses at the institute for credit.

JIR, already capping each incoming class at ten to twelve of its own accord,
refused any fixed admissions ratio, and Louis I. Newman urged Wise not to enter
into any agreement with the college whatsoever. "I am convinced that if HUC had
its way, it would destroy the institute in a moment," he wrote. The institute should
conserve its resources and be wary of "HUC 'diplomats'" as well as any arrangements that would impede JIR's development.[55]

Accordingly, the institute admitted sixteen new students into its entering
class, the largest in its history. In addition, intent on finding ideal placements for
the growing number of JIR graduates, Wise hired Morton Berman '26 as the
school's director of field activities, charging him with visiting every congregation

served by a JIR student or graduate and helping Wise secure jobs for all graduating seniors and alumni.

Significantly, many of their pulpits resembled B'rith Kodesh in Rochester, where a growing portion of the membership were aligning with the JIR outlook. Generally from Eastern European backgrounds, these Jews were attracted to Reform's liberalism but found its Protestant aesthetics off-putting and enjoyed more Hebrew liturgy, Jewish music, and ritual. Unlike the earlier generation, they believed in Jewish peoplehood and gravitated toward outspoken Jewish leaders.

With JIR's 1929 commencement, the institute could pride itself on launching thirty-two rabbis into positions across the country.[56] Wherever they served, they hoped to take on the task John Tepfer '27 had set out in the first issue of the *Quarterly*: throwing open the doors to Jews of all persuasions and imparting their interpretation of Judaism from platform and pulpit to all the world.[57]

At the ceremony, the CCAR's president, David Lefkowitz, called on Jewish leaders to create a new set of priorities in response to the changing complexion of American Jewry. Just as Leviticus mandated for a redistribution of wealth and property in ancient Israel every fifty years, he said, so, too, after five decades of mass immigration, did American Jewry need a "radical readjustment." The American Jewish population had grown from 230,000 to more than four million, and while young Jews enjoyed economic opportunity, they were losing their parents' zeal for Judaism. Calling the new JIR rabbis "ambassadors to the second generation,"[58] he urged them to seek not power but servitude, citing Rabban Gamliel's exhortation to his disciples in the Talmud: "Today, you shall be a servant to this people."[59]

Among the assembled, the call to serve weighed on no one more heavily than Wise. Though his national stature continued to rise, fueled by NBC radio broadcasts of his weekly sermons at Carnegie Hall and frequent press coverage of his involvement in secular and Jewish issues, he was struggling to sustain his many commitments in the face of declining health. Just a week earlier, he had stepped away from the presidency of the American Jewish Congress, though he would continue to serve as the organization's honorary president as well as vice president of the Zionist General Council.[60]

That summer, Stephen and Louise Waterman Wise traveled together to Zurich, not for a much-needed respite but to attend the sixteenth Zionist Congress where the Jewish Agency was established. Wise had opposed an agreement brokered by Louis Marshall and Chaim Weizmann to include non-Zionists on the Agency's governing bodies, and he now failed even in establishing safeguards to ensure that the agency would support Zionist aims in Palestine.[61] After Marshall was elected chair of the Jewish Agency Council for Uniting Zionists and Non-Zionists, Wise chose not to participate. He attended the Hebrew University

Board of Governors' meeting, went on to the World Religious Peace Conference in Frankfurt, helped organize the American Jewish Congress's Geneva Bureau, and then, in early September, he and Louise headed home.

En route to New York aboard the RMS *Berengaria*, the Wises received shocking news by radio: Louis Marshall had died from pancreatic disease while still in Zurich. Wise quickly released a statement paying tribute to the man with whom he had sparred for decades: "He was great in his devotion to his people's cause; he was great in his resolution to right his people's wrongs; he was great in his resistless passions to secure justice for his fellow-Jews in all lands." Fundamentally, Wise seemed to acknowledge, he and Marshall had shared the same overarching goals, even as they pursued radically different approaches.[62]

Wise had first challenged Marshall as a young rabbi brashly rejecting the pulpit at Emanu-El; no longer a marginal figure, and approaching the height of his career, Wise now sought to ensconce his approach in the heart of the very American Jewish institutions that Marshall and his circle had built.

To achieve this, he needed to continue preparing his young students for the challenges ahead. What precisely these would entail, of course, no one could know.

But ominous signs were evident that September. In the United States, after a decade of prosperity and a soaring stock market, the Federal Reserve was warning of excessive speculation. While the market was booming in the summer of 1929, steel production, car sales, and homebuilding were slowing, and banks were beginning to fail. Germany, for the moment, was enjoying relative peace and prosperity, thanks to enormous credit extended in recent years by American banks. The German economy's stability, however, rested on the well-being of the very institutions now subject to the Federal Reserve's concerns. Moreover, across Central Europe, antisemitism continued to rise—Morton Berman, who studied at the Hochschule as a Guggenheimer Fellow, reported visiting Vienna and seeing signs everywhere that said "All Juden Hinaus" (all Jews out). In Palestine, meanwhile, tensions were high following a summer of deadly riots that the British failed to quell peacefully.

With major crises brewing in the United States, Europe, and Palestine and with a cadre of alumni now positioned across the nation, the institute's approach would be put to the test. The challenge of effectively serving their people as rabbis in the battles ahead would prove greater, and the stakes higher, than anyone could imagine.

Figure 1. Young Stephen S. Wise. American Jewish Archives, Cincinnati, Ohio.

(*Below*) Figure 2. JIR faculty and students, circa 1927. (*Seated, from left to right*): Nathan Krass, Henry Slonimsky, Stephen S. Wise, Julian J. Obermann, Chaim Tchernowitz; (*second row*): Windsor P. Daggett, Abraham W. Binder, Harry S. Lewis, Nissan Touroff, Sidney E. Goldstein, Zwi Diesendruck, Salo Baron, Joshua L. Goldberg '26; (*third row*): Gershon Tchernowitz '27, David B. Alpert '29, Harry Kaplan '27, Maurice J. Bloom '27, John J. Tepfer '27, Mitchell S. Fisher '27, Samuel Teitelbaum '27. Courtesy of the Jacob Rader Marcus Center of the American Jewish Archives, Cincinnati, Ohio, at americanjewisharchives.org; identifications appear in Samuel E. Karff, *Hebrew Union College-Jewish Institute of Religion at One Hundred Years*.

(*Left*) Figure 3. JIR building on West Sixty-Eighth Street. American Jewish Archives, Cincinnati, Ohio.

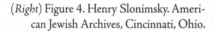

(*Right*) Figure 4. Henry Slonimsky. American Jewish Archives, Cincinnati, Ohio.

(*Left*) Figure 5. Salo W. Baron. Courtesy of the Department of Special Collections, Stanford University Libraries.

Figure 6. JIR student basketball team, date unknown. American Jewish Archives, Cincinnati, Ohio.

Figure 7. Irma Lindheim. Courtesy of Hadassah, the Women's Zionist Organization of America, Inc.

Figure 8. Hirsch Library, JIR. American Jewish Archives, Cincinnati, Ohio.

Figure 9. Stephen S. Wise addressing students in JIR Chapel. American Jewish Archives, Cincinnati, Ohio.

Figure 10. Helen Hadassah Levinthal holding the JIR certificate granting her the title *musmakah* ("ordained") that was awarded at her graduation in 1939. Despite the use of that word, however, the faculty was clear that her ordination was "in the literature of Israel," not as a rabbi. This photo appeared in a May 29, 1939, *New York World-Telegram* article, "Woman Passes Tests, but She Is Barred from Becoming a Rabbi Because Talmud Doesn't Recognize Her Sex in Synagogues."

Figure 11. Chaplain Harold Saperstein (*left center*) and Vicaire Andre (*center*), Catholic priest of Namur, Belgium, in 1945, with a group of Jewish children and displaced persons who found refuge in his home during the Nazi occupation. American Jewish Archives, Cincinnati, Ohio.

(*Right*) Figure 12. Chaplain Joseph Shalom Shubow '33 (*center*) witnesses the making of the first matzahs for German Jews who celebrated Passover in a traditional manner after the war. (*Left*) Lt. Col. Charles A. Albright, (*right*) a rabbi from Riga, an inmate of a displaced persons camp. Shubow was also awarded a Bronze Star. American Jewish Archives, Cincinnati, Ohio.

(*Left*) Figure 13. Jerome R. Malino '35 in 1946. American Jewish Archives, Cincinnati, Ohio.

(*Right*) Figure 14. Six JIR men in Palestine in early 1948 with Hebrew University in the background. (*Seated left to right*) Rabbi Albert Yanow '45, Leon Reinharth, Rabbi Jay R. Brickman '47. (*Standing left to right*) The first two men are unknown; third from left: Rabbi Marvin M. Reznikoff '38; fourth: Rabbi Jordan I. Taxon '47; fifth man is unknown; sixth: Morris H. Bell '49. American Jewish Archives, Cincinnati, Ohio.

III

METAMORPHOSIS

9

Early Transformation

O N OCTOBER 28, 1929, THE DAY AFTER SIMCHAT TORAH, THE DOW Jones Industrial Average plunged nearly 13 percent, wiping out billions of dollars in wealth followed by nearly as substantial a loss again the next day. The crash triggered a global Depression soon to impact every aspect of Jewish life in communities not only in the United States but also across the globe. The social and economic fallout from the Great Depression, the escalation of antisemitism and growth of fascist parties in Europe, and the British barriers blocking immigration into Palestine by European Jewry would require urgent response on the part of American Jewry.

For many, these crises heightened the importance of pursuing social justice, caring for *klal yisrael*, and Zionism. As financially struggling Jewish institutions sought to get food and clothing to individuals and families who had lost their savings and homes, the Free Synagogue's active social service model, created to meet the needs of first-generation immigrants, took on renewed relevance, as did Judaism's focus on economic equality and social justice. At the same time, as the economic depression spread to Germany, Hungary, and Romania, rising unemployment in those countries appeared to be fueling an alarming surge in antisemitic agitation and violence. In response, the number of European Jews seeking refuge in Palestine rose, which heightened American Jewish calls for the British to lift immigration restrictions and support the Yishuv.

Whereas many American Jewish leaders chose to focus on one or another of these issues, Wise and most JIR faculty, students, and alumni viewed them as inextricably linked. The prophetic social vision and Zionism were not merely compatible but indispensable to each other, Philip Bernstein told the Jewish Agency in London, and a large and growing body of American liberal Jews shared this outlook. True, he acknowledged, there were still anti-Zionists among them, but they belonged to "a passing generation, stubbornly clinging to the logic of 19th-century theories and evading the logic of contemporary Jewish life."

Bernstein and his peers also rejected the tactics of the patrician German Jewish leaders who had long dominated American Jewish life, and with Louis Marshall's passing, that era appeared to be coming to an end. Marshall's small, wealthy circle remained influential, without doubt, but their pianissimo political approach did not suit the young American Jews who were increasingly asserting their power en masse and confrontationally. In New York, especially, Jews had been staging a show of force through a series of mass gatherings demanding British accountability for the violence in Palestine. Twenty thousand filled Madison Square Garden for a protest in late August 1929, while Wise was still en route home from Europe, and a few weeks later, before a crowd of two thousand packed into Town Hall with another three thousand outside unable to get in, Wise demanded an investigation not *by* but *of* the British Mandatory government in Palestine.

Beyond engaging in public agitation of this kind, as Wise's international stature grew and conditions for European Jewry became more dire, he also began entering into the kinds of high level behind-the-scenes discussions for which he had long criticized Marshall. Indicative of this change, following the Town Hall protest, he pressed the matter in personal meetings with President Hoover and the prime minister of Britain. Still, his primary influence during this period stemmed from his mobilization of the American Jewish Congress to address a range of domestic as well as international issues, and his leadership in the Zionist movement, which was adopting more militant strategies. Of course, he also continued to lead the Free Synagogue as well as JIR, where he finally agreed to the board's request that he cease referring to himself as "acting president" and assume the permanent role.

The institute, its finances in a more precarious state than ever, faced multiple challenges during this period. Due to the continued push and pull of Jewish scholars across institutions globally, as well as the school's inability to offer much job security, retaining faculty proved difficult and the rotation of instructors became constant. At the same time, with synagogues and Jewish organizations across the country laying off staff and retrenching, employment prospects for students and alumni alike quickly went from plentiful to bleak.

Still, the need for leadership capable of addressing the unfolding crises was desperate, and collectively, faculty, students and especially alumni responded to the call, working on multiple fronts. Wise, long accustomed to having few kindred spirits in the rabbinate, took heart in being surrounded by a growing number of disciples who shared his convictions. JIR rabbis, including a few who worked particularly closely with Wise, got heavily involved both with social justice issues in the United States and with efforts on behalf of the Jews of Europe and Palestine. They organized at the synagogue and community levels, carried out research and advocacy for organizations including the American Jewish Congress and the ZOA, and many continued efforts to spread their integrated and activist approach into the mainstream. As in the 1920s, the mechanism that promised the greatest potential for doing so was the Reform rabbinate, represented by the Central Conference of American Rabbis, to which many JIR alumni belonged. With both the domestic and international crises taking on an unfathomable urgency, mustering American Jewry in a powerful broad-based response was crucial.

FACULTY

By this time, Slonimsky had become a central figure in the life of the institute, having been elected dean by the faculty several times and beloved by students for his broad literary knowledge and passion for teaching. Influential, too, were Salo Baron, Chaim Tchernowitz, and Harry Lewis. These men, along with Goldstein, Obermann, Touroff, and Binder represented JIR's core faculty in the mid-to-late 1920s.

In addition, Ralph Marcus, the young man who had assisted Kohut in the JIR library, began teaching Semitic philology after completing his doctorate at Columbia in 1927, and a year later, Shalom Spiegel, a Vienna-educated expert in biblical and medieval Hebrew literature arrived from Haifa. That year, Samson Benderly also joined the institute, replacing Isaac Berkson, who moved to Palestine to supervise the Yishuv's system of Hebrew schools.[1] And after observing firsthand congregations' bias against students with foreign accents, Wise enlisted Windsor Daggett, a teacher of dramatic diction at the American Laboratory Theatre and critic for *Billboard*, as speech coach.

Beyond this group, however, the institute continued to experience a great deal of turnover, as "permanent" faculty left for new posts in Europe and Palestine and Wise found replacement instructors from the United States and Europe. Gone were Reuben Levy, who accepted an appointment at Cambridge in 1926 as a lecturer in Persian, and Shalom Maximon, who joined HUC's School for Teachers in New York, after a salary dispute with Wise. Zevi Diesendruck, a young Viennese scholar of Modern Hebrew literature and Jewish philosophy, replaced Maximon and, like Baron, taught some of his courses *ivrit b'ivrit*, but he soon moved to Jerusalem to teach at Hebrew University.[2] Meanwhile, Harry Torczyner, a Hebrew philologist and Bible scholar at the Hochschule, also arrived as a visiting professor, much to the relief of students frustrated with Obermann's dry approach and, in Wise's view, "mania against East European Jews." That said, Wise ended up finding Torczyner "almost as difficult as Obermann"; he returned to the Hochschule while Obermann, for the time being, stayed.[3] Perhaps most disappointing for Wise, in the winter of 1927 Mordecai Kaplan had indicated he was finally prepared to join the institute, but then changed his mind once again.

Newman sympathized with Wise's predicament. "I suppose you remember Lightnin' Bill Jones who said he could drive a flock of bees across the desert without losing a single one," he wrote, referring to the 1918 Broadway hit *Lightnin'*. "I suppose Lightnin' Bill's job was child's play by the side of yours."[4] And the students seemed to take the flux in stride. In those years, Jacob Rudin recalled, though the institute was small with little money, "there was a crackle of excitement in the

air. It was a new school. Faculty members experimented with courses. The institute experimented with faculty members. Some courses were found wanting and
dropped. And so were some faculty members."[5]

Such was hardly the case, however, when just one month after the collapse of
the stock market, Salo Baron, one of the institute's most beloved faculty members,
was named to a prestigious post at Columbia University. The newly established Nathan J. Miller Chair of Jewish History, Literature and Institutions represented only
the second chair in Jewish studies in the United States (Wolfson held the first) and
the first serious recognition of Jewish history as a discipline in secular academe. The
position represented a milestone for Jewish studies as well as Jewish philanthropy
and inspired Jewish scholars, including some at the institute, to hope for similar appointments at other colleges and universities while prompting communal leaders,
including Solomon Freehof, a Chicago-based Reform rabbi and former professor at
HUC, to urge Jewish donors to increase their support for Jewish studies.[6] Jews were
already disproportionately generous in supporting university buildings and research
endeavors, Freehof argued, and institutions of higher education should now provide
a proper appreciation for the influence of Judaism in Western thought.[7]

Wise, who had been consulted during the search, felt proud that Columbia
had selected a JIR faculty member.[8] And Baron, out of a sense of loyalty to Wise
and JIR, negotiated an allowance to continue teaching at the institute on a visiting
basis. In the midst of the financial crisis, the arrangement suited JIR, which could
now retain Baron on the teaching staff at less than half the salary he had received
as a full-time professor.

STUDENTS

While retaining faculty proved challenging, JIR continued to attract young men
seeking to become rabbis, and in 1930, despite the poor employment prospects,
the institute received the largest number of applicants in its history. City College
and Harvard were the largest feeder schools, yielding ten JIR students each during
this period, but students came from all regions of the United States. A few women
enrolled in classes as well, including Dora Askowith, who had resumed her JIR
studies in 1928 while still teaching at Hunter College.[9]

When it came to recruitment, Wise's speaking engagements on college campuses were by far the most effective tool. The experience of Harold Saperstein '35,
a senior at Cornell when Wise visited campus, was typical. Seeing Sage Chapel
packed with thousands of university faculty and students, almost all non-Jewish,
listening raptly as Wise spoke, filled Saperstein with pride. Afterward, with trep-
idation, he approached Wise for their prearranged appointment. They went for a
walk in the rain, and Saperstein soon found himself "pouring out my heart to him
as though he were an old friend." He found the freedom JIR represented powerfully

compelling and decided to apply. Later that night, Wise spoke with Hillel students about Zionism. Ever since, Saperstein later reflected, "I have been subconsciously trying to catch the echo of Dr. Wise."[10]

During this period, a constant stream of leaders and diplomats from Washington and the capitals of Europe met with Wise in his office at the institute, as did countless individuals seeking his counsel or friendship, be they exiled, poor, or lonely. Observing Wise's interactions with this broad spectrum of humanity, and reflecting on them together, readied students for the rabbinate in ways as important as did the formal curriculum.

Wise, for his part, made sure JIR students were inculcated with the institute's ethos and expectations at each of the all-school events that punctuated the annual calendar. Typical were the messages conveyed at a dinner honoring Wise on his fifty-sixth birthday in 1930. To engender respect for the rabbinate among American Jewry, Louis I. Newman told more than two hundred guests assembled, JIR graduates needed to show backbone in the face of powerful opposition while also creating greater tolerance for challenging viewpoints. "If we can cultivate among our congregations a willingness to hear the right opinion at the wrong time, or the wrong opinion at the right time," he said, "then we are creating true liberalism in American Jewish congregations." Julian Mack told the same gathering that the institute is not concerned with training radical, Reform, Conservative, or Orthodox rabbis but those who "follow the dictates only of their own consciences."

Alumni

Wise developed close relationships with many of his students, but by 1930 he had an inner circle of alumni on whom he especially relied. These included the three who worked alongside him at the Free Synagogue and JIR, namely, Jacob Rudin, Morton Berman, and J. X. Cohen, and well as Louis I. Newman, JIR's one so-called honorary alumnus.

Particularly close with Rudin, Wise expressed dismay when the young rabbi decided to leave the Free Synagogue in 1930 for a position at Temple Beth-El of Great Neck. "I shall miss him," Wise told Newman, acknowledging the selfishness of wanting to keep Rudin indefinitely, especially given his promise for the congregational rabbinate. Wherever he goes, Wise consoled himself, "he will be the most effective and convincing testimony for the Institute." In fact, like Baron, Rudin arranged to continue working on behalf of JIR from his new position. "Dr. Wise never moved from the center of the orbit of my life, nor the Institute from the center of my interest," Rudin later recalled.

Fortuitously, just as Rudin headed for Great Neck, Newman, Wise's first protégé, returned to New York to serve as rabbi at Congregation Rodeph Sholom, the same pulpit Wise's father had long occupied. The surprising development resulted from a bit of tumult that broke out just after the congregation moved into its new home on West Eighty-Third Street, when their interim rabbi Mitchell Fisher (JIR '27) suddenly resigned. A vocal supporter of the Socialist Party and their presidential candidate Norman Thomas (whom Wise supported, as well), Fisher complained that as a rabbi he could not speak out forcefully without "immediate institutional restraint," and thus, he was leaving the profession. While neither Wise nor Newman believed Fisher, they were both elated when Newman was hired in his place. Now, notwithstanding their disagreement over Jabotinsky, Wise had another strong ally nearby, and he enlisted Newman to serve on the JIR board and teach homiletics.[11]

Social Justice

The class of 1930 heard a terse call to action at their commencement ceremony, where Sol Stroock, a prominent lawyer and Jewish philanthropist who months earlier had succeeded Louis Marshall as chairman of the board at JTS, addressed them. "You will be exemplars of social justice," he declared, and in no small way, he was right.[12]

That year, despite austerity measures at congregations across the country, the institute succeeded in securing employment for the entire class. JIR graduates now held fifty-nine positions across the country, with a majority serving in Reform congregations, along with a handful in Conservative or more traditional communities. While most were based in the Northeast, some of the more recent graduates assumed pulpits in Louisiana, Tennessee, Mississippi, Alabama, and Texas. Regardless of religious orientation or geographic locale, for the next several years, these rabbis faced a shared challenge: alleviating the suffering engulfing their communities due to the Great Depression.

Between "Black Monday" in October 1929 and the summer of 1932, the Dow plummeted 89 percent, thousands of banks failed, depositors lost more than a billion dollars in savings, and the nation's unemployment rate ballooned from 3.2 percent to 23.6 percent, amounting to twelve million people unable to find a job. Many had lost their life savings, homes, and farms, and more than two million were homeless. African American communities were hit especially hard, experiencing unemployment closer to 50 percent, as well as an escalation in racial violence, especially in the South. In 1931, for example, nine Black youths were falsely accused of raping two white women on a train near Scottsboro, Alabama, and despite ample evidence of their innocence, an all-white jury quickly convicted them and sentenced eight of the nine to death by electric chair. Ultimately, the Scottsboro case went to the Supreme Court, which in a landmark decision overturned the convictions. While the accused were spared execution, they were nonetheless forced to endure years of retrials and imprisonment. The infamous Scottsboro Affair became emblematic of the systemic racial injustice that plagued the United States.

JIR's young rabbis, driven by the spirit and teachings of the Hebrew prophets, saw a pressing need to protect the nation's most vulnerable. From their pulpits across the country, they preached political sermons supporting the plight of labor, fought to obtain relief for the unemployed and homeless, and worked with local as well as national organizations to combat rampant discrimination in employment, housing, and education based on race, religion, or creed. More than a few JIR graduates gravitated leftward. "The building of a better social order means radicalism of one kind or another," Philip Bernstein told a local PTA. "You can't find or abolish what is evil without offending vested interests, and that means trouble."

At the Free Synagogue, the Social Service Division's efforts took on renewed urgency. Using infrastructure created to address the immigrant community's hardship at the turn of the century, the congregation once again began distributing food and clothing at sites around the city. Meanwhile, Sidney Goldstein, as chair of the New York Board of Ministers' Committee on Unemployment, led a citywide effort to enlist all synagogues in providing relief. He urged congregations to offer temporary jobs, where possible, and to collect a day's salary every month from clergy and laity alike, to be allocated through an unemployment fund for those in greatest need.[13] He also worked with civic leaders on a long-range plan aimed at preventing a recurrence of the entire crisis.

Graduates brought the same approach to their local communities around the country. Joshua Goldberg '26 helped lead the distribution of emergency unemployment relief in Queens, and Schultz did the same in Brooklyn. Philip Bernstein, now a prominent leader of progressive reform in Rochester, became a forceful advocate for the city's settlement houses, missions, and educational institutions. He also promoted women's rights, a stance that prompted a number of his congregants to quit the synagogue after he defended the birth control movement and invited Margaret Sanger to speak from the pulpit.

Among rabbis in the North, the fight against racial discrimination and violence focused mainly on housing and employment. While Bernstein battled housing discrimination against African Americans in Rochester, Abram Goodman, serving a pulpit in White Plains, publicly condemned a wall of communal opposition that two Black doctors encountered when they bought homes in one of the city's exclusive sections. Decrying the burning of a cross on the lawn of one of the doctors, Goodman urged local Jews to refuse to sign a mutual agreement being circulated among property owners in two wealthy sections of the city that would have placed restrictions in all property deeds to forever prohibit the sale of land to African Americans.[14]

Many alumni worked with the American Jewish Congress on these issues, including Joshua Goldberg, Benjamin Schultz '31, Albert Ruskin '30, and J. X. Cohen '29. Of these, Cohen played a central role, serving with Wise on the Governing

Council, chairing the National Committee on Economic Problems, and direct-ing several major studies of employment discrimination against Jews and African Americans. To facilitate data gathering for these studies, Cohen hired undercover investigators to pose as Jewish and non-Jewish job applicants at firms in New York City and then compared and analyzed their reports.

Chaplaincy in hospitals, prisons, and social welfare institutions provided a pastoral approach to alleviating suffering during these Depression years, and Co-hen was tasked with engaging more members of the New York Board of Jewish Ministers in this work. This approach in many ways reflected the practical applica-tion of values he had explored as a senior at JIR, when he wrote his master's thesis on "Ancient and Modern Care of the Aged: A Study of Paupers, Poorhouses and Pensions." Throughout the 1930s, Cohen preached on all of these topics at the Free Synagogue's Sunday morning Carnegie Hall services.

Rabbis with pulpits in the South faced higher stakes when engaging in social activism, most notably when they challenged the system of white supremacy. Ben-jamin Goldstein '26 discovered this as soon as he involved himself in the Scotts-boro case while serving Temple Beth Or in Montgomery, Alabama. Goldstein, the only white clergyman to visit the accused in prison after their conviction, helped connect them with the American Communist Party's team of lawyers, the Inter-national Defense League, which agreed to take on the case and spurred a national campaign to protest this miscarriage of justice.

On Yom Kippur 1932, Goldstein defended the youths in his sermon. In do-ing so, he risked violent intimidation and more, for Montgomery's mayor informed the temple board that if Goldstein continued his involvement with the case, the Ku Klux Klan would organize a boycott of Jewish businesses across the city. After Goldstein spoke publicly on the matter again, this time at a rally for the Scottsboro Boys, Beth Or's president now demanded that Goldstein choose his political work or his job. A day later, the rabbi resigned, and upon receiving numerous threats, he soon moved back to New York. Several Beth Or members of the congregation told newspaper reporters that while they agreed with Rabbi Goldstein's views, in expressing them he posed an "open threat to the welfare of the congregation."[15]

Benjamin Goldstein spoke about his experience at JIR's 1933 commencement luncheon. "You must be equal to the duty that you accept upon entering the min-istry," he said, "namely, the obligation to speak and to act with courage." However, with his politics now gravitating toward Communism, he was, in fact, like Mitchell Fisher, questioning whether or not he belonged in the rabbinate at all.

KLAL YISRAEL AND ZIONISM
Far more typical among JIR graduates was the blending of liberal-to-radical pol-itics with Jewish nationalism. They shared neither the leftist view that class in-terests superseded the bond of Jewish peoplehood nor the anti-nationalist view

promulgated by early Reform Judaism, namely, that Judaism was purely a religion. Instead, many agreed with Maurice J. Bloom '27, rabbi of Temple Beth Jacob in Newburgh, New York, when he preached, "Any liberal movement not now Zionist is reactionary."[16]

In 1930, Wise and Jacob De Haas, the British-born Zionist and journalist, cowrote the *Great Betrayal*, a history of British policy toward Palestine up to the Passfield White Paper of 1930, in which they outlined their disappointment in Great Britain's failure to carry out the promise of the Balfour Declaration. That same year, the Lipsky and Brandeis factions of the ZOA finally reconciled, and Wise, Newman, and Mack joined the eighteen-member administrative council. Their shared goals entailed fighting the British cap on Jewish immigration into Palestine and building the social and economic infrastructure of the Yishuv.

Having returned to the ZOA in an official capacity, Wise worked out of his office at JIR, where faculty and students became accustomed to seeing world leaders coming and going. Robert P. Jacobs '33 recalled his wedding day, for example, when he was still a student and, like many of his classmates, had asked Wise to officiate. At the appointed time, a cab arrived to take Jacobs and Wise from the institute to the Hotel White for the ceremony. Jacobs ran up to Wise's office and pull him out of a meeting with a short, stocky man whom Wise introduced as Eduard Benes, the foreign minister of Czechoslovakia (soon to become president). The groom and his teacher then dashed downstairs and out the building. When, from the down the sidewalk, a square-jawed gray-haired man yelled, "Stephen! Stephen!" Wise invited him to share the back seat of the cab. While Jacobs shrank into his seat, the two older men fell into a heated debate over whether to see Brandeis or cable England. When the cab pulled up to the hotel, Jacobs helped his elders out and took Wise by the arm. Wise paused with a smile and, before turning to the business of getting Jacobs married, introduced him to Felix Frankfurter.[17]

During these years, as the American Jewish Congress continued investigating and publicizing the worsening conditions for Jewish communities in Central and Eastern Europe, including the growing menace of Nazism, Wise enlisted JIR faculty and alumni for a variety of assignments, including eyewitness reports. In the summer of 1930, for example, Nissan Touroff traveled to Soviet Russia and Poland to meet with Jewish leaders and observe the situation firsthand, and Philip Bernstein and Salo Baron (now teaching at Columbia as well as JIR) went to Romania for the same purpose. Baron documented the economic ruin and increasingly virulent antisemitism he witnessed, as well as the urgent need for American Jewry's help, in a formal report Wise requested for an upcoming meeting with the Romanian ambassador to the United States. Based on Baron's recommendations, Wise demanded immediate action by the Romanian government, including the dismantling of antisemitic organizations and propaganda machines, compensation for Jewish victims, and protection of all Jewish citizens.

When the ambassador refused, claiming such measures would incite Romanian nationalists who were threatening the lives of government officials, the AJC continued pressuring the Romanian government to shield its Jewish citizens from harm, to no avail.[18]

Wise also involved students and alumni in organizing for the Zionist movement, making the institute even more of a hub of activism. Zionist leaders regularly spoke on campus, including, for example, Judah Magnes, Nahum Sokolow, Nahum Goldmann, Solomon Goldman, and the poet Simon Halkin, who conducted discussions in Hebrew. "Indoctrination in Zionism continued under my former teacher," recalled Morton Berman, the Free Synagogue's assistant rabbi and director of field activities for JIR at this time. Just as Cohen took on significant responsibilities working under Wise for the American Jewish Congress, Berman did the same for the Zionist movement, joining Wise at ZOA executive meetings, couriering confidential correspondence between Wise, Brandeis, Frankfurter, and Mack, and assisting in the Zionist efforts of the AJC, as well.

JIR's faculty also engaged with the movement, most especially in Palestine, where they contributed their expertise to life on the Yishuv and furthered their own research. Berkson continued serving as superintendent of the Jewish school system there while Benderly taught in his place at JIR. Binder, having already published a collection of Palestinian Jewish songs and instrumentals, spent the summer of 1930 gathering new material while giving concerts in Jerusalem and Tel Aviv. Slonimsky and Moses Marcus, an instructor of Talmud at the institute, spent 1931–1932 in Palestine. "Forgive the ecstatic tone," Slonimsky wrote Wise, "but I could not help feeling that if only every Jew or every other Jew could be planted here in person, just to see the place, he would be won for the cause forever."

The faculty worked on building the movement in the United States, as well, teaching courses open to the public, like Baron's "Palestine and the Jewish Renaissance" series for West Side Zionists, and speaking to congregations at the invitation of JIR alumni. They also partnered with alumni like Mitchell Fisher, John Tepfer '27, and Michael Alper '30 to write and teach for Avukah, the American Student Zionist Federation, which sometimes held courses at the institute.

In 1932, Nissan Touroff left permanently for Palestine to continue his Hebrew scholarship in psychology and education. In his final address to the students at Commencement that year, he urged them to visit the Yishuv to "be inspired by the work of the pioneers" and to embrace Modern Hebrew as the key to Jewish renaissance. JIR alumni should make sure every congregation has a real Hebrew school, he said, and enlist their communities in the cause of Zionism regardless of whatever opposition might come their way. On cue, Binder concluded the ceremony by having all join in the singing of "Hatikvah."

In addition to preaching Zionism from their pulpits across the country, at least one-third of JIR alumni took leadership positions at the regional or national level of Zionist organizations including the ZOA, Avukah, and others. As regional president of the ZOA, for example, Maurice Bloom '27 organized the Hudson Valley, and Adolph Lasker '30 led a similar effort in Long Island. The senior leadership of Avukah included a strong JIR presence, with Samuel Blumenfield '30 serving as national president (he was on the ZOA's National Commission on Youth Education, too), Michael Alper '30 chairing the National Publications Committee and organizing the Avukah programs at JIR, and Lawrence Schwartz '28 on the National Culture Committee. Mitchell Fisher worked for Avukah in a variety of capacities as well, even introducing Albert Einstein on an Avukah radio program—Einstein lectured on Zionism in German while James Waterman Wise translated. A few alumni took positions of leadership in Young Judaea or the more radical Revisionists, and many others encouraged their congregations to support the movement politically and financially.

While speaking from the pulpit enabled rabbis to influence their congregations, mobilizing the rabbinate to cooperate across denominational lines could achieve much broader change. Recognizing this, Wise had proposed in 1929 that Reform and Conservative rabbis who shared his twofold commitment to social justice and Zionism unite around a single shared program for liberal Judaism. Conservative rabbis, especially, were lending strong support to the ZOA; and while they were slower to organize around matters of social justice, some were moving in that direction, too. Nonetheless, Wise's effort failed; while he had little trouble inspiring diverse rabbinical students to work together, he could do nothing comparable with ordained rabbis, whom he found less willing to work across party lines.[19]

CCAR

Instead, he turned to the Central Conference of Reform Rabbis, a remarkable change given the antipathy he had long felt toward the organization. For decades, the CCAR had expressed its anti-Zionism in a variety of resolutions, including opposition to the Balfour Declaration. In addition, going back to the CCAR's founding in 1889, only one Zionist had ever led the organization, namely, Rabbi Max Heller, a friend of Wise's who served as president from 1909 to 1911; far more typical were the anti-Zionist presidencies of Louis Wolsey and Hyman Enelow in the late 1920s and the non-Zionist approach of Morris Newfield, who became president in 1931. As a result, Wise rarely attended meetings.

However, beginning in 1929, he saw a potential opening. That year, while the conference remained officially opposed to political Zionism, it did express support for the Palestine Emergency Fund and the Jewish Agency. And more broadly, support for Zionism was growing within the conference, thanks to the JIR contingent along with a growing number of HUC graduates, chief among them Abba Hillel Silver '15. Rabbi at Cleveland's The Temple, one of the largest congregations in the country, Silver held prominence as a national Zionist leader and spokesman and frequently worked alongside Wise. Silver also served on the board of the CCAR, where he had a strong following among the college's recent alumni, a majority of whom supported Zionism.

As the Depression wore on, the CCAR attempted to address both the immediate demand for relief in Jewish communities across the country as well as the need for systemic change at the national level. At the conference's annual gatherings, Sidney Goldstein led sessions on the Free Synagogue's social service model, and urged the creation of synagogue social action committees that could work for broader reform. Congregations around the country were following the Free Synagogue's lead, and the CCAR itself was taking increasingly liberal stances on a variety of issues, pushed far to the left by its own Social Justice Committee, which in 1929 virtually embraced socialism. Predictably, such radicalism met resistance, particularly among rabbis who feared antagonizing wealthy congregants or fueling antisemitism, but this did not impede the CCAR from adopting exceedingly progressive stances throughout this period.[20]

With roughly 75 percent of all JIR alumni joining the CCAR, most of whom served in Reform congregations, Wise increased his own involvement and began attending meetings. Together with faculty like Henry Slonimsky and Harry Lewis, who were members as well, the JIR group formed a minority bloc aimed at moving the Reform rabbinate toward their outlook. Given how many HUC students shared their views on Zionism and social justice, the JIR rabbis could also anticipate allying with a good number of recent graduates from the college.

Tensions remained high, however, between the HUC graduates and their JIR counterparts, exacerbated by competition for scarce jobs. Both seminary presidents, Wise and Morgenstern alike, wielded a heavy hand in the job placement process, and in the tight market they fought hard to secure positions for their graduates. And while HUC men like Silver objected strongly to Morgenstern's continued opposition to Zionism, they nonetheless remained loyal to their alma mater.

For JIR graduates, these tensions were further exacerbated by the fact that leadership positions in the CCAR were held almost exclusively by HUC alumni. To remedy this, at Wise's urging, JIR alumni began vying for committee assignments. Wise and Goldstein did the same beginning in 1929, when they both joined the Social Justice Committee and helped shape its leftist positions. If the JIR group could penetrate the CCAR's entire committee structure, they could similarly wield influence on a broader array of issues. In strategizing their plan of attack, in 1930, Wise and the alumni instituted an annual dinner to be held in conjunction with each CCAR convention.

At the very first of these, in Providence, they had a specific goal in mind: Adding "Hatikvah," the Jewish national hymn sung at Zionist gatherings everywhere (including JIR's commencement), to the next edition of the *Union*

Hymnal.[21] Working together, with help from Silver and a handful of other HUC graduates, the JIR contingent successfully laid the groundwork. Wise then made the motion, declaring "Hatikvah" the one song loved by Jews across the world for expressing their imperishable aspirations for a creative Hebrew life. In the vote that followed, the CCAR passed the first pro-Zionist resolution in the rabbinical association's history.[22]

Though changing the hymnal hardly reflected a full about-face for the organization, the anti-Zionists recognized the symbolic power of including "Hatikvah" and planned to overturn the decision the following year. Taking the offense, Wise joined the Liturgical Literature Committee, and then, in 1931, the JIR group advanced a resolution requiring inclusion of all *five* of the song's verses—and this, too, passed. With the new prayerbook, Reform congregants in every corner of the country would now see the full Jewish national anthem as part of their liturgy.

That same year, fully one-third of the JIR contingent joined a total of nine different committees; unmistakably, they were preparing for more battles ahead. Wise joined the Committee on International Peace, just one of many steps he was taking out of concern for the worsening situation in Europe, where the Depression had hit hard and right-wing groups were on the rise.

With violent antisemitism spreading across Germany, protecting the Jews there and in neighboring countries now took precedence over all else for Wise. As early as 1930, he had alerted the American Jewish Congress that Hitler and his movement must be thwarted, and yet a year later, the Nazis had considerably grown in strength. Wise, virtually the only prominent American Jewish leader to recognize the gravity of the situation, urged a proactive response. While American Nazi supporters began organizing mass meetings of their own, the American Jewish Committee together with Jewish leaders in Germany advised patience; Hitler seemed too much of a fringe lunatic to pose a genuine threat.

As German elections approached in late winter of 1932, Wise galvanized the American Jewish Congress, working with his closest allies, including his son James, who was now editing *Opinion*, a journal of Jewish affairs, and J. X. Cohen. They had no time to lose; Hitler was running for president, and the Nazis aimed to capture more seats in the Reichstag.

Cohen worked at the local level, drawing on the same undercover methods he used to surveil employment discrimination in New York. That February, for example, he attended a Bund meeting in Yorkville, a heavily German American section of Manhattan then known for pockets of Nazi sympathizing. Posing as a Nazi supporter, he listened to an evening of speakers attacking world Jewry, Communists, and the anti-German boycott, then stood quietly amid a crowd of over one thousand singing the Nazi Party anthem "Horst-Wessel-Lied" and saluting "Heil Hitler." He documented the experience in his American Jewish Congress report,

"The Menace of Hitlerism to American Jewry."[23] Meanwhile, Wise continued to speak publicly against Hitlerism.

In March, just days before Germany's presidential election, the three lobbied Jewish as well as non-Jewish leaders to decry Nazism, with limited success. The Federal Council of Churches of Christ agreed to issue a statement drafted by the Wises and Cohen, but the National Conference of Jews and Christians refused, thanks in no small part to a Jewish contingent who opposed the idea, including Cyrus Adler, head of the American Jewish Committee. The Wise group encountered similar opposition from the National Seminar of Catholics, Jews, and Protestants.

While Hitler failed to win the presidency in Germany's elections that March, in the Reichstag elections held that July the Nazis swept nearly one-third of the popular vote, winning 230 out of 608 seats, the most held by any party. Hitler now demanded to be made chancellor.

Just a few weeks after the Reichstag elections, the American Jewish Congress convened Jewish leaders from twenty-five different countries in Geneva, to establish an international organization devoted to waging a defense against Hitlerism and protecting the increasingly besieged Jewish communities of Central and Eastern Europe.

The plan drew sharp criticism from the American Jewish Committee. Calling the Geneva conference "a last gasp in Jewish nationalism, as it is passing away," the committee's Samuel Schulman, rabbi at New York's Temple Emanu-El, accused the organizers of playing into the hands of the Hitlerites by lending credence to their charge that Jews were interfering in the internal affairs of Germany. "The Jews in every Western country today can speak for themselves," he said. "Wherever anti-Semitism exists, it is a local problem." The Jews in Germany were conducting themselves magnificently, he added, and in the end, antisemitism will be defeated "by what is best in German thought," along with an improved global economy.[24]

Wise took a very different approach to safeguarding Jewish rights. "Without continued protests against wrongs," he declared to the Geneva conference, they will come to be accepted as normal by perpetrator and victim alike. He pled for a united Jewish effort to protect the Jews of Europe and appealed to the Jewish masses to remain hopeful while standing together to save the Jewish people.

The battle between Wise and the American Jewish Committee continued that fall when Wise, back in New York and preaching the first of the fall services at Carnegie Hall, responded directly to Schulman's charge that he and the American Jewish Congress were playing into Hitler's hands. Those who base their views on non-Jewish opinions, he urged, should "get out of Jewish life."[25] As to Schulman's attack on Jewish nationalism, Wise responded at the CCAR conference in Cincinnati that November. "As a people, we have been too docile and acquiescent instead of being inflexibly self-insistent as Jews," he preached to the rabbis gathered Friday night at Plum Street Synagogue. Declaiming Reform Judaism's denial of Jewish peoplehood and "un-Jewish stress upon credo," he urged the conference to join the effort to support the creation of a World Jewish Congress.

The call was debated heatedly in ensuing days, but the JIR contingent could not yet bring a majority of the conference along with them; ultimately, neither side prevailed and the matter was deferred until the CCAR's June 1933 meeting.[26]

However, with the situation in Germany rapidly deteriorating, Schulman and his allies—the old guard of the Reform rabbinate—could no longer assume broad support within the CCAR for either their worldview or their tactics. Instead, a growing number of their colleagues, including forty graduates of the Jewish Institute of Religion, supported Wise's call for greater Jewish militancy and unity.

10

Reform's Volte-Face

WHILE THE REFORM RABBINATE WAVERED, WISE'S GROWING STATURE, and the growth of the organizations he led in the mid-1930s, signaled the extent to which Jews across the United States and internationally had come to share his commitments to social justice, Jewish peoplehood, and the establishment of a Jewish state in Palestine. In the face of an alarming combination of economic crises across the globe and rising fascism and state-sponsored antisemitism in Central Europe, these priorities, once considered marginal, now had the support of millions of Jews.

If ever there was a reason Wise created the Jewish Institute of Religion, it was to provide the Jewish world with rabbis prepared to confront the crises unfolding in the winter of 1933. On the domestic front, the Depression continued unabated, leaving millions of Americans unemployed, hungry, and without relief. For the Jews of Germany, meanwhile, the situation was turning dire; after Hitler was appointed chancellor on January 30, the Nazi regime immediately began implementing an antisemitic campaign of discriminatory legislation backed by widespread intimidation and violence. The American and British governments heightened the danger for German Jewry by refusing to lift immigration restrictions for those refugees seeking safe haven.

JIR's melding of particularist and universalist ideological commitments now became the essence of a broad call to battle that Wise issued not only to the cadre of rabbis he had trained but to the entire American Jewish community: In this time of dire need, it was critical that the bonds of Jewish peoplehood take primacy over credal differences and for all Jews to unite around aiding their kin in danger; at the same time, with democracy and civilization itself under threat, it was critical, too, for Jews to fight for justice and stand up against fascism everywhere. The call also had a tactical dimension, as Wise, the longtime critic of pianissimo diplomacy, became, in this moment, the representative leader for a growing number of American Jews demanding public, loud, and aggressive action.

Despite the popularity of this approach, those in the upper echelons of the American Jewish Committee, B'nai B'rith, and the leadership of Reform Judaism remained largely non-Zionist and inclined toward quiet diplomacy over public agitation. Given this divide, American Jewish organizations struggling to respond to the crisis in Germany were forced to line up on one side or the other, as two distinct ideological and tactical approaches, long at odds, were put to a test of contemporary relevance.

Each of the non-Orthodox American rabbinical seminaries stood clearly on one side of this divide or the other by virtue of its leadership. For just as Wise headed the American Jewish Congress as well as JIR, the committee was led by Cyrus Adler, president of JTS, and B'nai B'rith was led Alfred M. Cohen, chairman of HUC's board of governors. That the current dispute represented yet another manifestation of the long-standing conflict that pitted Wise against the leadership of the non-Orthodox movements did not bode well for cooperation. As in the past, but with the stakes much higher now, few showed a willingness to compromise. This included Wise, who, while publicly willing to explore unity, determinedly aimed to win over the opposition.

Although he and his circle had little chance of influencing the committee or B'nai B'rith, where they had no meaningful entrée, when it came to the Reform movement, graduates of the Jewish Institute of Religion were now uniquely positioned to bring real change. After ten years in operation, JIR had produced a cadre of fifty-seven rabbis who shared Wise's commitments and on whom he could call, and while some were based in Orthodox or Conservative congregations, a majority held pulpits in UAHC congregations and belonged to the CCAR. If JIR graduates could work together with like-minded HUC graduates, and with the support of the Eastern European Jews, who now made up a majority of Reform synagogue membership, they could potentially turn Reform Judaism into a force *for*, rather than *against*, their ideological synthesis and tactical approach.

During this period, Wise focused on the broader battles at hand, traveling frequently, fundraising, preaching to large crowds and organizing protests, while also serving as a rabbi-statesman of global stature who met regularly with heads of state, diplomats, and lawmakers. As he took on ever greater responsibilities at the national and international levels, he had little time or patience to engage directly with the leaders of Reform Judaism; instead, through his prominence, he influenced the movement from without while JIR alumni based at Reform congregations across the country led the charge from within.

GALVANIZING AMERICAN JEWRY AGAINST HITLER

Just a week after Hitler took power on January 30, 1933, Wise and Bernard Deutsch, president of the American Jewish Congress, met with the Weimar Republic's ambassador to the United States, Baron von Prittwitz, who refused their request that he publicly allay Jewish fears and instead tried to assuage them that Hitler's threats were mere campaign propaganda.[1] A day later, Wise and Deutsch recruited several JIR men to shape an emergency response. They included Salo

Baron, who was still teaching at the institute, as well as J. X. Cohen '29 and Israel Thurman, a member of JIR's board. Together with Joseph Tenenbaum, chair of the congress's executive committee, and Horace Kallen, they developed an activist strategy that JIR students, faculty, board members, and alumni would soon help implement. For the students, especially, the events that followed offered an intensive education in Wise's approach to rabbinical leadership.[2]

The planning group had to weigh a complex set of factors. The committee and B'nai B'rith, in urging quiet, behind-the-scenes diplomacy, were respecting the pleas of Jewish leaders within Germany who feared that American protests might incite the Nazi regime to carry out even more vindictive and violent attacks on their communities. At the same time, however, pressure was mounting from within the American Jewish Congress for bold and immediate action, including mass protests and a boycott of all German goods. They decided to pressure prominent Jewish and non-Jewish leaders to publicly decry the Nazi regime while also organizing large-scale demonstrations.

JIR's Harold Saperstein '35, like other students and alumni, threw himself into the protest movement. "It was my fate to be a student at the Institute during those early years when Hitler had first come to power," he recalled. "Of all the great Jewish leaders—it was Dr. Wise alone who recognized the true menace that Hitler represented to Israel and to the world.... Others attacked him bitterly—they condemned him for being outspoken—they accused him of notoriety seeking because he called great public meetings of protest."[3]

To initiate the campaign, the congress and Free Synagogue organized an anti-Nazi protest at Carnegie Hall featuring mainly non-Jewish speakers.[4] Then, on March 21, congress delegates convened at the Astor Hotel, where the depth of outrage over the attacks on German Jewry became apparent as several thousand people attempted to get through the doors. While New York City police called in reinforcements to manage the crowded streets surrounding the hotel, inside, speaker after speaker called for nationwide protests over the attacks on German Jewry. While Wise and the leadership fended off calls from the Jewish War Veterans and the Revisionists to join the boycott movement, they agreed to hold a major demonstration at Madison Square Garden the following week, to be broadcast across the nation and internationally.

On the last Sunday morning in March, before a capacity crowd at Carnegie Hall, Wise demanded that the German government cease all antisemitic activity and propaganda, end the economic exclusion of Jews from the life of Germany, protect Jewish life and property, and agree not to expel the "Ost-Juden" who had settled in Germany since 1914.[5] The next afternoon, twenty-two thousand protesters packed into the Garden, and thirty-five thousand more gathered in two overflow demonstrations on Forty-Ninth Street and in Columbus Circle, where the proceedings were broadcast over loudspeakers. Another one million gathered in synagogues and at rallies in two hundred cities across the country to listen by radio. Wise opened the meeting at 5:00 P.M., and for the next six hours politicians, labor leaders, clergy, and representatives from a wide variety of Jewish organizations addressed the crowd, including Israel Thurman as well as Rebekah Kohut, president of the World Union of Women and the one female speaker.[6] To conclude the evening, Rabbi Moses. S. Margolies, the eighty-year old president of the Orthodox Jewish Congregations of America, who had insisted on rising from his sickbed to attend, brought thousands to their feet when he offered a closing prayer for the Nazi persecution to cease.[7]

While three Orthodox rabbinical associations supported the demonstration and called for a day of fasting and prayer, the Reform and Conservative rabbinical and lay organizations refused to participate, as did the American Jewish Committee and B'nai B'rith.[8] Indeed, Louis I. Newman charged Cyrus Adler with pressuring the New York Board of Jewish Ministers to vote down resolutions urging members to preach on the German situation and announce the rally from their pulpits and of threatening Conservative rabbis that support for the protests could harm their careers.[9]

Adler, anticipating negative repercussions from the protests, defended his actions on numerous bases. For one, the committee felt an obligation to heed the Jewish leaders inside Germany who were begging their American counterparts to remain silent, lest the Nazis retaliate by instating even harsher measures. The committee worried, too, that protests would antagonize the American public, stoking antisemitism within the United States and lending credence to false accusations of an international Jewish conspiracy. In addition, Adler and his colleagues believed American Christians had more sway over Roosevelt than did American Jewry and could more likely influence the president to take a harder line against the Nazis. Thus, while not supporting the protests, the committee was working to mobilize a significant number of Protestants and liberal organizations to join the fight.[10]

None of the committee's concerns led Wise to change course. Rather, immediately following the Madison Square Garden rally, he took a leave of absence from running the institute and Free Synagogue in order to devote himself fully to the effort of preventing a "bacchanal of world anti-Semitism as has never been witnessed in modern times." Working out of his office on Sixty-Eighth Street, he brought more students and alumni into the effort.[11] Joshua Goldberg '26 headed up a speakers bureau for the congress, while Saperstein and Berman launched a monthly publication, the *Courier*, and devoted the first three issues to the next phase of protest.[12] Dora Askowith, still a student at the institute, worked with Louise Waterman Wise on organizing the Women's Division of the American Jewish Congress and called on Jewish women to play a central role in raising awareness of their sisters' plight abroad.[13]

With Roosevelt unresponsive to demands that he call on the German government to cease its campaign against the Jews,[14] Wise faced increasing pressure
for more militant action. In April, twelve hundred congress delegates representing a broad cross-section of labor, fraternal, religious, Zionist, and other organizations endorsed the anti-German boycott and targeted May 10 for the next mass
protest, to coincide with a Nazi book-burning planned for university towns across
Germany.

Once again, while the Union of Orthodox Jewish Congregations of America,
the Rabbi Isaac Elchanan Theological Seminary, the Union of Orthodox Rabbis
(established in 1901), and the Degel Harabonim (another council of Orthodox
Rabbis) all joined the protest, conspicuously absent were the American Jewish Committee and B'nai B'rith, who issued a joint statement calling the protest
"futile."[15] The CCAR, UAHC, Rabbinical Assembly, and United Synagogue of
America also withheld support, and Ludwig Vogelstein, president of the UAHC,
sent a letter to Reform congregations urging them not to participate.

Neither Adler nor Vogelstein's opposition, however, deterred American Jewry
from turning out on May 10 in an unprecedented show of force. In New York,
where Jewish shops and offices closed early, 250,000 demonstrators lined the
streets as Wise and leaders of the American Jewish Congress headed a parade
marching south from Madison Square Garden. Uniformed war veterans, school
and labor groups, rabbis in long black robes with their congregations, and thousands of singing children on floats and on foot, carrying banners, Zionist flags, and
anti-Hitler posters followed the route past City Hall and into Battery Park, where
speakers addressed the crowd late into the evening.[16] Finally, after singing "The
Star-Spangled Banner" and "Hatikvah," the gathering dispersed.[17]

In the ensuing weeks, renewed efforts to form an alliance among the congress, the committee, and B'nai B'rith proved no more effective than earlier talks
to align JIR, JTS, and HUC. Cyrus Adler, adamantly opposing public demonstrations, trusted that US and British governmental pressure would yield "less
drastic" policies on the part of the Nazis and adamantly opposed public demonstrations. Deutsch, in response, accused the committee of fighting the congress
more strongly than the Nazis, and maintained that American Jewry had a solemn
obligation to protest Hitler's policies of ruthless extermination. "To do less would
be short only of treason to the cause of our people," he told Adler.[18]

Throughout that spring, Wise continued to enlist JIR students and alumni
in the fight. At JIR's eighth commencement ceremony in June, he alerted the institute's five newest rabbis to the two most pressing challenges they would have to
face: fighting the social injustices of American society and confronting the tragedy
of German Jewry, which overshadowed all else. Criticizing the Reform leadership
for finding silence "strategically expedient," he urged the graduates to speak out and
prioritize Jewish national unity over religious schism. Historically, in travail, Jews

had "learned and proclaimed the oneness of God," he said; now, in equal anguish, "it is for you to affirm the oneness of God's people Israel."

Benjamin Goldstein '26, recently fired from his Montgomery pulpit after supporting the Scottsboro defendants, addressed civil rights at the luncheon following the ceremony and similarly implored the graduates to act with courage. Maurice Pekarsky '33, about to head to Palestine as the institute's latest recipient of the Guggenheimer Fellowship, acknowledged the responsibility borne by his classmates in this hour of need. "We hope to become worthy," he said. "May God help us."

That summer, JIR graduates continued to pursue Zionist and anti-Nazi activism in the broader Jewish community. Four alumni, for example, taught in the Zionist movement's Avukah School in Highland Falls, New York. Askowith organized "The School of the Jewish Woman" for Hadassah, where she taught alongside JIR faculty and local rabbis at the Spanish and Portuguese Synagogue around the corner from JIR. Joseph Shubow '33 took on direction of the American Jewish Congress's New England office, and Wendell Phillips '36 traveled to Denver and Salt Lake City to establish branches in those cities. Lawrence Schwartz '28 visited Germany and, upon his return, pressed the US immigration authorities to admit more German Jews.[19] Meanwhile, J. X. Cohen '29 began monitoring pro-Nazi activities in the New York area for the congress, including a German Day at Madison Square Garden that attracted eighteen thousand attendees.[20]

CHALLENGING REFORM

While Cohen remained silent at the Bund meeting, he and other JIR men had no compunction making themselves a disruptive force at the UAHC as well as the CCAR annual conventions during this period. In 1933 and 1934, JIR alumni challenged the national institutions of Reform Judaism repeatedly, even as Wise, always seeking ways to place the institute on more solid financial footing, signaled that he might be open to a merger with HUC.

First, at the UAHC convention in Chicago in June 1933, Cohen, together with Morton Berman, mounted an offensive by publicly protesting several statements Vogelstein made to the gathering of 1,500 representatives from Reform congregations across the country. In his opening remarks, the union's president condemned anti-Nazi protesters for "trying to meddle" in another nation's internal politics and claimed that their demonstrations "violated the amenities of Western civilization." Then, saying, "Jewish religion is the supreme tie which holds us together," he proposed that the two-year-old Synagogue Council of America henceforth serve as the mouthpiece for all American Jewry, which would have left no voice for the community's many secular, labor, cultural, and political organizations. Further infuriating the JIR men, Vogelstein thanked President Roosevelt on behalf of the UAHC for his "sympathy for those Jews and others who are suffering under the present German administration"—even though Roosevelt had thus far refused Wise's plea that he speak out against the Nazis' antisemitic campaign.

When Wise heard about Vogelstein's statements, including the message to Roosevelt, which he considered the "foulest betrayal of Jewish life," he telegrammed his views to Cohen and Berman, who promptly shared his missive with prominent delegates. A stormy debate ensued on the floor, as the JIR men pressed the union to endorse the protests against Hitler and Cohen accused Vogelstein of failing to represent the many Reform congregations that had joined the demonstrations on May 10. Finally, a compromise resolution passed praising the collective work of the congress, the committee, and B'nai B'rith.

"It was a good fight," Cohen reported to Wise, and while he, Berman, and their backers were hopelessly outnumbered, they felt the American Jewish Congress came through with newfound support among many Reform delegates.

Cohen and Berman then traveled to Milwaukee for the CCAR convention, where the situation in Europe and Roosevelt's far-reaching social legislation headed the agenda. While little was achieved concerning the international crisis, the conference united around a progressive legislative agenda on the domestic front, supporting governmental oversight of manufacturing, labor representation in industry management, limits on corporate profits, and a ban on the private manufacture of war materials. They also urged an end to racial injustice of the kind suffered by the Scottsboro defendants and called on congregations to support their rabbis' efforts fighting for civil rights.

Most significantly, the JIR contingent in Milwaukee helped vote an ardent Zionist, Felix Levy, to the position of vice president. While an avowed anti-Zionist, Samuel Goldenson of Pittsburgh, was, for now, taking the reins as president, Levy's selection meant that in all likelihood a Zionist would lead the CCAR two years hence—for the first time since Max Heller did so back in 1909.

Hastened by the growing number of JIR rabbis willing to press their ideological agenda, the CCAR's ambitious social justice platform and the election of a Zionist as vice president demonstrated that the Reform rabbinate was undeniably gravitating toward the JIR outlook.

Exploring a Merger with HUC

Ironically, however, even as JIR's influence climbed steadily, its financial situation continued to worsen despite Wise's efforts to generate revenue in a variety of ways. Therefore, out of necessity, the JIR board once again entered into discussions with HUC regarding consolidation.

Part of the institute's fiscal problems stemmed from Wise's extensive fundraising for organizations other than JIR. With the American Jewish Congress facing a deficit, the Zionist movement in greater need than ever, and the Free Synagogue stretched thin, he was repeatedly approaching the same individuals to fund multiple causes. Already deep in deficit, the institute took another significant hit in the fall of 1933 when the Walden School, which had been renting five JIR-owned buildings on Sixty-Eighth Street, abandoned their lease. The properties—in need of repair, still carrying a mortgage, and unlikely to house a new tenant soon—suddenly became not an asset but a liability. Wise exhorted JIR alumni to help the school. "I have the right to expect to hear from you immediately," he wrote. "If you wish that the Institute shall go on, you must make a real sacrifice in its behalf."[21] Wise's sixtieth birthday in March 1934 provided a welcome opportunity for fundraising celebrations at Carnegie Hall and in multiple galas across town, but even these did little to place the institute on secure financial footing.

The idea of a merger to relieve the Jewish community's burden of supporting so many seminaries had been floated by various funders and rabbis in the past, including Tobias Schanfarber, rabbi emeritus of KAM Temple of Chicago, who had recently called for HUC and JIR to combine under one roof and for RIETS and the Theological Seminary in Chicago to do the same. "Why should there be a double expenditure to do the work that one institution is capable of doing?" he wrote, calling the waste of money a sacrilege. "Certainly the future historian of American Judaism will have to put it down as a tremendous mistake that two theological seminaries having practically the same 'Richtung' were operating . . . when there was absolutely no necessity for more than one." Someone fearless should bring about this consummation, he concluded.

Felix Levy, vice president of the CCAR, attempted to do just that. For four years, he had tried to persuade the HUC board to reach out to JIR regarding a merger, to no avail. Now, with both seminaries in difficult financial straits, he told Wise, it was "the natural thing" to proceed with amalgamation. "You are far too valuable a man to spend yourself in causes which are taken care of by other organizations," Levy wrote. "You are needed elsewhere."[22] Moreover, he warned Wise that if one or the other seminary ultimately had to go out of business, the college, given its history and relationship with the UAHC, "would not efface itself."

Neither, of course, would JIR. Wise envisioned a merger in which both schools would continue, each providing different components of the training.[23] Negotiations moved forward only haltingly, however. HUC's president, Julian Morgenstern, was hardly eager to join forces with Wise and JIR, whom he blamed for the Reform rabbinate's growing support for Zionism. That a majority of the college's students now sympathized with Zionism hardly made the merger idea any more enticing.

REFORM IDEOLOGY IN FLUX
The swell in Zionist sentiment among Reform rabbis became even more apparent at the June 1934 CCAR convention in Wernersville, Pennsylvania. The first evening of the gathering, as Jews around the country had their radios tuned to the

broadcast from the Madison Square Garden Bowl where the Jewish heavyweight boxer Max Baer was facing off against Italy's Primo "the ambling Alp" Carnera, so, too, did Wise, J. X. Cohen and Martin Perley '34, who had driven together to the convention. Just after nine o'clock in the evening, the three men pulled into the hotel parking lot, and though Wise was scheduled to address the opening session, he insisted on remaining in the car for the full eleven rounds until, to the three rabbis' elation, Baer knocked out Carnera and became the first Jewish heavyweight boxing champion of the world. Within minutes of the final blow, Wise took to the podium and held the rapt attention of his colleagues, impressing young Perley as "a world champion Jewish leader still tingling with the excitement of listening to the crowning of a new world champion boxer, putting the lie to Hitler's characterization of Jews as an inferior species."[24]

Passions aroused by the Baer-Carnera match infused the rest of the conference, as Zionists and non-Zionists repeatedly came to verbal fisticuffs, and tensions remained high between HUC and JIR graduates, the latter of whom still represented a minority of the entire conference.[25] Nevertheless, a growing number were holding leadership positions on various committees, and overall, on the matter of Zionism, they were gaining allies (if not friends) among the HUC group. Acting as a unified block in Wernersville, the JIR and HUC Zionists managed to pass resolutions celebrating "the economic, cultural, social and spiritual progress of the new Palestine" and urging the British to facilitate more Jewish settlement there.[26]

The ideological outlook of CCAR rabbis was also in flux concerning religious practice, and the domestic and global political situation. As a result, many began to see the need for a "Revaluation of Reform Judaism." After Abraham Feldman, HUC '18, proposed adding the language of peoplehood to Reform's original characterization of Judaism as a religion, the rabbis in Wernersville moved forward a controversial proposal to replace the Reform platform issued in Pittsburgh in 1885 with an entirely new statement of principles.[27]

Reaching an agreement on these would not be easy, for divisions were emerging even among the Zionist rabbis, most of whom supported the Labor movement in Palestine, known as the Histadrut, while a smaller group aligned with the more militant Revisionist party led by Vladimir Jabotinsky. This divide went public in January 1935 after 241 out of 401 CCAR members signed a statement endorsing the Histadrut. Revisionists within the JIR contingent, including Morris Rose '26 and Louis I. Newman, took particular offense at the statement's release on the very day Jabotinsky arrived in the United States to meet with supporters. They issued a counter statement, not endorsing Revisionism, which they knew most Reform rabbis opposed, but upholding Zionism and social justice writ large rather than endorsing the Histadrut or any other particular party. In doing so, they attracted an unlikely mix of religious, pacifist, and Revisionist signatories, including graduates of HUC as well as JIR, but they also incurred the wrath of prominent CCAR members, including Abba Hillel Silver, Edward Israel, and Wise himself.

Wise, in response, preached on "Why Zionists Cannot Support Jabotinsky and Revisionism" at Carnegie Hall early that March. Revisionism ran counter to the social, democratic, and anti-militaristic ideals of Judaism and the Jewish people, he argued, and he criticized especially the party's disregard for the Arab population in Palestine. "The truth is that Revisionism is a species of Fascism in Yiddish or Hebrew," he said, "uttering its commands in the Hebrew language and therefore doubly baleful to us who believe that Hebrew should be the medium of a forward-looking hope, not of a dangerously reactionary movement."[28]

Wise had always encouraged his students to speak forthrightly, but thus far the dissenters—including his son—had largely come from the left. Now he watched with dismay as some of his dearest disciples joined the militant wing of the Zionist movement. Newman deplored Wise's sermon and said so from the dais at a Revisionist conference a few weeks later, where he spoke alongside Jabotinsky. Morris Rose published a letter in the *Jewish Bulletin* defending Revisionism against the charge of fascism.

More dissension broke out at the 1935 CCAR convention in Chicago when discussions began once again over the shaping of a new platform, for not all found the 1885 statement outdated. David Philipson, who had helped draft the Pittsburgh Platform a half-century earlier, urged his colleagues to beware "the advocacy of a political program."[29]

Nevertheless, there was no escaping the new thinking of many Reform rabbis. Zionism had become a top priority for many, and in response to both the Depression and the rise of fascism, the need to protect the most vulnerable members of society had also taken on urgency. Pacifism, by contrast, was losing adherents in the face of violent threats to Jewish communities in Europe as well as Palestine; in truth, the failure of the US and British governments to act on behalf of the Jews of Europe was leading some, for the first time, to consider armed defense a viable option.

The extent of the Reform rabbinate's changed thinking became evident in the debates that ensued on the floor of the 1935 convention. Following one of the most heated discussions in the CCAR's history, the rabbis voted 81 to 25 to shift their official position on Zionism from opposition to neutrality and to cooperate in the upbuilding of the Jewish community in Palestine. While Abba Hillel Silver and others failed to pass a resolution supporting the creation of a Jewish state, the election of Felix Levy as president increased the likelihood that such a statement would be adopted in the future. Meanwhile, Goldstein and the CCAR's Commission on Social Justice also made headway, garnering national headlines when the conference endorsed their recommendations for the "socialization" of certain businesses and a constitutional amendment that would enable the US Congress to enact legislation protecting labor and redistributing wealth.[30] The anti-war contingent, however, led by several JIR men, suffered a significant blow when a strongly worded pacifist resolution advanced by Victor Eppstein '29, Philip Bernstein '26, and Abram Goodman '28 met fierce opposition and was ultimately shelved.

Following the convention, Felix Levy appointed an eleven-member Commission on the Revaluation of Judaism to draft a new platform. When Wise received an invitation to serve as one of seven Zionists but the only JIR man in the group, he could not have been pleased about working with the commission's chair, Samuel Schulman, a nemesis since the two sparred over the Hochschule's cooperation with JIR in the summer of 1922; still, he felt the effort was "worth trying."[31]

While the CCAR commission represented an opportunity to formalize the ideological shift underway in the Reform rabbinate, Wise remained focused on the global situation. Just reelected as president of the American Jewish Congress, he had skipped the Chicago convention in order to travel to Palestine and then Lucerne, first for discussions with the World Zionist Congress and Jewish Agency leadership, and then to help the Committee of Jewish Delegations prepare for the inaugural meeting of the World Jewish Congress in 1936. This group, too, elected Wise as president, while its executive committee included JIR's board chair, Julian Mack, and alumnus Joshua Goldberg '26, now national secretary of the American Jewish Congress and rabbi of a Conservative congregation in Astoria, New York.

In September, aboard the steamer back to the United States, Wise learned that the Reichstag had passed the Nuremberg Laws, which deprived Jews of their German citizenship and prohibited them from marrying or engaging in sexual relations with non-Jewish Aryans. Never before had Jews faced persecution for their "blood" rather than their beliefs, and as soon as Wise disembarked in New York on September 18, he denounced the laws as criminal, demanding, "Why doesn't the civilized world intervene and protest against its destroying enemies?"[32]

American Jewry must intervene and protest, Wise determined, and to that end, he delegated most JIR responsibilities to Slonimsky, now dean, so that he could focus on urgent priorities: finding refuge for Jews fleeing Germany; sustaining the anti-German boycott; pressing the US and British governments to ease immigration restrictions and to impose sanctions on the Nazi regime for their antisemitic policies; convening the World Jewish Congress; raising money for Palestine; and heightening Americans' awareness of the threat Hitler posed not only to Jews but to democracy and civilization itself.

Slonimsky oversaw daily operations at the school, and despite its financial difficulties, the institute not only kept its doors open for rabbinical training but also began providing temporary shelter for Jews and non-Jews fleeing Nazi Germany under Hitler's policy of forced emigration. Thanks principally to the efforts of Louise Waterman Wise, the JIR board agreed to convert the house at 50 West Sixty-Eighth Street, which the Walden School had vacated a year earlier, into the first refuge in the United States explicitly designated for victims of Nazism. Run by the Women's Division of the American Jewish Congress, "Congress House" welcomed Jewish refugees and provided them with free short-term housing and food, instruction in English and Jewish history, and concerts and other recreational programming.

JIR students resided in the building, too, enabling them to learn about the horror unfolding in Germany from those who had experienced it firsthand. These refugees, unfortunately, represented just a tiny portion of all German Jews seeking entry into the United States, for the Roosevelt administration, refusing to abrogate Hoover's executive order, continued to let in far fewer immigrants than the official quota allowed.

Despite the weak economy, the demand for JIR rabbis remained stable and all ten members of the class of 1935 found positions spanning from Danbury, Connecticut, (Jerome Malino) to San Francisco (Saul White). In October 1935 a new class of eight arrived, selected from thirty-six applicants and bringing the total student body to thirty-two.[33]

The school's most difficult challenges were budgetary, including paying the faculty. The budget had been reduced by two-thirds, and after repeated cuts to faculty salaries, the institute was becoming increasingly reliant on instructors teaching out of their devotion to Wise and the students—hardly a sustainable model. In the fall of 1935, for example, after Baron's pay had already dropped from $3,000 in 1930 to $1,000 in 1934, the institute offered him even less, while still owing him $1,200 in postponed payments. "I have already gone to the extreme of possible concession," he told Mack, but he agreed to teach for $500.[34] Benderly taught his course for free.

Plainly the school could not remain open much longer without a massive infusion of cash or a merger of some kind, but no munificent donors were in sight, and nothing had come of the recent discussions with the college. JIR board member Joseph Hagedorn learned that some at HUC were insisting that amalgamation only happen if the institute was shut down and all faculty and students were moved to Cincinnati, which put a chill on further talks.

"If there were a will, a way could be found of uniting the two institutions," Wise told Felix Levy. "Merging, however, must not mean submerging."[35] This was just what Wise had told Emil G. Hirsch back in 1922 during the very first round of negotiations.

For all his other commitments, Wise tried to stabilize the institute financially. He urged the alumni to give, telling them, "the problem is in your hands" and again threatening that without their help the institute would soon close. He encouraged them to take out insurance plans with JIR as the beneficiary, and thirty-three complied. Even more agreed to impose a tax on their congregations, which garnered $4,543.50 via checks ranging from $4.50 to $650.[36] Wise, faculty, and several alumni also spoke regularly at congregations served by JIR graduates, always with the aim of meeting prospective donors.

But Wise focused most of his time shaping policy for the American Jewish Congress, fundraising for the American Zionist movement, and every week calling public attention to the crisis facing global Jewry in sermons at Carnegie Hall and mass meetings around the country. He advocated moving the Olympics from Berlin to Vienna, and when that failed, he called on Jewish athletes to boycott the Games. He pressed government officials to address Jewish concerns. Moreover, significantly, after a meeting with Roosevelt in January, he let go of his long-held misgivings about the president, convinced that in the role of trusted confidant, he could counteract advisors urging FDR not to aid the Jews of Germany. Hopeful that he could prevail, Wise pressed the president to end economic negotiations with the Nazis and publicly condemn Hitler's antisemitic campaign.[37]

And, he took on more. In December 1935, the United Palestine Appeal elected Wise chairman, and that winter, he set out to raise $3.5 million for the Yishuv. He also oversaw a coordinated effort by the American Jewish Congress and the Jewish Labor committee to strengthen the anti-German boycott. He took over editorship of *Opinion* from his son Jim, whose drift leftward was creating unease on the editorial board.[38] And early in the summer of 1936, while Wise was in Europe preparing to convene the World Jewish Congress, the ZOA unanimously elected him as president.

Wise also continued serving on the CCAR commission and had to be pleased when Samuel Cohon, HUC's professor of theology and a longtime Zionist going back to his days as a rabbinical student in Cincinnati a quarter of a century earlier, replaced Samuel Schulman as chair. With this new leadership, it suddenly appeared likely that a CCAR committee headed by a HUC professor and consisting of alumni from the college (with the exception of Wise) might put forward a platform reflecting the *JIR* perspective. This would mark a major turn in the twelve-year battle Wise had been waging with the Reform leadership by training rabbis with a progressive, pluralist, and Zionist outlook. Were the CCAR membership to adopt such a statement, Wise could essentially declare a truce—not with the entire movement but at least with its religious leadership, the Reform rabbinate.

Given the ideological breakdown of the CCAR, no such statement would pass without the support of JIR alumni, at least thirty of whom attended the convention in June 1936. Despite their support, however, opposition to Cohon's draft statement remained strong among the older HUC contingent, who lodged so many objections that the platform vote had to be postponed until the following year, at the 1937 convention in Columbus.

Soon after, Wise and Nahum Goldmann, along with three hundred representatives from thirty-two countries, met in Geneva for the opening session of the World Jewish Congress. In the streets outside, local Nazis shouted antisemitic slogans at the delegates, and Wise had to travel with a bodyguard due to threats on his life. Inside, the delegates battled over Jewish relief policies, Zionism, Communism, and other issues. On one matter, however, most agreed. Wise, appointed chairman of the executive, would direct that organization, too.

COLUMBUS PLATFORM

By 1937, many Reform leaders—lay as well as rabbinic—understood that to remain relevant, they urgently needed to update their platform. The UAHC acted first, passing a pro-Zionist resolution that January at the Biennial in New Orleans. "The time has come for all Jews to unite in activities leading to the establishment of a Jewish homeland in Palestine," the resolution stated, urging financial and moral support for the Yishuv.

The CCAR followed suit in May by adopting Cohon's updated version of "The Guiding Principles of Reform Judaism" at the convention in Columbus. The platform endorsed the upbuilding of Palestine as a Jewish homeland, though it still fell short of calling for the establishment of a Jewish state. It deemed the social service and social justice programs of Reform Judaism imperative, and in response to the threat of war abroad, it called for "spiritual and physical disarmament" and declared justice the condition for enduring peace. The platform also opened a path toward greater religious practice by supporting the retention and development of customs, symbols, and ceremonies in the home and synagogue.

Samuel Schulman, who came to Columbus prepared for a fight, nearly derailed the platform's passage. Unable to muster significant support for his own statement of principles, he did manage to push forward a resolution opposing the adoption of any platform at all, which resulted in a tied vote of 81–81. Only after Felix Levy, as president, stepped in to cast the deciding ballot in favor of proceeding did passage of the new platform become inevitable; the membership rallied in a show of unity, and David Philipson, symbolically and remarkably given his opposition to Zionism, made the motion for its adoption. This time, all but eight members voted in favor.

Notably, over the previous year, the CCAR's Commission on the Revaluation of Judaism had shrunk from eleven to five members and included neither Wise nor any JIR graduates. Nevertheless, the cadre he and the founders of JIR envisioned at the time of the institute's founding proved critical; JIR alumni now represented roughly 16 percent of the CCAR's membership, and without their votes, adoption of the Guiding Principles would have been impossible.

CONCLUSION

The Columbus Platform, as the document came to be known, signaled a pivotal change in the ideological trajectory of American liberal Judaism, as well as a significant victory for the founders, faculty, and graduates of JIR. Under different circumstances, the CCAR's endorsement of their outlook might have been reason to celebrate, for the change clearly went far beyond a mere statement of principles.

Their ideological approach stemmed from a commitment to the survival of the Jewish people and to democracy itself. Viewing these as inextricably linked, Wise and his corps of rabbis urged American Jews to fight publicly and aggressively for social justice, against antisemitic policies and practices in the United States and abroad, and for the establishment of a Jewish state. Many of the Eastern European immigrants and their children who now made up the vast majority of American Jewry were determined to fight for these, as well.

Wise's approach to the American rabbinate was spreading, too. His highly visible role as statesman, activist, preacher, and pastor demonstrated the power of rabbinic leadership not only to influence Jewish belief and practice but also to create movements for change within and beyond the Jewish community, while acting in defense of Jews and the vulnerable everywhere. Similarly, several foundational aspects of the Free Synagogue model had become prevalent, namely, congregational involvement in social service (which some called social action) and freedom of the pulpit.

However, in the summer of 1937, with the Nazis' campaign of antisemitic persecution escalating and Hitler's ambitions for European domination ever more apparent, the Jewish people were in grave danger. The long-sought consensus was largely wrought in response to these crises, which led American Jews to embrace the tactical responses associated with Wise and his contingent, including mass demonstrations and raising support of every kind for the Yishuv.

Similarly, it was these grim circumstances that led a majority of the Reform movement, including lay leaders as well as rabbis, to join the struggle.

11

The Legacy Crystalizes

THE INSTITUTE'S EFFORT TO ALIGN LIVED AMERICAN JEWISH EXPERI-
ence with the ideological shift expressed in the Columbus Platform proceeded, inevitably, in the context of the momentous events and tragedies of the
late 1930s and subsequent war years. During this period, the crucial work of rescuing European Jewry and establishing a homeland in Palestine dominated Wise's
attention. Necessarily, these struggles, which he waged principally through the
American and World Jewish Congresses and the Zionist movement, crowded out
virtually everything else, including the institute's needs. That the school fell to the
bottom of his priority list reflected not his lack of concern for the school but the
overwhelming urgency of the battle to save the Jewish people.

As the immense challenges of this tumultuous period tested the school's ability to translate its values and its ability to translate them into action, certain aspects of the mission fell away and others blossomed. The goal of creating a center
for Jewish scholarship came to fruition only partially in the shadow of the war.
And though women students continued seeking ordination at JIR, Wise, with the
support of most students and faculty, shut down that possibility at the institute for
good. At the same time, the institute's students and alumni, through their activism in this period—serving in the US armed forces, bringing aid to the survivors
of Nazism, and helping establish the State of Israel—fundamentally changed the
role of the American rabbinate in ways that surpassed the founders' original vision.
In addition, as most of these men, like Wise, integrated their activism into their
pulpit work, their involvement in the broader world helped transform the mindset
of their congregants and communities. By the end of the war, the values and approach most JIR alumni embodied were incontrovertibly in sync with the mindset
of much of American Jewry.

At this juncture, the leadership of Reform Judaism, seeking to reposition the
movement for growth in a newly competitive postwar landscape, finally acknowledged and embraced the changes wrought by the institute, and actively pursued a
merger. And although Wise and the JIR contingent negotiated an agreement that
preserved their core commitments to maintaining a New York school and serving *klal yisrael*, both were cut out of the final document following Wise's death in
1949. In ensuing years, in the face of opposition from HUC's Cincinnati-based

leadership, preserving JIR's mission proved challenging. Ultimately, the institute's nondenominationalism was lost, as HUC-JIR became singularly Reform.

During the final years of JIR's existence as an independent institution, the school's contributions in the realms of scholarship as well as the rabbinate, combined with its failure to spread the nondenominational model or to effectively respond to women seeking to become rabbis, crystalized the school's long-term legacy.

Scholarly Center

Wise's tireless work to engage American Jewish leaders, the US government, and the British in large-scale rescue efforts severely curtailed the resources he could devote to growing JIR's faculty, scholarly production, and library. Still, as the centers of Wissenschaft in Germany, Austria, and Hungary faced imminent collapse, Wise joined other American seminary heads in a desperate attempt to save as many of their faculty as possible, and despite the duress caused by the war, the institute remained, within its limited resources, a productive a center for teaching and research.

European Destruction

Wise always viewed JIR's scholarly mission in the context of the global shifts underway in Jewish higher learning. In the 1920s, while scholars, books, and manuscripts typically flowed from Europe to the United States and, to a lesser extent, Palestine, the trend was not entirely unidirectional. A majority of the visiting faculty Wise brought from Germany, for example, returned to their homes after teaching for just a semester or two. By 1938, however, the truth of Perles's forecast that American Jewry would have to salvage Jewish learning "from the wreckage of the European debacle" had become all too apparent, and obtaining an appointment in the United States was now a matter of life and death. Under the Nazis, all Jewish institutions of higher learning were eventually destroyed, and a countless number of their teachers, students, and alumni were murdered.

These included the "five seminaries of German-speaking lands" that once received aid from JIR. The Israelitisch-Theologische Lehranstalt was shut down along with all of Vienna's Jewish cultural institutions when the Germans annexed the city during the Anschluss of 1938.[1] During Kristallnacht in November of that year, the Jewish Theological Seminary of Breslau was attacked. While the faculty managed to clandestinely ordain the seminary's last two students in February 1939, most of its library was destroyed, teaching ended, and many students were sent to Buchenwald.[2] Berlin's Hildesheimer Seminary closed days after Kristallnacht, having transferred most of its library to Tel Aviv.[3] At the Hochschule, Leo Baeck continued teaching about a dozen students until July 1942, when the Nazis shut it down and confiscated its library.[4] That year, Regina Jonas (memorialized at Yad Vashem as "history's first female rabbi") was deported with her mother to Theresienstadt, where she continued serving as a rabbi until she and her mother were deported to Auschwitz and murdered on October 12, 1944.[5] Hungary's Landesrabbinerschule heroically attempted to save Jews from deportation by admitting all applicants, ultimately enrolling 174 students in 1944. However, that March, as soon as the Nazis occupied Hungary, they destroyed the seminary.[6]

Before that cataclysm, Wise joined Cyrus Adler and Julian Morgenstern of JTS and HUC, respectively, in an effort to save German scholars, though of the many strategies for Jewish rescue that he pursued, this was not where he was most effective, for the cash-strapped JIR was able to contribute very little to the endeavor. In contrast, HUC, with crucial funding provided by the National Federation of Temple Sisterhoods, successfully rescued seven students and eleven professors from Germany, including several of those Wise had considered for visiting faculty posts in the 1920s.[7]

However, Wise did bring two professors from Germany onto the JIR faculty in 1938, Guido Kisch, a lawyer and historian of German Jewry, and Ismar Elbogen. Kisch had been forced out of his teaching position at the University of Halle by the Nazis in 1933 and then taught for a short time at Prague University and the Jewish Theological Seminary of Breslau before immigrating to the United States in 1935. After arriving at JIR, he went on to have a long and productive scholarly career.

Elbogen, having spent his life providing intellectual leadership for the Reform movement of Germany as well as inspiration for hundreds of students at the Hochschule, remained in Germany until he could no longer safeguard the community. In 1938, sixteen years after Wise had hoped Elbogen might serve as the institute's first president, JIR, JTS, HUC, and Dropsie joined forces to provide the elder scholar refuge by bringing him to New York and together appointing him research professor. In the few years remaining before Elbogen died in 1943, he completed *A Century of Jewish Life*, intended as a sequel to Heinrich Graetz's *History of the Jews*. Picking up where Graetz work ended, Elbogen's opus covered the period from 1848–1939 in Europe, the United States, and Palestine and was published posthumously in 1944, translated from German into English by Moses Hadas.

During these years, despite Wise's primary focus on Europe and Palestine, the institute remained fully functioning. Tchernowitz produced two multivolume works on the development of Jewish law, while also founding *Bitzaron*, a Hebrew monthly, and authoring scores of political and biographical essays. Slonimsky became a dominant influence on several generations of JIR students, thanks to the free spirit and idealism he brought to his teaching of philosophy and work as dean. John Tepfer '27, after years of tutoring JIR seniors for no compensation, joined the faculty in rabbinics and taught history, as well, while Abraham W. Binder became a noted composer of orchestral, chamber, and synagogue choral works. Meanwhile, faculty turnover continued. In 1943, when Ralph Marcus left JIR for the University of Chicago and Shalom Spiegel left for JTS, to be replaced by Harry Orlinsky in the field of Bible and Simon Halkin in Hebrew literature.

Under the direction of I. Edward Kiev, a one-time student at JIR, the institute's library, which originated with the private collections of Wise, Emil G. Hirsch, and Marcus Brann, grew to include more than fifty thousand books, pamphlets, and rare manuscripts. The institute also had its own small press, which published papers by scholars including Israel Abrahams, Hugo Gressman, H. St. John Thackeray, and R. Travers Herford. Of more significant impact, early in 1938 Gershom Scholem, a Jerusalem-based scholar who had just published a pioneering article on Sabbatianism, came to New York at Spiegel's invitation to deliver a series of lectures at JIR on Jewish mysticism. Scholem used the opportunity to create a synthesis of his field from antiquity through Hasidism and delivered six talks in English and one in Hebrew. Had the JIR Press any funding at the time, it surely would have published the talks, which over the next three years Scholem turned into the pivotal work *Major Trends in Jewish Mysticism*.[8]

Throughout the 1940s, the institute remained a vibrant center of Jewish learning. With no shortage of applicants attracted to its pluralistic ethos, the school was able to maintain selectivity in admissions and high academic standards. Although the institute offered post-graduate research opportunities for alumni, only a few JIR graduates chose a scholarly professional path.

The ideal of training American scholars of Judaism failed to materialize not only at JIR during the Depression and subsequent war years but at most institutions of higher learning, Jewish as well as secular. While HUC's rescue effort added to the number of major Jewish scholars in the United States, and Wolfson and Baron thrived in their research at Harvard and Columbia, no additional chairs in the field were created during this period.

It took two more decades for Zunz and Geiger's dreams to come to fruition. Only in the 1960s did Jewish studies departments begin opening in American colleges and universities, supported through the generosity of American Jewish philanthropists who often preferred giving to prestigious secular institutions than to Jewish seminaries.

A Setback for Women

It would take even longer for the first female rabbi to be ordained in the United States. For a moment in 1922, when the faculty voted unanimously to train "men and women for the Jewish ministry," the institute stood on the precipice of radical change. Nevertheless, Wise, rather than seizing the moment as he so often did, chose the tactic of delay, ostensibly just for a year or two while the lack of housing and other "satisfactory arrangements" were worked out.[9] In retrospect, it appears that, while conceptually he may have supported opening the rabbinate to women, when presented with actual candidates, he chose to continue the traditional exclusion.

These candidates included Dora Askowith, who, still designated a "special student" at JIR in the 1930s, set her hopes on being admitted into the rabbinical program and paving the way for women desirous of becoming ordained. She delivered a student sermon at JIR titled "The Woman in the Rabbinate," in which she argued that Jewish tradition did not prohibit women's religious leadership, and she completed a majority of the curriculum. The faculty, however, refused her admission into the rabbinical program until she passed the second-year Hebrew examinations, which she never took. Askowith left the institute in 1937 to devote herself to teaching at Hunter College and writing, but she did not stop pressing for women's ordination.[10]

Next to challenge the barrier at JIR was Helen Levinthal, a young University of Pennsylvania graduate descended from a prominent Lithuanian rabbinical family. Her grandfather, Bernard Levinthal, immigrated to the United States in 1891 and became a world-renowned Orthodox rabbi who helped found RIETS, the American Jewish Committee, the Mizrachi Organization of America, and Agudat ha-Rabbanim. Her father, Israel Levinthal, a Zionist and Conservative rabbi who led the Brooklyn Jewish Center in Crown Heights, was one of the most popular preachers in New York. And her uncle, Louis Levinthal, lent further stature to the family as an influential Philadelphia attorney and judge, who eventually became president of the Jewish Publication Society as well as the Zionist Organization of America.

When Levinthal arrived at JIR in 1931 fresh out of college, Wise and the faculty were well aware of her prestigious family. Initially, Levinthal audited her courses while also studying at Columbia, where she earned a master's degree in 1932. Askowith writes, "I was the one who persuaded Miss Levinthal, later, to continue her work and at least to acquire the degree of 'Master of Hebraic Literature' even though she could not be admitted into the Rabbinate."[11] In 1935, Levinthal began taking courses for credit and progressing through the program. In 1937, she put forth her candidacy for ordination, thereby forcing a decision. In response, the entire faculty with the exception of Shalom Spiegel voiced their opposition, claiming Levinthal was "an average student with no special qualifications."[12] According to the historian Pamela Nadell, Wise later told Levinthal's father that the faculty actually believed Helen had done excellent work, but the time was not right for JIR to ordain a woman.[13] Nonetheless, Levinthal proceeded with the aim of completing all of the institute's rabbinical requirements.

Notably, across the Atlantic at the Hochschule in Berlin, the question of ordaining a woman as a rabbi had already been addressed a few years earlier. There, in 1930, twenty-eight-year-old Regina Jonas had completed her studies, including a final thesis titled "Can a Woman Hold Rabbinical Office?" which offered a ha-lakhic argument for women's fitness for the rabbinate. Her thesis supervisor, Edu-ard Baneth, professor of Talmud, approved the thesis and graded it "good" but died shortly thereafter, before he could administer the exam required for ordination. It is not clear whether or not Baneth would have ordained Jonas, but after his death the rest of the faculty refused to grant her more than a teaching diploma at grad-uation, along with recognition of her homiletical training and skills as a preacher.

Jonas went on to teach at several girls' schools in Berlin, but she did not aban-don her dream of becoming a rabbi. Finally, in December 1935, Rabbi Max Die-nemann, a prominent leader of German Reform Judaism, agreed to ordain her privately, and four days after he signed her *semikhah* (certificate of ordination), Leo Baeck, leader of the German Jewish community and a senior faculty member at the Hochschule, wrote to congratulate her. Through the late 1930s, the Berlin Jewish community employed her as "pastoral-rabbinic counselor," and she offici-ated at the Jewish Hospital while also preaching regularly in Berlin's liberal syn-agogues and lecturing to Jewish groups around the city. As conditions worsened, especially after Kristallnacht in November 1938, she focused her work on visiting the sick and caring for the elderly.[14] In February 1942, Baeck signed a certificate confirming her ordination, and she continued to minister even after being ordered into forced labor in a factory. That November, Jonas was deported with her mother to Theresienstadt, where she continued serving as a rabbi until she and her mother were deported to Auschwitz and murdered on October 12, 1944.[15]

In 1938, Helen Levinthal, as a student at JIR in New York, appears to have been unaware that in Germany the first female rabbi had already been ordained and was ministering to her fellow Jews suffering under Nazism. Levinthal com-pleted her thesis that year on Jewish law and women's suffrage, and after earning an honor grade from Chaim Tchernowitz,[16] she became the first woman to complete the rabbinical curriculum at an American Jewish seminary.[17]

However, Wise still chose to deny her entry into the rabbinate. Even award-ing Levinthal a master's of Hebrew literature (MHL) degree[18] dismayed her class-mates, who told Wise this would "detract from the dignity and force" of their own ordination.[19] Nonetheless, at the June 1939 ceremony, which Levinthal's father and grandfather attended, Wise awarded Helen Levinthal two JIR diplomas, the MHL along with a certificate in Hebrew that granted her the title *musmakah*, "or-dained," that, according to Nadell, Tchernowitz likely suggested.[20] Notwithstand-ing the language on that certificate, and the *Palestine Post* headline "First Woman Rabbi: Helen Levinthal Ordained in New York," JIR did not grant Levinthal the title rabbi.[21] Rather, the MHL was conferred upon JIR's "first woman graduate," as the *New York Times* accurately reported.[22]

Why did Wise, who fought so hard for women's suffrage and encouraged his own daughter to attend Yale Law School and join the female pioneers in that field, choose not to break down the barrier to ordaining women as rabbis? While Irma Lindheim, who pushed for ordination in the 1920s, lacked a college degree, and Dora Askowith perhaps lacked strong proficiency in Hebrew, certainly Helen Levinthal presented a compelling case, both on her own merits as an excellent student who completed all JIR requirements and wrote an honors thesis, and given the pressure applied by her father Israel Levinthal, among the most influential rabbis in the United States, who lobbied Wise on her behalf.

Wise's decision likely reflected a mix of political expediency and his own conflicted view of women's roles, particularly within the spheres of religion and the home. Israel Levinthal later recalled Wise asserting to him that JIR would ordain Helen if ever Israel's Orthodox father gave his approval.[23] The statement seems uncharacteristic because, while Wise did value his ties with certain Orthodox leaders, he was more than willing to defy the traditional establishment in order to advance his views. More significantly, Wise surely knew that a prominent Orthodox rabbi like Bernard Levinthal would never support women's ordination. If Wise indeed said this, he was likely signaling that, in fact, he had no intention of ordaining women.

Nadell suggests that the poor job market at the time may have been a factor. In the early 1920s, the demand for rabbis in the United States exceeded the supply, so women's entry into the profession represented a minimal threat to male rabbis' employment; in 1939, by contrast, the still all-male American rabbinate faced a shortage of jobs. With German rabbis seeking refuge in the United States and increasing the competition for pulpits already in scant supply, few rabbis had any interest in opening the field to women.[24]

Wise's complicated view of women must factor into the analysis, as well. On the one hand, he had long advocated publicly for legal and civil protections for women, and within his own family he was fully supportive of Louise Waterman Wise's extensive charitable work and political activism, and he consistently championed the professional aspirations of his daughter Justine, who became a distinguished judge on New York's Domestic Relations Court and the first woman in the state to hold a judicial post above magistrate.[25]

At the same time, Wise also preached and conducted himself in ways that hardly advanced women's freedom. From the pulpit, he linked notions of women's purity with women's responsibility to preserve not just the sanctity of marriage but the moral fiber of society, and he condemned those who challenged social and sexual conventions. Thus, his support for women's suffrage and equality was tempered by his ambivalence about changing women's roles in the domestic sphere and perhaps particularly in the Jewish family.

Complicating Wise's image as a devoted husband, despite his sermonizing on marital fidelity, he was known to have had at least one long-term extramarital affair and to engage in conduct long minimized as "womanizing." At the time, this conduct rarely garnered headlines, and it is impossible to know what, for Wise, this entailed.

Additionally, during the 1970s, Helen Lawrenson (who had been an editor and writer for *Vanity Fair* in the 1930s) described in her memoir two separate occasions during which she alleged Wise forced himself on her: the first in 1930 when, as a twenty-two-year-old journalist, she agreed to interview the fifty-six-year-old rabbi in his hotel room following his speech at Syracuse University, and then three years later when she interviewed him again, this time in his office at JIR.[26]

How did Wise's outlook and conduct regarding women align with his refusal to act on his early support for women entering the rabbinate? He was hardly unique in espousing an idealized but restrictive view of women's role in society at this time, particularly as a product of the Progressive Era, nor can his trespassing on his own calls for marital fidelity be seen as exceptional. As to the sexual coercion Helen Lawrenson alleged more than a quarter-century after Wise's death, the imposition of unwanted sexual relations by powerful men on subordinate women was rife, and not until the rise of sexual harassment law in the 1970s would it begin to be regulated in the workplace.[27]

Still, while the seeming contradiction between Wise's support for women's equality in certain spheres (including suffrage) versus his refusal to ordain women does fit sociocultural patterns of this era, the allegations of Wise's abusive attitude toward women suggests troubling gendered power relations. Relevant here is Wise's consistent assertion of male dominance and control, on the pulpit as well as behind closed doors. Despite his and his students' commitment to social justice and equality, long denied to Jewish men in the Christian and secular worlds, they refused to cede their own power over women in the workplace and the home.[28]

In the minds of Wise's own students, merely awarding a master's degree to a woman in their presence threatened to diminish the "dignity and force" of their ordination. They understood that their power and authority were at stake, for to some degree these were dependent on the exclusion of women, which enabled their notions about the sexes, and their sexual conduct, to go largely unchecked within the profession. Given the particular ideas and conduct that were normative at this time, Wise along with his students and colleagues had reason to worry that female rabbis would, indeed, challenge their assertion of power and authority.

In this light, Wise's willingness to quash the rabbinical aspirations of JIR's female students is less surprising, even in light of his support for his wife's and daughter's work in spheres outside the rabbinate. There were limits to his commitment to justice and equality for all, as Helen Levinthal, as well as Irma Lindheim and Dora Askowith before her, painfully discovered.

A New American Rabbinate Emerges Out of Wartime

It was by training a new kind of rabbi, albeit still a male rabbi, that JIR achieved its greatest impact. With the onset of war, the institute mobilized to meet the need for military chaplains, and alumni put themselves on the line in a variety of ways. Among those serving in the armed forces in Europe, some went beyond their assigned duties to bring aid to Jewish refugees or to help them immigrate to Palestine. As the extent of the Nazis' mass murder of European Jewry became apparent and support for a Jewish homeland among American Jewry increased, many JIR alumni intensified their Zionist activity, legal as well as illegal. Collectively, JIR alumni, having learned firsthand from Wise the power of a publicly engaged rabbinate, now modeled for their congregations and the broader American Jewish community powerful and effective forms of social activism grounded in the values of Judaism.

Military Chaplains

Three days after the bombing of Pearl Harbor, Wise put out the call for JIR alumni to take leave from their pulpits to meet the pressing need for military chaplains. "I realize that this might entail a great sacrifice on your part," he wrote, "but nothing short of the greatest sacrifice on the part of all of us will carry us through to victory."[29]

Many stepped up, including pacifists like Philip Bernstein '26 and Abram Goodman '28, who had long advocated global demilitarization. Bernstein, for example, who had condemned the US arms buildup while chairing the CCAR's Committee on International Peace in the late 1930s, now renounced his long held anti-war views in order to fight Nazism. After becoming head of the National Jewish Welfare Board's Committee on Army and Navy Religious Activities in 1942, he visited every major battlefront where US soldiers served and met thousands of Jewish GIs. Following the war, he served for another two years as advisor of Jewish Affairs to the US Army Commander in Germany, ensuring adequate food and housing for Jews in the displaced persons camps and, less successfully, urging Congress to permit their resettlement in the United States.[30]

Throughout the war, to accelerate the replenishment of chaplains to the military, the institute conducted three rounds of admissions each year and temporarily allowed college seniors to begin their JIR studies while still completing their BAs. Summer terms were added so students could qualify for ordination in three and a half years rather than four (graduates then needed to complete a year of civilian service before they could join the Chaplaincy Corps). The institute also assigned students and faculty to temporarily replace New York–area congregational rabbis who were away on active duty.

Meanwhile, in the late 1930s, JIR's board had increased to three the number of institute-owned buildings designated as Congress House. With the onset of war, when the flow of refugees ended, Louise Waterman Wise and her team of volunteers converted the buildings into Defense House, where they provided temporary housing and care for more than a quarter-million Allied soldiers and sailors, regardless of religion.[31]

Ultimately, fifty JIR graduates served as military chaplains in the US armed forces, representing just over one-third of the institute's 143 rabbis ordained between 1926 and 1945. They joined the Army, Navy, Marine Corps, and Merchant Marine and were deployed to the battlefields of Africa, Europe, Asia, and the Pacific. As but one example, Joshua Goldberg '26, who had fought in US Army artillery units during World War I, became the first rabbi commissioned as a Jewish chaplain in the US Navy, where he reached the rank of captain.[32]

While attending to the needs of service members abroad, these rabbis also provided support for Jewish communities where they still existed. Nearing the end of the war, some, like Abraham Haselkorn '32, worked with survivors of the concentration camps and with Jews who had spent the war years in hiding. Based in Central France in 1944, the Army unit in which Haselkorn served as captain discovered hundreds of Jewish children, most from Paris, hidden in the small farms and villages of the Loire Valley. They raised $3,500 to convert a local chateau into a group home and hired staff to care for those children whose parents had been killed or deported.

ZIONISM

That so many nations had closed their doors to Jews fleeing the Nazi genocide radicalized many in the Zionist movement, including a substantial number of JIR students and alumni who now saw a Jewish State as the sole path to Jewish survival. Some, on the left, devoted themselves to the Labor Zionist movement; others chose advocacy, speaking widely on the need for a Jewish state; and others further to the right got involved with an underground network sending material support to the Jewish militias in Palestine.

Wise made the connection between the Nazis' war against the Jews and the need for a Jewish homeland explicit for his students, as Herbert Friedman '43 recalled. In August 1942, Wise received a telegram drafted by Gerhart Riegner, the World Jewish Congress representative in Switzerland, alerting him of the Nazis' plan to deport and kill three and a half to four million Jews in Nazi-occupied territory. Riegner had already shared this information with US and British officials, and the British WJC representative, a member of Parliament, passed it on to Wise, as Riegner had requested. Wise immediately told Sumner Welles, undersecretary of state, who requested that the information not be publicized until the US government could confirm it. Wise complied, but while waiting, he shared the warning with other government officials, Jewish leaders, and students at JIR.[33] Herbert Friedman '43 recalled how, for Wise, the plight of European Jewry and the battle to create a Jewish state were intertwined:

He showed us the pain and frustration, as well as the glory, which accompanied these struggles. I shall never forget that moment in August 1942 when
he pulled from his pocket Gerhard Riegner's telegram from Geneva which
was the first formal charge accusing Hitler of intending to murder the entire Jewish population of Europe. And month after month, he continued to
relate to us how Under Secretary of State Sumner Welles urged him not to
publish the telegram until its information could be confirmed through the
State Department representative at the Vatican. Permission finally came ten
weeks later, with the statement to Wise that the United States government
"can now confirm and justify your deepest fears." We students learned from
Wise that our deepest obligation was to fight, at whatever cost, for the creation of a Jewish state in order to protect the security of the Jewish people.
We learned it through the burning passion of his eyes and voice—we learned
it week after week, year after year, from the manner in which he impacted our
very souls by exposing his own to us, his beloved students.[34]

JIR students and alumni rabbis expressed their Zionism in wide-ranging
ways. Many worked within their own communities, building support for ending
the British White Paper and establishing a Jewish sovereign state in Palestine.
Those in the CCAR, which remained divided despite the adoption of the Columbus Platform, helped pass a controversial 1942 resolution favoring the creation
of a Jewish army. Some JIR rabbis engaged in more direct action, lending aid to
Aliyah Bet, the illegal immigration of Jews into Palestine, and to the Jewish underground militias, including the Haganah as well as the Irgun. Still others would
eventually make their lives there, including Saadia Gelb '46, who helped found
Habonim and worked for Poale Zion before smuggling himself, his wife, and their
three children into Palestine in 1947.

A few examples illustrate the range of alumni efforts. Friedman, a US army
lieutenant responsible for rescuing Jewish refugees in southern Bavaria and getting
aid to the DP camps, was secretly recruited by David Ben-Gurion to assist the
Haganah in illegally transporting refugees to Palestine. Later, he was disciplined
for helping Gershom Scholem smuggle thousands of medieval religious manuscripts stolen by the Nazis to Hebrew University. Decommissioned with an honorable discharge, he returned to his pulpit in Denver, where he transported arms
and munitions for the Haganah.[35] Other JIR men engaged as well, including Max
Maccoby '38, who used the Free Synagogue of Westchester as a secret collection
point for the weaponry.[36]

Several graduates joined the more militant wing of the Zionist movement,
disregarding Wise's public denunciation of the Revisionist party and its leaders.
Louis I. Newman not only hosted Jabotinsky in his home and joined him in fundraising events but also, reportedly, used Congregation Rodeph Sholom as a storage

site for weapons being smuggled to the Irgun, over the objections of the synagogue's lay leadership.[37] Other JIR alumni involved with these efforts included Morris Rose '26, who presided over the New Zionist Organization of America, a Revisionist political organization, and Jacob Philip Rudin, the Free Synagogue's former assistant rabbi, who together with at least seven other JIR alumni joined the Committee for a Jewish Army, a group dedicated to sending military support to the Irgun.[38]

Students, too, ran guns. "As a passionate Zionist I worked for Americans for Haganah, securing large quantities of small weapons, which overflowed my locker at JIR, where they were stored until they were shipped to the freedom fighters in Eretz Israel," recalled Paul Steinberg '49, who entered the institute in June 1945 while still a senior at CCNY. Steinberg belonged to the last JIR class to be ordained prior to the merger with Hebrew Union College and in a few years would become dean of the New York School.[39]

The work of these JIR students and rabbis substantiated the premise that by training clergy differently, the institute could reshape the American rabbinate and thereby alter the course of American Jewish life. For over two decades, Wise and the faculty had imbued students with the tools and inspiration they needed, so that when the call to battle came, they were prepared to fight in ways that were new and unique to the American rabbinate. For some, whether in uniform or as civilians, that entailed dramatic rescue missions and gunrunning aimed at saving European Jewry and building a Jewish homeland; others, especially in the years before and after the war, chose the pursuit of universal justice and equality as their primary focus, in keeping with the prophetic values of Judaism.

And the model, which Wise honed in his own career and the earliest JIR-trained rabbis brought to their pulpits, became more widespread as rabbis from across the religious spectrum increasingly felt called to this kind of principled activism and outspoken public engagement. The change extended beyond the rabbinate, too. In the early 1920s, only pockets of American Jewry shared JIR's ideological outlook, and Wise's overall blueprint for American Judaism had yet to take hold. But now, for a majority of Jews across the United States, the broad commitment to *klal yisrael*, the creation of a Jewish homeland in Palestine, and the pursuit of universal social justice rooted in the prophetic tradition had become foundational.

Postwar Denominationalism and Merger: A Strained Embrace
In 1945, as the United States began preparing for a postwar period of growth and prosperity, American Jewish efforts to aid refugees and displaced persons in Europe continued, and the battle for a Jewish state in Palestine grew more militant. At the same time, American Jewry also turned inward, determined to strengthen a communal infrastructure that had declined during the Depression and war.

With Jewish servicemen returning home and many young Jews starting families, hundreds of new synagogues began cropping up across the country. These helped fuel the growth of Reform, Conservative, and Orthodox Judaism, each of which sought to deepen their influence among American Jewry by bolstering their membership numbers, bringing more congregations into their fold, and strengthening their respective seminaries. In this context, though small and nondenominational, JIR represented a formidable force within American Judaism. Indicatively, the Reform movement, for the first time in its history, recognized the institute as a serious contender.

The institute's strength lay not in the school's coffers, which were near empty, nor even, at this point, in Wise's leadership; though still at the helm, he was grieving for his people, battle-worn, and in great physical pain due to illness, and it was clear a successor would be needed soon. The real power of this small nondenominational seminary lay in its ability to continually generate rabbis who spoke, in many ways, for a broad swath of American Jewry. That year, the institute graduated fourteen new rabbis, its largest class ever, bringing the total number of JIR rabbinical alumni to 163. Several worked abroad, ten served full-time in the US military, and eighteen directed Hillel foundations; almost all the rest led congregations spread across the United States, roughly fifty of which were Reform.[40]

The leadership of the Reform movement recognized that, to keep up with the rapid growth of Conservative Judaism, they would have to embrace the JIR outlook while also neutralizing the competitive threat the institute posed as a second flank. Absorbing the New York School would accomplish both goals, determined the head of the union, Maurice Eisendrath. Wise and the JIR contingent saw possible gains in a merger, as well; perhaps by surrendering the school's independence, they could broaden its influence geographically as well as ideologically. This would also resolve the matter of succession, for clearly new leadership would soon be needed.

Despite the many potential benefits a merger offered, including the obvious economies of scale, the process of reaching an accord surfaced the old battle lines of 1922: one side Midwestern, fiercely denominational, and seeking dominance; the other New York–centric, pluralistic, and demanding equal standing. As a result, it would take over a decade for an uneasy but lasting agreement to be reached. To the despair of the most diehard JIR men, the entire process unfolded in a context where American Jewish denominationalism, which Wise had long deemed irrelevant and utterly contrary to the mission of JIR, was entering its heyday.

In the fall of 1945, Eisendrath shared internal memoranda from the Conservative movement with a select group of Reform colleagues. "The future of world Judaism rests in our hands," wrote Robert Gordis, president of the Rabbinical Assembly and a professor at JTS. "We, the Conservative movement, want to shape that future."[41] In like manner, Max Arzt, director of field activities at JTS, planned a fundraising message that emphasized, "The Seminary appeals to *all types of Jews, irrespective of their affiliation.*"[42]

With the Conservative movement planning such a broad recruitment effort, Eisendrath emphasized the importance of strengthening support for HUC and the union—and not just financially. "More basic is the obvious bid on the part of Conservative Judaism and the Jewish Theological Seminary for hegemony in American Jewish life and their direct challenge for supremacy on the American Jewish scene," he wrote. "If we believe that Liberal Judaism offers the most suitable way of life for American Jewry, if we feel that ours is the pattern for the future of American Israel, then we must be prepared more vigorously than ever to fight for our particular conviction and cause, both locally and nationally."[43]

Fighting for the cause, Eisendrath believed, would clearly entail raising money for Reform Judaism and attracting large numbers of unaffiliated Jews. As well, he now began seeking Wise's blessing for a merger of JIR and HUC.

Wise and the JIR group were wary. Not only had they no interest in sectarianism, but they also distrusted the leaders of Reform. Just five years earlier, seizing on a unique moment when the chairmanships of JIR and HUC were held by brothers, Julian and Ralph Mack, respectively, Wise had initiated merger talks, perhaps hoping that the familial bond would help yield an agreement. However, like previous discussions between the two schools, this discussion, too, which ensued from 1940 to 1942, resulted in little more than rancor. During that period, the college unilaterally committed to becoming solely a graduate school and ceased admitting undergraduates.[44] However, when the college insisted that JIR halt *all* admissions immediately and require its current students to spend most of their graduate studies in Cincinnati, negotiations broke down.

Further alienating Wise, in June 1942, HUC's president, Julian Morgenstern, joined a dissident group of CCAR rabbis who opposed the creation of a Jewish army and state and sought to reverse Reform Judaism's shift toward Zionism. Wise, still working to unify American Jewry in support of the movement, assailed the group, as did 757 Reform, Conservative, and Orthodox rabbis who signed a statement called *Zionism: An Affirmation of Judaism.* Though HUC students approved the statement in a 42–9 vote, it was clear that Wise could never agree to a merger that placed JIR under the authority of Julian Morgenstern.[45]

The JIR contingent emerged from these failed talks with two other sine qua nons, as well. First, they would never agree to an arrangement unless the merged rabbinical school represented all shades of opinion in Jewish life, in accord with JIR's original mission. Second, they would require assurance that a center of study would be maintained in New York. Given HUC's demands in 1942, they had little reason to expect either.

So when Eisendrath raised the merger possibility in 1945, Wise insisted on limiting discussions to two potential areas of cooperation: fundraising and a school of education the college planned to open soon in New York. Fundraising was the more urgent matter. Both the Reform and Conservative movements had ambitious campaigns underway, and JIR, too, had launched a Million Dollar Campaign, with Albert Einstein as honorary chair. Recently, JIR alumni serving in Reform congregations had approached Wise with a problem: The UAHC wanted their congregations to participate in its fundraising campaign, but neither their laity nor the rabbis themselves were inclined to support a drive that benefited the college alone, and not the institute.

As a compromise, Wise proposed including JIR in the UAHC-HUC fundraising effort. Not only could the fifty or so JIR alumni based in Reform congregations raise funds for the overall campaign, but an additional twenty-five JIR rabbis, he estimated, could bring their unaffiliated congregations into the UAHC, adding membership as well as revenue. In return, a portion of the money raised would accrue to JIR—say, $50,000 out of $90,000, were JIR to raise that much. Should the Reform movement *not* be interested in joint fundraising, JIR alumni were considering creating a union of congregations of their own.[46]

The veiled threat was real. The institute already had a separate rabbinical association in the form of its alumni body, which met regularly and helped members compete for pulpits against HUC and JTS graduates. JIR, and not the college, represented progressive Judaism in the New York area, amid the strengthening Orthodox and Conservative communities, whose national headquarters were also based there. Moreover, JIR had its Million Dollar Campaign, which, while unlikely to achieve its goal, would undoubtedly siphon at least some funds away from the UAHC drive. The last thing the Reform movement needed, while vying with Conservative Judaism, was more competition from JIR.

Thus, Eisendrath and other Reform leaders continued to coax Wise into merger negotiations, albeit without agreeing to cooperate on fundraising or any other matter. As part of their friendship campaign, HUC awarded Wise an honorary degree in December 1945. Having spurned the college as a young man, after Isaac Mayer Wise granted his request to remain in New York while preparing for HUC's advanced qualifying exams, and having been spurned himself by the college many times since, Stephen S. Wise would now become an honorary HUC alumnus. Still, he continued to fend off Eisendrath's warm advances.[47]

The turning point came after the UAHC's Biennial Conference in March 1946, where Eisendrath put forth an agenda for the Reform movement that reflected Wise's priorities in almost every regard. He called for the UAHC to "boldly and forthrightly disassociate itself from dogmatic anti-Zionism" and to create labor synagogues to show "we are something more than an upper and middle-class movement." The Union endorsed a statement of principles that condemned antisemitism and called for abrogation of the British White Paper, unlimited Jewish immigration into Palestine, banning the atomic bomb, and passage of federal fair employment legislation to combat discrimination in US hiring practices.

As well, the Biennial Council unanimously supported exploring a merger of HUC and JIR, after Eisendrath declared, "We need each other sorely." They also implicitly authorized the creation of a "House of Living Judaism" in New York, to serve as UAHC headquarters.[48]

Eisendrath, clearly, was in the process of transforming and empowering the union, which had not carried much influence for decades. Perhaps most contentious in the short term was his goal of moving the UAHC to New York. In the eyes of some leading Cincinnati Jews and others who refused to believe "the spirit of Reform and the spirit of New York could ever mix," as the historian Michael Meyer has written, this was tantamount to a declaration of war.[49] The move meant abandoning the wellsprings of Reform Judaism, they believed, and would inevitably mire the union in fractious politics with New York's radical Jews, on the one hand, and traditional congregations, on the other, surely marring the movement's religious character.

But for Eisendrath, for whom Cincinnati represented the past and New York the future, the move was essential, both to growing the Reform movement in the metropolitan area, where it languished, and to breaking Reform's isolation from *klal yisrael*. In addition, he believed that only by releasing the grip of the conservative Cincinnati leadership who opposed his progressive agenda, and locating the union in the heart of American Jewish life, could he make the pursuit of social justice a central activity of Reform Judaism.[50] Notably, by this point, New York's Jewish population had grown to two million, whereas Cincinnati's had declined to twenty-two thousand.[51]

Cognizant that his program reflected Wise's outlook in many ways, Eisendrath contacted Wise immediately after the 1946 Biennial. "It was a thrilling Convention which lifted Liberal Judaism to a new and exalted plane," he wrote. "We have now been given a mandate to press forward as a real people's movement." In light of this "decisive transformation in the spirit and character of the Union," Eisendrath added, Wise's lingering reservations concerning a closer bond between JIR and the union "should now be definitely dissipated."[52]

Though aware that with Eisendrath's ascendency Morgenstern's power was waning, Wise remained wary, even after Eisendrath assured him that the issues that had caused the earlier negotiations to break down no longer held. Wise did, however, agreed to resume talks, with the intention of focusing solely on joint fundraising and plans for the school of education.

Discussions, however, quickly turned to carrying out a full-fledged merger. A significant impediment for the JIR group was removed the following January when Julian Morgenstern announced his resignation. Wise also intended to resign, but only after an accord was reached. He had already stepped back from his responsibilities at the Free Synagogue in 1943, when his student Edward Klein '40 had been hired as assistant rabbi.

With the assurance that Morgenstern would never preside over JIR in a merged institution, in 1947 the institute awarded the college's outgoing president with an honorary degree, and issued one to the incoming president, Nelson Glueck, as well. One of the four HUC graduates who had conducted their doctoral studies together in Germany in the 1920s, Glueck was now professor of Bible and biblical archeology at the college, where the other three had also returned to serve. Blank now taught Bible, Marcus taught history, and Rothman had taught philosophy and then served as librarian until 1945.

Glueck was also the director of the American Society of Oriental Research in Jerusalem and conducted much of his research in Palestine. When the president-designate attended JIR's Founders Day dinner in March 1948, Slonimsky declared him a welcome guest, "not because he is a fine archaeologist, but because he has written a love-song on the River Jordan. A man in love with a landscape, with the landscape into which Israel has projected its soul and which it has drenched with its genius, is a man fit to be listened to and trusted."[53] That Glueck reportedly favored requiring every student in the merged school to spend a year at Hebrew University only made him more palatable as a partner in the negotiations and a potential president of the merged institution.

That June, the two sides settled on a plan for the new school, whose "Statement of Purpose" reflected the Reform movement's apparent acquiescence to JIR's two stipulations: "The HUC and the JIR resolve to unite for the strengthening and advancement of Judaism in America and throughout the world. The right to serve the Jewish people in its entirety (K'lal Yisroel), with freedom for faculty and students alike, is axiomatic. This united institution shall continue to maintain schools in Cincinnati and New York, with Nelson Glueck as President and Stephen S. Wise and Julian Morgenstern as Presidents Emeriti. Upon this union we invoke the blessing of God."

The JIR negotiators had insisted that publicity regarding the merger omit the word "Reform," and Eisendrath complied when he told the New York Times, "This unification of all the liberal Jewish forces in America into one dynamic and cohesive movement dedicated to a holy task indigenous to the soil and soul of America cannot but inspire and delight every liberal Jew in this country."

Addressing the denominational issue directly, the Journal of Jewish Education reported that the new school "will not be officially 'Reform' but rather 'Liberal' and 'progressive.'"[54] Indeed, this was just what Slonimsky had told the JIR faculty, which now included the journal article's author, Michael Alper, a philosopher of Jewish education and member of JIR's class of 1930.[55]

Glueck was inaugurated president of JIR on October 31, 1948. Henceforth, the two schools functioned as one, with the merger to become official pending legal approval from the state legislatures of New York and Ohio. At that time, Wise, as well as Morgenstern, would become presidents emeriti of the Hebrew Union College-Jewish Institute of Religion (HUC-JIR).

Wise, however, succumbed to stomach cancer before the final consolidation of HUC-JIR. He did, however, manage to visit the State of Israel before his death. He had celebrated the UN General Assembly's vote to partition Palestine on November 29, 1947, listening joyfully on the radio with his former student Philip Bernstein and, later that evening, delivering remarks at a Zionist rally in Madison Square Garden, where the crowd erupted in a standing ovation. The following summer, just months after Israel's establishment, he traveled there with Morton Berman, Bernstein's classmate. He shared the inspiration he experienced in a speech to Chicago's Decalogue Society of Lawyers in March 1949 when he received their award of merit:

> I want to say to you that there is a Jewish state today ... a little state. It is my state. It is the state of the Jewish people who dwell there today—800,000. In a year it will be a million and a hundred thousand. In five years it will be two million. I have beheld it most recently last July and August. Dr. Berman—he and I and others among you have beheld ... the miracle of miracles. If ever you are tempted to say the day of miracles has passed, go to the state of Israel and look upon it and let your hearts swell with pride and hope. Now Palestine is going to be a little state. It is going to be like Belgium or Holland or Denmark. But it is going to be a great state.[56]

The great orator gave his final address on his seventy-fifth birthday on March 17, 1949, before a crowd of more than twelve hundred, who gathered to honor him. His biographer, Melvin Urofsky, preserved the moment: "Wise slowly went to the rostrum, his hands shaking as he spread out his hand-written talk. It was unusual for him to do this, but he feared the emotions of the evening. Slowly and eloquently he listed his achievements, first among them Zionism, but he also spoke of all the work still unfinished. The forces opposed to freedom and individual dignity had not been defeated; they still threatened democracy and, he declared, so long as he had breath, he would oppose them. As he finished, he raised his fist and shouted 'I'll fight! I'll fight!' and the audience came roaring to its feet, the applause rolling on and on as Wise stood there with tears in his eyes."

He died four weeks later. As his body lay before the flower-banked altar in the dimly lit JIR chapel, a solemn procession of an estimated 7,500 New Yorkers paid tribute over two days. The funeral was held at Carnegie Hall, where Free Synagogue clergy Edward Klein '40, J. X. Cohen '29, and Sidney Goldstein officiated before a gathering of three thousand mourners, while another fifteen thousand lined the streets outside, and messages of condolences poured in from around the world. David Petegorsky, executive director of the American Jewish Congress, delivered the eulogy, praising Wise as a pioneer and fearless crusader for his people as well as the universal causes of justice, freedom, and peace.[57]

JIR's final commencement ceremony that June provided a poignant moment of reflection for those who had participated in JIR's opening in October 1922, when the first classes were held in temporary quarters at Temple Israel on West Ninety-First Street and Nissan Touroff had proclaimed the institute a new Yavneh. With few resources and formidable foes, its founders had proceeded with optimism, and twenty-seven years later, those who filled the chapel could celebrate not just the ordination of eight new rabbis in the class of 1949 but the fact that JIR had largely achieved its mission.

Despite having failed to create a secure endowment or reliable stream of revenue before the crash of 1929, and then finding fundraising virtually impossible amid the crises of the 1930s and 1940s, the institute nonetheless produced nearly two hundred rabbis, who, through their leadership in a wide variety of capacities, brought their outlook to bear at every level of American Jewish life. While Wise's death marked the end of his family's long rabbinical lineage, many of these men considered him a father and more than a handful named their sons Stephen.

Together, they carried on his legacy through their own rabbinates, seizing on the principle of free expression that Wise had held sacred as far back as 1906, when he demanded that Louis Marshall and the board of Temple Emanu-El not muzzle his pulpit. "In that one sentence, Wise struck the clarion note, the clanging of the bell of emancipation which liberated every one of us," Herbert Friedman told a group of rabbis years later, "and enabled us in the decades since to practice our profession without fear of harassment or rebuke. . . . We take this freedom for granted, as an inalienable right, but it was certainly not so until his sword flashed."

In asserting this freedom, JIR rabbis represented a new generation of American Jews. From their pulpits and rabbinical associations, as heads of educational and social welfare organizations, and in their work for the American Jewish Congress, the Zionist movement, and other causes, they advanced their shared commitment to *klal yisrael*, Zionism, and prophetic justice.

Wise had created the seminary that trained these rabbis in order to address a *spiritual* crisis in American Judaism. In 1922, he and the founders were aiming to fashion a renaissance in Jewish life and to transform American Jewry's relationship both to *klal yisrael* and to the secular world. At the time, Wise had no way of foreseeing how his ideological approach would be tested in the unfathomable battles that lay ahead. Less than a decade later, the entire Jewish world faced *material* crises previously inconceivable in kind and scale. While the institute itself was crushed by the weight of the Depression, followed by World War II and the

Holocaust, its impact grew exponentially as the work of JIR alumni and students revealed the relevance of their training and outlook. Following Wise's lead, they, too, sounded the alarm and tried to avert the impending disaster, and when tragedy struck, they endeavored to save as much of European Jewry as possible and to ensure that, somehow, Jewish life would emerge out of the destruction.

Thus, by 1949, as the institute was losing its autonomy, its impact on American Judaism was readily apparent and growing, most especially within the Reform movement. Both the UAHC and the CCAR now pledged full support for Israel while also demanding recognition for non-Orthodox rabbis and equal rights for non-Orthodox Jews. The UAHC, soon to relocate its headquarters to New York, joined with the conference to establish a Joint Commission on Social Action, dedicated to furthering international peace, social justice, and interracial harmony. The CCAR's Commission on Justice and Peace focused on racial equality, labor protections, and civil rights. And in the wake of the mass destruction of European Jewry, the importance of Jewish peoplehood—the bond shared by Jews across the world, regardless of belief or practice—appeared self-evident.

Reform Judaism's commitments in all of these areas, and the consensus that came to include all the major movements within twentieth-century American liberal Judaism, formed the real legacy of JIR.

A Reversal

Negotiations over the specifics of the merger continued after Wise's death, and to the JIR contingent's dismay, HUC's leadership reneged on the commitments expressed in the original Statement of Purpose. The final agreement omitted any language referencing either *klal yisrael* or the maintenance of a center of learning in New York. Wise would have despaired upon reading his morning paper the day after the statement's signing in January 1950, for the *New York Times* accurately reported that Hebrew Union College-Jewish Institute of Religion "became the only American Jewish Reform seminary today."[58]

JIR's nondenominationalism was extinguished. Not long before his death, Wise had observed that "the fires of Jewish sectarianism have died down," for the tragedy of recent years had "served to prove anew the Oneness of the Jewish fate, whatever the content of the faith of the Jews."[59] Instead, the Reform, Conservative, and Orthodox movements were now engaged in fierce competition to strengthen their own footholds.

If Glueck had his way, next on the chopping block would be the rabbinical school in New York. He did not seek to close operations on West Sixty-Eighth Street entirely, for two new endeavors, a School of Education and a School of Sacred Music, were now housed there. But in the spring of 1953, Glueck devised a way to position Cincinnati as the sole center of rabbinical training for the Reform movement.

That March, the HUC-JIR board of governors approved his so-called Unification Plan by a vote of 35–8, with only JIR alumni and New York–area lay leaders dissenting.[60] The plan would extend the five-year rabbinical program to six years, including two years of study for the Bachelor of Hebrew Letters degree in either New York or Cincinnati, followed by three years of graduate-level study conducted exclusively in Cincinnati, and then a yearlong internship in New York. All students, upon completion of five years of study, would be ordained in Cincinnati; then, after the year interning in New York, they would receive a diploma and a master's degree.

Functioning essentially as a preparatory program, the New York rabbinical school would meet the same fate Isaac Mayer Wise had assigned the Emanu-El Theological Seminary roughly seventy-five years earlier. While Glueck determined that upper-level students currently in New York could complete their requirements without having to move, all second-year students would have to transfer to Cincinnati that fall.

Students immediately refused, however, and broad resistance began to mobilize. The New York rabbinical student body voiced their unanimous opposition to a plan that, in their eyes, would compel every graduate-level rabbinical student to spend "his most important years of study" far from "the center and mainspring of Jewish life in America."[61] UAHC congregations in New York and Chicago passed resolutions condemning the plan, which would threaten the growth and development of Reform Judaism in a metropolitan area that was now home to more than two million Jews. A group of lay leaders and rabbis asked that implementation be deferred pending further study.

Glueck, calling the plan merely a matter of "inner administration" and "mechanics," had not formally consulted with either the UAHC or the CCAR before making it public, though Eisendrath had personally approved. Now he agreed to delay implementation as both organizations took up discussion of the matter. Still, that fall, when a broad contingent of rabbis, faculty, students, and congregational leaders appealed for full restoration of the rabbinical school in New York, including ordination, Glueck refused.

The first class to transfer from New York reluctantly began their studies in Cincinnati a year later, but opposition to further diminution of the New York School escalated, with Louis I. Newman, Morton Berman, Jacob Rudin, and Edward Klein leading the counterattack. Newman called Glueck's plan "mistaken, unworkable and injurious," and that spring, more than sixty-five congregations represented by the Federation of Reform Synagogues of Greater New York repeated the call for full restoration of the rabbinical school—still to no avail.[62]

Ultimately, it was Newman who delivered the coup de grâce to the Unification Plan.[63] He did so by turning to his mentor's playbook, replicating Stephen S. Wise's strategy of a quarter-century earlier.

In September 1955, while a second class of students transferred to Cincinnati, Newman opened a "Rabbinical Tutorial Program," similar to the summer school for rabbis that the Free Synagogue had opened in 1921. With little time to spare, he quickly assembled not only a board but sufficient faculty and students to open a full-fledged school called the Academy for Liberal Judaism. Newman served as director, and Jacob Manheimer, an attorney and former president of Newman's congregation, chaired the board. Faculty included Cyrus Gordon, Moses Hadas, Eugen Kullmann, and David Neiman teaching Bible, history, philosophy, and Mishnah, respectively, as well as Edward Klein in practical rabbinics, Newman in homiletics, and Gunter Hirschberg, Rodeph Sholom's cantor, in music and liturgy.[64] A dedication ceremony was held in October, and with an enrollment of twenty-two, including a handful of students who chose to transfer to the academy rather than move to Cincinnati under Glueck's order, classes began in November, housed temporarily at Rodeph Sholom.[65]

In keeping with the original mission of JIR, the academy restored the commitment "to serving [klal yisrael]" that had been dropped from the HUC-JIR merger agreement. Governed by the principle of free inquiry and the scientific method, the academy maintained "no creedal or ritual test for admission as a student or Faculty member" and aimed "to be inclusive with respect to varying viewpoints in Jewish belief and practice."[66] Most importantly, it would offer a full program of rabbinical training leading to ordination.

"The Academy for Liberal Judaism has been established in order to make it possible for men who wish to become Liberal Rabbis to study and be ordained in a full course of instruction and field work in New York City, the great laboratory of Jewish religious and community life," read publicity materials. "Such facilities for uninterrupted study leading to Ordination are not now available in New York City. The Academy seeks to fill this vacuum."

Glueck, facing effectively the same challenge Morgenstern had confronted in 1922 when JIR opened, seemed equally inclined to dig in his heels. However, other influential Reform leaders urged that he back down. "Unfortunately, we are confronted with a condition and not a theory," wrote Frank Weil, chairman of the college-institute's board of governors, to Jack Skirball, a wealthy HUC alumnus in Los Angeles who had served on the original committee that recommended Glueck's plan and upon whose support Glueck relied. As long as the UAHC would agree, Weil added, "I am afraid the solution requires the reopening of a complete school in New York." Maurice Eisendrath, head of the UAHC, was "beating his breast" and regretting his support for the plan, which, according to Weil, he now believed was a mistake.[67]

Solomon Freehof warned Glueck that if he did not abandon his plan, the academy would garner financial support from the New York Jewish community, and after graduating four or five classes, acquire its own momentum and continue indefinitely.

"Then the situation slips back to the status that we had before the merger," Freehof wrote Glueck. "There will be a separate Reform rabbinical school probably facing us with hostility and rivalry. There will be a new clique within the Conference and new competition for positions. Everything that we hoped to avoid by the merger will soon return to plague us."

"We would be better off if we had two semi-autonomous schools under your chancellorship, than two rival schools," Freehof concluded,[68] likely aware that Newman, Slonimsky, and others were considering breaking JIR off from HUC-JIR and consolidating the institute with the academy.[69]

At Glueck's recommendation, the board of governors reconstituted the committee that had created the Unification Plan to reappraise its original recommendations, and in February 1956, they listened to a series of speakers arguing for and against preserving the New York School. Just days before, the students in New York informed Glueck that the entire student body "refuses to attend the Cincinnati school." Cincinnati students objected to the plan, as well, viewing the sixth-year internship as excessive in light of a CCAR expectation that following ordination, all Reform rabbis serve as US military chaplains for two years.

That June, the committee recommended elimination of the sixth year and the reestablishment in New York of "a complete, strong and vigorous rabbinic school with a full course of five years, equivalent in all respects to the school heretofore and now carried on in Cincinnati." Factors cited included the increasing number of congregations in the United States and the attendant need for more rabbis and optimism regarding the financial position of both the UAHC and the college-institute. The committee also acknowledged widespread opposition to the plan, though no mention was made of the Academy for Liberal Judaism. The board of governors accepted the recommendation.

In announcing the decision, Glueck also shared plans to open a rabbinical program on a newly established campus in Los Angeles. Students would be able to take a two-year course leading to the Bachelor of Hebrew Letters degree and then complete their rabbinical training—in either Cincinnati *or* New York.[70]

Conclusion

B Y THE MID-1950S, IT WAS CLEAR THAT STEPHEN S. WISE AND THE JEW-
ish Institute of Religion, having started at the margins of Reform Judaism, had
succeeded in redefining the entire movement, as well as the wider world of liberal
Judaism.

For the next half-century, JIR's nearly two hundred graduates led hundreds
of Jewish communities and influenced untold tens of thousands of American Jews
from their positions in synagogues, Hillels, educational institutions, and other organizations around the country. In time, new generations took up the mantle in
ways at once new and reflective of the spiritual and moral reformation for which
Wise had called at the time of the institute's founding.

Simultaneously, HUC-JIR became a partner with the UAHC in advancing the very commitments that had led Stephen S. Wise and the Free Synagogue
to establish the Jewish Institute of Religion. Cementing the change within the
college-institute, Nelson Glueck enlisted two JIR men, Paul Steinberg and Alfred
Gottschalk, to help lead the school's expansion in New York, Los Angeles, and Jerusalem. Both men had formative experiences studying under Wise and the other
JIR faculty in the late 1940s and centered academic freedom, Zionism, *klal yisrael*,
and social justice in their public-facing leadership of the school.

That said, not until the 1970s, by which point Gottschalk had become president and Steinberg dean of the New York campus, would the college-institute
begin to make concrete strides toward gender equality. And it was not until the
beginning of the twenty-first century that the JIR's nondenominational model also
took hold.

POSTWAR PERIOD

In the immediate aftermath of World War II, when denominationalism remained
strong, the majority of JIR rabbis served in either Reform or Conservative congregations, where they generally brought renewed attention to traditional rituals
like the bar mitzvah, introduced more Hebrew into religious school training and
services, encouraged greater learning and support for Israel, and created opportunities for social service. These opportunities were increasingly called "social action."

As well, a handful stood out for their leadership within the mainstream denominations. Philip Bernstein '26, Jacob Rudin '28, and Jerome Malino '35 each served a term as president of the CCAR, and together with Harold Saperstein '35, they became legendary for their powerful preaching and lifelong activism in Jewish and progressive causes. Paul Steinberg '49, who followed Slonimsky as dean, spent his fifty-year career in senior administration at the college-institute until his death in 2005. Prominent figures in the Conservative movement included Arthur Chiel '46, a noted scholar of Jewish history, and Saul White '35, who became well-known in San Francisco as a civil rights and anti-war activist in the 1960s.

Other alumni took different paths. Roughly twenty served in Hillel, and a few devoted themselves to teaching and research. John Tepfer '27, for example, remained on the faculty of the New York School until his death in 1988, Samuel Blumenfield '30 became dean of the Chicago College of Jewish Studies, and Ephraim Fischoff '28 taught at the New School for Social Research as well as Hunter College. Harry Brevis '29 invented the International Hebrew Braille Code after entering the institute, having recently lost his eyesight and needing a system to study Talmud in Chaim Tchernowitz's class. Brevis went on to serve as a congregational rabbi in Batavia, New York, and as chaplain at Attica Prison before retiring to Los Angeles, where he lectured at HUC-JIR. Saadia Gelb '46 spent his life on Kibbutz Kfar Blum in Israel's Upper Galilee, working in government and as a truck driver and fisherman, while Morton Berman '26, after serving at Temple Isaiah Israel in Chicago for two decades, moved to Jerusalem in 1957 and joined the Keren Hayesod.

By the peak of these rabbis' careers, they had bequeathed their model of Jewish leadership to a new generation of American Jews, who made it their own. That is to say, while American rabbis from the liberal streams of Judaism mobilized in the 1960s and later around a different set of issues than those that engaged JIR rabbis in the 1930s and 1940s, they remained focused on the same core commitments. A few examples: After the establishment of the State of Israel in 1948, the Reform rabbinate expressed full support for Zionism. The Israel Movement for Reform and Progressive Judaism was established in 1958, and that year the first Reform synagogue opened in Jerusalem. While American Zionism waned in the early 1960s, Israel's victory in the Six-Day War of 1967 generated a resurgence of pride among liberal Jews. Building upon that, Rabbi Alexander Schindler (HUC-JIR '53), who became president of the UAHC in 1973 following Eisendrath's sudden death, pressed the union to join the Zionist movement officially. In 1976, a group of young Jews founded the Reform Kibbutz Yahel in the Arava, and a year later, the American Reform Zionist Association (ARZA) was formed. In 1978, ARZA's first delegation was seated in the World Jewish Congress.

Meanwhile, in the 1960s and 1970s, a new generation of rabbis dedicated to protecting *klal yisrael* across the globe was taking up the plight of Soviet Jewry.

Allan Levine (HUC-JIR '59), for example, one of the earliest rabbis to challenge
the complacency he saw in the American Jewish communal leadership's hesitation
to act, pressed for public rallies and nonviolent direct-action protests demanding
the USSR end its persecution of Jews and grant them the right to emigrate.[1] In
1966, the CCAR sent a mission to investigate the conditions of Jews in the Soviet
Union, and upon return to the United States these rabbis described the suffering
and isolation of their coreligionists and decried the state's antisemitic and repressive
policies. Eventually, many other rabbis joined the struggle by actively lobbying Congress and organizing mass demonstrations like the 250,000-person march held on
the eve of a summit between Mikhail Gorbachev and Ronald Reagan in December
1987. By the time of the Soviet Union's dissolution in 1991, most Soviet Jews seeking to emigrate had been permitted to do so.

And, just as JIR students between 1922 and 1950 learned to apply the teachings of the Hebrew prophets to contemporary social and economic issues in their
own communities, so, too, did many Reform rabbis and lay leaders devote themselves to confronting injustice over the next half-century. In 1961, the CCAR and
UAHC jointly established the Religious Action Center (RAC) as the political and
legislative arm of the Reform movement, and the RAC rapidly became the van-
guard of the Reform movement's efforts to achieve social justice in a range of areas.[2] This work increasingly became characterized within liberal Judaism as *tikkun
olam*, parlance drawn from kabbalistic literature meaning repair of a broken world
in which racial and economic equality remains elusive.

These movements—to support Israel and liberal Judaism *in* Israel; to fight
on behalf of oppressed Jews wherever they may be; and to pursue social justice
grounded in Jewish teachings—are part of the legacy of JIR and the generation
of rabbis and teachers who spread the intertwining model of *klal yisrael*, Zionism,
and the prophetic call.

Hebrew Union College-Jewish Institute of Religion
At the college-institute, Glueck advanced this model as well, relying heavily on the
leadership of Steinberg and Gottschalk, both of whom credited their JIR experience for shaping their lifelong commitment to serving the Jewish people.

Steinberg, who once ran guns for the Haganah out of his locker in the school's
basement, received the Guggenheimer Fellowship when he graduated in 1949,
which enabled him to work and study in Israel for a year. He directed the Hillel at the University of California, Berkeley for several years before serving as a
congregational rabbi in Westchester until the mid-1950s, when Glueck appointed
him dean of the new School of Education and School of Sacred Music, which
were housed alongside the rabbinical school in the building on West Sixty-Eighth
Street. In 1960, he became dean of the Rabbinical School, as well, and in 1962 he
was asked by Glueck to oversee the construction of a new campus in Jerusalem,

which was completed in 1963. After the Six-Day War in 1967, the college-institute began requiring all rabbinical students to spend a year in residence at the Jerusalem School, and a formal Year-in-Israel Program was inaugurated in 1971. Steinberg later recalled, "As a lifelong Zionist, nothing could have pleased me more."[3]

Gottschalk, who was born into a traditional family in Oberwesel, Germany, in 1930, witnessed the violence of Kristallnacht, and soon afterward, he and his parents managed to immigrate to New York just before entry for German Jews became nearly impossible. As a teenager living in Brooklyn in the early 1940s, he attended American Jewish Congress gatherings where Wise's anti-Hitler orations influenced him to become a rabbi. After the war, while pursuing his bachelor's degree at Brooklyn College, he enrolled in pre-rabbinic courses at JIR and thus had the opportunity to study directly with Wise, Slonimsky, John Tepfer, and other faculty who together imbued him with the JIR ethos. He joined the rabbinical program in 1952, but soon after, as part of Glueck's effort to diminish the New York School, his class was forced to relocate to Cincinnati despite their unanimous protest. As secretary of the New York School's Student Organization, Gottschalk was listed on a June 1953 letter to the board of governors expressing disapproval of the Unification Plan.[4]

Though he completed his studies in Cincinnati, Gottschalk carried the ideals of Wise and the Jewish Institute of Religion with him for the rest of his life. Immediately after his ordination in 1957, Glueck hired him onto the faculty and administration, and in 1959, he became dean of the recently established Los Angeles School, where he opened a School of Jewish Communal Service, the Rhea Hirsch School of Education, and the Magnin School of Graduate Studies.

Gottschalk succeeded Glueck as president in 1971 and led the school through a period of growth for the next twenty-five years. This included the relocation of the New York School from its site on West Sixty-Eighth Street adjacent to the renamed Stephen Wise Free Synagogue to a new building near New York University in Greenwich Village in 1979.[5] His achievements, however, must be seen in light of the independent investigation conducted for the college-institute in 2021, which reported a consistent and decades-long pattern of alleged sexual misconduct by Gottschalk toward women including students, alumni and staff.[6]

While Wise and the founders of JIR succeeded, to a large extent, in reshaping American liberal Judaism, in two crucial ways they missed the mark: by failing to act on the faculty's 1923 vote in favor of admitting women, which would have enabled the American Jewish community to benefit from women's rabbinical leadership long before 1972, when Sally Priesand became the first woman ordained in the United States; and in their belief that the end of denominationalism was imminent. Here, they underestimated both the staying power of the various streams of Judaism and American Jewry's desire to replicate the denominational structure of American Protestantism. Neither issue was seriously addressed until the various streams of American Judaism had flourished in the latter part of the twentieth century.

Did it occur to Wise that the magnitude of JIR's impact would have been greater had his notion of pluralism in rabbinical leadership included women? Irma Lindheim, Dora Askowith, and Helen Levinthal all made the case forcefully, and the latter two, even after leaving the institute, never gave up the fight for women's ordination.

Askowith continued her professional career as an adjunct professor of history at Hunter College while also writing several books, publishing more than one hundred articles, advising the Menorah Society, and remaining active in the Zionist movement and women's organizations. Pressing not her own case but that of all Jewish women, she published a letter in the *New York Times* in 1947 in favor of women's ordination and soon after, upon learning of the merger, asked Wise and Glueck if they planned to ordain women. Wise thanked her for the inquiry and wrote that in the course of time, "we will take up your suggestion about Women being offered degrees . . . but there are many other more urgent problems which must first be considered and settled."[7] Almost a decade later, in 1956, Askowith wrote an article for *Judaism* magazine, arguing that traditional Jewish law does not overtly oppose women in the rabbinate. She died in 1958.[8]

After receiving her master's degree from JIR in 1939, Helen Levinthal married, raised children, and chose the path of active volunteerism, particularly within Hadassah and her Conservative synagogue. Not until news broke in 1971 that the college-institute would soon ordain Priesand as a rabbi did Levinthal resume the battle for her own ordination. She had, after all, fulfilled all the requirements, and this time, she had a new ally. Amid all the attention being paid to Priesand, Earl Stone, one of Levinthal's former classmates who decades earlier had opposed her ordination, urged Alfred Gottschalk, president of HUC-JIR, to right the institute's wrong of 1939. Gottschalk acknowledged that Levinthal (now Helen Levinthal Lyons) had completed the curriculum, but nonetheless he failed to act.

Fourteen years later, when JTS ordained the first Conservative female rabbi in 1985, Stone and Levinthal made the request of Gottschalk once again, and still he refused to act. Finally, after further pressure, in 1988, Paul Steinberg, then dean of the faculty in New York, bestowed on Levinthal an award for pioneering "new directions in higher Jewish learning and scholarship for women." Never ordained, she died less than a year later.[9]

By this time, women represented about 45 percent of HUC-JIR's rabbinical student body. Few were aware of the unsuccessful battles for ordination fought in the past by Askowith and Levinthal, as well as Neumark and Lindheim; nor did they know that Levinthal was seeking reparations for Wise's denial of her ordination in 1939. Even as Gottschalk and Steinberg fended off her request, a segment of the student body was pressuring them on a different but related front—for the ordination of openly gay and lesbian rabbis. That battle, expanded to include LGBTQ Jews, was eventually won, as well. Still far from representing the Jewish people's full racial and cultural diversity, the Reform rabbinate was finally at least opening to a broader array of backgrounds and perspectives.

As to the denominational issue, while in 1921 Wise had derided religious labels as "fatuous and impermanent," the various streams of Judaism to which he was referring only gained strength during his lifetime, and even more so after his death, when each entered a period of accelerated and long-term expansion. Wise failed to anticipate that the norms of 1950s American culture would include membership in a house of worship and institutional affiliation, both of which fueled denominational growth.

Still, his intuition was correct; post-denominational Judaism *would* blossom, but not until the twenty-first century. In retrospect, several changes took place that made this possible. First, the various non-Orthodox streams of Judaism all came to embrace as essential the original pillars of Wise's outlook—*klal yisrael*, Zionism, and social justice. Then, they repaired one of the central flaws in the original model—namely, the exclusion of women and LGBTQ Jews from the rabbinate. Finally, they each became far more inclusive in relation to the diverse liturgical and halakhic practices of their clergy and membership. As a result, in the eyes of many, the distinctions between Reform, Conservative, and Reconstructionist Judaism fell away, along with any rationale for preserving them.

Yet, while these mainstream denominations were becoming increasingly similar, a growing number of liberal Jews in the 1990s and early 2000s were opting out of the emerging institutional consensus because they found it lacking on matters of inclusion and social justice. These included intermarried Jews seeking to remain part of the Jewish community along with their spouses and children but repelled by the ambivalence if not disdain they encountered in the denominational world.[10] With the increasingly multiracial and multiethnic composition of many Jewish families reflected in neither the leadership nor the membership of mainstream denominations, many felt a sense of exclusion that some feminist and queer Jews experienced for similar reasons. In addition, some non- or anti-Zionist Jews were troubled by denominational leaders who appeared impervious to dissent in relation to Israel. Finally, not unlike the founders of the Jewish Institute of Religion, a significant number of American Jews simply believed American liberal Judaism had become stale and outdated and was desperately in need of an overhaul.

As a result, at the turn of the twenty-first century, new nondenominational seminaries began emerging on the American Jewish landscape, addressing these contemporary concerns while also, in important respects, following in the footsteps of JIR. They appealed particularly to a new generation of Jews who valued neither institutional membership nor affiliation for its own sake, and notably, these schools shared, in a broad sense, the same liberal ideology and curricular model that JIR pioneered. Many function simultaneously as a seminary, graduate school, and professional school, insist on academic freedom for faculty as well as students, and offer traditional text study alongside Modern Hebrew, professional development, and fieldwork while emphasizing contemporary problems in rabbinical leadership. Most, though not all, also require a period of study in Israel.

In addition, these seminaries uphold a foundational commitment to diversity and pluralism. Here, they surpass the Jewish Institute of Religion in the area most sacred to Wise: serving *klal yisrael*. For when it came to rabbinical training, Wise had a blind spot; despite the many different battles he fought in the name of freedom and social justice, he and the institute withheld the opportunity to enter the rabbinate from all Jewish women, including those who had studied at JIR and pressed for their own ordination.

FACING THE FUTURE

At the start of the 1920s, Wise responded to dramatic change underway in American Jewish life by creating a fresh approach that was reflective of the new generation's aspirations and relevant to the crises he saw brewing in the broader world. Then, in the tradition of American as well as Jewish seminary founders who came before him, he set out to train leaders capable of advancing that approach. "We must build anew," declared Mitchell Fisher '27 in the *JIR Quarterly* in 1924, expressing the convictions of a student body determined to shape a renaissance in Jewish life.[11] JIR prepared them with the tools to do this, and the model they created proved lasting.

Notes

INTRODUCTION

1. *Tikkun olam* refers to social justice and *klal yisrael* to Jewish peoplehood.

2. "Jewish Institute of Religion," Jewish Institute of Religion Nearprint Box 1, Nearprint Special Topics. American Jewish Archives, Cincinnati, OH (hereafter, JIR Nearprint Box 1).

3. Grace E. Speights, Sharon P. Masling, Martha B. Stolley, Jocelyn R. Cuttino, and Ira G. Rosenstein, *Report of Investigation into Allegations of Misconduct at Hebrew Union College-Jewish Institute of Religion*, Investigation conducted by the Philadelphia law firm Morgan Lewis (New York: Hebrew Union College-Jewish Institute of Religion, November 3, 2021.

4. Louis I. Newman, "Rabbi Stephen S. Wise," speech delivered at dinner tendered by the Citizens Committee celebrating Wise's sixtieth birthday, Hotel Astor, New York, NY, March 19, 1934. Box 13, folder 7, Louis I. Newman Collection. American Jewish Archives, Cincinnati, OH.

CHAPTER 1

1. The school was originally named "New College" and took on the surname of John Harvard, its first major benefactor, in 1639.

2. See Roger L. Geiger, *The History of American Higher Education: Learning and Culture from the Founding to World War II* (Princeton, NJ: Princeton University Press, 2014).

3. Joseph M. White, "The Diocesan Seminary and the Community of Faith: Reflections from the American Experience." *U.S. Catholic Historian* 11, no. 1 (1993): 4.

4. Geiger, *The History of American Higher Education*, 196.

5. White, "The Diocesan Seminary and the Community of Faith," 6–7.

6. The school became Oberlin College in 1850. See J. Brent Morris, *Oberlin, Hotbed of Abolitionism: College, Community, and the Fight for Freedom and Equality in Antebellum America* (Chapel Hill: University of North Carolina Press, 2014), 23–27.

7. See James Fraser, *Schooling the Preachers: The Development of Protestant Theological Education in the United States, 1740–1875* (Lanham, MD: University Press of America, 1988).

8. David Ellenson, "President's Report," *HUC-JIR Annual Report 2009–2010*. Hebrew Union College-Jewish Institute of Religion, accessed September 10, 2021, huc.edu/sites/default/files/News-Events/presidents-report/09-10.pdf.

9. Moshe Carmilly-Weinberger, "One Hundred Years of the Seminary in Retrospect," in *The Rabbinical Seminary of Budapest, 1877–1977: A Centennial Volume*, ed. Moshe Carmilly-Weinberger, 3 (New York: Sepher-Hermon, 1986).

10. Lance J. Sussman, *Isaac Leeser and the Making of American Judaism* (Detroit, MI: Wayne State University Press, 1995), 235–36.

11. Moshe Carmilly-Weinberger, *The Rabbinical Seminary of Budapest, 1877–1977: A Centennial Volume* (New York: Sepher-Hermon, 1986), xi.

12. David Ellenson, *Rabbi Esriel Hildesheimer and the Creation of a Modern Jewish Orthodoxy* (Tuscaloosa: University of Alabama Press, 1990), x.

13. Michael A. Meyer, *Response to Modernity: A History of the Reform Movement in Judaism* (New York: Oxford University Press, 1988), 241–42.

14. Bruce L. Ruben, *Max Lilienthal: The Making of the American Rabbinate* (Detroit: Wayne State University Press, 2011), 154–55.

15. Gershon Greenberg, "The Dimensions of Samuel Adler's Religious View of the World: Adler's Career (1809–91)." *Hebrew Union College Annual* 46 (1975), 381n17: Sinai IV, 1 (1859), 52–53; Sinai VI, 7 (1861), 231; and Sinai VI, 8 (1861), 26.

16. Leon A. Jick, "Bernhard Felsenthal: The Zionization of a Radical Reform Rabbi," *Jewish Political Studies Review* 9, no. 1/2 (1997): 6 and 12n3; and Emma Felsenthal, *Bernhard Felsenthal, Teacher in Israel, Selections from His Writings with Biographical Sketch and Bibliography* (New York: Oxford University Press, 1924), 22.

17. Greenberg, "The Dimensions of Samuel Adler's Religious View of the World," 381n19; *Die Deborah*, June 30, 1865, 210.

18. Sussman, *Isaac Leeser and the Making of American Judaism*, 238–40. Also see Bertram W. Korn, "The First American Jewish Theological Seminary: Maimonides College, 1867–1873," in *Eventful Years and Experiences: Studies in Nineteenth Century American Jewish History* (1954), 151–213.

19. Meyer, *Response to Modernity*, 260–61.

20. Michael A. Meyer, "Part One: A Centennial History," in *Hebrew Union College-Jewish Institute of Religion at One Hundred Years*, ed. Samuel E. Karff (Cincinnati: Hebrew Union College Press, 1976), 16.

21. Max Lilienthal, June 5, 1868. Quoted in Stephen G. Mostov, "A 'Jerusalem' on the Ohio: The Social and Economic History of Cincinnati's Jewish Community, 1840–1875" (PhD diss., Brandeis University, 1981), 143.

22. Jonathan D. Sarna, "'A Sort of Paradise for the Hebrews': The Lofty Vision of Cincinnati Jews," in *Ethnic Diversity and Civic Identity: Patterns of Conflict and Cohesion in Cincinnati since 1820*, ed. Henry D. Shapiro and Jonathan D. Sarna (Urbana: University of Illinois Press, 1992), 131–32.

23. Meyer, *Response to Modernity*, 261.

24. For a discussion of rabbinical training in the European Jewish seminaries, see David Ellenson and Lee Bycel, "A Seminary of Sacred Learning: The JTS Rabbinical Curriculum in Historical Perspective," in *Tradition Renewed: A History of the Jewish Theological Seminary of America, Vol. II*, ed. Jack Wertheimer, 528–30 (New York: Jewish Theological Seminary of America, 1997).

25. Meyer, *Response to Modernity*, 262.

26. Bertram W. Korn, "The Temple Emanu-El Theological Seminary of New York City," in *Essays in American Jewish History*, ed. Jacob Rader Marcus, 359–71 (New York: Ktav Publishing House, 1975).

27. See Lance Sussman, "The Myth of the Trefa Banquet: American Culinary Culture and the Radicalization of Food Policy in American Reform Judaism," *American Jewish Archives Journal* 57, no. 1/2 (2005): 29–52.

28. Meyer, *Response to Modernity*, 270.

29. Jeffrey S. Gurock, "Yeshiva Students at the Jewish Theological Seminary," in *Tradition Renewed: A History of the Jewish Theological Seminary of America, Vol. I*, ed. Jack Wertheimer, 476–78 (New York: Jewish Theological Seminary of America, 1997).

30. The synagogue was located at 44 East Broadway, and JTS was located at Fifty-Ninth Street and Lexington Avenue.

31. Gurock, "Yeshiva Students at the Jewish Theological Seminary," 475.

32. Eitan Kastner, "Yeshiva College and the Pursuit of a Jewish Architecture," *American Jewish History* 96, no. 2 (2010): 142.

33. Samson D. Oppenheim, "The Jewish Population of the United States," *The American Jewish Year Book* 20 (1918): 32.

34. Dana Evan Kaplan, "The Rise and Fall of American Jewish Denominationalism," in *Contemporary American Judaism: Transformation and Renewal* (New York: Columbia University Press, 2009), 146.

35. Melvin I. Urofsky, *A Voice That Spoke for Justice: The Life and Times of Stephen S. Wise* (Albany: State University of New York Press, 1982), 1–3.

36. Robert Shapiro, "A Reform Rabbi in the Progressive Era: The Early Career of Stephen S. Wise" (PhD diss., Harvard University, 1984), 20.

37. Davidson saw great promise in Wise, to whom he would later write, "You will devise a twentieth century Judaism fitted to meet the needs of the present day." Melvin I. Urofsky, *A Voice That Spoke for Justice: The Life and Times of Stephen S. Wise* (Albany: State University of New York Press, 1982), 9 and 374n21.

38. Isaac Mayer Wise to Stephen S. Wise, September 4, 1892. My thanks to Dr. Gary Zola for clarifying the record.

39. Urofsky, *A Voice That Spoke for Justice*, 9–10.

40. Lance J. Sussman and Malcolm H. Stern, eds., *Reform Judaism in America: A Biographical Dictionary and Sourcebook* (Westport, CT: Greenwood, 1993), 226.

41. Urofsky, *A Voice That Spoke for Justice*, 22–24.

42. Melvin Weinman, "The Attitude of Isaac Mayer Wise toward Zionism and Palestine," *American Jewish Archives Journal* 3, no. 2 (January 1951): 8.

43. Urofsky, *A Voice That Spoke for Justice*, 28–29.

44. See Benny Kraut, *From Reform Judaism to Ethical Culture: The Religious Evolution of Felix Adler* (Cincinnati, OH: Hebrew Union College Press, 1979).

45. Urofsky, *A Voice That Spoke for Justice*, 33.

46. "One Institution for Rearing Rabbis?" *American Hebrew*, May 25, 1900.

47. See Mel Scult, "Schechter's Seminary," in *Tradition Renewed: A History of the Jewish Theological Seminary of America Vol. I*, ed. Jack Wertheimer (New York: Jewish Theological Seminary of America, 1997), 47–85.

48. Halakhic Judaism adheres to traditional legal codes of Judaism.

49. Urofsky, *A Voice That Spoke for Justice*, 36–44.

50. Urofsky, *A Voice That Spoke for Justice*, 49.

51. "If I am to accept a call to the pulpit of Temple Emanu-El, I do so with the understanding that I am to be free, and that my pulpit is not to be muzzled," Wise wrote. "An Open Letter from Stephen S. Wise to the Members of Temple Emanu-El of New York," January 5, 1906. Box 5, folder 8, Stephen S. Wise Collection. American Jewish Archives, Cincinnati, OH (hereafter, Stephen S. Wise Collection).

52. "Rev. Dr. Wise Surprises Emanu-El Trustees," *New York Times*, January 7, 1906, 5.

53. "Rev. Dr. Wise Surprises Emanu-El Trustees," *New York Times*, January 7, 1906, 5.

54. See Peter S. Onuf, *The Mind of Thomas Jefferson* (Charlottesville: University of Virginia Press, 2007).

55. Carl Hermann Voss, *Rabbi and Minister: The Friendship of Stephen S. Wise and John Haynes Holmes* (Cleveland, OH: World, 1964), 17; and Urofsky, *A Voice That Spoke for Justice*, 61.

56. While Wise was an early advocate of free seating, he did not invent the model. Concerns about unfair church seating systems in the United States date back at least as far as colonial New England. A system of assigning seats to family members gradually gave way to systems of pew rental and sale. While hereditary privileges no longer obtained, seating continued to be determined by wealth. Only with the rise of the Social Gospel movement did calls for free seating gain traction in liberal Protestant as well as many Catholic churches. In 1903, Temple Beth El

of Detroit, Michigan, under the leadership of Rabbi Leo Franklin, became the first American synagogue to adopt the practice. While the change was initially implemented as a temporary measure for practical reasons, the congregation made it permanent in 1904, and Franklin became an advocate for free seating for ethical as well practical reason. That year, Stephen S. Wise urged his congregants at Temple Beth Israel in Portland, Oregon, to create a "free synagogue" with free seating and voluntary dues, arguing the matter purely on principle. In 1905, Beth Israel successfully implemented the system, and soon after, Wise turned his sights on creating a "free synagogue" in New York. See Jonathan D. Sarna, "Seating and the American Synagogue," in *Belief and Behavior: Essays in the New Religious History*, ed. Philip R. Vandermeer and Robert P. Swierenga (New Brunswick, NJ: Rutgers University Press, 1991).

57. *From the First Address by Dr. Wise (Preliminary to the Founding of the Free Synagogue, April 1907)*, Box 5, folder 8, Stephen S. Wise Collection.

58. "Many Flock to Hear Free Synagogue Plans," *New York Times*, January 28, 1907, 7.

59. Urofsky, *A Voice That Spoke for Justice*, 62.

60. Urofsky, *A Voice That Spoke for Justice*, 62–64; and "Brief Biographical Sketch of Stephen S. Wise," March 17, 1934. Box 5, folder 8, Stephen S. Wise Collection.

61. Urofsky, *A Voice That Spoke for Justice*, 65.

62. While most Reform congregations in the United States did not hold Sunday morning services, about three dozen did, using the weekday liturgy. Generally, these services featured a lengthy sermon or lecture and had a serious rather than celebratory tone. See Meyer, *Response to Modernity*, 290.

63. Urofsky, *A Voice That Spoke for Justice*, 65.

64. Joe Rooks-Rapport, "Louise Waterman Wise," in *Jewish Women in America: An Historical Encyclopedia*, Paula E. Hyman and Deborah Dash Moore, eds. (New York: Routledge, 1997) 1482–84. After Louise Wise's death, the Free Synagogue Child Adoption Committee was renamed Louise Wise Services and was presided over by Justine Wise Polier (Louise and Stephen's daughter). In the 1950s and 1960s, Polier led the professionalization of the organization and shifted its mission toward serving children of color. Louise Wise Services closed in 2004 amid charges of ethical violations and abuses. Jonathan E. Lazarus, "Louise Wise Services Did What?," Jewish Standard, April 14, 2021, https://jewishstandard.timesofisrael.com.

65. Urofsky, *A Voice That Spoke for Justice*, 91–115.

66. "Yishuv" is a term used to refer to the Jewish community in Palestine during the decades prior to the establishment of the State of Israel in 1948.

67. "Jewish National Organizations in the United States," *American Jewish Year Book* 16 (1914–1915): 282.

68. Urofsky, *A Voice That Spoke for Justice*, 120.

69. Urofsky, *A Voice That Spoke for Justice*, 135, 146.

70. Later, the Free Synagogue of Westchester would be established in Mount Vernon, New York. "The First Ninety Years." Stephen Wise Free Synagogue, accessed July 6, 2013, www.swfs.org; and "A History of Significance." Sinai Free Synagogue, accessed August 7, 2013, www.sinaifreesynagogue.org.

71. These included Abraham Cronbach, Bernard Cantor, and others. In 1922, Abraham Cronbach became a professor at HUC, where he remained until his retirement in 1950. Bernard Cantor was killed by Soviet troops in 1920 while on a mission for the Joint Distribution Committee in the Ukraine with Israel Friedlaender, a JTS professor who was also killed. See Louis I. Newman, "Communication." *American Jewish Historical Quarterly* 58, no. 4 (1969): 532–33. Regarding the Free Synagogue idea in the context of synagogue economics, see Daniel Judson, *Pennies for Heaven: The History of American Synagogues and Money* (Waltham, MA: Brandeis University Press, 2018).

72. Urofsky, *A Voice That Spoke for Justice*, 183 and 393n4.

73. Herbert I. Bloom, "Stephen S. Wise and the Dynamics of Liberal Judaism: Founders Day Address," delivered at HUC-JIR, New York City, March 13, 1953, pp. 3–4. Bloom reportedly viewed letters shared with him by Louis I. Newman and I. Edward Kiev, including this one from Richard Gottheil to Stephen S. Wise, July 18, 1910. Stephen S. Wise papers, collection, Robert D. Farber University Archives & Special Collections, Brandeis University, Waltham, Massachusetts.

74. William Samuel Tepper, "I Dwell Among the People: A Biography of Rabbi Louis Israel Newman," rabbinical thesis (Hebrew Union College-Jewish Institute of Religion, Cincinnati, OH, 2008), 7. The intercollegiate Menorah Association stemmed from Harvard's Menorah Society, founded in 1906 to help Jewish students engage intellectually with the humanistic values of Judaism. In 1913, similar groups on campuses across the United States joined together to form the Menorah Association, which grew to include about eighty chapters.

75. Tepper, "I Dwell Among the People," 10.

CHAPTER 2

1. Stephen S. Wise, "The Idea of the Free Synagogue," *Jewish Tribune*, April 8, 1927.

2. Stephen S. Wise, "Liberal Judaism," in *Free Synagogue Pulpit Sermons and Addresses by Stephen S. Wise, Volume VI, 1920–1921* (New York: Bloch, 1921), 6.

3. Wise, "Liberal Judaism," 9.

4. Wise, "Liberal Judaism," 21.

5. Deborah Dash Moore, *Urban Origins of American Judaism* (Athens: University of Georgia Press, 2014), 162.

6. See UAHC board meeting minutes 1921; temporary source is Russell Silverman, *The Union for Reform Judaism 1873–2009: A History According to the Minutes of the Organization*, 72; *American Jewish Yearbook: 1900–1901*, 67; *American Jewish Yearbook: 1920–1921*, 313; and *Hebrew Union College-Jewish Institute of Religion Alumni Directory*. Retrieved from huc.edu/alumni/alumni-directory.

7. See Scult, "Schechter's Seminary," in *Tradition Renewed*, 43–102.

8. Sarna, "A Sort of Paradise for the Hebrews," 136 and 157.

9. Barbara S. Malone, *Rabbi Max Heller: Reformer, Zionist, Southerner, 1860–1929* (Tuscaloosa: University of Alabama Press, 1997), 128. For more on this incident, see also Meyer, *Response to Modernity*; Jonathan D. Sarna, *JPS: The Americanization of Jewish Culture 1888–1988: A Centennial History of the Jewish Publication Society* (Philadelphia: Jewish Publication Society, 1989); and Yaakov Ariel, "Kaufmann Kohler and His Attitude Toward Zionism: A Reexamination," *American Jewish Archives Journal* 43, no. 2 (1991): 207–23.

10. Malone, *Rabbi Max Heller*, 167–68.

11. Summer School for Rabbis and Rabbinical Students, Prospectus 1921. Box 11, folder 11, JIR Records.

12. Minutes of a meeting of the Special Committee appointed to consider the desirability and the practicability of organizing an institute for the training of rabbis, held at the Free Synagogue House, November 2, 1920. Minutes of Meetings of the Board of Trustees Committees, Vol. I: November 2, 1920–May 24, 1932 (hereafter, JIR Board Minutes). These minutes are kept in the Klau Library at the Hebrew Union College–Jewish Institute of Religion's New York School.

13. JIR Board Minutes.

14. Bernard Martin, "The Religious Philosophy of Emil G. Hirsch," *American Jewish Archives Journal* 4, no. 2 (June 1952): 66.

15. See Tobias Brinkmann, *Sundays at Sinai: A Jewish Congregation in Chicago* (Chicago: University of Chicago Press, 2012).

16. Letter from Free Synagogue Committee to UAHC Executive Board, May 1921, included

in "Open Letter to the President of the Union of American Hebrew Congregations from Committee of Free Synagogue on the Jewish Institute of Religion," Appendix C, 21. Jewish Institute of Religion Nearprint Box 1, Nearprint Special Topics. American Jewish Archives, Cincinnati, OH (hereafter, JIR Nearprint Box 1).

17. Letter from Free Synagogue Committee to UAHC Executive Board, May 1921, included in "Open Letter to the President of the Union of American Hebrew Congregations from Committee of Free Synagogue on the Jewish Institute of Religion," Appendix C, 21. JIR Nearprint Box 1.

18. Wise, "Liberal Judaism," 5.

19. Letter from Free Synagogue Committee to UAHC Executive Board, May 1921, included in "Open Letter to the President of the Union of American Hebrew Congregations from Committee of Free Synagogue on the Jewish Institute of Religion," Appendix C, 21. JIR Nearprint Box 1.

20. Stephen S. Wise to Richard Gottheil, April 27, 1921. Box 3, folder 5, Stephen S. Wise Manuscript Collection.

21. Letter from Free Synagogue Committee to UAHC Executive Board, May 1921, included in "Open Letter to the President of the Union of American Hebrew Congregations from Committee of Free Synagogue on the Jewish Institute of Religion," Appendix C, 21. JIR Nearprint Box 1.

22. "An Offer and an Acceptance," *Free Synagogue Bulletin*, June 5, 1921. Box 9, JIR Records.

23. Summer School for Rabbis and Rabbinical Students Prospectus 1921. JIR Nearprint Box 1.

CHAPTER 3

1. "Slightly Facetious," *Jewish Times*, April 29, 1921.

2. Stephen S. Wise to Louis Grossmann, December 12, 1921. Box 17, folder 9, JIR Records.

3. See Solomon Lowenstein, "Dr. Lee K. Frankel: 1867–1931." *American Jewish Year Book* 34 (1932): 121–40. Frankel was a charter member of the board of trustees of the Federation for the Support of Jewish Philanthropic Societies of New York City, and in 1925, he would become a founding board member and vice president of the Training School for Jewish Social Work. He remained heavily involved until his death in 1931.

4. Stephen S. Wise to Emil G. Hirsch, January 25, 1922. Box 19, folder 14, JIR Records.

5. J. Dorsey Callaghan, "Dr. Franklin's Life Was One of Service," *Detroit Free Press*, August 9, 1948. JIR Press Clipping Book, JIR Records.

6. Stephen S. Wise to Leo M. Franklin, February 28, 1922. Box 9, folder 3, JIR Records.

7. Stephen S. Wise to Leo M. Franklin, February 28, 1922. Box 9, folder 3, JIR Records.

8. "Who knows but that it may be given to us in some senses to be serviceable to the College by the very spirit and methods which are to obtain in the Jewish Institute of Religion." Stephen S. Wise to Leo M. Franklin, February 28, 1922. Box 9, folder 3, JIR Records.

9. Stephen S. Wise to Emil G. Hirsch, January 25, 1922. Box 19, folder 14, JIR Records.

10. "To Erect Synagogue House, But Dr. Wise's Congregation Will Still Worship in Carnegie Hall," *New York Times*, February 13, 1922.

11. Minutes, Dinner Meeting of Committee on Jewish Institute of Religion [n.d., circa 1921]. Box 11, folder 11, JIR Records.

12. Daniel P. Hays, Chairman of UAHC, to Lee K. Frankel, Chairman, Free Synagogue Committee, April 6, 1922. In "Open Letter to the President of the Union of American Hebrew Congregations from Committee of Free Synagogue on the Jewish Institute of Religion," Appendix A, p. 14: Dr. Stephen S. Wise Makes a Proposal to the Union, the Committee's Reply. JIR Nearprint Box 1.

13. "Open Letter to the President of the Union of American Hebrew Congregations from Committee of Free Synagogue on the Jewish Institute of Religion," April 20, 1922, p. 6. JIR Nearprint Box 1.

14. "Open Letter to the President of the Union of American Hebrew Congregations from Committee of Free Synagogue on the Jewish Institute of Religion," April 20, 1922, p. 7. JIR Nearprint Box 1.

15. Attendance at the Committee's first dinner meeting included Stephen S. Wise, Sidney E. Goldstein, Julian W. Mack, Mollie Fels, Bertha Guggenheimer, Louise Waterman Wise, Susan Goldstein, Edmund I. Kaufmann, Herbert M. Kaufmann, Armand Baer, Richard Gottheil, Maurice Harris, Max Weis, Charles Bloch, Walter S. Hilborn, Frederick Guggenheimer, and Israel N. Thurman. Mack was selected chair. [Note: Bertha Guggenheimer's husband was Max Guggenheimer of Lynchburg, died 1912; Frederick Guggenheimer appears not to be related.] Minutes, Dinner Meeting of Committee on Jewish Institute of Religion, n.d. Box 11, folder 11, JIR Records.

16. Kallen, Horace M. "Julian William Mack, 1866–1943," *American Jewish Year Book* 46 (1944): 35–46.

17. Julian W. Mack to Stephen S. Wise, March 4, 1922. Box 25, folder 13, JIR Records.

18. Mary Ruth Yoe, "Edward Hirsch Levi," *University of Chicago Magazine* 92, no. 4 (April 2002): accessed January 1, 2019, magazine.uchicago.edu/0004/features/levi2.html.

19. Stephen S. Wise to Emil G. Hirsch, Jan 25, 1922. Box 19, folder 14, JIR Records.

20. Elliot Weinbaum, "Mary Fels 1863–1953," *Jewish Women's Archive*, accessed December 22, 2018, jwa.org/encyclopedia/article/fels-mary.

21. The following attended the March 26, 1922, dinner meeting: Armand Baer, Charles Bloch, Joseph and Mollie Fels, Walter S. Hilborn, Rabbi Sidney E. and Susan Goldstein, Prof. Richard Gottheil, Frederick L. Guggenheimer, Bertha Guggenheimer, Rabbi Maurice Harris, Herbert M. Kaufmann, Hon. Julian Mack, Israel N. Thurman, Rabbi J. Max Weis, and Rabbi Stephen S. and Louise Waterman Wise. JIR Board Minutes, March 26, 1922.

22. Daniel P. Hays, Chairman, UAHC to Lee K. Frankel, Chairman, Free Synagogue Committee, April 6, 1922. In "Open Letter to the President of the Union of American Hebrew Congregations from Committee of Free Synagogue on the Jewish Institute of Religion," April 20, 1922, Appendix A, 14. JIR Nearprint Box 1.

23. Daniel P. Hays, Chairman, UAHC to Lee K. Frankel, Chairman, Free Synagogue Committee, April 6, 1922, JIR Nearprint Box 1.

24. Max Heller to Stephen S. Wise, April 28, 1922. Box 18, folder 15, JIR Records.

25. Stephen S. Wise to Louis Grossmann, December 12, 1921. Box 17, folder 9, JIR Records.

26. Stephen S. Wise to Julian W. Mack, n.d. [ca. 1922]. Box 25, folder 13, JIR Records.

27. Stephen S. Wise to Emil G. Hirsch, January 25, 1922. Box 19, folder 14, JIR Records.

28. Emil G. Hirsch to Stephen S. Wise, n.d. [ca 1922]. Box 19, folder 14, JIR Records.

CHAPTER 4

1. Stephen S. Wise to Harry S. Lewis, May 19, 1922. Box 24, folder 15, JIR Records.

2. The Committee identified the following scholars for consideration: Harry Austryn Wolfson (philosophy, Harvard University); Max Leopold Margolis, (biblical philology, Dropsie College); Raphael Mahler (history, teaching in Jewish secondary schools in Poland); Israel Efros, (philosophy and Hebrew poetry, and director, Baltimore Hebrew College); Jacob Mann (Jewish history, Hebrew College in Baltimore in 1920, and then Hebrew Union College ca. 1921); Ismar Elbogen (liturgy, the Hochschule in Berlin); Felix Perles (Koenigsberg); George Foot Moore (Bible and history, Harvard University); Richard Gottheil (Semitics, Columbia University); Israel Abrahams (rabbinic literature, Cambridge University); and Mordecai Kaplan (Midrash and philosophy, Jewish Theological Seminary of America). Minutes, Dinner Meeting of Committee on Jewish Institute of Religion, ca. 1921. Box 11, folder 11, JIR Records.

3. "The difficulty is that I won't have any man without meeting him face to face and getting

something of what I conceive to be his reactions to men," Wise wrote. Stephen S. Wise to Louis Grossmann, December 12, 1921. Box 17, folder 9, JIR Records.

4. Isadore Twersky, "Harry Austryn Wolfson (1887–1974)," *American Jewish Year Book* 76 (1976): 104.

5. Lewis S. Feuer, "Recollections of Harry Austryn Wolfson," *American Jewish Archives Journal* 28, no. 1 (1976): 30.

6. Horace M. Kallen to Stephen S. Wise, December 8, 1921. Box 40, folder 2, JIR Records.

7. Max L. Margolis to Stephen S. Wise, May 30, 1922. Box 26, folder 6, JIR Records.

8. Meyer, "Part One: A Centennial History," in *Hebrew Union College-Jewish Institute of Religion at One Hundred Years*, ed. Samuel E. Karff (Cincinnati, OH: Hebrew Union College Press, 1976), 66–67.

9. Arthur Kiron, "ARC MS6—Max Leopold Margolis Collection." Finding aid at the Library of the Herbert D. Katz Center for Advanced Judaic Studies, Penn Libraries, accessed August 16, 2013, www.library.upenn.edu.

10. As with other prospective faculty, Wise wanted to be sure Margolis would be willing to devote time to teaching and not only to research. "I know you respect him as a scholar," Wise explained to Hirsch, "but we ought to try to get men who are teachers and who can be a real influence in the lives of the younger men." Stephen S. Wise to Emil G. Hirsch, January 25, 1922. Box 19, folder 14, JIR Records.

11. Mel Scult, "Mordecai Kaplan, the Teachers Institute, and the Foundations of Jewish Education in America," *American Jewish Archives Journal* 38, no. 1 (1986): 57–84. "*Ivrit b'ivrit*" literally means "Hebrew in Hebrew" and refers to a method of teaching Hebrew through language immersion in the classroom.

12. Mordecai M. Kaplan, "A Program for the Reconstruction of Judaism," *Menorah Journal* 6 (1920): 182–84.

13. Mel Scult, "Mordecai M. Kaplan: Challenges and Conflicts in the Twenties," *American Jewish Historical Quarterly* 66, no. 3 (1977): 401–16.

14. Memo of a meeting held in the study of Dr. Wise, January 3, 1927. Present: Judge Mack, Dr. Wise, Dr. Kohut, Professor Kaplan. Box 22, folder 11, JIR Records. According to Mel Scult, though Wise later stated in his autobiography that he had Kaplan in mind for the presidency of JIR, he never extended an official offer. Later, Wise considered Kaplan for a deanship, but this too never transpired. See Mel Scult, *Judaism Faces the Twentieth Century: A Biography of Mordecai M. Kaplan* (Detroit: Wayne State University Press, 1993), 411n29; and Stephen S. Wise, *Challenging Years: The Autobiography of Stephen Wise* (New York: G. P. Putnam's Sons, 1949), 136.

15. Stephen S. Wise to Rabbi Goldman (likely, Solomon Goldman), 1922 (n.d.). Box 22, folder 11, JIR Records.

16. Richard Gottheil to Stephen S. Wise, May 24, 1922. Box 16, folder 18, JIR Records.

17. "Funeral Services Held for Dr. Nissan Touroff, Noted Educator," Jewish Telegraph Agency, April 3, 1953, accessed January 1, 2019, archive.jta.org/1953/04/03/archive/funeral-services -held-for-dr-nissan-touroff-noted-educator.

18. Goldberg, P. Selvin. "The Manchester Congregation of British Jews 1857–1957: A Short History." Manchester: Manchester Congregation of British Jews, 1957, accessed January 1, 2019, jacksonsrow.awardspace.com/manchester_cong/manchester_congregation.htm#CHAPTER 10.

19. *The Annual*, 1926, 10. JIR Nearprint Box 1.

20. Stephen S. Wise to Harry S. Lewis, May 19, 1922. Box 24, folder 15, JIR Records.

21. For more on Joel Blau, see Maurice Wohlgelernter, ed., *History, Religion, and Spiritual Democracy: Essays in Honor of Joseph L. Blau* (New York: Columbia University Press, 1980).

22. Carsten Wilke, "From Talmud Torah to Oriental Studies: Itineraries of Rabbinical

Students in Hungary," in *Modern Jewish Scholarship in Hungary: The "Science of Judaism" between East and West* (Berlin: Walter de Gruyter, 2016), 179.

23. Stephen S. Wise to Charles Foster Kent, April 19, 1922. Box 22, folder 18, JIR Records.

24. Glenn T. Miller, *Piety and Profession: American Protestant Theological Education, 1870–1970* (Grand Rapids, MI: William B. Eerdmans, 2007), 162.

25. "He (or the Chairman of his committee) insists upon an answer in fifteen days, or Dr. Wise will immediately set out upon a tour of the West to raise money for the support of the proposed college in New York," Shohl wrote. Charles Shohl to rabbis serving UAHC congregations, April 11, 1922. In "Open Letter to the President of the Union of American Hebrew Congregations from Committee of Free Synagogue on the Jewish Institute of Religion," April 20, 1922, Appendix B, 17. JIR Nearprint Box 1.

26. Stephen S. Wise to Emil G. Hirsch, April 14, 1922. Box 19, folder 14, JIR Records.

27. The open letter resembled in form the open letter Wise had crafted fifteen years earlier after he rejected the Emanu-El pulpit, which he published as part of an effort to elicit support for his new Free Synagogue. *Open Letter to the President of the Union of American Hebrew Congregations from Committee of Free Synagogue on the Jewish Institute of Religion*, April 20, 1922, p. 3. JIR Nearprint Box 1.

28. Emil G. Hirsch to Stephen S. Wise, Apr 26, 1922. Box 19, folder 14, JIR Records.

29. John Haynes Holmes to Stephen S. Wise, April 25, 1922. Box 20, folder 2, JIR Records. In 1918, Holmes resigned from the American Unitarian Association over its support for the war, and he later attempted but failed to convince his congregation to leave the denomination and become an independent church. Voss, *Rabbi and Minister*, 152, 157; and John Haynes Holmes, "A Statement: On the Future of This Church" (Church of the Messiah, 1918; Project Gutenberg, 2006), www.gutenberg.org.

30. Farewell Sermon delivered by Kaufmann Kohler on May 27, 1922, *Hebrew Union College Monthly* 8, no. 8 (1922): 226.

31. Kaplan worried that allying himself with the Free Synagogue would jeopardize the support he received from his traditional backers and believed he could better achieve his aims by remaining at the Conservative Seminary. Gottheil tried to assure Kaplan that not everyone at JIR was affiliated with the Free Synagogue. Richard Gottheil to Stephen S. Wise, May 24, 1922, and May 27, 1922. Box 16, folder 18, JIR Records.

32. Stephen S. Wise to Mordecai M. Kaplan, May 31, 1922. Box 22, folder 11, JIR Records. Over the course of the twenties, three separate sets of negotiations took place. Kaplan's biographer, Mel Scult, has described these in Scult, *Judaism Faces the Twentieth Century*.

33. Scult, *Judaism Faces the Twentieth Century*, 269.

34. Scult, *Judaism Faces the Twentieth Century*, 268.

35. Richard Gottheil to Steven S. Wise, May 27, 1922. Box 16, folder 18, JIR Records.

36. Julian W. Mack to Max L. Margolis, June 20, 1922. Box 26, folder 6, JIR Records.

37. Julian W. Mack to Stephen S. Wise, June 30, 1922. Box 25, folder 13, JIR Records.

38. Stephen S. Wise to Emil G. Hirsch, n.d. Box 19, folder 14, JIR Records.

39. Emil G. Hirsch to Stephen S. Wise, June 2, 1922. Box 19, folder 14, JIR Records.

40. Stephen S. Wise to Emil G. Hirsch, June 14, 1922. Box 19, folder 14, JIR Records.

41. Telegram from Julian W. Mack to Stephen S. Wise, June 11, 1922. Box 25, folder 13, JIR Records.

42. Julian W. Mack to Stephen S. Wise, June 16, 1922. Box 25, folder 13, JIR Records.

43. Julian W. Mack to Stephen S. Wise, June 16, 1922. Box 25, folder 13, JIR Record.

CHAPTER 5

1. Scult, "Schechter's Seminary," in *Tradition Renewed*, 63.

2. Yaakov Ariel, "A German Rabbi and Scholar in America: Kaufmann Kohler and the Shaping of American Jewish Theological and Intellectual Agendas," *European Judaism: A Journal for the New Europe* 45, no. 2 (2012): 59–77.

3. "Wise" refers to Isaac Mayer Wise, founder of Hebrew Union College and no relation to Stephen S. Wise. Stephen S. Wise to Richard J. H. Gottheil, April 27, 1921. Box 3, folder 5, JIR Records.

4. Kohut believed JIR would best be served by scholars fluent in English and comfortable with American customs. George A. Kohut to Stephen S. Wise, 1922 n.d. Box 23, folder 1, JIR Records.

5. Michael A. Meyer, "Two Persistent Tensions within Wissenschaft Des Judentums," *Modern Judaism* 24, no. 2 (2004): 105–19.

6. See Michael Brenner, *The Renaissance of Jewish Culture in Weimar Germany* (New Haven, CT: Yale University Press, 1998).

7. Lisa Silverman, *Becoming Austrians: Jews and Culture between the World Wars* (Oxford: Oxford University Press, 2012).

8. Bela Bodo, "Hungarian Aristocracy and the White Terror," *Journal of Contemporary History*, 45, no. 4 (2010): 704.

9. Raphael Patai, *Jews of Hungary: History, Culture, Psychology* (Detroit: Wayne State University Press, 1996), 474.

10. Stephen S. Wise to Louis Grossmann, December 12, 1921. Box 17, folder 9, JIR Records.

11. In the case of each candidate, Wise wanted to be sure "he is the man to do our kind of work." Stephen S. Wise to Emil G. Hirsch, January 25, 1922. Box 19, folder 14, JIR Records.

12. Years earlier, HUC's board of governors had expressed interest in bringing Abrahams to Cincinnati as a candidate for the presidency following Isaac Mayer Wise's death. After considering the idea, he declined. Robert S. Liberles, "Wissenschaft des Judentums Comes to America: A Chapter in Migration History, 1890–1935," in *Tradition Renewed: A History of the Jewish Theological Seminary of America, Vol. I*, ed. Jack Wertheimer (New York: Jewish Theological Seminary of America, 1997), 333.

13. Memorandum of Meetings of Stephen S. Wise with Israel Abrahams, Claude Montefiore, Israel Mattuck, and Travers Herford. 1922, n.d. Box 5, folder 1, Stephen S. Wise Collection. American Jewish Archives, Cincinnati, OH (hereafter, Stephen S. Wise Collection).

14. Umansky, Ellen M. "Jewish Historical Studies." *Jewish Historical Studies* 47, no. 1 (2015): 245–47.

15. Stephen S. Wise to Sidney E. Goldstein, June 22, 1922. Box 16, folder 15, JIR Records.

16. Memorandum of Meetings of Stephen S. Wise with Israel Abrahams, Claude Montefiore, Israel Mattuck, and Travers Herford. 1922, n.d. Box 5, folder 1, Stephen S. Wise Collection. American Jewish Archives, Cincinnati, OH (hereafter, Stephen S. Wise Collection).

17. Ismar Elbogen (in German) to Stephen S. Wise, June 19, 1922. Box 19, folder 15, JIR Records.

18. "Elbogen, Ismar." *Encyclopaedia Judaica*, ed. Michael Berenbaum and Fred Skolnik, 2nd ed., 6 (Macmillan Reference USA, 2007), 291.

19. Jacques K. Mikliszanski, "Tchernowitz, Chaim," *Encyclopaedia Judaica*, ed. Michael Berenbaum and Fred Skolnik, 2nd ed., 19, Macmillan Reference USA, 2007, 567. Also, Joseph Turner, "The Notion of Jewish Ethnicity in Yehezkel Kaufmann's *Golah Venekhar*," *Modern Judaism* 28, no. 3 (October 2008): 257–82.

20. Jacques K. Mikliszanski, "Tchernowitz, Chaim." *Encyclopaedia Judaica*, ed. Michael Berenbaum and Fred Skolnik, 2nd ed., 19 (Macmillan Reference USA, 2007), 567; and Solomon Zeitlin, "Jewish Learning in America," *Jewish Quarterly Review* 45, no. 4 (1955): 582–616.

21. "In the Article about R. Travers Herford," ca. 1923, n.d. Box 19, folder 6, JIR Records.

22. Memorandum of Meetings of Stephen S. Wise with Israel Abrahams, Claude Montefiore, Israel Mattuck, and Travers Herford. 1922, n.d. Box 5, folder 1, Stephen S. Wise Collection.

23. Stephen S. Wise to R. Travers Herford, June 28, 1922. Box 19, folder 6, JIR Records.

24. Stephen S. Wise to Sidney Goldstein, July 1, 1922. Stephen S. Wise Collection, Series 4, folder 7. Brandeis University Archives and Special Collections, Waltham, Massachusetts.

25. Sidney Goldstein to Stephen S. Wise, June 16, 1922. Box 5, folder 1, Stephen S. Wise Collection.

26. Stephen S. Wise to Emil G. Hirsch, June 29, 1922. Box 19, folder 14, JIR Records.

27. Wise's 1922 handwritten diary. Box 7, folder 1, Stephen S. Wise Collection.

28. Robert L. Hetzel, "German Monetary History in the First Half of the Twentieth Century," *Federal Reserve Bank of Richmond Economic Quarterly* 88, no. 1 (2002): 6.

29. Jacob Rader Marcus, *United States Jewry, 1776–1985: Volume 3, The Germanic Period, Part 2* (Detroit: Wayne State University Press, 1993), 510

30. Brenner, *The Renaissance of Jewish Culture in Weimar Germany*, 64.

31. Robert Liberles, *Salo Wittmayer Baron: Architect of Jewish History* (New York: New York University Press, 1995), 53.

32. Yael Unterman, "Nehama Leibowitz, Teacher and Bible Scholar, Reviewed by Marla L. Frankel," *Nashim: A Journal of Jewish Women's Studies & Gender Issues* 18 (2009): 246; and Alan T. Levenson, "The 'Triple Immersion': A Singular Moment in Modern Jewish Intellectual History?" in *Three-Way Street: Jews, Germans, and the Transnational*, ed. Jay Howard Geller and Leslie Morris (Ann Arbor: University of Michigan Press, 2016), 55.

33. Yehoyada Amir, "Guttmann, Julius," in *Encyclopaedia Judaica*, 2nd ed., ed. Michael Berenbaum and Fred Skolnik, 8 (Macmillan Reference USA, 2007), 157–58.

34. Harry Torczyner eventually took the name Naphtali Herz Tur-Sinai.

35. Stephen S. Wise memorandum, July 4, 1922. Stephen S. Wise Collection, Series 4, folder 7. Brandeis University Archives and Special Collections, Waltham, Massachusetts.

36. Enrico Lucca, *Guide to the Perles Family Collection 1837–1937*, Leo Back Institute of Jerusalem, accessed January 4, 2019, digifindingaids.cjh.org/?pID=2851741#a18.

37. Stephen S. Wise memorandum, July 4, 1922. Stephen S. Wise Collection, Series 4, folder 7. Brandeis University Archives and Special Collections, Waltham, Massachusetts.

38. Stephen S. Wise to Sidney Goldstein, July 14, 1922. Stephen S. Wise Collection, Series 4, folder 7. Brandeis University Archives and Special Collections, Waltham, Massachusetts.

39. Stephen S. Wise to Ismar Elbogen, 1922 ca. July. Box 19, folder 15, JIR Records.

40. Stephen S. Wise to Ismar Elbogen, n.d. [ca. July 1922]. Box 19, folder 15, JIR Records.

41. Stephen S. Wise's 1922 handwritten diary. Box 7, folder 1, Stephen S. Wise Collection.

42. Salo W. Baron, "Israelitisch-Theologische Lehranstalt," in *Encyclopaedia Judaica*, ed. Michael Berenbaum and Fred Skolnik, 2nd ed., 10 (Macmillan Reference USA, 2007), 754–55.

43. Stephen S. Wise to Hirsch Perez Chajes, June 22, 1922. Box 5, folder 2, JIR Records.

44. "Council Formally Approves Mandate," *New York Times*, July 24, 1922.

45. "Jews Celebrate Mandate," *New York Times*, July 24, 1922.

46. Cable from Ismar Elbogen to Stephen S. Wise, n.d. Box 19, folder 15, JIR Records.

47. B'h is an abbreviation for the Hebrew *b'ezrat hashem*, "with God's help." Stephen S. Wise to Sidney Goldstein, July 14, 1922. Stephen S. Wise Collection, Series 4, folder 7. Brandeis University Archives and Special Collections, Waltham, Massachusetts.

48. Stephen S. Wise to Bertha Guggenheimer, August 3, 1922. Box 17, folder 19, JIR Records.

49. Stephen S. Wise's 1922 handwritten diary. Box 7, folder 1, Stephen S. Wise Collection.

50. Stephen S. Wise to Ismar Elbogen, August 3, 1922. Box 19, folder 15, JIR Records.

51. Stephen S. Wise to Charles Bloch, August 3, 1922. Box 3, folder 13, JIR Records.

52. "True, we haven't the men for good and all," he told Bloch, "but I don't know that I would

want any one of them for good and all. I think our plan is a much wiser one—to try a great number of men and then to endeavor to keep as permanent teachers the different men whom we find most suitable." Stephen S. Wise to Charles Bloch, August 3, 1922. Box 3, folder 13, JIR Records.

53. Sidney E. Goldstein to Stephen S. Wise, July 21, 1922. Box 16, folder 15, JIR Records.

54. Sidney E. Goldstein to Stephen S. Wise, August 4, 1922. Box 16, folder 15, JIR Records.

55. Sidney E. Goldstein to Stephen S. Wise, July 21, 1922. Box 16, folder 15, JIR Records.

56. "Dr. Joshua Bloch, Rabbi, Author, 67, Chief of Jewish Division of Public Library Until 1956 Dies—Taught at NYU," *New York Times*, September 27, 1957; and *The Annual*, 1926, 14. JIR Nearprint Box 1, JIR Records.

57. Sidney E. Goldstein to Stephen S. Wise, August 4, 1922. Box 16, folder 15, JIR Records.

58. Stephen S. Wise to Charles Bloch, August 3, 1922. Box 3, folder 13, JIR Records.

59. Stephen S. Wise to Charles Bloch, August 3, 1922. Box 3, folder 13, JIR Records.

60. Stephen S. Wise to Ismar Elbogen, August 3, 1922. Box 19, folder 15, JIR Records.

61. "As I see things, including the remuneration of Wolfson, Abrahams, Perles, Elbogen, Turoff, Block, and the special lecturers, Moore, Lake, Herford, secretarial and registrar expenses, I think we are already committed up to $35,000, so I am going to move slowly in the matter of getting Krauss in Vienna," Wise wrote. Wise also expressed concern about the conflict in which Mack was involved at Harvard over President Lowell's imposing an admissions quota on Jews. Stephen S. Wise to Julian Mack, August 3, 1922. Box 25, folder 13, JIR Records.

62. Verena Dohrn, "Seminary," trans. Anna Lipphardt and Rebecca Stuart, YIVO Encyclopedia of Jews in Eastern Europe, www.yivoencyclopedia.org.

63. Stephen S. Wise to Sidney E. Goldstein, August 7, 1922. Box 16, folder 15, JIR Records.

64. Stephen S. Wise to Sidney E. Goldstein, August 7, 1922. Box 16, folder 15, JIR Records.

65. Stephen S. Wise to Julian Mack, August 3, 1922. Box 25, folder 13, JIR Records.

66. Stephen S. Wise's 1922 handwritten diary. Box 7, folder 1, Stephen S. Wise Collection.

67. Ismar Elbogen to Stephen S. Wise, August 22, 1922. Box 19, folder 15, JIR Records.

68. Cyrus Adler to Samuel Schulman, May 29, 1922. Folder 205, Records of the American Jewish Joint Distribution Committee of the Years 1921–1932, JDC NY Archives.

69. Ismar Elbogen (in German) to Stephen S. Wise, August 23, 1922. Box 19, folder 15, JIR Records.

70. Cable from Stephen S. Wise to Stephen S. Wise (JIR), handwritten, n.d. Box 19, folder 15, JIR Records.

71. Cable from Julian W. Mack and Lee K. Frankel to Ismar Elbogen, August 26, 1922. Box 19, folder 15, JIR Records.

72. Cable from Louis D. Brandeis to Ismar Elbogen, August 26, 1922. Box 19, folder 15, JIR Records.

73. Stephen S. Wise to Albert Mosse, August 29, 1922. Box 19, folder 15, JIR Records.

74. Memorandum from Stephen S. Wise aboard Cunard R.M.S. "Aquitainia," 1922, n.d. Box 5, folder 1, Stephen S. Wise Collection.

75. Stephen S. Wise to Albert Mosse, August 29, 1922. Box 19, folder 15, JIR Records.

76. Memoranda from Stephen S. Wise aboard Cunard R.M.S. "Aquitainia," 1922, n.d. Box 5, folder 1, Stephen S. Wise Collection.

77. Chas. H. Joseph, "Random Thoughts," *Detroit Jewish Chronicle*, September 8, 1922.

CHAPTER 6

1. Nissan Touroff to Stephen S. Wise, September 20, 1922. Box 38, folder 6, JIR Records.

2. *Free Synagogue Bulletin*, November 27, 1921. Box 9, JIR Records.

3. Henry L. Feingold, "Investing in Themselves: The Harvard Case and the Origins of the Third American-Jewish Commercial Elite," *American Jewish History* 77, no. 4 (1988): 530. Also,

Nitza Rosovsky, *The Jewish Experience at Harvard and Radcliffe* (Boston: Harvard University Press, 1986), 6–7.

4. Feingold, "Investing in Themselves," 540n36.

5. Feingold, "Investing in Themselves," 540 and 543.

6. "Lowell Tells Jews Limit at Colleges Might Help Them," *New York Times*, June 17, 1922, 1.

7. Feingold, "Investing in Themselves," 547.

8. Horace M. Kallen, "Julian William Mack, 1866–1943." *American Jewish Year Book*, 46 (1944–1945), 34–46.

9. "Jews See Race Ban in Harvard Queries," *New York Times*, September 20, 1922.

10. These included University of Pennsylvania, University of Chicago, University of California-Berkeley, Johns Hopkins University, Harvard University, and Columbia University. See Paul Ritterband and Harold S. Wechsler, *Jewish Learning in American Universities: The First Century* (Bloomington: Indiana University Press, 1994), 52–76.

11. The *Menorah Journal* was published bimonthly by the Intercollegiate Menorah Association, dedicated "to the study and advancement of Jewish culture and ideas." In 1922, the association included seventy-three societies, and five thousand members. *American Jewish Year Book* 24 (1922–23), 242.

12. Pamela S. Nadell, "'The Synagog Shall Hear the Call of the Sister': Carrie Simon and the Founding of the NFTS," in *Sisterhood: A Centennial History of Women of Reform Judaism*, ed. Carole B. Balin, Dana Herman, Jonathan D. Sarna, and Gary P. Zola (Cincinnati: Hebrew Union College Press, 2013), 39.

13. Pamela Susan Nadell, *Women Who Would Be Rabbis: A History of Women's Ordination 1889–1985* (Boston: Beacon, 1999), 27, 65, 68, and 71; and "American Rabbis Approve Ordination of Women," *B'nai B'rith Messenger*, August 25, 1922.

14. Nadell, *Women Who Would Be Rabbis*, 95.

15. Harry S. Lewis to Stephen S. Wise, June 12, 1922. Box 24, folder 15, JIR Records.

16. Stephen S. Wise to Charles Bloch, August 3, 1922. Box 3, folder 13, JIR Records.

17. Stephen S. Wise to Emil G. Hirsch, January 25, 1922. Box 19, folder 14, JIR Records; and unsigned letter to Julian W. Mack, September 7, 1922. Box 25, folder 13, JIR Records.

18. JIR Board Minutes, special committee appointed to consider desirability and practicability of organizing an institute for the training of rabbis, November 2, 1920. Box 11, folder 11, JIR Records.

19. Wise told Mack, "Enrollment thus far twenty college graduates from all over country proves validity contention my access to university youth enormous importance in moving men choose ministry." Cable from Stephen S. Wise to Julian W. Mack, n.d. [ca. June 1922]. Box 25, folder 13, JIR Records. Sidney Goldstein to Stephen S. Wise, August 4, 1922. Box 16, folder 15, JIR Records.

20. Emil G. Hirsch is using the German term "marktschreierisch" here to mean "overly promotional."

21. *The Annual*, 1926, p. 24. JIR Nearprint Box 1.

22. "Ten Rabbis Graduated from Jewish Institute of Religion: Claude Montefiore and Chaim Bialik Granted Honorary Degrees," *Reform Advocate*, May 29, 1926. Free Synagogue Scrapbook. Box 9, JIR Records; and *The Annual*, 1926, p. 27. JIR Nearprint Box 1.

23. Several entering students, including Parker and Rose, had studied at the New School for Social Research, founded in 1919 by a group of progressive scholars including several pacifists; other students took classes at the New School during their years at JIR.

24. JIR did not admit all applicants, and not all admitted applicants chose to attend. In addition, not all who attended the institute qualified to graduate. Indeed, the faculty explicitly warned applicants upon acceptance that admission did not guarantee graduation, and a number

of students either dropped out or were dismissed. Maurice Teschner, for example, during his first semester at JIR in the fall of 1922, misrepresented his standing at the institute by claiming he was a senior. After speaking with him, Wise and Goldstein determined that his "lack of plasticity, independent manner" and the serious problem he had created at the beginning of his tenure as a student were not in the interests of JIR, and at their urging, Teschner left the institute. Faculty meeting minutes, December 21, 1922. Box 9, folder 7, JIR Records.

25. Sidney E. Goldstein to Stephen S. Wise, July 20, 1923. Box 16, folder 15, JIR Records.

26. Stephen S. Wise to Julian W. Mack, September 7, 1922. Box 25, folder 13, JIR Records.

27. "Dr. Max Meyer," *New York Times*, December 31, 1981.

28. Nadell, *Women Who Would Be Rabbis*, 76–77.

29. According to historian Shulamit Reinharz, the questioning of Norvin Lindheim's loyalty was fueled by antisemitism; his prison term lasted until 1924, but in 1928 he was declared innocent. See Shulamit Reinharz, "Irma Rama' Lindheim: An Independent American Zionist Woman," *Nashim: A Journal of Jewish Women's Studies & Gender Issues* 1 (1998): 106–9.

30. Nadell, *Women Who Would Be Rabbis*, 74.

31. Stephen S. Wise to Charles Bloch, August 3, 1922. Box 3, folder 13, JIR Records.

32. Philip Bernstein, baccalaureate address at the Jewish Institute of Religion, June 5, 1942. Box 6, folder 2, JIR Records.

33. Dinner Meeting of Committee on Jewish Institute of Religion minutes, n.d. [ca. 1921]. Box 11, folder 11, JIR Records.

34. Shabbat Shuvah is the sabbath that falls between Rosh Hashanah and Yom Kippur, when rabbis typically deliver sermons focused on repentance and forgiveness.

35. The schedule was formulated at a meeting in Stephen S. Wise's home with Wise, Sidney E. Goldstein, Maurice I. Harris, Joel Blau, Harry Lewis, Joshua Bloch, Louis I. Newman and J. Max Weis, September 27, 1922. Box 9, folder 7, JIR Records.

36. Faculty administering the exams included Nathan Krass, Harry Lewis, Joshua Bloch, Nissan Touroff, and J. Max Weis. Faculty meeting minutes, October 6, 1922. Box 9, folder 7, JIR Records.

37. Faculty meeting minutes, October 6, 1922. Box 9, folder 7, JIR Records.

38. Faculty course assignments included: history (Elbogen), Bible (Perles), Jewish religion (Perles), Talmud (Lewis or Blau), Midrash and homiletics (Blau), liturgy (Elbogen), social service (Goldstein), principles and methods of education (Touroff, in Hebrew); and Modern Hebrew literature and composition (Blau and Touroff). Faculty meeting minutes, October 8, 1922. Box 9, folder 7, JIR Records.

39. Faculty meeting minutes, October 5 and 8, 1922. Box 9, folder 7, JIR Records.

40. Faculty meeting minutes, October 3, 1922. Box 9, folder 7, JIR Records. Shabbat Bereshit is the sabbath when the Torah-reading cycle restarts with the first portion in Genesis. "Bereshit" means "In the beginning," which are also the first words of the Torah.

41. Faculty meeting minutes, October 8, 1922. Box 9, folder 7, JIR Records.

42. *Free Synagogue Bulletin*, October 15, 1922. Box 9, JIR Records.

43. Israel Goldstein to Stephen S. Wise, October 4, 1922. Box 16, folder 14, JIR Records.

44. Dinner meeting of Committee on Jewish Institute of Religion, n.d. [ca. 1921]. Box 11, folder 11, JIR Records.

45. "Harris, Maurice," *Encyclopaedia Judaica*, ed. Michael Berenbaum and Fred Skolnik, 2nd ed., 8, Macmillan Reference USA, 2007, 363–64; and "The Graduating Class," *The Annual*, 1926, 30. JIR Nearprint Box 1.

46. Stephen S. Wise to Charles Bloch, September 26, 1922. Box 3, folder 13, JIR Records; and faculty meeting minutes, September 25, 1922. Box 9, folder 7, JIR Records.

47. Present were the two German scholars, no doubt weary from their journey; Goldstein,

Wise's assistant rabbi; Harry Lewis, the institute's British-born chaplain; George Alexander Kohut, the bibliographer; Wise's longtime allies in the Zionist movement, Richard Gottheil from Columbia and Rabbi Louis I. Newman, who had recently left the Bronx Free Synagogue to work alongside Harris at Temple Israel; local rabbis Joel Blau and J. M. Weis; and, youngest of all, Joshua Bloch, librarian and instructor. Only Touroff was missing. Faculty Meeting minutes, October 11, 1922. Box 9, folder 7, JIR Records.

48. Stephen S. Wise to Richard Gottheil, n.d. [ca. 1922]. Box 16, folder 18, JIR Records.

49. Faculty Meeting minutes, October 11, 1922. Box 9, folder 7, JIR Records.

50. Faculty Meeting minutes, November 2, 1922. Box 9, folder 7, JIR Records.

51. Faculty Meeting minutes, October 18, 1922, and December 21, 1922. Box 9, folder 7, JIR Records.

52. Faculty Meeting minutes, November 16 and December 21, 1922. Box 9, folder 7, JIR Records.

53. Faculty Meeting minutes, November 2, 1922. Box 9, folder 7, JIR Records.

54. Faculty Meeting minutes, December 6, 1922. Box 9, folder 7, JIR Records.

55. Faculty Meeting minutes, December 28, 1922. Box 9, folder 7, JIR Records.

56. "And America Shall Lead Them: An Interview with Professor Ismar Elbogen and Dr. Felix Perles," *American Hebrew*, October 20, 1922. JIR Nearprint Box 1.

57. "America as the Center of Jewish Culture," *Detroit Free Chronicle*, November 3, 1922.

58. Elbogen's courses included "Development of Jewish Liturgy," "An Introduction to the Study of Judaism," "Jewish Historical Sources," and "Historical Problems of the Talmud." Perles taught "Critical Study of Psalms and Prophets," "History of the Jewish Religion from the Babylonian Exile to the Close of the Talmud" (in German), and "Introduction to the Old Testament Literature," including the Apocrypha and Pseudepigraphia. *Free Synagogue Bulletin*, November 26, 1922. See also "America as the Center of Jewish Culture," *Detroit Free Chronicle*, November 3, 1922.

59. Tom Miller, "The Lost Adolph Lewisohn Mansion—9 West 57th Street," in *Daytonian in Manhattan*, April 16, 2018, accessed August 3, 2019, daytoninmanhattan.blogspot.com /2018/04/the-lost-adolph-lewisohn-mansion-9-west.html. See also Stephen Birmingham, "*Our Crowd": The Great Jewish Families of New York* (New York: Harper and Rowe, 1967), 357.

60. "Burlesque Auction in Lewisohn Home," *New York Times*, January 1, 1923.

61. List of guests invited to the reception, accepted. Box 24, folder 24, JIR Records.

62. List of guests invited to the reception, accepted. Box 24, folder 24, JIR Records.

63. Addresses in honor of Professor Ismar Elbogen and Dr. Felix Perles, New York, December 6, 1922, p. 2–3. *Free Synagogue Bulletin* 1921–1928 [Scrapbook], Box 9, JIR Records.

64. Initially, Kaplan refused Wise's invitation to speak at the gathering, suggesting that other, more accomplished scholars should do so. Only after Wise insisted that Kaplan was the only man from the seminary he could with self-respect include on the program did his colleague relent. Mordecai M. Kaplan to Stephen S. Wise, November 21, 1922. Box 22, folder 11, JIR Records.

65. Addresses in honor of Professor Ismar Elbogen and Dr. Felix Perles, New York, December 6, 1922, pp. 4–5. *Free Synagogue Bulletin* 1921–1928 [Scrapbook], Box 9, JIR Records.

66. Addresses in honor of Professor Ismar Elbogen and Dr. Felix Perles, New York, December 6, 1922, p. 6.

67. Addresses in honor of Professor Ismar Elbogen and Dr. Felix Perles, New York, December 6, 1922, pp. 6–7.

68. Addresses in honor of Professor Ismar Elbogen and Dr. Felix Perles, New York, December 6, 1922, p. 13.

69. Addresses in honor of Professor Ismar Elbogen and Dr. Felix Perles, New York, December 6, 1922, p. 12.

70. Addresses in honor of Professor Ismar Elbogen and Dr. Felix Perles, New York, December 6, 1922, p. 11.

71. Addresses in honor of Professor Ismar Elbogen and Dr. Felix Perles, New York, December 6, 1922, p. 16.

72. Stephen S. Wise to Hirsch P. Chajes, January 1, 1923. Box 5, folder 2, JIR Records.

73. Leo Baeck to Stephen S. Wise, December 1, 1922. Box 2, folder 11, JIR Records.

74. Cable from Julian Obermann to Stephen S. Wise, December 23, 1922. Box 28, folder 5, JIR Records.

75. Cecil Roth, "I.A.," Israel Abrahams Memorial Issue, *Institute Quarterly* 2, no. 1 (November 1925), 19–20.

76. JIR Board minutes, Executive Committee, December 18, 1922, and February 16, 1923. See also Stephen S. Wise to Emil G. Hirsch, November 7, 1922. Box 19, folder 14, JIR Records.

77. "The Synagogue has been from the beginning ready to share, and more than share my own service with the Institute which, of course, I serve, and will throughout my life serve, without one penny of remuneration. My one compensation is the privilege of providing two scholarships, bearing my mother's and my wife's names," Wise states in the 1926 *Annual.* "The History of the Institute: An Interview with Dr. Wise," *The Annual,* 1926, 34–35. JIR Nearprint Box 1.

78. "Dr. Emil G. Hirsch, Noted Orator, Dies," *New York Times,* January 8, 1923.

79. Greenberg, "The Dimensions of Samuel Adler's Religious View of the World," 377–412.

80. Norval White and Elliot Willensky with Fran Leadon, *AIA Guide to New York City, Fifth Edition* (Oxford University Press, 2010), 393. "The New York Institute of Religion," *Jewish Guardian,* London, England, November 16, 1923; and "The New York Institute of Religion," *Jewish Guardian,* London, England, November 16, 1923.

81. *Encyclopedia of Library and Information Science,* s.v. "Seminary Libraries"; Stephen S. Wise to Richard Gottheil, December 12, 1922. Box 16, folder 18, JIR Records; and JIR Board minutes, Executive Committee, December 18, 1922.

82. "Jewish Institute of Religion: An Estimate," *Free Synagogue Bulletin,* November 26, 1922. Box 9, JIR Records. See also Harold Berman, "The Jewish Institute of Religion," *Reform Advocate,* November 11, 1922, 43–44.

Chapter 7

1. Zev Eleff, "'The Envy of the World and the Pride of the Jews': Debating the American Jewish University in the Twenties," *Modern Judaism* 31, no. 2 (2011): 236.

2. Leslie B. Alexander and Milton D. Speizman, "The Graduate School for Jewish Social Work, 1924–40: Training for Social Work in an Ethnic Community," *Journal of Education for Social Work* 19, no. 2 (1983): 8.

3. Louis I. Newman, "Is a Jewish University in America Desirable: A Thorough Discussion of One of the Most Burning Problems of Our Day," *Jewish Tribune,* October 27, 1922. Newman's idea came to fruition in 1948 with the founding of Brandeis University.

4. Daniel P. Kotzin, *Judah L. Magnes: An American Jewish Nonconformist* (Syracuse University Press, 2010), 171 and 174.

5. Einstein opened his remarks in Hebrew. Norman Bentwich, Devorah Getzler, Jerry Barasch, and Shared Gilboa, "Hebrew University of Jerusalem," *Encyclopaedia Judaica,* edited by Michael Berenbaum and Fred Skolnik, 2nd ed., 8, Macmillan Reference USA, 2007, 740–44.

6. Sheldon Blank, "Autobiography." Unpublished manuscript, 1988.

7. "The Institute trains men for Jewish scholarship and the rabbinate. It is not concerned with the label of the rabbi, whether he be orthodox, or reform or conservative." "Institute of Religion Dedicated: Rabbi Stephen Wise Leads Exercises In New $500,000 New York Edifice," *Jewish Review and Observer,* April 1924. Free Synagogue Scrapbook. Box 9, JIR Records.

8. Stephen S. Wise, "As I See Myself," written for the *Jewish Exponent*, ca. March 1926. Free Synagogue Scrapbook. Box 9, JIR Records.

9. See Mark Kligman, "Reestablishing a 'Jewish Spirit' in American Synagogue Music: The Music of A. W. Binder," in *The Art of Being Jewish in Modern Times*, ed. Barbara Kirshenblatt-Gimblett and Jonathan Karp (Philadelphia: University of Pennsylvania Press, 2008), 270–87.

10. JIR Board Minutes, April 2, 1923.

11. Harry Lewis, Joel Blau, Maurice Harris, and Louis I. Newman.

12. Feuer, "Recollections of Harry Austryn Wolfson," 30.

13. "Harvard Bans Discrimination," *Reform Advocate*, April 14, 1923.

14. The report was issued April 7, 1923. Jerome Karabel, *The Chosen: The Hidden History of Admission and Exclusion at Harvard, Yale, and Princeton* (Boston: Houghton Mifflin, 2005), 100. See also Feingold, "Investing in Themselves," 550.

15. Karabel, *The Chosen*, 101–2; and Feingold, "Investing in Themselves," 551. See also Stephen Steinberg, "How Jewish Quotas Began," *Commentary* (September 1971), 67–76.

16. JIR Board Minutes, Executive Committee, January 17, 1923.

17. JIR Board Minutes, Executive Committee, April 2, 1923.

18. JIR Board Minutes, Executive Committee, May 24, 1923.

19. "The Jewish Institute of Religion is ready to accept these conditions, and pursuant thereto to tender to Harvard University the services of Professor Wolfson in the fields in which he has been active at Harvard, for a semester in each academic year, without compensation by the University, the Institute paying him his full compensation as Professor," Wise wrote. Stephen S. Wise to the President and Fellows of Harvard College, April 7, 1923. Box 40, folder 2, JIR Records.

20. Pound mentioned Slonimsky by name in his *Cantos*. Jonathan Malino, "Haff you gno bolidigal basshunts? . . .' (Canto 77/152–3): Ezra Pound and 'Doktor' Slonimsky." Paper presented at the Twenty-First Ezra Pound International Conference, Rapallo, Italy, July 2005.

21. "Dr. Henry Slonimsky, 86, Dead; Educator Also Active in Religion," *New York Times*, November 14, 1970.

22. Frank Goodnow, "Annual Report of the President of the Johns Hopkins University," *Johns Hopkins University Circular Baltimore 1916*, ns, no. 1, 281 (Baltimore, MD: Johns Hopkins University Press, 1916): 90; "Hebrew Union College News: Activities of Faculty and Students," *Union Bulletin* 12, nos. 4–5 (Cincinnati: Union of American Hebrew Congregations, April–May 1922): 8; and Eugene B. Borowitz, "Henry Slonimsky 1884–1970," Proceedings and Addresses of the American Philosophical Association 44 (1970–1971): 226.

23. Jacob Billikopf to Stephen S. Wise, January 29, 1923. Box 34, folder 1, JIR Records.

24. Stephen S. Wise to Jacob Billikopf, April 3, 1923. Box 34, folder 1, JIR Records.

25. Stephen S. Wise to Jacob Billikopf, April 3, 1923. Box 34, folder 1, JIR Records.

26. The Alexander Kohut Memorial Collection of Judaica was the university's first major gift of Judaica and included many rare works. Kohut also financed the publication of works by Yale faculty and in later years created a Kohut Book Fund at the Yale Library and a Kohut Publication Fund at the Yale Graduate School. He bequested to the university 950 volumes of his private library. Leon Nemoy, "George Alexander Kohut," *Yale University Library Gazette* 9, no. 4 (April 1935): 96.

27. JIR Board Minutes, Executive Committee, May 24, 1923.

28. JIR Board Minutes, Executive Committee, May 24, 1923.

29. JIR Board Minutes, Executive Committee, May 24, 1923.

30. Nadell, *Women Who Would Be Rabbis*, 71.

31. According to the February 1923 faculty meeting minutes, "The question of admitting women as regular students to the Institute was considered at length. This matter was brought up for consideration as a result of a request from Mrs. Lindheim to be permitted to become

a regular student. It was the consensus of opinion that in view of the lack of proper facilities, such as dormitories, etc. for women, that the matter should be disposed of for about two years. It was clearly understood by all those present that it was not against the principles of the Institute to admit women students but as Dr. Abrahams pointed out, it might add to the burden of the founding of the Institute. While Dr. Goldstein expressed the hope that in time it might be possible to admit women in all departments of the work, he was strongly opposed to admitting women at present as either regular or special students. He felt there was a lack of seriousness among the students and would like to cultivate a more severe atmosphere. This he felt could be done easier without women than with them. It was therefore decided that for the time being women can only be admitted as auditor to the Extension Courses, but to permit the three women already members of the Institute to remain." Faculty meeting minutes, February 2, 1923. Box 9, folder 7, JIR Records.

32. Faculty Meeting minutes, March 7, 1923, and May 4, 1923. Box 9, folder 7, JIR Records.

33. Faculty Meeting minutes, April 20, 1923. Box 9, folder 7, JIR Records.

34. Faculty Meeting minutes, March 26, 1923. Box 9, folder 7, JIR Records.

35. Irma Lindheim to Julian W. Mack, August 23, 1929. Box 28, folder 5, JIR Records.

36. Faculty Meeting minutes, April 20, 1923. Box 9, folder 7, JIR Records.

37. Stephen S. Wise to Max Weis, December 14, 1922. Box 6, folder 10, JIR Records. Also, Faculty Meeting minutes, May 4, 1923. Box 9, folder 7, JIR Records.

38. Mitchell S. Fisher to "Friend," November 7, 1923. Box 36, folder 3, JIR Records.

39. Stephen S. Wise to Reuben Levy, July 26, 1923. Box 24, folder 22, JIR Records.

40. Sidney E. Goldstein to Stephen S. Wise, July 18, 1923. Box 37, folder 1, JIR Records.

41. Faculty Meeting minutes, September 14, 1923. Box 9, folder 7, JIR Records.

42. Stephen S. Wise to Edmund I. Kaufmann, March 21, 1923. Box 22, folder 14, JIR Records.

43. Stephen S. Wise to Edmund I. Kaufmann, March 21, 1923. Box 22, folder 14, JIR Records.

44. "Institute of Religion," *Free Synagogue Bulletin*, May 20, 1923. Box 9, JIR Records. Also, Martin A. Meyer, "Emanuel," April 6, 1923.

45. "Institute Notes," *Free Synagogue Bulletin*, April 22, 1923. Also, Faculty Meeting minutes, April 20, 1923. Box 9, folder 7, JIR Records.

46. Kaplan was paid $6,000 and he believed Ginzberg, Marx, and Davidson were paid the same. Hyamson received $2,000 and Kaplan did not know what Levine and Finkelstein were paid. "Adler told me more than once that, had the Seminary been better situated financially, I would have long ago received an increase. I presume the same holds true of the other members of the faculty who find it hard to make ends meet on their present income." Mordecai M. Kaplan to Stephen S. Wise, January 25, 1923. Box 22, folder 11, JIR Records.

47. Stephen S. Wise to Mordecai M. Kaplan, February 23, 1923. Box 22, folder 11, JIR Records.

48. Mordecai M. Kaplan to Stephen S. Wise, March 4, 1923. Box 22, folder 11, JIR Records.

49. JIR Board Minutes, Executive Committee, October 18, 1923.

50. Mordechai Zalkin, "Tchernowitz, Hayim," YIVO Encyclopedia of Jews in Eastern Europe, accessed July 26, 2020, yivoencyclopedia.org/article.aspx/Tchernowitz_Hayim.

51. Faculty Meeting minutes, March 26, 1923. Box 9, folder 7, JIR Records.

52. Stephen S. Wise to Hirsch P. Chajes, n.d. Box 5, folder 2, JIR Records. Stephen S. Wise to Hirsch P. Chajes, November 8, 1923. Box 5, folder 2, JIR Records. Faculty Meeting minutes, March 26, 1923. Box 9, folder 7, JIR Records.

53. "I have been ready the last few months to consider an offer from you," Kaplan told Wise. Mordecai M. Kaplan to Stephen S. Wise, July 1, 1923. Box 22, folder 11, JIR Records; also: "You may recall that from the beginning,—nearly two years ago,—I had invited you and urged you

to become co-founder of the Jewish Institute of Religion. I understood your viewpoint, and I respected it," Wise told Kaplan. Since then, "I was somewhat reluctant to see you because every time we met I felt I had hurt you by pressing you unduly to ally yourself with the Institute and its work. I felt it was a tremendous problem for you." Stephen S. Wise to Mordecai M. Kaplan, July 26, 1923. Box 22, folder 11, JIR Records.

54. Mordecai M. Kaplan to Stephen S. Wise, August 29, 1923. Box 22, folder 11, JIR Records.

55. Sidney E. Goldstein [memo] to Stephen S. Wise, July 10 and July 12, 1923. Box 16, folder 15, JIR Records.

56. Scult, *Judaism Faces the Twentieth Century*, 271.

57. Nathan Ausubel, "The True Story of the Man Who Built Up the Jewish Room of the New York Public Library," *Freedom: Morning Freiheit Magazine Section*, October 28, 1944, accessed August 7, 2013, legacy.www.nypl.org.

58. Edwin H. Anderson to Stephen S. Wise, October 6, 1923. Box 27, folder 18, JIR Records.

59. Memo of meeting with Stephen S. Wise and Edwin H. Anderson at the New York Public Library, November 12, 1923. Box 27, folder 18, JIR Records.

60. JIR Board Minutes, Executive Committee, November 28, 1923.

61. Edwin H. Anderson to Stephen S. Wise, February 18, 1924, and Stephen S. Wise to Edwin H. Anderson, February 29, 1924. Box 27, folder 18, JIR Records.

62. JIR Board Minutes, Executive Committee, March 18, 1924.

63. G. E. Von Grunebaum, "Ralph Marcus (1900–1956)," *Journal of Near Eastern Studies* 16, no. 3 (July 1957): 143–44.

64. Harry A. Wolfson to Stephen S. Wise, January 14, 1924. Box 40, folder 2, JIR Records.

65. Cable from Harry A. Wolfson to Stephen S. Wise, February 9, 1924. Box 40, folder 2, JIR Records.

66. Stephen S. Wise to Julius Guttmann, November 9, 1923. Box 17, folder 11, JIR Records. "Institute Notes," *Free Synagogue Bulletin*, January 27, 1924. Box 9, JIR Records.

67. Richard Gottheil to Stephen S. Wise, November 19, 1923. Box 16, folder 18, JIR Records.

68. Richard Gottheil to Stephen S. Wise, November 10, 1923. Box 16, folder 18, JIR Records.

69. JIR Board Minutes, Executive Committee, December 26, 1923.

70. Tchernowitz remained on the JIR faculty until his death in 1949. "Dr. Tchernowitz, Talmudic Scholar, Author and Editor of Bitzaron, Hebrew Monthly, Dies at 78—His Pen Name Rav Tzair," *New York Times*, May 16, 1949.

71. Stephen S. Wise to Albert M. Greenfield, March 28, 1924. Box 17, folder 3, JIR Records.

72. Stephen S. Wise to Edmund I. Kaufmann, March 21, 1923. Box 22, folder 14, JIR Records.

73. JIR Board Minutes, addition to Executive Committee meeting, January 30, 1924.

74. Stephen S. Wise to Julian W. Mack, May 8, 1924. Box 25, folder 13, JIR Records.

75. Stephen S. Wise to Julian W. Mack, May 8, 1924. Box 25, folder 13, JIR Records.

76. JIR Board Minutes, April 20, 1924.

77. These were the houses located at 32, 34, and 36 West Sixty-Eighth Street. Stephen S. Wise to Edmund I. Kaufmann, June 14, 1924. Box 22, folder 14, JIR Records.

78. Edmund I. Kaufmann to Stephen S. Wise, June 5, 1924. Box 22, folder 14, JIR Records.

79. Stephen S. Wise to Edmund I. Kaufmann, June 14, 1924. Box 22, folder 14, JIR Records.

80. See J. Wesley Null, *Peerless Educator: The Life and Work of Isaac Leon Kandel* (New York: Peter Lang, 2007).

81. The Jewish National Library would eventually be housed at the Hebrew University.

82. For more on Joel Blau, see Wohlgelernter, ed., *History, Religion, and Spiritual Democracy*.

83. Memo of meeting with Stephen S. Wise and Joel Blau, December 31, 1923. Box 3, folder 11, JIR Records.

84. Joel Blau to Stephen S. Wise, September 25, 1924. Box 3, folder 11, JIR Records.

85. Stephen S. Wise to Louis Grossmann, November 10, 1924. Box 17, folder 9, JIR Records.

86. Memo of meeting held with Stephen S. Wise, Julian W. Mack, George A. Kohut, and Mordecai M. Kaplan in Wise's study, January 3, 1927. Box 22, folder 11, JIR Records.

87. "'Rav Zair,' First of Hebrew University Faculty, to Lecture in U.S.," *Detroit Jewish Chronicle*, August 31, 1923.

88. "'Rav Zair,' First of Hebrew University Faculty, to Lecture in U.S.," *Detroit Jewish Chronicle*, August 31, 1923.

89. Stephen S. Wise to Julian W. Mack, February 3, 1925. Box 25, folder 14, JIR Records.

90. Stephen S. Wise to Julian W. Mack, February 3, 1925. Box 25, folder 14, JIR Records.

91. See Paul Ritterband and Harold S. Wechsler, *Jewish Learning in American Universities*, 117–21; and Feuer, "Recollections of Harry Austryn Wolfson," 25–50.

92. Stephen S. Wise to Gerson B. Levi, February 25, 1925. Box 24, folder 17, JIR Records.

93. Louis Grossmann to Stephen S. Wise, March 4, 1925. Box 17, folder 9, JIR Records.

94. *The Annual*, 1926, 36. JIR Nearprint Box 1.

95. Radiogram from Julian W. Mack to Stephen S. Wise, June 25, 1923. Box 25, folder 13, JIR Records.

96. Stephen S. Wise to Bertha Guggenheimer, February 24, 1925. Box 17, folder 19, JIR Records.

97. "Hebrew Union College Endowment Fund Passes Million Dollar Mark," *Jewish Daily Bulletin*, June 2, 1926. "Reform Jews Join Orthodox in Seminary Endowment," *Jewish Daily Bulletin*, November 15, 1923. "Jewish Theological Seminary to Have Library Building Through Generosity of Felix M. Warburg and Mortimer Schiff," *Jewish Daily Bulletin*, October 28, 1924.

98. Barry W. Holtz, "How One Man Shaped American Jewish Education," *Jewish Daily Forward*, August 26, 2011. Henry Slonimsky, "The Jewish Institute of Religion," *Jewish Education News* 1, no. 9 (June 1926). JIR Nearprint Box 1. Faculty Meeting minutes, June 5, 1925. Box 9, folder 7, JIR Records.

99. Solomon Lowenstein, "Dr. Lee K. Frankel 1867–1931," *American Jewish Year Book* 34 (1932–1933): 126. "Guide to the Records of the Graduate School for Jewish Social Work (New York, NY), undated, 1925–1950," American Jewish Historical Society, accessed July 28, 2020, digifindingaids.cjh.org/?pID=109156.

100. Shalom Vemunah, "In the Jewish Institute of Religion," *Jewish Advocate*, February 21, 1924. Free Synagogue Scrapbook, box 9, JIR Records.

101. Jacob X. Cohen, "Jewish Institute of Religion Reactions and Responses to Dr. Horace M. Kallen's 'Can Judaism Survive in the United States,'" n.d. Jacob Xenab Cohen Papers 1904–1971, box 2, folder 1.

102. Jacob Philip Rudin, "Concerning a King," Founder's Day Address, Hebrew Union College-Jewish Institute of Religion, New York, March 12, 1954. Jacob Philip Rudin Papers 1920–1959, box 2, folder 3.

103. "Schedule First Term, 1925–1926." JIR Nearprint Box 2.

104. Herbert A. Friedman, "Stephen S. Wise—The Giant of His Time: Moralist, Zionist, Pluralist," Founder's Day Address, Hebrew Union College-Jewish Institute of Religion, Cincinnati, March 10, 1993. Rabbi Herbert A. Friedman Collection, 1930–2004, box 8, folder 1. American Jewish Archives, Cincinnati, OH, accessed July 28, 2020, collections.americanjewisharchives.org/ms/ms0763/ms0763.008.001.pdf.

105. Harold I. Saperstein, "Recollections of Stephen Wise," May 1989. Stephen S. Wise, Reminiscences of Wise by Students. American Jewish Archives, Cincinnati, OH.

106. Stephen S. Wise to Homer Folks, March 2, 1923. Box 9, folder 3, JIR Records. Faculty Meeting minutes, February 2, 1923. Box 9, folder 7, JIR Records.

107. Harold I. Saperstein, "A Prince in Israel: Tribute to S. S. Wise." Text of Sermons in "Witness from the Pulpit, 1933–1959," box 6, folder 6. American Jewish Archives, Cincinnati, OH.

108. "Schedule First Term, 1925–1926." JIR Nearprint Box 2.

109. I. Edward Kiev and John J. Tepfer, "Jewish Institute of Religion," *American Jewish Yearbook* 49 (1947–1948), 95.

110. "Philip S. Bernstein Papers." Introduction to the register description at the River Campus Libraries, University of Rochester, accessed July 10, 2013, www.lib.rochester.edu.

111. By the fall of 1923, about fifteen High Holy Day pulpits had expanded into regular weekend positions.

112. Sidney E. Goldstein to Stephen S. Wise, August 2, 1924. Box 16, folder 15, JIR Records.

113. JIR Board Minutes, Executive Committee, November 28, 1923.

114. Faculty Meeting minutes, November 8, 1923. Box 9, folder 7, JIR Records.

115. JIR Board Minutes, memo from Chairman regarding conversation with Julian Morgenstern, November 5, 1923.

116. Stephen S. Wise to Louis Grossmann, November 10, 1924. Box 17, folder 9, JIR Records.

117. Jewish Institute of Religion *Annual Catalogue 1924–1925*, 9. JIR Nearprint Box 2.

118. Stephen S. Wise to Hirsch P. Chajes, January 1, 1923. Box 5, folder 2, JIR Records. Stephen S. Wise to Robert T. Herford, December 27, 1922. Box 19, folder 6, JIR Records.

CHAPTER 8

1. *American Hebrew*, November 29, 1924.

2. Philip Bernstein, baccalaureate address at the Jewish Institute of Religion, June 5, 1942. Box 6, folder 2, JIR Records.

3. Robert P. Jacobs, *By Reason of Strength* (St. Louis Rabbinical Association, 1998), 22.

4. Shalom Vemunah, "In the JIR," *Jewish Advocate*, February 21, 1924.

5. Vemunah, "In the JIR," *Jewish Advocate*, February 21, 1924.

6. Vemunah, "In the JIR," *Jewish Advocate*, February 21, 1924.

7. Young Judaea, a Zionist youth organization, was founded in 1909 under the auspices of the Zionist Organization of America. It is now affiliated with Hadassah.

8. Harold I. Saperstein and Marc Saperstein, *Witness from the Pulpit: Topical Sermons, 1933–1980* (Lanham, MD: Lexington, 1999), 148.

9. "Concerning a King," Founder's Day Address by Jacob Philip Rudin, Rabbi of Temple Beth-El of Great Neck, HUC-JIR, New York, March 12, 1954. Box 2, folder 3, Jacob Philip Rudin Records.

10. Shalom Vemunah, "In the JIR," *Jewish Advocate*, February 21, 1924.

11. John Tepfer, "Editorial: The Jewish Institute Quarterly," *Jewish Institute Quarterly* 1, no. 4 (May 1925): 116–17.

12. "Upperclassmen in Religious Work during Holidays," *Free Synagogue Bulletin*, October 1927. Box 9, JIR Records.

13. JIR Board Minutes, Administration Committee, June 9, 1923. Sidney E. Goldstein to Stephen S. Wise, August 10, 1923. Box 16, folder 15, JIR Records.

14. JIR Board Minutes, Executive Committee, November 28, 1923.

15. *Free Synagogue Bulletin*, September 26, 1926. Box 9, JIR Records.

16. *Free Synagogue Bulletin*, January 1923. Box 9, JIR Records.

17. Jacob X. Cohen, "A Year's Work of the Free Synagogue, NY Social Service Department." Box 2, folder 7, Jacob Xenab Cohen Papers.

18. *Free Synagogue Bulletin*, October 1927. Box 9, JIR Records.

19. *Free Synagogue Bulletin*, October 1927. Box 9, JIR Records.

20. *Free Synagogue Weekly Bulletin*, September 25, 1928. Box 11, folder 11, JIR Records.

21. "Dr. Wellisch, Herzl's Close Coworker, Dies," *Daily Bulletin*, November 8, 1926.

22. Urofsky, *A Voice That Spoke for Justice*, 230–31.

23. "First Graduations at Jewish Institute," *New York Times*, May 27, 1926.

24. Tchernowitz quotation from "Chaim Nachman Bialik Receives Degree of Doctor of Hebrew Literature from Jewish Institute of Religion," *Jewish Daily Bulletin*, May 27, 1926. 3.

25. "Mrs. Bertha Guggenheimer Leaves $125,000 Bequests," *JTA*, March 14, 1927.

26. "Rabbi Wise Advises Religious Exchanges," *New York Times*, May 23, 1926.

27. "Jewish School in First Graduation," *World*, May 27, 1926. Free Synagogue Scrapbook, Box 9, JIR Records.

28. JIR 1928 Commencement program. Box 3, folder 5, Jacob Philip Rudin Papers.

29. Louis I. Newman to Stephen S. Wise, February 22, 1929. Box 13, folder 2, Louis I. Newman Papers.

30. Philip S. Bernstein Papers finding aid, River Campus Libraries, University of Rochester, accessed August 1, 2020, rbscp.lib.rochester.edu/finding-aids/D269.

31. Louis I. Newman to Stephen S. Wise, September 22, 1929. Box 13, folder 2, Louis I. Newman Papers.

32. Meyer, *Response to Modernity*, 302.

33. Robert A. Seigel, "Cronbach, Abraham," in *Encyclopaedia Judaica*, 2nd ed., edited by Michael Berenbaum and Fred Skolnik, 306. Vol. 5. Detroit, MI: Macmillan Reference USA, 2007.

34. "Institute Notes," *Free Synagogue Weekly Bulletin*, March 3, 1929. Box 11, folder 11, JIR Records.

35. Stephen S. Wise to Louis I. Newman, February 18, 1929. Box 13, folder 2, Louis I. Newman Papers.

36. Louis I. Newman to Stephen S. Wise, February 22, 1929. Box 13, folder 2, Louis I. Newman Papers.

37. "Taxes for 1930." Box 37, folder 7, JIR Records.

38. *The Annual*, 1926, p. 36. JIR Nearprint Box 1.

39. "Dr. Wise is Honored on Eve of Birthday," *New York Times*, March 17, 1929.

40. Stephen S. Wise to Abram I. Elkus, March 2, 1925. Box 8, folder 10, JIR Records.

41. "Dr. Wise Dedicates Glens Falls Synagogue," *Free Synagogue Bulletin*, October 10, 1926.

42. "Jews Contribute $1,245,000 to $10,000,000 Fund of Harvard," *JTA*, January 1, 1924.

43. When Wise approached Mack about the possibility of soliciting Littauer for JIR, Mack steered him away; Littauer had more contributions to make at Harvard, and before asking him to support JIR as well, Mack planned to raise from him funding for the New School for Social Research. Julian W. Mack to Stephen S. Wise, December 28, 1927. Box 25, folder 14, JIR Records.

44. "Columbia University Seeks Professor to Occupy Jewish Chair," *JTA*, August 22, 1929.

45. Meyer, "Part One: A Centennial History," 114.

46. "Union Will Discuss New Finance Plan in April," *JTA*, March 3, 1924.

47. "Hebrew Union College Endowment Fund Passes Million Dollar Mark," *JTA*, June 2, 1926.

48. Meyer, "Part One: A Centennial History," 116.

49. Finding Aid to the Union for Reform Judaism Records. 1873–2011 Manuscript Collection No. 72.

50. "Cincinnati College to Be Separated from Union of American Hebrew Congregations," *JTA*, December 26, 1924.

51. Hasia R. Diner, *Julius Rosenwald: Repairing the World* (New Haven, CT: Yale University Press, 2017), 107.

52. Meyer, "Part One: A Centennial History," 116.

53. *News Bulletin of JIR*, April 1930 and December 1931.

54. Julius Rosenwald to Adolph Ochs, January 15, 1925. Box 3, folder 5, Hebrew Union College Records. Quoted in Diner, *108*.

55. Louis I. Newman to Stephen S. Wise, July 24, 1929. Box 13, folder 2, Louis I. Newman Papers.

56. *News Bulletin of JIR*, October 1929.

57. John Tepfer, "Editorial: The Jewish Institute Quarterly," 117.

58. "Jewish Institute to Graduate Five," *Jewish Daily Bulletin*, May 22, 1929.

59. David Lefkowitz, JIR Commencement address, May 27, 1929. Box 5, folder 12, JIR Records.

60. "Dr. Stephen S. Wise Retires from American Jewish Congress Presidency," *Jewish Daily Bulletin*, May 20, 1929.

61. "Herzl Termed Epochal by Dr. Wise in London," *New York Times*, July 19, 1929.

62. "Marshall Funeral Plans Indefinite," *New York Times*, September 13, 1929.

CHAPTER 9

1. "American Heads Palestine Hebrew Education System," *Jewish Daily Bulletin*, March 22, 1928.

2. Diesendruck would return to the United States in 1930 to occupy the chair in Jewish Philosophy at Hebrew Union College in Cincinnati, where he served until his death in 1940.

3. Stephen S. Wise to Louis I. Newman, April 24, 1929. Box 13, folder 2, Louis I. Newman Papers; Stephen S. Wise to Louis I. Newman, April 19, 1929. Box 13, folder 2, Louis I. Newman Papers.

4. Louis I. Newman to Stephen S. Wise, May 8, 1929. Box 13, folder 2, Louis I. Newman Papers.

5. Jacob Philip Rudin, Founder's Day address at HUC-JIR in New York, March 12, 1954. Box 2, folder 3, Jacob Philip Rudin papers.

6. In 1934, Freehof would become rabbi of Rodef Shalom Congregation in Pittsburgh, where he remained until he retired in 1966.

7. Solomon Freehof, "The Jewish Chair at Columbia," *American Israelite*, May 30, 1930.

8. Stephen S. Wise to Ismar Elbogen, December 18, 1929. Box 5, folder 8, JIR Records.

9. Nadell, *Women Who Would Be Rabbis*, 79.

10. Harold Saperstein, "Tribute to Stephen S. Wise," April 22, 1949. Box 6, folder 6, Harold I. Saperstein Papers.

11. Tepper, "I Dwell Among the People," 29.

12. *News Bulletin of JIR*, June 1930.

13. "Synagogues Organize for Service in Unemployment Crisis," *JTA*, December 2, 1930.

14. "White Plains Rabbi Aids Negroes' Fight on Exclusion," *JTA*, April 24, 1930.

15. Leonard Dinnerstein, "A Neglected Aspect of Southern Jewish History," *American Jewish Historical Quarterly* 61, no. 1 (1971): 63.

16. Maurice J. Bloom, "The Messiah of Liberal Judaism," sermon delivered March 20, 1931, at Temple Beth Jacob, Newburgh, New York. Box 1, folder 4, Maurice J. Bloom Papers.

17. Robert P. Jacobs, "Stephen Wise Takes Command." Reminiscences of Wise by his students, SC-13528.

18. Morris Frommer, "The American Jewish Congress: A History, 1914–1950 Volume I" (PhD diss., Ohio State University, 1978), 243–46.

19. Michael A. Meyer, "Abba Hillel Silver as Zionist Within the Camp of Reform Judaism," in *Abba Hillel Silver and American Zionism*, ed. Mark A. Raider, Jonathan D. Sarna, and Ronald W. Zweig (London: Frank Cass, 1997).

20. Meyer, *Response to Modernity*, 313.

21. Louis I. Newman to William H. Fineshriber, January 5, 1931. Box 13, folder 4, Louis I. Newman Papers; William H. Fineshriber to Louis I. Newman, January 7, 1931. Box 13, folder 4, Louis I. Newman Papers.

22. "Reform Rabbis Approve Inclusion of Revised Version of Ancient Kol Nidrei Prayer and Hatikvah in New Union Hymnal," *Jewish Daily Bulletin*, June 30, 1930.

23. Jacob X. Cohen, "Memorandum of Meeting of Das Bund Der Freunde Das Neue Deutschland Held at Turn Halle, Tuesday, December 5, 1933." Box 1, folder 2, Jacob Xenab Cohen Papers.

24. "Dr. Samuel Schulman Sees Agency as Most Promising Instrument for Jewish Unity," *JTA*, September 23, 1932.

25. "Wise Advises Jews Who Base Views on Non-Jewish Opinions to Get Out of Jewish Life," *JTA*, September 26, 1932.

26. "Central Conference of American Rabbis Defers Action on World Congress," *JTA*, November 7, 1932.

CHAPTER 10

1. Frommer, "The American Jewish Congress," 307.

2. Morton M. Berman, "Zionist Reminiscences." Box 1, folder 9, Morton Mayer Berman Papers.

3. Harold I. Saperstein, "A Prince in Israel: Tribute to Stephen S. Wise," April 22, 1949. Box 6, folder 6, Harold I. Saperstein Papers.

4. "Congress Postpones Session on American Problems," *JTA*, February 26, 1933.

5. "250,000 Jews Here to Protest Today," *New York Times*, March 27, 1933.

6. Kohut would soon join the JIR board.

7. "Vast crowds flock to monster demonstration at Madison Square Garden to express indignation against Nazi excesses," *JTA*, March 29, 1933.

8. "Rabbinical Associations Proclaim Fast for Next Monday," *JTA*, March 24, 1933.

9. Frederick A. Lazin, "The Response of the American Jewish Committee to the Crisis of German Jewry, 1933–1939," *American Jewish History* 68, no. 3 (March 1979): 292.

10. Lazin, "The Response of the American Jewish Committee to the Crisis of German Jewry, 1933–1939," 292–93.

11. "Jewish Congress Fight Against Nazi Outrages Renewed in Urgent Call," *JTA*, April 16, 1933.

12. Harold I. Saperstein, "A Prince in Israel: Tribute to Stephen S. Wise," April 22, 1949. Box 6, folder 6, Harold I. Saperstein Papers.

13. Dora Askowith, "Women Have Role in Congress," *Congress Courier*, June 30, 1933.

14. Frommer, "The American Jewish Congress," 323.

15. "Confer Jointly, Act in Unison, Rabbis Urge Conflicting Jewish Bodies," *JTA*, May 2, 1933.

16. "Jews of World Join in Great Demonstration Against Hitler Persecutions in Germany," *JTA*, May 12, 1933; "100,000 March Here in 6-Hour Protest Over Nazi Policies," *New York Times*, May 11, 1933.

17. Louis I. Newman, "A Tribute to Doctor Wise." Box 13, folder 7, Louis I. Newman Papers.

18. *Congress Courier*, May 19, 1933.

19. "Urge Government to Permit Entry of German Refugees, Rabbi Schwartz Advises," *JTA*, September 8, 1933.

20. Jacob X. Cohen, "Memorandum of Meeting of Das Bund Der Freunde Das Neue Deutschland Held at Turn Halle, Tuesday, December 5, 1933." Box 1, folder 2, Jacob Xenab Cohen Papers.

21. Stephen S. Wise to Harry Kaplan, October 11, 1933. Box 4, folder 1, Harry Kaplan Papers.

22. Felix Levy to Stephen S. Wise, January 10, 1934. Box 18, folder 15, JIR Records.

23. Stephen S. Wise to Felix Levy, January 12, 1934. Box 18, folder 15, JIR Records.

24. Martin Perley, May 4, 1989. Reminiscences of Wise by his students, SC-13528.

25. "Rabbis Confer Thursday," *New York Times*, June 12, 1934.

26. "Resolution Adopted by the CCAR: Palestine, 1934," Central Conference of American Rabbis, accessed August 2, 2020, www.ccarnet.org.

27. Shawn Ilene Hellman, "Revising a Collective Identity: The Rhetorical Traditions of Reform Judaism in America, 1885–1999" (PhD diss., The University of Arizona, 2003), 137–138; and 1934 *CCARY* 44:182–83.

28. "Dr. Wise Withdraws His Support from the Revisionist Movement," *JTA*, March 12, 1935.

29. "Rabbis Back Share-Wealth Program," *Jewish Daily Bulletin*, June 27, 1935.

30. "Social Amendment Is Urged on Rabbis," *New York Times*, June 28, 1935.

31. Stephen S. Wise to Louis I. Newman, October 30, 1935. Box 13, folder 8, Louis I. Newman Papers.

32. "Wise Back, Says Crime of Nuremberg Was Expected," *JTA*, September 18, 1935.

33. "Admissions 1935–1936." Box 1, folder 5, JIR Records.

34. Salo W. Baron to Stephen S. Wise, June 4, 1936. Box 3, folder 2, JIR Records.

35. Stephen S. Wise to Felix Levy, May 18, 1936. Box 18, folder 15, JIR Records.

36. "Contributions from Alumni Congregations 1935–1936." Box 1, folder 11, JIR Records.

37. Urofsky, *A Voice That Spoke for Justice*, 274–75.

38. Urofsky, *A Voice That Spoke for Justice*, 253.

Chapter 11

1. Salo W. Baron, "Israelitisch-Theologische Lehranstalt," in *Encyclopaedia Judaica*, 2nd ed., ed. Michael Berenbaum and Fred Skolnik, 754–55. Vol. 10. Detroit, MI: Macmillan Reference USA, 2007. *Gale eBooks*, accessed August 2, 2020, link-gale-com.silk.library.umass.edu/apps/doc.

2. "Juedisch-Theologisches Seminar, Breslau," in *Encyclopaedia Judaica*, 2nd ed., ed. Michael Berenbaum and Fred Skolnik, 572. Vol. 11. Detroit, MI: Macmillan Reference USA, 2007. *Gale eBooks*, accessed August 2, 2020, link-gale-com.silk.library.umass.edu/apps/doc.

3. Leo Jung, "Rabbiner-Seminar Fuer das Orthodoxe Judentum," in *Encyclopaedia Judaica*, 2nd ed., ed. Michael Berenbaum and Fred Skolnik, 19–20. Vol. 17. Detroit, MI: Macmillan Reference USA, 2007. *Gale eBooks*, accessed August 2, 2020, link-gale-com.silk.library.umass.edu/apps/doc.

4. Michael A. Meyer, "Hochschule Fuer Die Wissenschaft Des Judentums," in *Encyclopaedia Judaica*, 2nd ed., ed. Michael Berenbaum and Fred Skolnik, 300. Vol. 9. Detroit, MI: Macmillan Reference USA, 2007. *Gale eBooks*, accessed August 2, 2020, link-gale-com.silk.library.umass.edu/apps/doc.

5. Regina Jonas, who was born in Berlin in 1902, was ordained in 1935 at a liberal seminary. Because no congregation was willing to offer a pulpit to a female rabbi, she served in clergy positions in nursing homes, hospitals, and prisons before her deportation and death. Liz Elsby, "I Shall Be What I Shall Be"—The Story of Rabbiner Regina Jonas," Yad Vashem: The World Holocaust Remembrance Center, https://www.yadvashem.org.

6. Alexander Scheiber, "Landesrabbinerschule," in *Encyclopaedia Judaica*, 2nd ed., ed. Michael Berenbaum and Fred Skolnik, 470. Vol. 12. Detroit, MI: Macmillan Reference USA, 2007. *Gale eBooks*, accessed August 2, 2020, link-gale-com.silk.library.umass.edu/apps/doc.

7. David Ellenson and Jane F. Darlin, "Mothers and Sons, Sisters and Brothers: Women of Reform Judaism and Hebrew Union College-Jewish Institute of Religion," in *Sisterhood: A Centennial History of Women of Reform Judaism*, ed. Carole B. Balin, Dana Herman, Jonathan D. Sarna, and Gary P. Zola (Cincinnati, OH: Hebrew Union College Press, 2013), 79.

8. Yaacob Dweck, "Gershom Scholem and America," *New German Critique* 44, no. 3 (November 2017): 65–66.

9. Stephen S. Wise to Charles Bloch, August 3, 1922. Box 3, folder 13, JIR Records.

10. Nadell, *Women Who Would Be Rabbis*, 79 and 241n68: Dora Askowith to Stephen S. Wise, August 2, 1948. Box 2, folder 8, JIR Records.

11. Dora Askowith to Stephen S. Wise, August 2, 1948, Box 2, Folder 8, JIR Records.

12. Nadell, *Women Who Would Be Rabbis*, 81. It may be noted that the faculty did not always discern the rabbinical promise in their students. Sidney Goldstein, for example, wrote to Wise in the early 1930s, "I have just seen the four men passed by the other members of the Faculty yesterday. You must pardon me if I tell you that I am dreadfully disappointed in the group. There is not one in the four with any outstanding gift or a touch of distinction. Instead of examining I talked with them for sometime and they belong clearly to the B C or D groups. There is not an A among them. What is the use of trying to train such mediocre men for leadership. Would it not be better, in view of the situation today in the American rabbinate, to declare a moratorium on admissions? The four men to whom I refer are Malino, Saperstein, Jacobson, White." As it turned out, each of these members of the class of 1935—Jerome Malino, Harold Saperstein, Abraham I. Jacobson, and Saul E. White—had a long and successful career in the rabbinate, and Malino, Saperstein, and White were among the leading American rabbis of their generation. Sidney E. Goldstein to Stephen S. Wise, September 24, 1931. Box 16, folder 16, JIR Records.

13. Nadell, *Women Who Would Be Rabbis*, 82.

14. Nadell, *Women Who Would Be Rabbis*, 85–87; and Elisa Klapheck, "Regina Jonas," in *Jewish Women: A Comprehensive Historical Encyclopedia*, February 27, 2009. Jewish Women's Archive, accessed February 27, 2021, jwa.org/encyclopedia/article/jonas-regina.

15. Nadel, *Women Who Would Be Rabbis*, 85–87 and 114–16; and Elizabeth Sarah, "The Discovery of Fräulein Rabbiner Regina Jonas: Making Sense of Our Inheritance," *European Judaism: A Journal for the New Europe* 28, no. 2 (Autumn 1995): 91–98.

16. Nadell, *Women Who Would Be Rabbis*, 84.

17. Nadell, *Women Who Would Be Rabbis*, 80.

18. Nadell, *Women Who Would Be Rabbis*, 84.

19. Nadell, *Women Who Would Be Rabbis*, 84.

20. Nadell, *Women Who Would Be Rabbis*, 84–85.

21. "First Woman Rabbi," *Palestine Post*, June 20, 1939, p. 2.

22. "Jews Are Warned on Wasting Effort," *New York Times*, May 29, 1939.

23. Nadell, *Women Who Would Be Rabbis*, 82.

24. Nadell, *Women Who Would Be Rabbis*, 99. During the 1930s, HUC, JIR, JTS, Yeshiva University, and Dropsie joined with others on the National Committee on Refugee Jewish Ministers devoted to rescuing as many German rabbis, rabbinical students, and scholars as possible. One means of obtaining non-quota immigration visas entailed creating short-term rabbinical positions with low pay for qualified clergy. Many of those who entered the United States this way went on to have successful rabbinical careers.

25. Joyce Antler, "Justine Wise Polier," *Jewish Women: A Comprehensive Historical Encyclopedia*. March 20, 2009. Jewish Women's Archive, accessed February 28, 2021, jwa.org/encyclopedia/article/polier-justine-wise.

26. Helen Lawrenson, *Stranger at the Party* (New York: Random House, 1975), 44–47.

27. See Reva B. Siegel, "A Short History of Sexual Harassment," in *Directions in Sexual Harassment Law*, ed. Catharine A. MacKinnon and Reva B. Siegel (New Haven, CT: Yale University Press, 2004).

28. On the ways American notions of masculinity, as well as power dynamics related to gender, have benefitted Jewish men at the expense of women in the home and workplace, see Keren R. McGinity, "The Unfinished Business of the Sexual Revolution," *American Jewish History* 104, nos. 2/3 (April/July 2020): 207–13.

29. Stephen S. Wise to Maurice J. Bloom, December 10, 1941. Box 1, folder 1, Maurice J. Bloom Papers.

30. "Philip S. Bernstein Papers, Register Description," River Campus Libraries, University of Rochester, accessed August 2, 2020, rbscp.lib.rochester.edu/3323.

31. Rooks-Rapport, "Louise Waterman Wise," in *Jewish Women in America*, 1483.

32. "Jewish Institute of Religion Report of Activities 1938–1939." Box 5, folder 1, Stephen S. Wise Collection.

33. United States Holocaust Memorial Museum, "The Riegner Telegram," *Holocaust Encyclopedia*, United States Holocaust Memorial Museum, accessed August 2, 2020, encyclopedia. ushmm.org/content/en/article/the-riegner-telegram.

34. Herbert A. Friedman, "Stephen S. Wise," in *Hebrew Union College-Jewish Institute of Religion Founders' Day Exercises*, March 10, 1993. Box 8, folder 1, Rabbi Herbert A. Friedman Collection.

35. "Biographical Sketch," Rabbi Herbert A. Friedman Collection, American Jewish Archives, accessed August 2, 2020, fa.americanjewisharchives.org/friedman/biographical-sketch/.

36. "A History of Significance," Sinai Free Synagogue, accessed August 2, 2020, www.sinai-freesynagogue.org.

37. Philip Miller, "Rabbi Louis I. Newman," in *Rhode Island Jewish Historical Notes* 14, no. 3 (November 2005): 450.

38. Joanna Maura Saidel, "Revisionist Zionism in America: The Campaign to Win American Public Support 1939–1948," (PhD diss., University of New Hampshire, 1994).

39. Paul M. Steinberg, "50 Years at the College-Institute," *Chronicle* 65 (Hebrew Union College-Jewish Institute of Religion, 2005), 17.

40. *News Bulletin of JIR*, June 1945.

41. Robert Gordis to "Dear Colleague," September 10, 1945. Box 39, folder 7, JIR Records.

42. Max Arzt to Members of the Rabbinical Association, n.d. (ca. September 3, 1945). Box 39, folder 7, JIR Records.

43. Maurice N. Eisendrath to "Dear Friend," November 9, 1945. Box 39, folder 7, JIR Records.

44. Tepper, "I Dwell Among the People," 80.

45. Monty Noam Penkower, "The Genesis of the American Council for Judaism: A Quest for Identity in World War II," *American Jewish History* 86, no. 2 (June 1998): 184.

46. Stephen S. Wise draft letter to Maurice Eisendrath, January 17, 1945. Box 39, folder 7, JIR Records.

47. Stephen S. Wise to Maurice Eisendrath, March 13, 1946. Box 18, folder 16, JIR Records.

48. "Reform Jewry Urged to Repudiate Anti-Zionism," *News from the Union of American Hebrew Congregations*, March 4, 1946. Box 39, folder 7, JIR Records.

49. Michael A. Meyer, "From Cincinnati to New York: A Symbolic Move," in *The Jewish Condition: Essays on Contemporary Judaism Honoring Rabbi Alexander M. Schindler*, edited by Aron Hirt-Manheimer (New York: UAHC Press, 1995), 302 and forward.

50. See Meyer, "From Cincinnati to New York."

51. Sarna, "A Sort of Paradise for the Hebrews," 157.

52. Maurice Eisendrath to Stephen S. Wise, March 8, 1946. Box 39, folder 7, JIR Records.

53. *News Bulletin of the Jewish Institute of Religion*, June 1948.

54. Michael Alper, "Educational Notes and News," *Journal of Jewish Education* 19, no. 3 (1948): 61–63.

55. JIR faculty minutes, June 25, 1949.

56. This was Wise's last recorded speech. Audio provided by Dr. Gary Zola, director, American Jewish Archives, Cincinnati, OH. See also "Rabbi S. S. Wise Gets '48 Decalogue Honor," *New York Times*, March 13, 1949.

57. "18,000 Pay Tribute at Rites for Wise," *New York Times*, April 23, 1949.

58. Hebrew Union College-Jewish Institute of Religion merger agreement. Office of the President 20.A4–1. American Jewish Archives, Cincinnati, OH; "2 Jewish Colleges Merged in Seminary," *New York Times*, January 26, 1950.

59. Michael Alper, "The Institute Is Different," *Sentinel*, April 22, 1948.

60. Tepper, "I Dwell Among the People," 87.

61. The Student Body, HUC-JIR, New York School to A. B. Cohen, June 17, 1953. Box A4–1, MS-20, Office of the President 1947–1956.

62. Louis I. Newman, "A Mistaken, Unworkable and Injurious Plan," in *The Case Against the "Unification Plan" Regarding the Hebrew Union College-Jewish Institute of Religion*. Merger 20.Ala-21.4. American Jewish Archives, Cincinnati, OH; "The Jewish Institute of Religion Restored as Full School," in *Rodeph Sholom Chronicle*, August 1, 1956.

63. I am grateful to Dr. Gary Zola for applying the term "coup de grâce" to this context.

64. Tepper, "I Dwell Among the People," 99.

65. "The Jewish Institute of Religion Restored as Full School," in *Rodeph Sholom Chronicle*, August 1, 1956.

66. See Academy for Liberal Judaism, Nearprint. Louis I. Newman and David Neiman to "Dear Friend," n.d. Academy for Liberal Judaism Nearprint. American Jewish Archives, Cincinnati, OH.

67. Frank Weil to Jack Skirball, November 7, 1955. Newman folder, American Jewish Archives, Cincinnati, OH.

68. Solomon B. Freehof to Nelson Glueck, February 2, 1956. Merger folder, American Jewish Archives, Cincinnati, OH.

69. "Students for Reform Rabbinate to Be Able to Graduate in New York," *JTA*, June 4, 1956.

70. "Students for Reform Rabbinate to Be Able to Graduate in New York," *JTA*, June 4, 1956.

Conclusion

1. Marc Dollinger, *Black Power, Jewish Politics: Reinventing the Alliance in the 1960s* (Waltham, MA: Brandeis University Press, 2018), 137.

2. Dollinger, *Black Power, Jewish Politics*, 173. See also "Civil Rights & Voting Rights," Religious Action Center, accessed April 10, 2021, rac.org/issues/civil-rights-voting-rights.

3. Steinberg, "50 Years at the College-Institute," 17.

4. The Student Body, HUC-JIR, New York School to A. B. Cohen, June 17, 1953. Box A4–1, MS-20, Office of the President 1947–1956.

5. "Dr. Alfred Gottschalk, *z"l*, Former President and Chancellor Emeritus of HUC-JIR," HUC-JIR News, September 14, 2009, huc.edu/news/article/2009/dr-alfred-gottschalk-zl-former-president-and-chancellor-emeritus-huc-jir.

6. Grace E. Speights, Sharon P. Masling, Martha B. Stolley, Jocelyn R. Cuttino, and Ira G. Rosenstein, *Report of Investigation into Allegations of Misconduct at Hebrew Union College-Jewish Institute of Religion*, Investigation conducted by the Philadelphia law firm Morgan Lewis (New York: Hebrew Union College-Jewish Institute of Religion, November 3, 2021.

7. Stephen S. Wise to Dora Askowith, August 16, 1948. Box 2, folder 8, JIR Records.

8. Nadell, *Women Who Would Be Rabbis*, 107–8.

9. Nadell, *Women Who Would Be Rabbis*, 112.

10. This was reflected in part by policies long held by HUC-JIR, JTS, and RRC barring intermarried Jews from their rabbinical and cantorial programs. The Reconstructionist Rabbinical College changed that policy and began accepting students with non-Jewish partners in 2015.

11. Mitchell S. Fisher, "A Reconstruction of Modern Religion," *Jewish Institute Quarterly* 1, no. 1 (November 15, 1924): 7–8.

Bibliography

ARCHIVAL AND MANUSCRIPT COLLECTIONS
American Jewish Historical Society, New York, NY
American Jewish Archives, Cincinnati, OH
American Jewish Joint Distribution Committee Archives, New York, NY
Archives and Special Collections, Brandeis University, Waltham, MA
Klau Library, Hebrew Union College-Jewish Institute of Religion, New York, NY
Schlesinger Library, Radcliffe Institute, Harvard University, Cambridge, MA
Archives, Temple Emanu-El, New York, NY

NEWSPAPERS
American Hebrew
Detroit Free Press
Detroit Jewish Chronicle
Jewish Daily Bulletin
Jewish Daily Forward
Jewish Education News
Jewish Telegraph Agency
Kansas City Jewish Chronicle
Light of Israel
New York Times
New York World-Telegram
The World

OTHER PERIODICALS
American Jewish Year Book
American Jewish Congress Courier
Free Synagogue Weekly Bulletin
Hebrew Union College Monthly
HUC-JIR Chronicle
Jewish Institute Quarterly
Jewish Institute of Religion Annual
News Bulletin of the Jewish Institute of Religion
The Reform Advocate
The Union Bulletin

REMEMBRANCES, REPORTS, SERMONS, AND SPEECHES
Berman, Morton M. "Zionist Reminiscences." Box 1, folder 9, Morton Mayer Berman Papers.
    American Jewish Archives, Cincinnati, OH.
Blank, Sheldon. "Autobiography." Unpublished manuscript, 1988.
Bloom, Herbert I. "Stephen S. Wise and the Dynamics of Liberal Judaism." Founders Day

Address, Hebrew Union College-Jewish Institute of Religion, New York, March 13, 1953. American Jewish Archives, Cincinnati, OH.

Bloom, Maurice J. "The Messiah of Liberal Judaism." Sermon, Temple Beth Jacob, Newburgh, NY, March 20, 1931. Box 1, folder 4, Maurice J. Bloom Papers. American Jewish Archives, Cincinnati, OH.

Ellenson, David. "President's Report." *HUC-JIR Annual Report 2009–2010*, Hebrew Union College-Jewish Institute of Religion, 2010.

Friedman, Herbert A. "Stephen S. Wise—The Giant of His Time: Moralist, Zionist, Pluralist." Founders Day Address, Hebrew Union College-Jewish Institute of Religion, Cincinnati, March 10, 1993. Rabbi Herbert A. Friedman Collection, box 8, folder 1. American Jewish Archives, Cincinnati, OH.

Goodnow, Frank. "Annual Report of the President of the Johns Hopkins University." *Johns Hopkins University Circular* 1916, ns, no. 1, whole number 281. Baltimore, MD: Johns Hopkins University Press, 1916.

Hirsch, Emil G. "The Free Synagogue." Pamphlet reprint from *The Reform Advocate*, 1907.

Holmes, John Haynes. "A Statement: On the Future of This Church." Church of the Messiah, 1918. Project Gutenberg, 2006. www.gutenberg.org.

Jacobs, Robert P. *By Reason of Strength*. St. Louis Rabbinical Association, 1998.

———. "Stephen Wise Takes Command." Reminiscences of Wise by his students, SC-13528. American Jewish Archives, Cincinnati, OH.

Kohler, Kaufmann. Farewell Sermon delivered on May 27, 1922. *Hebrew Union College Monthly* 8, no. 8 (1922): 221–27.

Levi, Gerson B. "Fragments of a Sermon Preached on Saturday Afternoon, March 15th, Before the Students of the Jewish Institute of Religion, New York." *The Reform Advocate* 67, no. 8 (March 22, 1924). Box 24, folder 17, JIR Records. American Jewish Archives, Cincinnati, OH.

Rudin, Jacob Philip. "Concerning a King." Founder's Day Address, Hebrew Union College-Jewish Institute of Religion, New York, March 12, 1954. Jacob Philip Rudin Papers 1920–1959, box 2, folder 3. American Jewish Archives, Cincinnati, OH.

Saperstein, Harold I. "Tribute to Stephen S. Wise." April 22, 1949. Box 6, folder 6, Harold I. Saperstein Papers. American Jewish Archives, Cincinnati, OH.

———. "Recollections of Stephen Wise." May 1989. Stephen S. Wise, Reminiscences of Wise by his students, SC-13528. American Jewish Archives, Cincinnati, OH.

Speights, Grace E., Sharon P. Masling, Martha B. Stolley, Jocelyn R. Cuttino, and Ira G. Rosenstein. *Report of Investigation into Allegations of Misconduct at Hebrew Union College-Jewish Institute of Religion*, Investigation conducted by the Philadelphia law firm Morgan Lewis. New York: Hebrew Union College-Jewish Institute of Religion, November 3, 2021.

Steinberg, Paul M. "50 Years at the College-Institute." *Chronicle* 65, Hebrew Union College-Jewish Institute of Religion, 2005.

Journal Articles

Alexander, Leslie B., and Milton D. Speizman. "The Graduate School for Jewish Social Work, 1924–40: Training for Social Work in an Ethnic Community." *Journal of Education for Social Work* 19, no. 2 (1983): 5–15.

Ariel, Yaakov. "A German Rabbi and Scholar in America: Kaufmann Kohler and the Shaping of American Jewish Theological and Intellectual Agendas." *European Judaism: A Journal for the New Europe* 45, no. 2 (2012): 59–77.

———. "Kaufmann Kohler and His Attitude Toward Zionism: A Reexamination." *American Jewish Archives Journal* 43, no. 2 (1991): 207–23.

Band, A. J. "Jewish Studies in American Liberal Arts Colleges and Universities." *American Jewish Yearbook* 67 (1966): 1–30.

Bodo, Bela. "Hungarian Aristocracy and the White Terror." *Journal of Contemporary History* 45, no. 4 (2010): 704.

Borowitz, Eugene B. "Henry Slonimsky 1884–1970," Proceedings and Addresses of the American Philosophical Association 44 (1970–1971): 226.

Brenner, Michael. "An Unknown Project of a World Jewish History in Weimar Germany: Reflections on Jewish Historiography in the 1920s." *Modern Judaism* 13, no. 3 (1993): 249–67.

Cohen, Naomi W. "American Jewish Reactions to Anti-Semitism in Western Europe, 1875–1900." *Proceedings of the American Academy for Jewish Research* 45 (1978): 29–65.

Dalin, David G. "Cyrus Adler, Non-Zionism, and the Zionist Movement: A Study in Contradictions." *AJS Review* 10, no. 1 (1985): 55–87.

Dinnerstein, Leonard. "A Neglected Aspect of Southern Jewish History." *American Jewish Historical Quarterly* 61, no. 1 (1971): 52–68.

Dweck, Yaacob. "Gershom Scholem and America." *New German Critique* 44, no. 3 (November 2017): 61–82.

Eleff, Zev. "'The Envy of the World and the Pride of the Jews': Debating the American Jewish University in the Twenties." *Modern Judaism* 31, no. 2 (2011): 229–44.

Engel, David. "Crisis and Lachrymosity: On Salo Baron, Neobaronianism, and the Study of Modern European Jewish History." *Jewish History* 20, no. 3/4 (2006): 243–64.

Engelman, Uriah Zvi. "Jewish Statistics in the US Census of Religious Bodies (1850–1936)." *Jewish Social Studies* (1947): 127–74.

Feingold, Henry L. "Investing in Themselves: The Harvard Case and the Origins of the Third American-Jewish Commercial Elite." *American Jewish History* 77, no. 4 (1988): 530–53.

Feuer, Lewis S. "Recollections of Harry Austryn Wolfson." *American Jewish Archives Journal* 28, no. 1 (1976): 25–50.

Glueck, Nelson, and Shalom Spiegel. "Stephen Samuel Wise." *Proceedings of the American Academy for Jewish Research* 18 (1948): xxiii–xxv.

Goren, Arthur A. "The View from Scopus: Judah L. Magnes and the Early Years of the Hebrew University." *Judaism* 45, no. 2 (1996): 199–225.

Greenberg, Gershon. "The Dimensions of Samuel Adler's Religious View of the World: Adler's Career (1809—91)." *Hebrew Union College Annual* 46 (1975): 377–412.

Greenspahn, Frederick E. "The Beginnings of Judaic Studies in American Universities." *Modern Judaism* 20, no. 2 (2000): 209–25.

Gurock, Jeffrey S. "An Orthodox Conspiracy Theory: The Travis Family, Bernard Revel, and the Jewish Theological Seminary." *Modern Judaism* 19, no. 3 (1999): 241–53.

———. "A Stage in the Emergence of the Americanized Synagogue Among East European Jews: 1890–1910." *Journal of American Ethnic History* 9, no. 2 (1990): 7–25.

Hetzel, Robert L. "German Monetary History in the First Half of the Twentieth Century." *FRB Richmond Economic Quarterly* 88, no. 1 (2002): 1–35.

"In Memoriam Julian W. Mack 1866–1943." *Social Service Review* 17, no. 4 (1943): 506–8.

Jick, Leon A. "Bernhard Felsenthal: The Zionization of a Radical Reform Rabbi." *Jewish Political Studies Review* 9, no. 1/2 (1997): 5–14.

Kallen, Horace M. "Julian William Mack, 1866–1943." *American Jewish Year Book* 46 (1944–1945): 35–46.

Kaplan, Mordecai M. "A Program for the Reconstruction of Judaism." *Menorah Journal* 6 (1920): 182–84.

Kastner, Eitan. "Yeshiva College and the Pursuit of a Jewish Architecture." *American Jewish History* 96, no. 2 (2010): 141–61.

Katz, Emily Alice. "Pen Pals, Pilgrims, and Pioneers: Reform Youth and Israel, 1948–1967." *American Jewish History* 95, no. 3 (2009): 249–76.

Kelly, Robert Lincoln. "Tendencies in Theological Education in America." *Journal of Religion* (1924): 16–31.

Kiev, I. Edward, and John J. Tepfer. "Jewish Institute of Religion." *American Jewish Yearbook* 49 (1947–1948): 91–100.

Kotzin, Daniel P. "An Attempt to Americanize the Yishuv: Judah L. Magnes in Mandatory Palestine." *Israel Studies* 5, no. 1 (2000): 1–23.

Kraut, Benny. "Not So Strange Bedfellow: Felix Adler and Ahad Ha'am." *American Jewish Archives Journal* 37, no. 2 (1985): 305–8.

Lamberti, Marjorie. "The Reception of Refugee Scholars From Nazi Germany in America: Philanthropy and Social Change in Higher Education." *Jewish Social Studies* 12, no. 3 (2006): 157–92.

Lazin, Frederick A. "The Response of the American Jewish Committee to the Crisis of German Jewry, 1933–1939." *American Jewish History* 68, no. 3 (March 1979): 283–304.

Lowenstein, Solomon. "Dr. Lee K. Frankel: 1867–1931." *American Jewish Year Book* 34 (1932): 121–40.

McGinity, Keren. "The Unfinished Business of the Sexual Revolution." *American Jewish History* 104, no. 2/3 (April/July 2020): 207–13.

Medoff, Rafael. "The Emergence of American Zionism." *American Jewish History* 86, no. 3 (1998): 367–376.

Meyer, Michael A. "Two Persistent Tensions Within Wissenschaft Des Judentums." *Modern Judaism* 24, no. 2 (2004): 105–19.

Miller, Philip. "Rabbi Louis I. Newman." *Rhode Island Jewish Historical Notes* 14, no. 3 (November 2005): 443–54.

Myers, David N. "A New Scholarly Colony in Jerusalem: The Early History of Jewish Studies at the Hebrew University." *Judaism* 45, no. 2 (1996): 142–60.

Nadell, Pamela Susan. "'Opening the Blue of Heaven to Us': Reading Anew the Pioneers of Women's Ordination." *Nashim: A Journal of Jewish Women's Studies and Gender Issues* 9 (2005): 88–100.

Newman, Louis I. "Communication." *American Jewish Historical Quarterly* 58, no. 4 (1969): 532–33.

Orlinsky, Harry M. "Jewish Biblical Scholarship in America." *Jewish Quarterly Review* 45, no. 4 (1955): 374–412.

———. "Jewish Biblical Scholarship in America (Continued)." *Jewish Quarterly Review* 47, no. 4 (1957): 345–53.

Penkower, Monty Noam. "The Genesis of the American Council for Judaism: A Quest for Identity in World War II." *American Jewish History* 86, no. 2 (June 1998): 167–94.

Raider, Mark, A. "The Aristocrat and the Democrat: Louis Marshall, Stephen S. Wise and the Challenge of American Jewish Leadership." *American Jewish History* 94, no. 1–2 (2008): 91–113.

Reinharz, Shulamit. "Irma 'Rama' Lindheim: An Independent Zionist Woman." *Nashim: A Journal of Jewish Women's Studies and Gender Issues* 1 (winter 1988): 106–35.

Roth, Cecil. "I.A.," Israel Abrahams Memorial Issue, *Institute Quarterly* 2, no. 1 (November 1925), 19–20.

Sarah, Elizabeth. "The Discovery of Fräulein Rabbiner Regina Jonas: Making Sense of Our Inheritance." *European Judaism: A Journal for the New Europe* 28, no. 2 (Autumn 1995): 91–98.

Sarna, Jonathan, D. "Two Jewish Lawyers Named Louis." *American Jewish History* 94, no. 1–2 (2008): 1–19.

Schiffman, Marlene R. "The Library of the Jewish Institute of Religion, 1922–1950." *Jewish Book Annual* 48 (1990–1991): 183–96.

Scult, Mel. "Mordecai M. Kaplan: Challenges and Conflicts in the Twenties." *American Jewish Historical Quarterly* 66, no. 3 (1977): 401–16.

Simon, Rita J., Angela J. Scanlan, and Pamela S. Nadell. "Rabbis and Ministers: Women of the Book and the Cloth." *Sociology of Religion* 54, no. 1 (1993): 115–22.

Stein, Herman D. "Jewish Social Work in the United States, 1654–1954." *American Jewish Year Book* 57 (1956): 2–98.

Steinberg, Stephen. "How Jewish Quotas Began." *Commentary* (September 1971): 67–76.

Strauss, Lauren B. "Staying Afloat in the Melting Pot: Constructing an American Jewish Identity in the *Menorah Journal* of the 1920s." *American Jewish History* 84, no. 4 (1996): 315–31.

Sussman, Lance. "The Myth of the Trefa Banquet: American Culinary Culture and the Radicalization of Food Policy in American Reform Judaism." *American Jewish Archives Journal* 57, no. 1/2 (2005): 29–52.

Turner, Joseph. "The Notion of Jewish Ethnicity in Yehezkel Kaufmann's *Golah Venekhar*." *Modern Judaism* 28, no. 3 (October 2008): 257–82.

Twersky, Isadore. "Harry Austryn Wolfson (1887–1974)." *American Jewish Year Book* 76 (1976): 99–111.

Umansky, Ellen M. "Jewish Historical Studies." *Jewish Historical Studies* 47, no. 1 (2015): 245–47.

Unterman, Yael. "Nehama Leibowitz, Teacher and Bible Scholar, Reviewed by Marla L. Frankel." *Nashim: A Journal of Jewish Women's Studies & Gender Issues* 18 (2009): 243–48.

Von Grunebaum, G. E. "Ralph Marcus (1900–1956)." *Journal of Near Eastern Studies* 16, no. 3 (July 1957): 143–44.

Wechsler, Harold S, and Paul Ritterband. "Jewish Learning in American Universities: The Literature of a Field." *Modern Judaism* 3, no. 3 (1983): 253–89.

Weinman, Melvin. "The Attitude of Isaac Mayer Wise toward Zionism and Palestine." *American Jewish Archives Journal* 3, no. 2 (January 1951): 3–23.

Wenger, Beth S. "Memory as Identity: The Invention of the Lower East Side." *American Jewish History* 85, no. 1 (1997): 3–27.

White, Joseph M. "The Diocesan Seminary and the Community of Faith: Reflections from the American Experience." *U.S. Catholic Historian* 11, no. 1 (1993): 1–20.

Yoe, Mary Ruth. "Edward Hirsch Levi." *University of Chicago Magazine* 92, no. 4 (2000).

Zeitlin, Solomon. "Jewish Learning in America." *Jewish Quarterly Review* 45, no. 4 (1955): 582–616.

Book Chapters

Baird, Robert J. "Boys of the Wissenschaft." In *Judaism Since Gender*, edited by Miriam Peskowitz and Laura Levitt, 86–94. New York: Routledge, 1997.

Ellenson, David H. "Denominationalism: History and Hopes." In *Jewish Megatrends: Charting the Course of the American Jewish Future*, edited by Sidney Schwarz, 94–106. Woodstock, VT: Jewish Lights, 2013.

Ellenson, David, and Jane F. Karlin. "Mothers and Sons, Sisters and Brothers: Women of Reform Judaism and Hebrew Union College-Jewish Institute of Religion." In *Sisterhood: A Centennial History of Women of Reform Judaism*, edited by Carole B. Balin, Dana Herman, Jonathan D. Sarna, and Gary P. Zola, 72–85. Cincinnati, OH: Hebrew Union College Press, 2013.

Glatzer, Nahum N. "The Beginnings of Modern Jewish Studies." In *Studies in Nineteenth-Century*

Jewish Intellectual History, edited by Alexander Altmann, 27–45. Cambridge, MA: Harvard University Press, 1964.

Gurock, Jeffrey S. "Yeshiva Students at the Jewish Theological Seminary." In *Tradition Renewed: A History of the Jewish Theological Seminary of America, Vol. I*, edited by Jack Wertheimer, 471–513. New York: Jewish Theological Seminary of America, 1997.

Klapper, Melissa R. "The History of Jewish Education in America, 1700–2000." In *The Columbia History of Jews and Judaism in America*, edited by Marc Lee Raphael, 189–216. New York: Columbia University Press, 2008.

Kligman, Mark. "Reestablishing a 'Jewish Spirit' in American Synagogue Music: The Music of A. W. Binder." In *The Art of Being Jewish in Modern Times*, edited by Barbara Kirshenblatt-Gimblett and Jonathan Karp, 270–87. Philadelphia: University of Pennsylvania Press, 2008.

Korn, Bertram. "The Temple Emanu-El Theological Seminary." In *Essays in American Jewish History to Commemorate the Tenth Anniversary of the Founding of the American Jewish Archives under the Direction of Jacob Rader Marcus*, 359–71. Cincinnati: American Jewish Archives, 1958.

Levenson, Alan T. "The 'Triple Immersion': A Singular Moment in Modern Jewish Intellectual History?" In *Three-Way Street: Jews, Germans, and the Transnational*, edited by Jay Howard Geller and Leslie Morris, 46–65. Ann Arbor: University of Michigan Press, 2016.

Meyer, Michael A. "Abba Hillel Silver as Zionist Within the Camp of Reform Judaism." In *Abba Hillel Silver and American Zionism*, edited by Mark A. Raider, Jonathan D. Sarna, and Ronald W. Zweig, 9–31. London: Frank Cass, 1997.

——. "From Cincinnati to New York: A Symbolic Move." In *The Jewish Condition: Essays on Contemporary Judaism Honoring Rabbi Alexander M. Schindler*, edited by Aron Hirt-Mannheimer, 302–13. New York: UAHC Press, 1995.

——. "Part One: A Centennial History." In *Hebrew Union College-Jewish Institute of Religion at One Hundred Years*, edited by Samuel E. Karff, 1–283. Cincinnati: Hebrew Union College Press, 1976.

Myers, David. "The Ideology of Wissenschaft des Judentums." In *History of Jewish Philosophy*, edited by Daniel H. Frank and Oliver Leaman, 706–20. London: Routledge, 1997.

Nadell, Pamela S. "'The Synagog Shall Hear the Call of the Sister': Carrie Simon and the Founding of NFTS." In *Sisterhood: A Centennial History of Women of Reform Judaism*, edited by Carole B. Balin, Dana Herman, Jonathan D. Sarna, and Gary P. Zola, 19–48. Cincinnati: Hebrew Union College Press, 2013.

Rooks-Rapport, Joe. "Louise Waterman Wise." In *Jewish Women in America: An Historical Encyclopedia*, edited by Paula E. Hyman and Deborah Dash Moore, 1482–84. New York: Routledge, 1997.

Sarna, Jonathan D. "Seating and the American Synagogue." In *Belief and Behavior: Essays in the New Religious History*, edited by Philip R. Vandermeer and Robert P. Swierenga, 189–206. New Brunswick, NJ: Rutgers University Press, 1991.

——. "'A Sort of Paradise for the Hebrews': The Lofty Vision of Cincinnati Jews." In *Ethnic Diversity and Civic Identity: Patterns of Conflict and Cohesion in Cincinnati Since 1820*, edited by Henry D. Shapiro and Jonathan D. Sarna, 131–64. Urbana: University of Illinois Press, 1992.

Siegel, Reva B. "A Short History of Sexual Harassment." In *Directions in Sexual Harassment Law*, edited by Catharine A. MacKinnon and Reva B. Siegel, 1-39. New Haven, CT: Yale University Press, 2004.

Wilke, Carsten. "From Talmud Torah to Oriental Studies: Itineraries of Rabbinical Students in Hungary." In *Modern Jewish Scholarship in Hungary: The 'Science of Judaism' between East and West*, edited by Tamas Turan and Carsten Wilke, 75–98. Berlin: Walter de Gruyter, 2016.

BOOKS

Adams, John Quincy. *A History of Auburn Theological Seminary, 1818–1918*. Auburn, NY: Auburn Seminary Press, 1918.

Adler, Cyrus. *I Have Considered the Days*. Philadelphia: Jewish Publication Society of America, 1941.

American Jewish Archives and Jacob Rader Marcus Center of the American Jewish Archives. *Essays in American Jewish History to Commemorate the Tenth Anniversary of the Founding of the American Jewish Archives Under the Direction of Jacob Rader Marcus*. Cincinnati: American Jewish Archives, 1958.

Barnard, Harry. *The Forging of an American Jew: The Life and Times of Judge Julian W. Mack*. New York: Herzl, 1974.

Birmingham, Stephen. *"Our Crowd": The Great Jewish Families of New York*. New York: Harper and Rowe, 1967.

Brenner, Michael. *The Renaissance of Jewish Culture in Weimar Germany*. New Haven, CT: Yale University Press, 1998.

Brinkmann, Tobias. *Sundays at Sinai: A Jewish Congregation in Chicago*. Chicago: University of Chicago Press, 2012.

Cardin, Nina Beth, and David Wolf Silverman. *The Seminary at 100: Reflections on the Jewish Theological Seminary and the Conservative Movement*. New York: Rabbinical Assembly and the Jewish Theological Seminary of America, 1987.

Carmilly-Weinberger, Moshe, ed. *The Rabbinical Seminary of Budapest, 1877–1977: A Centennial Volume*. New York: Sepher-Hermon, 1986.

Cherry, Conrad. *Hurrying Toward Zion: Universities, Divinity Schools, and American Protestantism*. Bloomington: Indiana University Press, 1995.

Coffin, Henry Sloane. *A Half Century of Union Theological Seminary, 1896–1945: An Informal History*. New York: Scribner, 1954.

Cohen, Gerson D. *An Embarrassment of Riches: On the Condition of American Jewish Scholarship in 1969*. New York: Ktav, 1970.

Cohen, Judah M. *The Making of a Reform Jewish Cantor: Musical Authority, Cultural Investment*. Bloomington and Indianapolis: Indiana University Press, 2009.

Cohen, Naomi Wiener. *American Jews and the Zionist Idea*. New York: Ktav, 1975.

———. *A Dual Heritage: The Public Career of Oscar S. Straus*. Philadelphia: Jewish Publication Society of America, 1969.

———. *Encounter with Emancipation: The German Jews in the United States, 1830–1914*. Philadelphia: Jewish Publication Society of America, 1984.

———. *Jacob H. Schiff: A Study in American Jewish Leadership*. Hanover, NH: Brandeis University Press, 1999.

———. *Not Free to Desist: The American Jewish Committee, 1906–1966*. Philadelphia: Jewish Publication Society of America, 1972.

Cohen, Rich. *The Fish That Ate the Whale: The Life and Times of America's Banana King*. New York: Farrar, Straus and Giroux, 2012.

Dawley, Powel Mills. *The Story of the General Theological Seminary: A Sesquicentennial History, 1817–1967*. New York: Oxford University Press, 1969.

Dicker, Herman. *Of Learning and Libraries: The Seminary Library at One Hundred*. New York: Jewish Theological Seminary of America, 1988.

Diner, Hasia R. *Julius Rosenwald: Repairing the World*. New Haven, CT: Yale University Press, 2017.

Dollinger, Marc. *Black Power, Jewish Politics: Reinventing the Alliance in the 1960s*. Waltham, MA: Brandeis University Press, 2018.

———. *Quest for Inclusion: Jews and Liberalism in Modern America*. Princeton, NJ: Princeton University Press, 2000.

Ellenson, David. *Rabbi Esriel Hildesheimer and the Creation of a Modern Jewish Orthodoxy*. Tuscaloosa: University of Alabama Press, 1990.

———. *After Emancipation: Jewish Religious Responses to Modernity*. Cincinnati: Hebrew Union College Press, 2004.

Felsenthal, Emma. *Bernhard Felsenthal, Teacher in Israel: Selections from His Writings, with Biographical Sketch and Bibliography*. New York: Oxford University Press, 1924.

Fraser, James. *Schooling the Preachers: The Development of Protestant Theological Education in the United States, 1740–1875*. Lanham, MD: University Press of America, 1988.

Geiger, Roger L. *The History of American Higher Education: Learning and Culture from the Founding to World War II*. Princeton, NJ: Princeton University Press, 2014.

Goldman, Karla. *Beyond the Synagogue Gallery: Finding a Place for Women in American Judaism*. Cambridge, MA: Harvard University Press, 2009.

Goldsmith, Emanuel S., Mel Scult, and Robert M. Seltzer. *The American Judaism of Mordecai M. Kaplan*. New York: New York University Press, 1990.

Goldstein, Sidney E. *The Synagogue and Social Welfare: A Unique Experiment (1907–1953)*. New York: Bloch, 1955.

Goren, Arthur A. *New York Jews and the Quest for Community: The Kehillah Experiment, 1908–1922*. New York: Columbia University Press, 1970.

Gottheil, Richard J. H. *The Life of Gustav Gottheil: Memoir of a Priest in Israel*. Williamsport, PA: Bayard, 1936.

Greene, Daniel. *The Jewish Origins of Cultural Pluralism: The Menorah Association and American Diversity*. Bloomington: Indiana University Press, 2011.

Gurock, Jeffrey S. *From Fluidity to Rigidity: The Religious Worlds of Conservative and Orthodox Jews in Twentieth Century America*. Ann Arbor: Jean and Samuel Frankel Center for Judaic Studies, University of Michigan, 1998.

———. *The Men and Women of Yeshiva: Higher Education, Orthodoxy, and American Judaism*. New York: Columbia University Press, 1988.

Gurock, Jeffrey S., and Jacob J. Schacter. *A Modern Heretic and a Traditional Community: Mordecai M. Kaplan, Orthodoxy, and American Judaism*. New York: Columbia University Press, 1997.

Handy, Robert T. *A History of Union Theological Seminary in New York*. New York: Columbia University Press, 1987.

Hofstadter, Richard, and Walter P. Metzger. *The Development of Academic Freedom in the United States*. New York: Columbia University Press, 1955.

Hyamson, Albert M. *Jews' College, London, 1855–1955*. London: Jews' College, 1955.

Hyman, Paula E., and Deborah Dash Moore, eds. *Jewish Women in America: An Historical Encyclopedia* (New York: Routledge, 1997).

Judson, Daniel. *Pennies for Heaven: The History of American Synagogues and Money*. Waltham, MA: Brandeis University Press, 2018.

Kaplan, Dana Evan. *Contemporary American Judaism: Transformation and Renewal*. New York: Columbia University Press, 2009.

Kaplan, Mordecai Menahem, and Mel Scult. *Communings of the Spirit: The Journals of Mordecai M. Kaplan*. Detroit: Wayne State University Press and the Reconstructionist Press, 2001.

Karabel, Jerome. *The Chosen: The Hidden History of Admission and Exclusion at Harvard, Yale, and Princeton.* Boston: Houghton Mifflin, 2005.

Karff, Samuel E., ed. *Hebrew Union College-Jewish Institute of Religion at One Hundred Years.* Cincinnati: Hebrew Union College Press, 1976.

Kirshenblatt-Gimblett, Barbara, and Jonathan Karp. *The Art of Being Jewish in Modern Times.* Philadelphia: University of Pennsylvania Press, 2008.

Korn, Bertram W. *Eventful Years and Experiences: Studies in Nineteenth Century American Jewish History.* Cincinnati: American Jewish Archives, 1954.

Kotzin, Daniel P. *Judah L. Magnes: An American Jewish Nonconformist.* Syracuse: Syracuse University Press, 2010.

Krasner, Jonathan B. *The Benderly Boys and American Jewish Education.* Waltham, MA: Brandeis University Press, 2011.

Kraut, Benny. *From Reform Judaism to Ethical Culture: The Religious Evolution of Felix Adler.* Cincinnati, OH: Hebrew Union College Press, 1979.

Lawrenson, Helen. *Stranger at the Party: A Memoir.* New York: Random House, 1975.

Liberles, Robert. *Salo Wittmayer Baron: Architect of Jewish History.* New York: New York University Press, 1995.

Malone, Barbara S. *Rabbi Max Heller: Reformer, Zionist, Southerner, 1860–1929.* Tuscaloosa: University of Alabama Press, 1997.

Marcus, Jacob Rader. *United States Jewry, 1776–1985: Volume 3, The Germanic Period, Part 2.* Detroit: Wayne State University Press, 1993.

Marcus, Jacob Rader, Abraham J. Peck, and Jeffrey S. Gurock. *The American Rabbinate: A Century of Continuity and Change, 1883–1983.* Hoboken, NJ: Ktav, 1985.

Meyer, Michael A. *Response to Modernity: A History of the Reform Movement in Judaism.* New York: Oxford University Press, 1988.

Miller, Glenn T. *Piety and Profession: American Protestant Theological Education, 1870–1970.* Grand Rapids, MI: William B. Eerdmans, 2007.

Moore, Deborah Dash. *At Home in America: Second Generation New York Jews.* New York: Columbia University Press, 1981.

———. *Urban Origins of American Judaism.* Athens: University of Georgia Press, 2014.

Morris, J. Brent. *Oberlin, Hotbed of Abolitionism: College, Community, and the Fight for Freedom and Equality in Antebellum America.* Chapel Hill: University of North Carolina Press, 2014.

Nadell, Pamela Susan. *Women Who Would Be Rabbis: A History of Women's Ordination, 1889–1985.* Boston: Beacon, 1998.

Null, J. Wesley. *Peerless Educator: The Life and Work of Isaac Leon Kandel.* New York: Peter Lang, 2007.

Onuf, Peter S. *The Mind of Thomas Jefferson.* Charlottesville: University of Virginia Press, 2007.

Olitzky, Kerry M., Lance J. Sussman, and Malcolm H. Stern, eds. *Reform Judaism in America: A Biographical Dictionary and Sourcebook.* Westport, CT: Greenwood, 1993.

Patai, Raphael. *Jews of Hungary: History, Culture, Psychology.* Detroit: Wayne State University Press, 1996.

Puckett, Dan J. *In the Shadow of Hitler: Alabama's Jews, the Second World War, and the Holocaust.* Tuscaloosa: University of Alabama Press, 2014.

Raider, Mark A. *The Emergence of American Zionism.* New York: New York University Press, 1998.

Rakeffet-Rothkoff, Aaron. *Bernard Revel: Builder of American Jewish Orthodoxy.* Philadelphia: Jewish Publication Society of America, 1972.

Reinharz, Shulamit, and Mark A. Raider. *American Jewish Women and the Zionist Enterprise.*

Waltham, MA: Brandeis University Press and Hanover, NH: University Press of New England, 2005.

Ritterband, Paul, and Harold S. Wechsler. *Jewish Learning in American Universities: The First Century*. Bloomington: Indiana University Press, 1994.

Rosovsky, Nitza. *The Jewish Experience at Harvard and Radcliffe*. Boston: Harvard University Press, 1986.

Ruben, Bruce L. *Max Lilienthal: The Making of the American Rabbinate*. Detroit: Wayne State University Press, 2011.

Rudin, A. James. *Pillar of Fire: A Biography of Stephen S. Wise*. Lubbock: Texas Tech University Press, 2015.

Saperstein, Harold I. *Witness from the Pulpit: Topical Sermons, 1933–1980*. Edited with introductions and notes by Marc Saperstein. Lanham, MD: Lexington, 2001.

Sarna, Jonathan D. *American Judaism: A History*. New Haven, CT: Yale University Press, 2005.

———. *JPS: The Americanization of Jewish Culture, 1888–1988: A Centennial History of the Jewish Publication Society*. Philadelphia: Jewish Publication Society, 1989.

Sarna, Jonathan D., and Nancy H. Klein. *The Jews of Cincinnati*. Cincinnati: Hebrew Union College-Jewish Institute of Religion, 1989.

Schwarz, Leo W. *Wolfson of Harvard: Portrait of a Scholar*. Philadelphia: Jewish Publication Society of America, 1978.

Scult, Mel. *Judaism Faces the Twentieth Century: A Biography of Mordecai M. Kaplan*. Detroit: Wayne State University Press, 1993.

Seidel, Esther. *Women Pioneers of Jewish Learning: Ruth Liebrecht and Her Companions at the "Hochschule fur die Wissenschaft des Judentums" in Berlin 1930–1934*. Berlin: Judische Verlagsanstalt, 2002.

Silverman, Lisa. *Becoming Austrians: Jews and Culture between the World Wars*. Oxford: Oxford University Press, 2012.

Sperling, David S., Baruch A. Levine, and B. Barry Levy. *Students of the Covenant: A History of Jewish Biblical Scholarship in North America*. Atlanta: Scholars, 1992.

Sussman, Lance J. *Isaac Leeser and the Making of American Judaism*. Detroit: Wayne State University Press, 1995.

Urofsky, Melvin I. *American Zionism From Herzl to the Holocaust*. Garden City, NY: Anchor, 1975.

———. *Louis D. Brandeis: A Life*. New York: Pantheon, 2009.

———. *A Voice That Spoke for Justice: The Life and Times of Stephen S. Wise*. Albany: State University of New York Press, 1982.

Vandermeer, Philip R., and Robert P. Swierenga. *Belief and Behavior: Essays in the New Religious History*. New Brunswick, NJ: Rutgers University Press, 1991.

Voss, Carl Hermann. *Rabbi and Minister: The Friendship of Stephen S. Wise and John Haynes Holmes*. Cleveland, OH: World, 1964.

Wertheimer, Jack, ed. *Tradition Renewed: A History of the Jewish Theological Seminary*. 2 vols. New York: Jewish Theological Seminary of America, 1997.

Wise, James Waterman. *Liberalizing Liberal Judaism*. New York: The Macmillan Company, 1924.

Wise, Stephen Samuel. *Challenging Years: The Autobiography of Stephen Wise*. New York: G. P. Putnam's Sons, 1949.

———. *Free Synagogue Pulpit Sermons and Addresses by Stephen S. Wise, Volume VI, 1920–1921*. New York: Bloch, 1921.

———. *Free Synagogue Pulpit Sermons and Addresses by Stephen S. Wise and Others, Volume VII, 1921–1924*. New York: Bloch, 1924.

Wise, Stephen Samuel, and Carl Hermann Voss. *Stephen S. Wise: Servant of the People*. Philadelphia: Jewish Publication Society of America, 1969.

Wohlgelernter, Maurice, ed. *History, Religion, and Spiritual Democracy: Essays in Honor of Joseph L. Blau*. New York: Columbia University Press, 1980.

DISSERTATIONS, THESES, AND UNPUBLISHED PAPERS

Frommer, Morris. "The American Jewish Congress: A History, 1914–1950 Volume I." PhD diss., Ohio State University, 1978.

Heilbrunn, Bernice A. "Faith as Motive for Reform: Emil G. Hirsch and Chicago Jewish Progressives." PhD diss., University of Houston, 2012.

Hellman, Shawn Ilene. "Revising a Collective Identity: The Rhetorical Traditions of Reform Judaism in America, 1885–1999." PhD diss., University of Arizona, 2003.

Malino, Jonathan. "'Haff you gno bolidigal basshunts? . . .' (*Canto* 77/152–3): Ezra Pound and 'Doktor' Slonimsky." Paper presented at the Twenty-First Ezra Pound International Conference, Rapallo, Italy, July 2005.

Mostov, Stephen Gross. "A 'Jerusalem' on the Ohio: The Social and Economic History of Cincinnati's Jewish Community, 1840–1875." PhD diss., Brandeis University, 1981.

Saidel, Joanna Maura. "Revisionist Zionism in America: The Campaign to Win American Public Support 1939–1948." PhD diss., University of New Hampshire, 1994.

Shapiro, Robert Donald. "A Reform Rabbi in the Progressive Era: The Early Career of Stephen S. Wise." PhD diss., Harvard University, 1984.

Silverman, Russell. *The Union for Reform Judaism 1873–2009: A History According to the Minutes of the Organization*. n.p., 2011.

Sobel, Ronald B. "A History of New York's Temple Emanu-El: The Second Half Century." PhD diss., New York University, School of Education, Health, Nursing, and Arts Professions, 1980.

Tepper, William Samuel. "I Dwell Among the People: A Biography of Rabbi Louis Israel Newman." Rabbinical thesis, Hebrew Union College-Jewish Institute of Religion, 2008.

Veit, Lauren L. "The Hebrew Union College School for Teachers in New York City (1923–1932) in Historical Perspective." MARE thesis, Hebrew Union College-Jewish Institute of Religion, New York School of Education, 1991.

Index

Page numbers in italics indicate figures.
Stephen S. Wise's name is represented in some entries by the initials SSW.

Abrahams, Israel, 42, 73–74, 75, 77, 81, 86, 106, 110, 113, 115, 125, 186, 219n2, 222n12, 224n61, 229–30n31
academic freedom, 2, 33–34, 37–38, 53, 55–56, 59
ACLU. *See* American Civil Liberties Union
Addams, Jane, 25
Adler, Cyrus, 41, 58, 60, 65, 66, 67–68, 83, 84, 103, 105, 118, 122, 142, 166, 169, 171–72, 185, 230n46
Adler, Felix, 19, 36, 76
Adler, Samuel, 12–13, 19, 29
advertising, JIR and, 93–94
Agudat ha-Rabbanim, 187
AJC (American Jewish Congress), 4, 26, 37, 159–60, 165–67, 172, 174; and anti-Nazism, 170–72; Geneva Bureau, 144; investigation of conditions of Central and Eastern European Jews, 161; *Opinion*, 135; SSW and, 26, 37, 44, 71, 131, 143, 154, 161–62, 165–67, 178, 180; and war relief, 71; Women's Division, 171, 179
Akademie für die Wissenschaft des Judentums, 71
Aldington, Richard, 112
Aliyah Bet, 193
Alper, Michael, 162, 163, 199
Alpert, David B., *145*
"amalgamated synagogue," proposed, 116–17, 120–21, 123–24
American Academy in Rome, 135
American Civil Liberties Union (ACLU), 25, 37
American Hebrew (newspaper, New York), 20, 101–2, 130

Americanization, JTS and, 16
American Jewish Committee, 26, 166, 168–70, 187
American Jewish Congress (AJC). *See* AJC (American Jewish Congress)
American Jews, 36, 130, 143; and changing times, 153–55; opposition to Hitler, 169–73
American Judaism, spiritual crisis in, 201–2
American School of Oriental Research, Jerusalem, 135, 199
American Unitarian Association, 221n29
Anderman, Zwi, 94–95, 137
Anderson, Edwin, 119
Andover Theological Seminary, 9
Andre, Vicaire, *149*
Anshe Emeth congregation, Albany, New York, 12
anti-German boycott, 165, 172, 178, 180
antisemitism, 19, 70, 102, 131, 164, 180–81, 182, 197, 208, 226n29; antisemitic bias, in Christian scholarship, 62, 75; in Germany, 71, 78, 165–68, 170, 171–72, 174, 178, 180; growth and spread of, 130, 144, 153, 161, 165–67; at Harvard, 58, 90–91
antislavery movement, 10
ARZA (American Reform Zionist Association), 207
Arzt, Max, 196
Askowith, Dora, 95–96, 133, 135, 156, 171, 173, 189, 190, 210; "The Woman in the Rabbinate," 187
Avukah (American Student Zionist Federation), affiliated with the Zionist

Organization of America, 162–63. *See also* ZOA (Zionist Organization of America)
Avukah School, Highland Falls, New York, 173

Baeck, Leo, 79, 105–6, 184, 188
Baer, Max, 176
Balfour Declaration, 26, 31, 72, 74, 79, 80, 161, 163
Baneth, Eduard, 188
Baron, Salo, 124–25, *145*, *146*, 155–56, 157, 161, 162, 169–70, 179, 186
Beit Hamidrash Lechochmat Yisrael (Hebrew name for JIR), 98–102
Bell, Morris H., *150*
Benderly, Samson, 124, 155, 162, 179
"Benevolent Empire," 10
Ben-Gurion, David, 193
Berkson, Isaac, 124, 155, 162
Berlin, SSW visit to (1922), 76–78. *See also* Hochschule für die Wissenschaft des Judentums (Berlin)
Berman, Morton, 95, 98, 136–37, 142–44, 157–58, 162, 171, 173–74, 200, 203, 207
Bernstein, Philip, 98, 127, 131, 135–37, 153, 159, 161, 178, 191, 200, 207; as member of first JIR class, 94–95, 97
b'ezrat hashem, "with God's help," 80, 223n47
b'h. See b'ezrat hashem, "with God's help"
Bialik, Hayyim Nahman, 71, 75, 78, 135–36
Billikopf, Jacob, 112
Binder, Abraham W., 110, 125, 126, 134, *145*, 155, 162, 185–86
Bitzaron (Hebrew monthly), 185
Blank, Sheldon, 109, 199
Blau, Joel, 62, 68, 121–22, 226n35, 226n38, 226–27n47
Blau, Ludwig, 82–83, 100–101, 122
Bloch, Charles, 32, 49, 81–82, 92, 93, 96–97, 219n15, 219n21, 223–24n52
Bloch, Edward, 49
Bloch, Joshua, 81–82, 106, 116, 118–19, 122, 128, 226n35
Bloch, Theresa, 49
Bloch Publishing, 49
Bloom, Maurice J., *145*, 161, 163
Blumenfield, Samuel, 163, 207
B'nai B'rith, 168–70, 172

Board of Delegates of American Israelites, 13
Brandeis, Louis D., 25–26, 40, 49, 72, 84, 96, 161, 162
Brandeis University, 228n3
Breslau, Isadore, 137
Breslau, SSW visit (1922), 78
Brevis, Harry, 207
Brickman, Jay R., *150*
Britain, and Jewish immigration into Palestine, 153, 161
British Mandate for Palestine, 72, 79–80
Brooklyn Jewish Center (Crown Heights), 187
Brown, Elmer E., 103
Buber, Martin, and *De Jude* journal, 71
Budapest, SSW visit (1922), 80, 82–83, 105

Calvinists, 9
Cambridge University, 73–74
Cantor, Bernard, 216n71
Cassuto, Umberto, 79
"cathedral" Judaism, SSW and, 116–17
CCAR (Central Conference of American Rabbis), 20, 172; Columbus Platform, 2, 181–82; Commission on Justice and Peace, 202; Commission on the Revaluation of Judaism, 178, 181; Commission on Social Justice, 177–78; Committee on International Peace, 165; convention (Milwaukee, 1933), 174; convention (Wernersville, Pennsylvania, 1934), 175–76; convention (Chicago, 1935), 177–78; and emerging presence of JIR rabbis, 138–43, 154, 164–65; investigation of conditions of Soviet Jews, 208; Liturgical Literature Committee, 165; RAC (Religious Action Center), 208; and "Revaluation of Reform Judaism," 176; Social Justice Committee, 164; and Unification Plan, 203; and women's rabbinical ordination, 92, 113; and Zionism, 163–65, 176–78, 180
CCNY (City College of New York), 18, 90, 156
censorship, 33
Central Conference of American Rabbis (CCAR). *See* CCAR (Central Conference of American Rabbis)
Central Synagogue (New York City),

proposed merger with Free Synagogue, 116–17, 123–24

Chajes, Hirsch Perez (chief rabbi of Vienna), 74, 79, 105, 117–18

chaplaincy, 61–63, 160; military chaplains, 191–92

Chicago, 14, 31

Chicago Sinai Congregation, 35–36, 38, 49, 53–54, 106

Chiel, Arthur, 207

child labor, 25

church seating systems, 215n56

Cincinnati, 17; Jewish population, 31, 198; as seat of Reform Judaism, 31; as sole center of rabbinical training for Reform Judaism, 202–5; I. M. Wise and, 12–14

City College, New York. See CCNY (City College of New York)

classroom teaching, American-style, 114–16

clergy: demand for, 10; training of, 9–11

clergy, Protestant: recruited for JIR faculty, 62–63, 68, 75, 128; teach in Summer School (1921), 39; women in, 92

Cohen, Alfred M., 169

Cohen, Hermann, 77, 112

Cohen, Jacob X., 126, 134, 137, 157–60, 162, 165, 166, 170, 173–74, 176, 200

Cohon, Samuel, 180, 181

college graduates, seminaries and, 37, 90, 95

colleges and universities: as competitors in fundraising, 141; quota system to limit Jewish enrollment, 58, 90–91, 111, 124, 224n61

Collegio Rabbinico Italiano (Florence), 70, 75

Columbia University, 18, 90, 95, 120; Nathan J. Miller Chair in Jewish History, Literature and Institutions, 141, 156; Teachers College, 96, 127

Columbus Platform, 2, 181–82

Commission on Industrial Relations (federal), 25

Committee for a Jewish Army, 194

Committee of Jewish Delegations, 178

Committee on the Jewish Institute of Religion, 48–50

competition: in fundraising, 140–43; for students, 93–94

Congregation Bene Yeshurun (Cincinnati), 12

Congregation Beth El (Albany, New York), 11–12

Congregation Beth Elohim (Brooklyn), 17

Congregation Beth Israel (Portland, Oregon), 19, 37, 216n56

Congregation B'nai Jeshurun (New York City), 99; Sisterhood for Personal Service, 18–19

Congregation Rodeph Sholom (New York City), 17, 157–58, 193–94

Congress House (New York City), 179; as Defense House, 191–92

Conservative Judaism, 21, 171; and interdenominational competition, 202; postwar, 195–200. See also JTS (Jewish Theological Seminary)

contemporary Jewish issues, in JIR rabbinical training, 126–27

contemporary Jewish scholarship, 103–4

Courier (monthly publication), 171

Cronbach, Abraham, 138–39, 216n71

Daggett, Windsor, 145, 155

Davidson, Israel, 103, 230n46

Davidson, Thomas, 18, 32, 57, 215n37

Degel Harabonim, 172

De Haas, Jacob, Great Betrayal (with SSW), 161

denominationalism, 3, 52; postwar, 195–200. See also nondenominationalism

Detroit Jewish Chronicle, 102

Deutsch, Bernard, 169, 172

Dewey, John, 60, 96, 103, 127

Dienemann, Max, 188

Diesendruck, Zevi, 145, 155, 235n2

Doolittle, Hilda ("H.D."), 112

Dropsie College, 17, 33, 42, 56, 57, 58, 59, 65, 103, 118, 185, 219n2, 238n24

Dr. Williams's Library and Trust, London, 75

Dubin, Abraham, 95, 137

Dubnow, Simon, 75–76

Dvir publishing house, 71

Efros, Israel, 42, 219n2

Einhorn, David, 12, 15, 35

Einstein, Albert, 109, 163, 197, 228n5

Eisendrath, Maurice, 138, 203–4, 207; and HUC-JIR merger, 195–200

Elbogen, Ismar, 42, 74–78, 80–86, 97, 99,

100, 101–6, 109, 110, 117, 118, 122,
123, 141, 185, 219n2, 224n61, 226n38,
227n58; *A Century of Jewish Life*, 185
Eliot, Charles William, 124
Ellenson, David, 11
Elliott, John Lovejoy, 39
Emanu-El Theological Seminary (New York
City), 15–16, 99, 203; failure of, 30–31
employment: for JIR rabbis, 136–38, 158,
179; for JIR students, 115–16. *See also*
pulpits, rabbinical
Enelow, Hyman, 163
English Jews, 72
Eppstein, Victor, 137, 178
equity and inclusiveness, 5
Erlau (Hungary), 83
Erlich, Arnold B., 18
Ethical Culture movement, 19, 36, 39
ethical monotheism, 21
Etz Chaim Yeshiva (New York City),
16–17, 59
European Jews, post–World War I, 70–73
European models, for American Jewish sem-
inaries, 11
European scholars, recruitment of, 41–42,
69–86, 89–90, 101–2, 109
Evangelicalism, 10
exchange of faculty, JIR and Hochschule,
78–79, 83–85
exchange proposal, for JIR and HUC, 48

factionalization, of American Jewish life, 15
faculty: competition for, 109; joint appointments for, 111–12; part-time, 111;
permanent, 93, 110–13; recruitment of,
41–42, 55–63, 69–70, 73–86, 110–
13, 117–18, 121–22, 124–25, 219n3,
220n10, 222n11, 223n52; visiting, 56,
73–74, 78, 105–6, 109, 184. *See also*
HUC (Hebrew Union College); JIR
(Jewish Institute of Religion); JTS (Jewish Theological Seminary)
fascist parties, European, rise of, 153
FAZ (Federation of American Zionists),
19, 25
Federal Council of Churches of Christ, 166
Federation for the Support of Jewish Philanthropic Societies of New York City,
218n3

Federation of Jewish Charities, Philadelphia,
112
Federation of Reform Synagogues of Greater
New York, 203
Feldman, Abraham, 176
Fels, Mary ("Mollie"), 50, 84, 219n15,
219n21
Felsenthal, Bernard, 12–13
fieldwork program, JIR and, 96–97, 127, 131,
134–35, 142–43. *See also* JIR (Jewish In-
stitute of Religion)
Fischoff, Ephraim, 137, 207
Fisher, Mitchell, *145*, 158, 163, 212
Five Seminary Fund, 105–6, 124
Foakes-Jackson, F. J., 33, 63, 103
foreign accents, bias against, 100, 136–37,
155
Frankel, Lee K., 46,47, 51, 66, 84, 125, 218n3
Frankel, Zacharias, 11, 70, 78
Frankfurter, Felix, 72, 161, 162
Franklin, Leo, 216n56
Franzblau, Abraham, 108
freedom of the pulpit, 22–23, 28, 37, 201,
215n51
free dues, 28
Freehof, Solomon, 156, 204–5, 235n6
free pews, 28, 215n56
Free Synagogue (New York City), 28, 39,
44, 54, 140, 170–71, 199, 221n31; Child
Adoption Committee (Louise Wise Services), 216n64; founding of, 23–25; and
hiring of JIR students and graduates,
134, 137; and negotiations with UAHC
over planning for JIR, 46–52; *Open Letter to the President of UAHC…*, 63–64;
and planning for JIR, 35–39, 47, 63–64,
66–68; proposed merger with Central
Synagogue, 116–17, 123–24; renamed
Stephen Wise Free Synagogue, 209;
sharing SSW's service with JIR, 228n77;
Social Service Department, 24–25, 134,
159; social service model, 153, 164. *See
also* Summer School for Rabbis and Rabbinical Students (1920, 1921)
Free Synagogue of Westchester (Mount Vernon, New York), 137, 193, 216n70
Free Synagogue model, 32, 34–35, 182
Free Synagogue movement, 26–27, 30, 32
Freidus, Abraham Solomon, 119

Friedlaender, Israel, 69, 216n71

Friedman, Herbert, 192–93

fundraising, 3–4; for European rabbinical seminaries, 105–6; Free Synagogue and, 140; and HUC-JIR merger, 197; for JIR, 46–48, 50, 66–67, 110, 116–17, 120–21, 123–24, 139–43, 201; UAHC-HUC, 197. See also JIR (Jewish Institute of Religion)

Gamoran, Emanuel, 138

Geiger, Abraham, 36, 70

Gelb, Saadia, 193, 207

gender discrimination, 5, 95–96, 113–14, 133, 149, 186–90, 206, 210, 238n28

Georgetown College, 9

German Jews, 71

German language, spoken by Wise family, 17

Germany: Nazi, 165–68; Nuremberg Laws, 178

Gersoni, Henry, 18

Ginzberg, Louis, 69, 80, 93, 230n46

Glueck, Nelson, 109, 199, 202–3, 206, 208–9, 210; Unification Plan, 203–5

Goldberg, Joshua, 137, 145, 159, 171, 178, 192

Goldenson, Samuel, 174

Goldman, Solomon, 162

Goldmann, Nahum, 162, 180

Goldstein, Benjamin, 98, 101, 113, 117–18, 128, 137, 160, 173, 177

Goldstein, Israel, 99

Goldstein, Sidney, 24–25, 27, 33, 40, 62, 68, 75, 81–82, 93, 95, 134, 145, 159, 200, 226n35, 229–30n31, 238n12

Goodman, Abram, 137, 159, 178, 191

Gordis, Robert, 195–96

Gordon, Cyrus, 204

Gottheil, Gustav, 14–16, 18–19, 31, 119

Gottheil, Richard, 18–19, 25, 26–27, 31, 38, 41–42, 48–49, 57, 60–61, 65, 69, 76, 84, 98, 100, 106, 107, 113, 119–20, 128, 217n73, 219n15, 219n21, 219n2, 221n31, 226–27n47

Gottschalk, Alfred, 206, 209–10

Graetz, Heinrich, History of the Jews, 185

Grant, Percy, 39

Great Depression, 153, 158–60, 164, 168

Great Synagogue (Vienna), 18

Greenfield, Albert M., 112

Gressman, Hugo, 186

Grossmann, Louis, 45–46, 53, 57, 122, 128

guest preachers, practice of, at Free Synagogue, 24

Guggenheimer, Bertha, 96, 136, 140, 219n15, 219n21; as JIR board member, 50

Guggenheimer, Frederick, 40, 219n15, 219n21

Guggenheim family, 141–42

Guttmann, Julius, 77, 78, 79, 117, 119–20

Guttmann, Michael, 77

Ha'am, Ahad, 59–60, 75

Habonim, 193

Hadas, Moses, 185, 204

Hadassah, 96, 135, 173, 233n7

Haganah, 193, 194, 208

Hagedorn, Joseph, 179

halakhah. See Jewish law (halakhah)

Halkin, Simon, 162, 186

Har Sinai Congregation (Baltimore), 12

Harris, Rabbi Maurice, 99, 219n15, 219n21, 226n35

Harvard, 1, 15, 9–10, 42, 57–58, 59, 68, 74, 95, 111–12, 113, 115, 120, 128, 132, 136, 141, 156, 186, 213n1 (ch. 1), 219n2, 234n43; admissions quota on Jews, 58, 90–91, 111, 124, 224n61; Board of Overseers, 41, 49, 57–58, 91; Divinity School, 62–63, 104; "highest seventh" plan, 111; and Jewish studies, 108, 123; Littauer and, 122–23, 141, 234n43; Menorah Society, 217n74; Nathan Littauer Chair in Jewish Literature and Philosophy, 122–23; Wolfson and, 91, 122–23, 229n19

Haselkorn, Abraham, 192

"Hatikvah," 164–65

Hays, Daniel, 46, 50, 104

Hebrew language. See Modern Hebrew language

Hebrew Paedagogium (Vienna), 71, 125

Hebrew Teachers College, 61

Hebrew University (Jerusalem), 42, 109, 118, 143–44, 150, 193; Jewish National Library, 121, 231n81

Heller, James, 33, 138

Heller, Max, 33, 51, 138, 163, 174

Herend (Hungary), 83

Herford, R. Travers, 75, 81, 186, 224n61

Hertz, Joseph, 18

Herzl, Theodor, 19, 71

Heyman, Hannah, 120–21

Hilborn, Walter, 139, 219n15

Hildesheimer, Esriel, 17, 70

Hildesheimer Seminary (Berlin), 184

Hirsch, Emil G., 35–36, 38–39, 46, 49–50, 53–54, 63, 64, 66, 73, 76, 84, 86, 93, 99, 102, 106–7, 119, 120, 142, 179, 186, 220n10, 225n20

Hirsch Library, JIR. See JIR (Jewish Institute of Religion): Samuel and Emil Hirsch Library

Hirsch, Samuel, 35, 106

Hirschberg, Gunter, 204

Histadrut (Labor movement in Palestine), 176

Hochschule Agreement, 78–79, 83–85, 117

Hochschule für die Wissenschaft des Judentums (Berlin), 11, 16, 36, 54, 69–70, 74, 76–78, 94, 105–6, 141, 184, 187–88

Hoffseyer, Benjamin, 95, 100

Holdheim, Samuel, 14, 29

Holmes, John Haynes, 39, 64, 221n29

homiletics, in rabbinical training, 61–63

Hoover, President Herbert, 154

Horthy, Adm. Miklós, and "White Terror" (Hungary), 72, 83

HTC (Hebrew Teachers College, Boston), 57

HUC (Hebrew Union College), 13–15, 17, 20, 30–31, 36, 45–46, 59, 69, 94, 112, 130, 185, 235n2; advantages of, 50–51; and competition for students, 93–94; fundraising, 124, 141–42; German rabbis, rescue of, 238n24; growth of, 91–92; Margolis and, 58–59; opposition to JIR, 127–28; proposed admissions ratio, 142; proposed merger with JIR, 3, 174–75, 179, 183–84, 194–200; proposed merger with JTS, 20–21, 31; School for Teachers, 108; and thesis requirement, 101; Wolfson and, 122–23; and women's rabbinical ordination, 92, 113

HUC alumni, and CCAR, 164–65

HUC-JIR (merged institution), 199–200, 202–5, 208–9; campus in Jerusalem, 208–9; Los Angeles branch, 205, 209; School of Education, 202; School of Sacred Music, 202; "Statement of Purpose," 199; Unification Plan, 203; women students, 210–11; Year-in-Israel Program, 209

Hungarian Jews, 72, 83

Hunter College, 90, 95

immigrants, American Jewish, 11, 16–17, 44; second-generation, 31–32

inclusivity, JTS model of, 16

Intercollegiate Menorah Association, 132, 217n74, 225n11

interdenominational rabbinical cooperation, 163

interfaith dialogue, 61–63, 130, 136

intermarriage, 211, 240n10

International Defense League, 160

International Hebrew Braille Code, 207

Irgun, 193–94

Israel, SSW visit to (1948), 200

Israel, Edward, 138

Israelitisch-Theologische Lehranstalt (Vienna), 11, 70–72, 78–79, 94, 125, 184

Israel Movement for Reform and Progressive Judaism, 207

Isserman, Ferdinand, 138

Istituto Convitto Rabbinico (Collegio Rabbinico Italiano [Padua]), 11

"ivrit b'ivrit" (Hebrew in Hebrew), 60, 68, 116, 127, 155, 220n11. See also Modern Hebrew language

Jabotinsky, Vladimir, 138, 158, 176–77, 193–94

Jacob Joseph School, 95

Jacobs, Henry, 18–19

Jacobs, Robert P., 132, 161

Jacobson, Abraham I., 238n12

JDC (Joint Distribution Committee), 83–84, 105

Jellinek, Adolf, 18

Jesuits, 9

Jewish Agency, 178; Council for Uniting Zionists and Non-Zionists, 143–44

Jewish Bulletin, 177

Jewish Center (Orthodox), 60

Jewish congregations, growing number of, 130. See also names of synagogues

Jewish Institute of Religion. See JIR (Jewish Institute of Religion)

Jewish Institute Quarterly, 133–34

Jewish law (halakhah), 21, 30, 95, 118, 126, 188, 211, 215n48

Jewish peoplehood, 52–53, 59, 72–73, 143, 168–69

Jewish People's University (Petrograd), 76

Jewish Publication Society, 187

Jewish Publication Society, Bible translation (1917), 58

Jewish scholars, recruitment of, 41–42, 56–57

Jewish studies, 91, 97, 108–9, 114–16, 122–23, 156, 186. *See also* Wissenschaft des Judentums

Jewish Theological Seminary (JTS). *See* JTS (Jewish Theological Seminary)

Jewish Theological Seminary of Breslau, 11, 184

Jewish Times (Baltimore), 44–45

Jews' College, London, 11, 70

"Jew without label," 106

JIR (Jewish Institute of Religion), 1–2, 36, 108, 130, 136, *145–48*, 184–86, 218n8; and admission of women, 92–93, 95–96, 209–11, 229n31; admissions, 90, 95, 132, 136, 142–43, 225n24; adoption of four-year program, 116; all-school events, 157; as Beit Hamidrash Lechochmat Yisrael, 98–102; board of directors, 48–50; budget, 50, 82, 124, 179, 224n61; as center of Jewish learning, 185–86; commencement, 143–44, 172–73, 201; and competition for students, 93–94; course distributions, 98; curriculum development, 97, 100–102, 109–10, 114–16, 125–29, 226n35; disciplinary issues, 100–101; faculty, *145*, 185–86, 226–27n49; faculty biases, 100; faculty chairs, 120, 124; faculty course assignments, 226n38, 227n58; faculty engagement with Zionist movement, 162–63; faculty hiring, 111–13, 222n11; faculty joint appointments, 111–12; faculty recruitment, 41–42, 55–63, 73–86, 110–13, 117–18, 121–22, 124–25, 219n3, 220n10, 222n11, 223n52; faculty retention, 128, 154; faculty salaries, 111–12, 119, 179, 230n46; faculty turnover, 155–56; fieldwork program, 96–97, 127, 131, 134–35, 142–43; financial issues,

174–75, 179–80; first cadre, 94–98, 130–44; first faculty meeting, 99–100; Free Synagogue shares SSW's service with, 228n77; fundraising, 46–47, 110, 116–17, 120–21, 123–24, 139–43, 201; German rabbis, rescue of, 238n24; gifts and bequests, 120–21; graduating class of 1945, 195; Guggenheimer Fellowship, 136, 173; honorary degrees, 135–36, 199; initial evaluations of students, 97–98; *Jewish Institute Quarterly*, 133–34; JIR Press, 186; job security, 117; Master of Hebrew Literature degree, 135, 188; Million Dollar Campaign, 197; as new Yavneh, 89, 201; nondenominationalism, 2, 52–55, 93, 109–10, 128, 132, 184, 202–5, 228n7; opening reception, 102–5; opposition to, 50, 55, 63–68; ordination of first graduates, 135–36; part-time faculty, 111; permanent faculty, 110–13; planning for, 34–39, 44–52; and postwar "new American rabbinate," 191–94; proposed admissions ratio, 142; proposed merger with HUC, 3, 174–75, 179, 183–84, 194–200; public courses, 162; and rabbinical ordination for women, 113–14, 183; rabbinical training, 42–43, 61–63, 125–29; rabbinical training for women, 133; real estate, 106–7, 121, 140, 175, 178–79; Samuel and Emil Hirsch Library, 81, 106–7, 119, *148*, 186; *Scope and Purpose*, 128; speech coaching, 155; student awards and prizes, 136; student body, 50, 90–98, 114, 132–35, *145*, *147*, 156–57, 179, 225n19; student recruitment, 156–57; student sermons, 126; students' outside employment, 115–16; temporary location at Temple Israel (New York City), 99; thesis requirement, 101, 126, 135; tuition, 34–35; visiting faculty, 56, 73–74, 78, 105–6, 109, 184; work for victims of Nazism, 178–79. *See also* academic freedom; employment; JIR alumni; rabbinical training; rabbis, JIR

JIR alumni, 157–58; and CCAR, 164–65; and Zionism, 192–94

Johnson-Reed Act (1924), 130

Joint Commission on Social Action (UAHC and CCAR), 202

Jonas, Regina, 185, 237n5; "Can a Woman Hold Rabbinical Office?" 188
Journal (newspaper, New York), 19
Journal of Jewish Education, 199
JTS (Jewish Theological Seminary), 16–17, 69, 103, 124, 130, 185, 214n30; and competition for students, 93–94; German rabbis, rescue of, 238n24; growth of, 91–92; name changed to Jewish Theological Seminary of America (JTSA), 21; proposed merger with HUC, 20–21, 31; Rabbinical School, 60; and rabbinical training, 29–30; Teachers Institute, 57, 60, 92, 95; and thesis requirement, 101
Judaism (magazine), 210
Juedisch-Theologisches Seminar of Breslau, 70, 76–78

Kallen, Horace, 33, 58, 126, 170
KAM Temple (Chicago), 175
Kandel, Isaac, 121
Kaplan, Harry, *145*
Kaplan, Mordecai, 42, 57, 59–61, 65, 66, 68, 89, 95, 96, 103–4, 109, 117–18, 122, 124, 142, 155, 219n2, 220n14, 221nn31–32, 227n64, 230n46, 230–31n53; "Program for the Reconstruction of Judaism," 60
Kaufmann, Edmund, 121 219n15
Kaufmann, Yehezkel, 75
Keneseth Israel (Philadelphia), 35
Kent, Charles Foster, 39, 62
Keren Hayesod, 40
Kibbutz Kfar Blum, 207
Kibbutz Yahel (Reform), 207
Kiev, I. Edward, 186, 217n73
Kisch, Guido, 185
klal yisrael, 1, 153, 160–63, 183, 194, 198, 201–2, 204, 206–8, 211–12, 213n1 (Intro.)
Klein, Edward, 199–200, 203–4
Kohler, Kaufmann, 15, 20–21, 33, 35, 37–38, 41, 52, 59, 69; opposition to JIR, 64–65, 67–68
Kohut, Alexander, 18, 49, 107, 229n26
Kohut, George A., 18, 49, 62, 69, 76, 97, 112, 119, 155, 220n14, 222n4, 226–27n47, 229n26
Kohut, Rebekah, 103, 171, 236n6

Krass, Nathan, 122, *145*
Krauss, Samuel, 82, 122
Ku Klux Klan, 91, 160
Kullmann, Eugen, 204

Lake, Kirsopp, 63
Landesrabbinerschule (Hungary), 185
Lane Theological Seminary (Cincinnati), 10
Lasker, Adolph, 163
Lauterbach, Jacob, 93
Lawrenson, Helen, 190
Leeser, Isaac, 13
Lefkowitz, David, 143
Lehman, Irving, 58
Leibowitz, Nehama, 76
Levi, Gerson, 119
Levine, Allan, 208
Levine, Joseph, 79, 223n47
Levine, Morris D., 230n46
Levinthal, Bernard, 187, 189
Levinthal, Helen, *149*, 187–89, 190, 210
Levinthal, Israel, 187, 189
Levinthal, Louis, 187
Levy, Felix, 174–75, 177, 179, 181
Levy, J. Leonard, 124
Levy, Reuben, 116–17, 128, 155
Lewis, Harry S., 56, 61–62, 68, 92, 97, 126, 128, *145*, 155, 164, 226n35, 226n38
Lewisohn, Adolph, 102–5
liberal Judaism, American, 1–6, 29, 36–37, 43, 50, 84, 100, 102, 134–35, 163, 181–82, 196, 198, 202, 206, 208–9, 211
Liberal Judaism, in England, 74, 106, 136
Liberal Synagogue (London), 74
library, JIR. *See* JIR (Jewish Institute of Religion): Samuel and Emil Hirsch Library
Liebman, Joshua Loth, 138
Lilienthal, Max, 14
Lindheim, Irma, 96, 113–15, 127, 133, 136, 135, *147*, 189, 190, 210, 229–30n31
Lindheim, Norvin, 96, 135, 226n29
Littauer, Lucius, 123, 141, 234n43
London, SSW visit (1922), 73–76
Loth, Moritz, 13
Lowell, A. Lawrence, 91

Maccoby, Max, 193
Mack, Julian, 25, 41–42, 49, 53, 57–58, 66–67, 84, 91, 96, 109, 111, 157, 178,

196, 219n15, 219n21, 224n61, 225n19, 234n43; and JIR faculty recruitment, 117–18

Mack, Ralph, 196

Magnes, Judah, 42, 84, 109, 118, 162

Mahler, Raphael, 42, 219n2

Maimonides College (Philadelphia), 13, 16

Malino, Jerome, *150*, 207, 238n12

Malter, Henry, 118

Manchester (UK) Congregation of British Jews, 61–62

Manheimer, Jacob, 204

Mann, Jacob, 42, 219n2

Marcus, Jacob Rader, 76, 109, 199

Marcus, Moses, 162

Marcus, Ralph, 119, 155, 186

Margolies, Moses S., 171

Margolis, Max, 18, 33, 42, 57–59, 65–66, 219n2, 220n10

Margulies, Samuel Hirsch, 70

Mariampol Synagogue (New York City), 16–17, 214n30

Marmorstein, Arthur, 117

Marshall, Louis, 20–22, 26, 31, 103, 124, 142–44, 201

Marx, Alexander, 69, 103, 230n46

Mattuck, Israel, 74

Maximon, Shalom, 124, 155

McGiffert, Arthur C., 103

Mendes, Henry Pereira, 16

Menorah Journal, 91, 93–94, 225n11

Metz (France), 11

Meyer, Martin A., 27, 116, 137

Meyer, Max, 95, 134, 137

Meyer, Michael, 14, 142, 198

military chaplains, 191–92

Miller, Linda Rosenberg, 141

Mizrachi Organization of America, 187

Modern Hebrew language, 97, 100, 127

Montagu, Lily, 74

Montefiore, Claude, 74, 136

Montefiore College (Ramsgate, UK), 61–62

Moore, George Foot, 62–63, 104, 219n2, 224n61

Morais, Sabato, 16, 20

Morgenstern, Julian, 45–47, 127–28, 175, 185, 196, 198

Morgenthau, Henry, Sr., 24

Mosse, Albert, 83–85

NAACP (National Association for the Advancement of Colored People), 25

Nadell, Pamela, 187–89

National Committee on Refugee Jewish Ministers, 238n24

National Conference of Jewish Charities, 46; planning a Graduate School for Jewish Social Work, 108

National Conference of Jews and Christians, 166

National Federation of Temple Sisterhoods, 92, 185

nationalism, Jewish, 2, 4. *See also* Zionism

National Seminar of Catholics, Jews, and Protestants, 166

Nazism, German, *149*, 165–68

Nazi sympathizers, American, 165–67

Neiman, David, 204

Neumark, David, 92, 122

Neumark, Martha, 92, 94, 113, 210

Newfield, Morris, 163

Newman, Louis I., 5, 27, 97, 99, 108, 137–39, 142, 155, 157–58, 171, 176–77, 193–94, 203, 217n73, 226n35; and Academy for Liberal Judaism, 204; Rabbinical Tutorial Program, 204

New School for Social Research (New York), 58, 127, 225n23, 234n43

New York Board of Jewish Ministers, 171

New York City, 17; Jewish population, 16, 31, 36, 198

New York Public Library, 118–19

New York School of Social Work, 46

New York Times, 91, 135, 188, 199, 202, 210

New Zionist Organization of America, 194

nondenominationalism, 2, 4, 52, 106, 184, 202–5, 209–11; JIR and, 2, 52–55, 67, 93, 109–10, 128, 132, 184, 202–5, 228n7

non-Zionism, 168–69

numerus clausus: Harvard and, 91, 111; "Jewish Law" (Hungary), 7

Oberlin Collegiate Institute (Oberlin College), 10, 37

Obermann, Julian, 82, 106, 112–16, 118, 120, 128

Ochs, Adolph S., 103, 124, 141

Oko, Adolph, 119

"One Institution for Rearing Rabbis?" (*American Hebrew* symposium), 20
Orlinsky, Harry, 186
Orthodox Judaism, 16, 85–86, 171, 202; postwar, 195–200. *See also* RIETS (Rabbi Isaac Elchanan Theological Seminary)

pacifism, 25, 95, 177–78
Palestine, *150*; SSW visit (1922), 80
Palestine Post, 188
Paris, SSW visit (1922), 75–76
Parker, Benjamin, 98
Pekarsky, Maurice, 173
Perles, Felix, 42, 77–81, 84, 99, 101–5, 110, 219n2, 224n61, 226n38
Perley, Martin, 176
Petegorsky, David, 201
Philipson, David, 177, 181
Phillips, Wendell, 173
Pittsburgh Platform, 28, 33, 177
pluralism, 3, 25, 136, 210, 212
Poale Zion, 193
post-denominational Judaism, 211
Pound, Ezra, 112, 229n20
Priesand, Sally, 209, 210
professionalization of the rabbinate, 36–37. *See also* rabbinical training; *names of seminaries*
progressivism, 2, 22, 35, 125, 174
prophetic Judaism, 29, 32, 72, 153, 159, 208
Protestantism, 10. *See also* clergy, Protestant
publishing: Jewish, 71; Yiddish, in Vienna, 71
publishing, Jewish, 49
pulpits, rabbinical: "all week," 134; competition for, 139; full-time, 136; for High Holy Days, 96–97, 134, 233n111; for JIR students, 134; weekend, 134; year-long, 134
Puritans, 9

quota system to limit Jewish enrollment in colleges and universities, 58, 90–91, 111, 124, 224n61

Rabbi Isaac Elchanan Theological Seminary (RIETS). *See* RIETS (Rabbi Isaac Elchanan Theological Seminary)
Rabbiner-Seminar fuer das Orthodoxe Judentum (Berlin), 11, 17, 70, 105

rabbinical academies, ancient, 89
Rabbinical Assembly, 172
rabbinical lineage, 95
rabbinical promise, identifying, 238n12
Rabbinical Seminary of Budapest, 11, 70, 82
rabbinical training: and academic freedom, 33–34, 228n7; in European Jewish seminaries, 214n24; JIR's curricular innovation in, 125–29; JIR's plan for, 37, 42–43; JIR's recruitment for, 61–63; perceived need for, 28–30; and planning for JIR, 57; SSW's views on, 26–27
rabbis: African American, 5; demand for, 17; German, rescue of, 238n24; HUC, 138; LGBT, 5, 211; salaries of, 47; shortage of, 30, 36, 47, 96, 130, 134; shortage of jobs for, 189; transgender, 5; women as, 5, 133, 186–90, 209–11, 237n5
rabbis, JIR, 201; as "ambassadors to the second generation," 143; entry into congregations, 131; first group of, 136–38; postwar service, 206–8; and social justice, 154–55; wartime service, 191–92
racial injustice, 25, 158–59, 174
radical Judaism, 53
radical Reformers, 1, 12, 15, 35, 43, 52, 106
Rathenau, Walther, 76
Realgymnasium (Vienna), 71
Reconstructionist Rabbinical College, 240n10
Reform Advocate, 36, 49, 107
Reform Judaism, 14, 20–21, 24, 51, 127, 171, 202; and emerging presence of JIR rabbis, 131, 138–43; JIR alumni's challenge to, 173–74; and non-Zionism, 168–69; and planning for JIR, 35–39, 44–52; postwar, 195–200; shifting ideology of, 175–81; SSW's critique of, 29–30, 44; statement of principles, 15; and Zionism, 175–81, 207. *See also* HUC (Hebrew Union College)
Reichel, Leo, 98
Reinharth, Leon, *150*
Reinharz, Shulamit, 226n29
Revel, Bernard, 17, 42, 108, 142
Revisionism, 138, 163, 170, 176–77, 193–94
Reznikoff, Marvin M., *150*
Riegner, Gerhart, 192, 193
RIETS (Rabbi Isaac Elchanan Theological

Seminary), 17, 30, 52, 57, 95, 108, 172, 175, 187
Rodef Shalom Congregation (Pittsburgh), 124, 235n6
Romania, 161
Roosevelt, President Franklin D., 180
Rose, Morris, 95, 97–98, 137–38, 176–77, 194
Rosenwald, Julius, 67, 141–42
Rosenzweig, Franz, 71
Rosh Hashanah, 96–97
Roth, Cecil, 124
Rothman, Walter, 109
Rudin, Jacob, 126, 132–33, 137, 155–58, 194, 203
Ruskin, Albert, 159

Saint Mary's Seminary (Baltimore), 9
SAJ (Society for the Advancement of Judaism), 57, 60
San Francisco, 14
Sanger, Margaret, 159
Saperstein, Harold, 149, 156–57, 170–71, 207, 238n12
Sarna, Jonathan D., 13–14
Schanfarber, Tobias, 175
Schechter, Solomon, 21, 41, 60, 69, 106
Schiff, Jacob, 20–21, 24, 31
Schiff, Mortimer, 124
Schiff family, 141–42
Schindler, Alexander, 207
Scholem, Gershom, 186, 193
Schorr, Henry, 98, 126
Schulman, Samuel, 83–85, 166–67, 178, 181
Schultz, Benjamin, 159
Schwartz, Lawrence, 163, 173
Schwarz, Adolf, 78–79
Scottsboro Affair, 158, 160, 173–74
Semel, Jacob, 120–21
seminaries, Catholic, 9–10
seminaries, Jewish, 11–17, 52, 55; closed to women, 85–86; nondenominational, 211–12; and Wissenschaft scholarship, 69–70. See also rabbinical training
seminaries, Protestant, 10, 34, 37, 41. See also clergy, Protestant
seminaries, role of, 5, 9–11
seminar system, German-style, 114–16

Semitics programs, 18, 27, 42, 56, 59, 85, 91, 106
sexual harassment, 5
Shabbat, 134; Shabbat Bereshit, 98, 226n40; Shabbat Shuvah, 97, 226n34
Shohl, Charles, 48, 63–64, 65, 67, 221n25
Shubow, Joseph, 150, 173
Silver, Abba Hillel, 138, 163–64, 177
Simon, Carrie, 92
Six-Day War (1967), 207
Skirball, Jack, 204
Slobodka, Lithuania, yeshiva at, 57
Slonimsky, Henry, 112, 120, 128, 145, 146, 155, 162, 164, 178, 185, 199
Social Gospel movement, 22–23, 28, 36–37, 39, 41, 62, 68, 215n56
social justice, 19, 27–28, 36, 39–40, 44, 61, 127, 138–39, 153–54, 158–60, 163–64, 168, 174, 181–82, 198, 208, 211–12
social service, 23–24, 35, 37, 40–41, 50, 56, 61–63, 95, 97, 126–28, 153, 164, 181–82, 206
Sokolow, Nahum, 162
Soviet Jews, 208
Spanish and Portuguese Synagogue (New York) City, 173
Spektor, Yitzhak Elhanan, 75
Spiegel, Shalom, 155, 186–87
Steinberg, Paul, 194, 206–10
Stone, Earl, 210
Strauss, Leo, 76
Strauss, Nathan, Jr., 103
Stroock, Sol, 158
Summer School for Rabbis and Rabbinical Students (1920, 1921), 32–35, 39–41
Sunday morning services, Reform congregations and, 216n62
Sussman, Lance, 15
Synagogue Council of America, 173
Szold, Henrietta, 96, 135

Täubler, Eugen, 71
Taxon, Jordan I., 150
Tchernowitz, Chaim ("Rav Tzair"), 75, 77, 117–18, 120, 128, 145, 155, 185, 188, 231n70
Tchernowitz, Gershon, 145
Teitelbaum, Samuel, 145
Temple, The (Cleveland), 163

Temple Beth El (Detroit), 215n56
Temple Beth El (Glens Falls, New York), 140
Temple Beth-El (Great Neck, New York), 157
Temple Beth El (New York City), 15, 83
Temple Beth Or (Montgomery, Alabama), 160
Temple B'rith Kodesh (Rochester, New York), 136, 143
Temple Emanu-El (New York City), 12–14, 19, 108, 122–23, 141, 166, 201; SSW's candidacy for rabbi at, 21–22, 37, 215n51
Temple Emanu-El (San Francisco), 27, 137
Temple Israel (New York City), 108; as temporary location for JIR, 99
Temple Peni-El (New York), 62, 121
Tenenbaum, Joseph, 170
Tepfer, John, 145, 185, 207
Teschner, Maurice, 226n24
Thackeray, H. St. John, 186
Theological Seminary (Chicago), 175
Thurman, Israel, 34, 47–48, 170–71, 219n15, 219n21
tikkun olam, 1, 208, 213n1 (Intro.)
Torczyner, Harry (later Naphtali Herz Tur-Sinai), 77, 79, 117, 155
Touroff, Nissan, 57, 61, 68, 81–82, 89, 97, 98, 99, 110–11, 145, 155, 161–62, 201, 226n36, 226n38, 226–27n47
Training School for Jewish Social Work (New York City), 125, 218n3
"trefa banquet" (HUC, 1883), 15, 52
Triangle Shirtwaist Factory fire, 25
Tulane University, 141
Turner, Bernard, 98
Tur-Sinai, Naphtali Herz. See Torczyner, Harry (later Naphtali Herz Tur-Sinai)

UAHC (Union of American Hebrew Congregations), 13–15, 20, 104, 172; Biennial Conference (1946), 197–98; convention (Chicago, 1933), 173–74; and emerging presence of JIR rabbis, 138–43; fundraising, 141–42, 197; and HUC-JIR cooperation, 139–43; and JIR planning, 42–43, 45–52; opposition to JIR, 63–64, 66–67, 127–28; RAC (Religious Action Center), 208; rejection of Free Synagogue proposal for JIR, 51–52; relocation to New York,

198, 202; and Unification Plan, 203; and Zionism, 181
Union Hymnal, 165
Union of American Hebrew Congregations (UAHC). See UAHC (Union of American Hebrew Congregations)
Union of Orthodox Jewish Congregations of America, 172
Union of Orthodox Rabbis, 172
union rights, 25
United Hebrew Charities (New York City), 46
United Israel Appeal, 40
United Palestine Appeal, 180
United States Constitution, Nineteenth Amendment, 92
United Synagogue of America, 172
University of Berlin, 69
University of Chicago Divinity School, 37
University of Halle, 17
University of London, 95
University of Marburg, 112
Urofsky, Melvin, 200
UTS (Union Theological Seminary), 37, 103

Vienna: SSW visit (1922), 78–79, 82; as Zionist center, 71
Vogelstein, Ludwig, 172–74
von Prittwitz, Baron, 169

Wald, Lillian, 103
Walden School, 175
Warburg, Felix, 83, 124
Weil, Frank, 204
Weisz, Joseph Hirsch (SSW's paternal grandfather; chief rabbi of Erlau), 17
Weizmann, Chaim, 42, 143
Welles, Sumner, 192
White, Saul E., 207, 238n12
Wilson, President Woodrow, SSW's relationship with, 25–26
Wise, Aaron (father of SSW), move to US, 17
Wise, Isaac Mayer, 3, 11–14, 16, 18–20, 31, 51–52, 197, 203, 222n3, 222n12
Wise, James Waterman (son of SSW), 23, 95, 163; decision to leave JIR, 135; as editor of Opinion, 135, 165; Liberalizing Liberal Judaism, 135
Wise, Louise Waterman (wife of SSW), 19–20, 50, 143–44, 171, 178, 189, 191–92,

219n21; and founding of child adoption agency, 25, 47, 50, 216n64

Wise, Sabine de Fischer Farkashazy (mother of SSW), 17

Wise, Stephen S., *145, 148,* 215n37, 219n15, 219n21; and ACLU, 25, 37; and AJC, 26, 37, 44, 71, 131, 143, 154, 161–62, 165–67, 178, 180; and anti-Nazism, 165–67, 169–73, 178; assertion of male dominance, 190; and Balfour Declaration, 72; candidacy for rabbi at Temple Emanu-El, New York, 21–22, 215n51; and "cathedral" Judaism, 116–17; and CCAR, 163–65, 180; college years, 18; and Committee of Jewish Delegations, 178; critique of Reform Judaism, 29–30; death and funeral, 200–201; donation of personal library to JIR, 106–7; early education, 18; and editorship of *Opinion,* 180; European tour (1922), 73–86; and FDR, 180; final address, 200; and Five Seminary Fund, 105–6; and Free Synagogue, 23–25, 131, 197–98; and fundraising for JIR, 174–75; *Great Betrayal* (with De Haas), 161; health, 40, 143, 195; and homiletics, 121–22, 131; honorary HUC degree, 197; and HUC-JIR merger, 196–200; influence on American Judaism, 182; and interdenominational rabbinical cooperation, 163; and interfaith alliance, 62, 136; international efforts and influence, 154, 161–62, 169, 180, 185; and Jewish immigrants, 17, 44; and Jewish peoplehood, 18, 52–53, 59, 72–73, 168–69, 172–73; and Jewish statehood, 79; as JIR acting president, 99, 106, 116–17; and JIR faculty recruitment, 73–86, 111–13, 118–19; and JIR fundraising, 140–41; as JIR president, 46, 154; and JIR rabbinical training, 126–27; and JIR student body, 131, 156–57; legacy, 201–2; mix of pulpit responsibilities with public engagement, 130–31; move to Portland, OR, 19–22; "Open Letter to the Members of Temple Emanu-El of New York," 22, 221n27; preparation for rabbinate, 18; private *semikhah* (ordination), 18; and progressivism, 22, 35; and prophetic Judaism, 72; on rabbinical training, 26–27;

and Reform Judaism, 44; relationship with Woodrow Wilson, 25–26; return to New York from Portland, 23; at 16th Zionist Congress, 143–44; on smoking, 127; service shared by Free Synagogue and JIR, 228n77; students' admiration of, 94, 96, 133; studies in Vienna, 18, 52; and Summer Schools (1920, 1921), 32–35; and threats to his life, 181; translation of ethical treatise by Solomon ibn Gabirol (dissertation), 19; travel to Europe (1922), 73–85; travel to Palestine (1922), 80; and United Palestine Appeal, 131, 180; views on women and women's ordination, 92–93, 186–90; visit to State of Israel, 200; and warning of Nazi genocide against Jews, 192–93; "Why Zionists Cannot Support Jabotinsky and Revisionism" (sermon), 177; and Wissenschaft scholarship, 69–70, 73; and World Jewish Congress, 180–81; and Zionism, 19, 44, 110, 154, 162; and ZOA, 131, 161, 180

Wise (Polier), Justine (daughter of SSW), 23, 189, 216n64

Wissenschaft des Judentums, 11, 41, 69–70, 91, 99–100, 104, 118; Hochschule and, 76–78; women's absence from, 85–86

Wissenschaft model, 70, 73

Wolfson, Harry Austryn, 42, 57–58, 59, 61, 77, 108, 110–12, 113, 115, 116, 119–20, 124, 128, 141, 156, 186, 219n2, 224n61, 229n19; and Littauer Chair, 122–23; opposition to Harvard's numerus clausus, 91

Wolsey, Louis, 163

women: absent from JIR initial faculty recruitment, 85–86; and admission to JIR, 92–93, 95–96, 209–11, 229n31; in Protestant clergy, 92; and rabbinical training and ordination, 92–93, 113–14, 133; as rabbis, 5, 133, 186–90, 209–11, 237n5

women's suffrage, 25

World Jewish Congress, 4, 167, 178, 180–81, 192, 207

World Religious Peace Conference, 144

World Union of Women, 171

World War I, 25–26

World Zionist Congress, 178

World Zionist Congress (Second; Basel), 19, 79

Worrell, William, 40

Yale, 9, 39, 62, 68, 95, 112–13, 120, 132, 189; Alexander Kohut Memorial Collection of Judaica, 229n26

Yanow, Albert, *150*

Yellin, David, 121, 122, 124, 125

Yeshiva College (New York City), 42, 108, 142; Yeshiva University, 238n24

yeshiva model of learning, Orthodox and, 16

Yishuv, 25, 216n66

Young Judaea (Zionist youth organization), 132, 163, 233n7

Zeitlin, Solomon, 118

Zemurray, Samuel, 141

Zion College (Cincinnati), 12, 13

Zionism, 38, 44, 74, 96, 110, 153, 208, 211; CCAR and, 163–65; cultural, 59–60; HUC rabbis and, 138; JIR alumni and, 138, 192–94; in JIR curriculum, 125, 127; and JIR faculty recruitment, 57, 59–60; JIR rabbis and, 160–63; JIR students and, 95, 132

Zionism: An Affirmation of Judaism, 196

Zionist Congress (1897), 19

ZOA (Zionist Organization of America), 4, 40, 49, 138, 163, 187, 233n7

Zunz, Leopold, 70, 91, 102, 104, 186